Here, in comparisons of the Latin and the Anglo-Saxon genius, are heroic characters of the nineteenth century.

Great writers, great travelers, great solitaries, great agitators, great lovers—men and women, great patriots, great failures, great soldiers, great empire-builders—the range of selection is wide. And, as with the original Plutarch, the comparisons not only bring out with new clarity the individual traits of the several portraits, but also reveal the characteristic differences in the two great racial strains placed side by side.

A MODERN PLUTARCH

BY THE SAME AUTHOR

Novels

THE MASK
THE WALL
BABEL
THE NEW CANDIDE
MIRANDA MASTERS
O'FLAHERTY THE GREAT

Plays

SPORT OF GODS

Poems

IN EXILE

Biography

A MODERN PLUTARCH

HERMAN MELVILLE

From *Some Personal Letters of Herman Melville and a Bibliography*
by Meade Minnigerode
Courtesy of The Brick Row Book Shop, Inc.

A Modern Plutarch

Being an Account of Some Great Lives in the Nineteenth Century, together with Some Comparisons between the Latin and the Anglo-Saxon Genius

By

JOHN COURNOS

Illustrated

"Character is fate"

THE BOBBS-MERRILL COMPANY
Publishers *Indianapolis*

FIRST EDITION

Printed in the United States of America

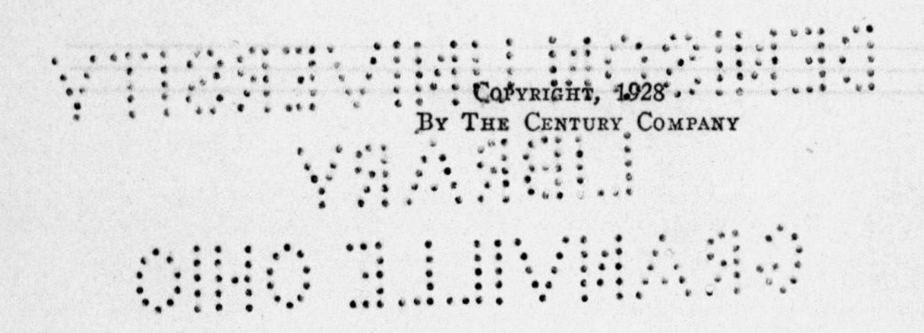

To

William Lyon Phelps
That Rare Thing
A Gentleman
Whose Kindness Is Herein
Remembered

NOTE

I wish to express my indebtedness to Mr. D. L. Chambers for his helpful cooperation in working out the plan of this book. But for him it would not have presented the semblance of unity which I hope is evident in its final shape.

J. C.

NOTE

I wish to express my indebtedness to Mr. D. L. Chambers for his helpful cooperation in working out the plan of this book. But for him it would not have presented the semblance of unity which I hope is evident in its final shape.

J. C.

FOREWORD

It may appear presumptuous to call this book *A Modern Plutarch.* It may seem even more presumptuous to call it anything else. This is because the fundamental idea upon which the book is based is so obviously borrowed from the author of the ancient *Lives* that to ignore the source of one's borrowing would be enough to bring the cry of "Thief!" upon one's head. Thus, the author of the present book finds himself between the devil and the sea. Is one the less a thief for acknowledging one's theft? And, as the saying goes, one may as well be hanged for a sheep as a lamb.

Plutarch's *Lives* were, in the first place, studies of famous characters of the Greek and Latin races; in the second, they were given supplementary value by the comparisons devised by the author, enabling him to point out the specific characteristics which distinguished the men of the one race from those of the other. The Plutarch method is one which may be employed to as great advantage to-day as in Plutarch's day. The present author has sought to apply it to certain heroic characters of the nineteenth century, who, because their personalities have experienced the storm and stress of the age in which they lived, may be called its Titans. The century, in the main, belonged to the Latins and the Anglo-Saxons; what conflict may be said to have existed in the great social body has been a conflict between so-called Latin and so-called Anglo-Saxon temperaments, often in the same individual. At all events, these have been the "progressive" races, whose existence, accelerated by devices of intercommunication and speed, have to some degree become confused one with the other, producing in the result a human network exceeding in complexity the Greco-Latin pattern traced by Plutarch and rendering any effort at comparison fascinating but precarious.

For the sake of greater clarity and precision, it has been thought best to exclude the Slavic elements; however absorbing these may be, they do not offer so much the spectacle of a conflict between two European temperaments as a most violent imaginable war between the European and the Asiatic conceptions of life. Peter the Great tried to veer Russia into the stream of European life and thought; he merely succeeded in creating a combustible element which exploded in 1917-18. This would make its own story and need not concern us here.

Voluminous biographies have been written about the persons treated in these studies, and I can not pretend to have added to the already exhaustive facts. I have attempted no more than the bare outline of each life, and I have tried to make the telling interesting, where possible casting my material in a form approximating a story, and concentrating on some episode in each life which is the culminating irony of that life, dramatic in essence. I trust, above all, that the average reader, for whom these narratives have been written, will find them as simple and as straightforward as the material will allow.

I have, for the most part, chosen the lives of personages which will make the legends of the future, myths for some future Shakespeare to work on, even as the stories of Plutarch have already served, and to good purpose, the Shakespeare we know. These lives, bound between the covers of a single volume, should bear witness to the truth that the human thirst for adventure is not quenched, is in fact eternal, and that the adventure of to-day differs from the adventure of the ancients in externals rather than in the spirit.

Human nature is very much the same that it was, and character still remains the guiding fate. But there is, in spite of the diversity of types presented, a unity which belongs to the time in which they lived.

There has been latterly, to my mind, a deplorable tendency to depreciate the great by exposing their human, "all-too-human" qualities. I say "deplorable" because it seems to me that the human weakness of great men renders them not less heroic but more so, since it alone makes the handicap which hinders them in their aspiration to become gods. It is their weakness, in the stress of heroic striving, which is that "one touch of nature" that links them with humanity. And it makes for that drama and irony which is the essential force in their lives. We may dream of becoming Olympians, but we are as yet Titans. When, if ever, we become Olympians, we shall cease striving. And, in that sense, there is a bit of the Titan in most of us. We are removed from the great only in the degree of energy which the poet Blake calls "Eternal Delight," and which takes account for what men call "good" and "evil."

These sketches are short; the materials from which they were extracted are exhaustive. They have been written with the deliberate intention of exciting the average man, of stimulating him to the fascinations of history and biography. If they should stir the reader sufficiently to impel him to go to the more detailed biographies mentioned in my Acknowledgments, they will have handsomely served their purpose.

J. C.

CONTENTS

CONTENTS—*Continued*

LIST OF ILLUSTRATIONS

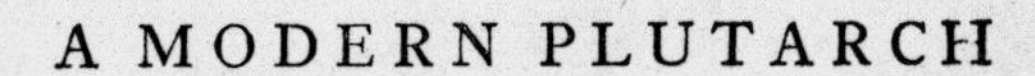

A MODERN PLUTARCH

A MODERN PLUTARCH

MARK TWAIN—A TRAGIC AMERICAN

THE great man lay in his bed, awake and restless. He was tired, too tired to sleep. There had been lately many nights like this—wakeful weary nights, with thoughts, terrible thoughts, for companions. He was getting to be old, to be sure; he had reached his allotted threescore and ten—an age when a man is supposed to take comfort in a life lived abundantly and well. And his life—could anything have been more fulsome, more rich in happenings, in good fortune, and what-not? It had all been, in its way, a fairy tale. Born in a backwoods hovel, amid dire poverty, he had had his share, and more than his share, of the good things of life; he had consorted with men in high places, with the great ones of the earth. Where civilized men dwelt, there men knew his name, and where his name was known, there his quaint humor acted like a lighted fuse to bless men with explosive laughter. And a greater gift than laughter the gods could not give men. The great man who thus lay in the dark, troubled and sad, was Samuel Clemens, better known as Mark Twain.

Like a child who had never grown up, he had always hated the dark. Day, always, had meant action to him, and for a man overflowing with irrepressible energy, action was everything. When one was active, there was no time for thought. Contemplation for him was always associated with sadness. And night was a time for contemplation, therefore for repentance, for regret for things done or seen in the day or in the night. There had been tragedies of which he had had the ill luck to be a witness. There was the slave man he had seen struck down with a chunk of slag for some small offense; he had seen him die. There was the young emigrant who was stabbed with a bowie knife by a drunken comrade; he had seen the red blood gush from his breast. There was the case of the rowdy young brothers and their harmless old uncle: one of them held the old man down with his knees on his breast while the other tried repeatedly to kill him with a revolver which wouldn't go off. He had happened along just then, of course!

Then there was the case of—— But never mind! For one man, he had seen a perfect host of tragedies.

Why should he, of all men, have been chosen to witness so much misfortune? How often had he asked himself the question? And the answer was never uncertain, and always the same. Something in him—perhaps his teaching and training—enabled him to see deeper into these tragedies than the average man could have done. And he knew why they crossed his path. He tried to disguise it from himself, but down in the secret deeps of his troubled heart he knew, and as he had said somewhere before—"and I *knew* I knew." And again he repeated to himself as he had often done before, "They were inventions of Providence to beguile me to a better life." Did all this sound curiously innocent and conceited? Yet each time he thought of it there had seemed nothing strange about it. It was "quite in accordance with the thoughtful and judicious ways of Providence"—as he understood them. Certainly, at one time, it would have in no wise astonished him "if Providence had killed off that whole community in trying to save an asset like me." "It would have seemed just the thing, and well worth the expense." *Why* Providence should have been so anxious about him in particular it had never then occurred to him to ask. Had all that been an illusion? What were the odds? Illusions were useful; with them one lived, without them one merely existed. If only he could have kept his. If only—— But curse night, anyway! What thoughts were born in the womb of darkness!

Those tragedies! He had taken them all to himself, he had tallied them off in turn as they happened, saying to himself in each case, with a sigh, "Another one gone—and on my account; this ought to bring me to repentance; the patience of God will not always endure." And yet he had been foolish enough to believe that it would. "That is,"—as he had written down in his *Autobiography,* the one book in which he had told the whole truth, and nothing but the truth, the book which was so terrible that he had decided it would not see the light of day until a hundred years after his death—"I believed it in the daytime; but not in the night. With the going down of the sun my faith failed and the clammy fears gathered about my heart. It was then that I repented. Those were awful nights, nights of despair, nights charged with the bitterness of death. After each tragedy I recognized the warning and repented; repented and begged; begged like a coward, begged like a dog; and not in the interest of those poor people who had been extinguished for my sake, but only in my *own* interest." It seemed selfish when he looked back on it now.

For a moment the thought of the book gave him a curious pleasure. He, the man who had made thousands laugh, and laugh like children, would give them a different kind of medicine. He gave vent to a mordant chuckle, unusual to him. . . . But his thoughts would not be turned aside. . . .

There was a time when these thoughts would not stand the test of daylight. Invariably, they "faded out and shredded away and disappeared in the glad splendor of the sun. They were the creatures of fear and darkness, and they could not live out of their own place." So he had once thought. But of late these pestiferous thoughts and repentances had a way of raising their heads in the sun's light; they distressed him as they distressed others, for, in order to escape their full venom, he consigned them to writing; men had shared his abounding mirth, it was only right that they should also share his lugubrious doubts. Had he not but lately written down a few pertinent facts concerning Man? Man "was not made for any useful purpose . . . his working himself up out of the oyster bed to the present position was probably matter of surprise and regret to the Creator. . . . For his history, in all climes, all ages and all circumstances, furnishes oceans and continents of proof that of all creatures that were made he is the most detestable. Of the entire brood he is the only one—the solitary one—that possesses malice." And that being the basest and most hateful of all instincts, passions, vices, "that one thing puts him below the rats, the grubs, the trichinæ." More than that: he is "the only creature that inflicts pain for sport. . . . Also—in all the list he is the only creature that has a nasty mind." And he had written a great deal more in the same vein.

Mark Twain, the universally beloved, the favorite of his own countrymen, would show them that life was not the mirth-provoking horse-play he had once pretended it was. "As from the grave"—since his book would not see the light until he was dead—he would challenge the whole of humanity and put it on judgment for its cruelties, lies, hypocrisies, those "blacknesses and rottennesses" of character; in spite of various charms and graces man undoubtedly possessed, he alone, of all creatures, was not free. This book, his *Autobiography,* would be his last will and testament. It would free his own conscience, as it would awaken (so he hoped) the consciences of those who forgot that there was a conscience. To this fancy he clung as to a straw. It was a last illusion.

The great man again gave his half-mordant chuckle in the dark. "Poor Yorick," indeed! But those who fondle his skull shall have to add, "I did not know him at all well! This man was full of quips and of gibes, but his voice from the grave sings another tune."

His blood coursing through his enfeebled body tingled with a perverse satisfaction, but his mind was tempestuous and alive, filled with an active despair. It took stock of his universe, verging again and again on reminiscence, always returning to himself, the core of himself. "What a man sees in the human race," he had recorded in a marginal note in one of his books, "is merely himself in the deep and honest privacy of his heart. Byron despised the race because he despised himself. I feel as Byron did, and for the same reason." And now the thought, born out of his brain, came back to haunt him.

There was no doubt of it. He did despise himself. Always he had despised himself. At first only a little, but like a malignant germ his self-despisal grew, developed, until now it reached its full bloom. Of its ultimate florescence he became aware, as it were, suddenly, at the very moment his wife, dear Livy—God bless her!—passed from this life. Oh, God! Why couldn't he have gone with her? That would have been easier than this eternal doubt, this eternal self-questioning, to which there could be no answer until the eternal darkness itself should offer its ultimate release by swallowing him.

Yet it seemed folly that he, of all men, should feel like

that. What manifold blessings had not been showered on his head! What man would not have exchanged places with him? Out of a hovel he came, "a puny baby with a wavering promise of life," and he grew into a big sturdy man, attractive of feature and full of life, fated to seduce fame and fortune and to bring kings and princes and giants of intellect knocking at his door. And he had had a wife he loved and children he loved and friends he loved, and thousands and tens of thousands of men to love and honor him. What more could a man want? Yet he had found the heart to write: "If you pick up a starving dog and make him prosperous, he will not bite you. That is the principal difference between a dog and a man." And again: "It takes your enemy and your friend, working together, to hurt you to the heart: the one to slander you and the other to get the news to you."

This, surely, was misanthropy. Let them call it what they will. What did it matter? Anyhow, it was the privilege of clowns to suffer melancholy. Did not the great clown Grimaldi himself go incognito to see a doctor for a cure for his spleen, only to be advised to see the great Grimaldi perform? The truth was, his own performance gave Mark Twain no pleasure. He had entered into the spirit of it only in so far as he had to perform a good job. The thing was distasteful to him. It was marvelous how well he managed to conceal it. When he and Mr. Cable were giving a public reading together, Mark had astonished his colleague by exclaiming, with a groan: "Oh, Cable, I am demeaning myself—I am allowing myself to be a mere buffoon. It's ghastly. I can't endure it any longer!" He remembered it now, and the memory added to his pain; for he had been young then, and had he followed his star——But what was the use of thinking about it now? Besides, he was a believer in destiny; there was a beginning somewhere, and that beginning, with a helpless inevitability, led to that ultimate product known as Mark Twain. Thus he consoled himself; yet something deep within him revolted at the thought, refused to be comforted; his mood savored of that infinite distress which a mortal suffers on finding himself cheated by the gods. Here was no mere "failure" in life, but a man who could confess to being frightened at the proportions of his prosperity and who could say, not wholly with pleasure, "It seems to me that whatever I touch turns to gold." After his first great success, with all life before him, he could still put a pistol to his head and refrain from pulling the trigger only because he lacked the courage. In short, he plucked the grapes, and did not find them sour, yet longed for some more unattainable fruit.

His achievements, in their way, were prodigious. He knew that, yet he thought little of them. They were admired, praised, they caused tides of laughter to lap native and foreign shores; but they had been so easy, so facile to him; they rolled like so much dirt off a body at the application of soap; while all the time, underneath, tempests raged within him, and at the heart was a conflagration, which, like Moses' burning bush, would burn and burn and yet remain unconsumed. He but dimly suspected that it was this terrible energy of his, unused and often abused, that caused his distress, and though the energy now lessened, the repentance for what he had lost and for God's gifts he had not used was prodigious. Had he not said in his happiest youth: "What is *a man* without energy? Nothing—nothing at all. What is the grandest thing in *Paradise Lost*—the Arch-Fiend's terrible energy! What was the greatest feature in Napoleon's character? His unconquerable energy. . . . To-day, if I were a heathen, I would rear a statute to Energy, and fall down and worship it!"

And he had added that a man was one who took up a line of action, and *followed* it out, *in spite of the very devil!* Had he himself done this? He thought, no. He had danced and cut capers and had indulged in horse-play, and the hat he had passed around was again and again filled with shekels; he had enjoyed that too in its way; but there were moments when his heart ached or was in revolt and his mind thought distressing thoughts, and in the privacy of his chamber he gave vent to expressive profanity. Once, following such an outburst, he had said placidly:

"In certain trying circumstances, urgent circumstances, desperate circumstances, profanity furnishes a relief denied even to prayer."

Even to the devil must be given his due. Lately he had been giving some thought to the fellow, and, like Heine, had come to the conclusion that he was, after all, not as black as he had been painted. There was this eternal contradiction in life, and the so-called good and the so-called bad were so horribly mixed up that it was sometimes hard to distinguish one from the other. There was this question of energy. He thought it good. Was it not the source and foundation of life? Yet, undoubtedly, everything which was called bad proceeded from energy. There was this same Napoleon whom he so much admired. Napoleon was a great man, and a much-beloved man, too; but no one yet called Napoleon a *good* man. Indeed, there were not a few who thought him the very incarnation of Satan. There was himself, Mark Twain. He generally (so he assumed) passed for a good man. And he *was* good. Everybody had conspired to make him good, from his mother, whom he had loved as a son should love his mother, to his beloved wife, Livy, and to his best friend, William Dean Howells. They all had combined to "edit him." Between them, they managed to expurgate every "unclean" thought, every "unclean" word, so that the large public should find no offense in his work. It all now came back to him:

Livy. "I think some other word would be better than 'stench.' You have used that pretty often."

Mark Twain. "But can't I get it in *any*where? You've knocked it out every time. Out it goes again. And yet 'stench' is a noble good word."

Livy. "I hate to have your father pictured as lashing a slave boy."

Mark Twain. "It's out, and my father is whitewashed."

Livy. "Change 'breech-clout.' It's a word that you love and I abominate. I would take that and 'offal' out of the language."

Mark Twain. "You are steadily weakening the English tongue, Livy."

And so on, and so on.

Yet he had been young once and he had day-dreamed and he had chased phantoms invisible to other men. He had said: "I must go on chasing until I marry, *then* I am done with literature and all other bosh—that is, literature wherewith to please the general public. I shall write to please myself then." He had not kept to his word. And so he despised himself. Again he had said: "I have been used to obeying my family all my life." Well, why shouldn't he? He had loved his family. He was a man of tender heart. He hated to inflict pain. And now he had a glimmering of the truth: Art was "a jealous mistress," it did not yield willingly because he had given so much of his love elsewhere. But now something rose up in him, his ego perhaps, and protested. In a dim way, floundering among his thoughts, he discerned something. He saw in himself the national symbol, the symbol of a whole race of pioneers, who from their initial effort to achieve material security developed into men whose one thought was the accumulation of possessions, whose measuring-stick for success was prosperity. He was the giant Gulliver tied down by Lilliputians, he was the victim and the sacrifice of the large multitude of small men bent on crippling him. He was a Niagara of energy, not pouring over, unencumbered and free, but harnessed for power, for utility. Oh, yes, he had been useful. To men weary after their day's work, he had given amusement. He had been a circus and a vaudeville to them; he had vied with the best of clowns and beaten them on their own ground. He had entered into the spirit of the performance, he had done his best in that line, and while it lasted he forgot himself. But afterward—oh, afterward! The sadness, the laceration of the spirit that he had undergone.

His daughter, Susy, alone had seen through the disguise. She alone had suspected what he was capable of. How keenly he had felt her death! How he valued that little note-book she had left behind! He could remember almost by heart those sentences which meant so much to him. "Papa has done a great deal in his life I think that is good and very remarkable, but I think if he had had the advantages with which he could have developed the gifts which he has made no use of in writing his books . . . he could have done *more* than he has, and a great deal more, even. He is known to the public as a humorist, but he has much more in him that is earnest than that is humorous." And again: "He is as much of a philosopher as anything. I think he could have done a great deal in this direction if he had studied while young . . . in a great many such directions he has greater ability than in the gifts which have made him famous."

He could not bear to go on thinking about Susy, that gentle creature who was now more of a dream to him than a human being, a vanished dream that bore away to the grave something that was himself. He tried to think of other things.

Night, night, what thoughts thy accursed darkness brings! These thoughts come, and prostrate man, with all the will in the world, can not stay them.

Yet there had been in his life happy, unforgettable nights, nights he had again and again longed for, nights which were no more to return. These were the nights on the Mississippi when he piloted craft through the darkness of the great river. It was no easy job, either. There were a thousand things to learn, a thousand obstacles to overcome. He had to engrave on his mind, in the manner of a most precise map, every straight line, every bend, every danger-point, every detail of the vast waterway, however minute and elusive. It offered him beauty on starry nights, a keen sense of power on those of dense mist; he was king here in this pilot-box, he was poet, too; and his pay was mighty good, not at all to be sneezed at. "I used to have inspirations," he had once said, "as I sat there alone those nights. I used to imagine all sorts of situations and possibilities. Those things got into my books by and by and furnished me with many a chapter. I can trace the effect of those nights through most of my books in one way and another." Above all, he felt his kinship there. It was the one thing he had thoroughly mastered. His was the hand that guided the craft through the darkness, and that craft was his world, his kingdom; and none could gainsay him. His responsibility was great, and he was complete master here. And all this required courage, character and determination. The greater world he was yet to encounter had taught him nothing that he had not learned here.

Life on the Mississippi had its tragedy for him too, as on that terrible unforgettable night when his brother Henry, whom he greatly loved, with more than a hundred others, lost his life in the explosion of the *Pennsylvania,* lingering in agony for days before he gave up the ghost, while the pilot sat at his side and watched with sad and tender eyes. He held himself to blame for Henry's death. If it were not for him, Henry would never have been there. There were other reasons why he held himself culpable. And but a few nights before he had had a dream, a most vivid dream. He saw Henry, a corpse, lying in a metallic burial-case in the sitting-room, supported on two chairs. On his breast lay a bouquet of flowers, white, with a single crimson bloom in the center. Fool that he had been, why hadn't he warned his brother off? And yet, and yet, there was the thought. If he dreamed that, was it not a sort of prophecy rather than a warning? For he believed that what was to be had to be, and that men's lives were as predestined as the course of the stars. Nevertheless, he suffered agonies of remorse, and the memory of his brother's death wove itself into the fabric of his life, to haunt him of nights.

Try as he would, he could not understand the Creator's plan. Was all this necessary?

Fortune, to be sure, had been kind to him, even lavish. In that sense, he had had more than his deserts. But he had got into that state when he was happy only when he was up and doing things, traveling, writing or speaking. There was pleasure in looking down on a sea of enthralled faces, in feeling the tense silence of the great throng preliminary to their breaking into explosive guffaws. There was unspeakable delight in the applause of a whole nation which hung on his words, whether written or spoken. There was sap to the ego, however uncertain one was as regards one's own worth, in the calls of the world's great men, in the shower of invitations from the most exalted quarters of the earth. This was enough to overwhelm any man. Yet he could not get around the one dubious fact: in quiet moments of reflection, and sometimes in the hours of the long nights, thoughts (God knew where they came from!) came to trouble him, and sometimes dreams—curious dreams, repeatedly recurring. Hardly a month passed that he did not dream of being in reduced circumstances, and of his being obliged to go back to the river for a living. He loved to think about those days, but there was always something sickening, he mused, in the thought that he was obliged to go back to them; and usually in his dream he was just about to start into a black shadow without being able to tell whether it was Selma Bluff, or Hat Island, or only a black wall of night.

Another dream of that kind which he had frequently was that he was being compelled to go back to the lecture platform. He hated this dream worse than the other. In it he was always getting up before an audience with nothing to say, trying to be funny, trying to make the audience laugh, realizing all the time that he was only making silly jokes. The members of the audience appeared to realize that too, and pretty soon they began to get up and leave. This dream always ended by his standing there in the semi-darkness talking to an empty house.

God, it was ghastly! It made him feel afraid. Like a child, he lay in that darkness, possessed by uncomfortable fears. What had he, the great Mark Twain, to fear? Yet he did fear, with a great unreason. Unreason? He was not sure. The ghost of "what he might have been" knocked on some innermost door. He did not really want the things he had got; he did not want the degrees and honors the world had conspired to confer on him; he did not want to be caged and always to be struggling against the wires. He wanted to be out, out, out! He wanted to soar like an eagle, like a free bird.

Ah, yes, Susy had known. Only Susy. He had put his

love of Susy into his *Joan of Arc,* one of the few books he loved writing. It had been an early dream, this picture of a young girl who was innocent and yet wise. "Be ye wise as serpents and innocent as doves." Decidedly, there was something in that. It was curious, that that page from the history of Joan of Arc should have come flying along the pavement straight into his hands—at Hannibal, of all places. He had been then but a boy, and the page described the "maid" in the cage at Rouen in the fortress, and the two ruffian English soldiers who had stolen her clothes. There was a short description and some dialogue: her reproaches and their ribald replies.

This dust-soiled page had been a turning-point in his life, and awakened his interest in history and in humankind. Into his own book about Joan he had put all the love and tenderness of which he was capable and he looked upon it as upon a beloved child—as upon Susy. And life was like that: the good die young, or they invite crucifixion. And humanity was like that: it consisted of the crucified and the crucifiers. The really good are not afraid; come what may, they think their thoughts and speak them; they live their lives undaunted; they leave material possessions, go and save their souls; they face cruelty, ridicule and what-not, for treasure not to be counted in dollars. He himself had said: "We may not doubt that society in heaven consists mainly of undesirable persons." And it was so. He felt he had, somehow, failed himself. He had not lived up to that being in him which was different from the appearance he presented to the world. He was like two persons, like "those extraordinary twins" of his story. They were the Siamese variety. "Whenever Luigi had possession of the legs, he carried Angelo to balls, rumshops, Sons of Liberty parades, horse-races, campaign riots, and everywhere else that could damage him with his party and his church; and when it was Angelo's week, he carried Luigi diligently to all manner of moral and religious gatherings, doing his best to regain the ground he had lost."

That was Mark Twain. That, also, was "this great big ignorant nation," America. He had borne his double burden, now facing this way, now that. After his wife's death, and when he had reached seventy, he had said:

"Threescore years and ten! It is the scriptural statute of limitations. After that you owe no active duties; for you the strenuous life is over. You are a time-expired man, to use Kipling's military phrase; you have served your term, well or less well, and you are mustered out."

Mustered out! If only that were true. For he had added, in the manner of an afterthought, that seventy years is "the time of life when you arrive at a new and awful dignity; when you may throw aside the decent reserves which have oppressed you for a generation, and stand unafraid and unabashed upon your seven-terraced summit and look down and teach unrebuked."

That was putting the horse after the cart, of course. The fact was, he looked upon his attainment of threescore and ten as a release. A release from what? A release from the lie which he had been living. He needed to confess, to tell the world that he was not what he appeared to be. Only to his friend Twichell he had lately written the truth:

"Am I honest? I give you my word of honor (privately) I am not. For seven years I have suppressed a book which my conscience tells me I ought to publish. I hold it my duty to publish it. There are other difficult duties which I am equal to, but I am not equal to that one."

A pity Livy hadn't liked the book. Well, he could hardly expect her to. How she had loathed it, shuddered over it, would not so much as listen to the last half of it, or allow him to publish any part of it. Her not liking it spoiled his happiness; it was like the proverbial fly in the ointment. By gad, he would publish the book yet, this pet of his, *What is Man?*—even if he had to do it anonymously! But why shouldn't he use his name and give the document the full weight of his reputation? He couldn't do that—no, not quite yet. Perhaps, later. But, oh, how he longed to let go, to cry out his secret thought from the housetops, to fill the land with his challenge, to tell them all that he had deceived them long enough, that their thoughts were not his thoughts, that their ways were not his ways. He longed to see the look of astonishment on their faces; the faces of those who had come to see him cut capers and found instead a Hebrew prophet pouring out his vituperation on a humanity which had no principles and did not know how to live. And he wanted to make up for lost time, to let that which had been dammed up in him for such a long time pour over in great torrents to overwhelm those who had conspired to make him a clown and had come to see him indulge in horse-play and turn somersaults. But seventy years was a very long time; how was he ever to make it up? And the strength of youth was gone; he was an enfeebled old man, and it would require violence on his part to break away from ties wrought in a long lifetime. Could he do it? He raised his head from the pillow, tried to pierce the darkness, and fell back again. A fearful conflict raged within his heart. What if it was too late! Too late!

Now he was like Samson, whose one desire was to pull down the structure of life and to bury himself and those others in the ruins. Too late! a voice cried within him. Samson had grown too old. The length of his white hair would not help him now.

A reaction set in. The mood in which he had the other day spoken to his friend Rogers seized him. Rogers had happened to suggest that he might find relief from the pressure of social demands in the city in his country home. And he had answered fiercely, "The country home I need is a cemetery!" Again, there was the time when he had said to his friend, "Rogers, I don't know what you think of it, but I think I have had enough of this world, and I wish I were out of it!" And what did Rogers say to that? Rogers, prosperous man and financier, answered, "I don't say much about it, but that expresses my view."

The thought of death, which now for him could not be so far off, deflected his thoughts to his early childhood, to the night his father, John Clemens, lay in that tiny hovel at Hannibal in the last sleep of death. Earlier in the day the gentle man had beckoned to Pamela, his lovely daughter now approaching her twenties, and, putting his arm around her neck and kissing her for the first time in years, had said, "Let me die." And, without another word, the good man had breathed his last. He had been upright, honest, and something of an idealist. He had ended life with less than he had begun.

And now Mark Twain remembered his horrible remorse. He had suddenly realized what he had lost, how wild he had been, how often he had disobeyed his father. They were trifling things in themselves, yet his heart had ached with a great ache at the thought of them, and that now his father would never know how his son had loved him. His mother had seen his grief, and, taking him by the hand, led him into the room where his father lay.

"It is all right, Sammy," she had said. "What's done is done, and it does not matter to him any more; but here by the side of him now I want you to promise me——"

His eyes full of tears, he had flung himself into her arms.

"I will promise anything," he had sobbed, "if you won't make me go to school! Anything!"

She had held him tight, reflecting; then said:

"No, Sammy; you need not go to school any more. Only promise me to be a better boy. Promise not to break my heart."

And so he had promised. He would be an upright, faithful and industrious man, like his father. He would keep that promise for ever. And he had kept it. He had not broken his mother's heart. No. But he had, somehow, broken his own. A glimmer of the truth was beginning to break on his weary brain.

That same night, after the funeral, a strange thing had happened. His mother and sister had been sleeping together, when he, attired in white, had appeared in their room, and advanced like one in sleep.

"Sam!" Mrs. Clemens had called.

He had made a reply, but still in sound sleep he had fallen to the floor. Night after night, for many nights, he had walked in his sleep.

And now, reliving the memory, he was a boy again. . . . He was romping the fields round Hannibal. He was at his interminable pranks. He was a boy. . . . Then, suddenly, he roused himself. He could not stand his thoughts any longer. Imps of darkness that they were, they had been sent to torture him. He rose from his bed; his giant form half tottered, fumbled toward the light. . . .

ANATOLE FRANCE—AN OLYMPIAN

1

ANATOLE FRANCE had the rare, one may almost say unique, fortune of being a man of genius who passed through this life without experiencing in his person the stress and sorrow which, for reasons unrevealed, nearly always fall to the lot of the great ones of the earth. He lived in an Ivory Tower, a tall structure on a mountain peak, with windows on all sides, from which, gazing down on the earth, he noted the folly of men, and setting it all down good-naturedly on paper,—he would have preferred papyrus,—he forced a smile to faces which might have remained solemn. He began as a dreamer, he emerged as a man of reason; in his late years he made the effort to descend from his tower to speak to his fellow beings more intimately; still smiling, a look of pity is said to have crept into his eyes; the so-called skeptic was more human than he had first appeared. Still unruffled, his mind ever turned on the congealed past, his face never abandoned its mask of Olympian calm.

As his life was devoid of tragedy, so in his work also he will live as an artist and a thinker, and not as a man of tragedy. He was, perhaps, aware that the felicity of the ecstasy of emotion was denied him; his attitude is made clear in the unconscious irony with which one of his Abbés speaks: "It is a great infirmity to think. God preserve you from it, my son, as He has preserved His greatest saints and the souls whom He loves with especial tenderness and destines to eternal felicity."

2

Anatole France was born on April 16, 1844, French of the French; more strictly speaking, Parisian of the Parisians. His birth took place in a house of the Quai Malaquais; the house was later demolished with others to give place to the École des Beaux Arts. Though the house is gone, it still lives in *My Friend's Book*. There was his bedroom which encompassed the child's world, since it was here that he had had his most vivid experiences: his dreams.

"In this room the most extraordinary adventures befell me. . . . No sooner had I lain down than the strangest individuals began to move in procession about me. They had noses like storks' bills, bristling mustaches, protuberant bellies and legs like chanticleer's. They came in, one after another, showing themselves in profiles, each with a single goggle eye in the middle of his cheek, bearing brooms, skewers, guitars, squirts and other instruments that I knew not. . . . I never went to sleep. You can imagine one would not care to close one's eyes in such company as that, and I kept mine wide open. And yet, here is another marvel! I would suddenly find the room flooded with sunlight and no one in it but my mother in her pink dressing-gown, and I could not for the life of me imagine how the night and the weird folk had vanished. 'What a boy you are for sleep!' my mother would say with a laugh."

From this house the family moved to Number Nine Quai Voltaire, where Anatole's father, an unusual man, *le père France,* as he was called, but whose real name was François Noel Thibault, carried on his bookselling business. The son adopted his father's nickname, which is an abbreviation of the name François. The elder Thibault was a countryman from Anjou, and to this peasant strain in the son has been ascribed that aspect of his genius which endowed his work with the spirit of folklore. Monsieur Thibault had a robust mind; he was a devout supporter of Catholicism and Monarchy, both of which his son was to repudiate; his shop on the Quai Voltaire attracted some of the boldest intellects of the day, whose talk young Anatole absorbed with a mind which was slow but retentive. He grew up in an atmosphere of books. There, on the *quais,* as he himself says, "old books form part of the landscape. The Seine was my delight. . . . I admired the river, which by day mirrored the sky and bore boats on its breast, and by night decked itself with jewels and sparkling flowers."

But life was not all books; he was a child who saw ghosts and indulged in reveries and day-dreams; not at all the sort of thing to be expected of one who was to develop into the greatest satirist of the time. It is true that his satire was not to hinder him from being at the same time a poet. That, while possessing the power of second sight, he saw even as a boy the humorous side of things, is made clear by his subsequent confession concerning his school life. He went to the Collège Stanislas where his own mood was out of tune with the methods of discipline and mass instruction. He was hardly happy there. "From my childhood onward, I have always been in love with solitude," he said, looking back on his school life, "the thought of a glade in the wood, of a rivulet in a meadow, was enough to send me, as I sat there on my form, into transports of desire and love and longing that almost amounted to despair. Perhaps I should have fallen sick with grief in that dreadful school had I not been saved by a gift which I have retained all through my life, the gift of seeing the comic side of things." School life, as he saw it, was degrading, but it was dreadfully funny; what the masters thought of the boy did not, after all, as things turned out, matter so much as what the boy thought of his masters; he lived to revenge himself amply by exposing their comic ineptitude. Paris and home were his real school, "Ah!" he exclaimed, "home is a famous school!"

Genius and school are often in conflict. It did not take him long to perceive that he was "somewhat different from the others, without knowing whether that difference was for my good or ill." And the feeling perturbed him. On the one hand, the masters were trying to cram his head with the classics that he might pass his examinations creditably; on the other, his visionary mind, unconsciously in love with beauty, took from the classics something which escaped the masters. He loved their spirit, not their letter. "Sophocles, Euripides," he exclaims, "they opened the gates of an enchanted world to me. To the *Alcestis* and the *Antigone* I owe the noblest dreams that ever schoolboy was visited by. As I sat at my ink-stained desk, my head buried in my dictionary, forms of godlike beauty passed before my vision; I beheld arms of gleaming ivory falling upon snowy tunics; I heard voices sweeter than the sweetest melody mourning most musically."

Little wonder, then, that lost in the contemplation of his beloved Paris from the towers of Notre Dame, the visionary youth had lost his turn for the *viva voce,* with disastrous results to his examination papers. Such a thing had never happened to any one before in the history of the Sorbonne!

"There," he says, recalling the episode, "I reigned over Paris. The Seine flowed on amid the housetops, domes and towers, and the eye followed it into the blue distance till the silver thread of it was lost among the green hills. Beneath my feet lay fifteen hundred years of glory and great deeds, of crime and misery, an ample subject for my yet unformed and unpractised mind to meditate upon. I know not of what I stayed there dreaming, but when I arrived within the gates of the old Sorbonne I had missed my turn."

For six months, he is lost in the *Odyssey,* which earns him many punishments. "Often enough I collided with a baker's boy with his basket on his head, dreaming his dreams as I was dreaming mine; or else I would suddenly feel on my cheek the hot breath of some unlucky horse tugging at his load." Above all, it is the classics which attract him, Homer, Virgil, Horace and the rest. To him they speak their secrets, into his nostrils they breathe their own mysterious undying life. In the light of their genius he reads all history, interprets the life that is, and the life yet to come. His is a desperate attachment, and he is intuitively guided by their spirit; he is not clear enough in his own mind for the tribute he is to pay later: "Without them the beauty of the French genius would be gone. We are Latins. The milk of the she-wolf is in our blood."

There was at least one master at school for whom young Anatole entertained a high regard, Monsieur Dubois, whom he immortalizes under his real name in *The Bloom of Life.* This fine old man "who held his head erect, bowed with elegance, and displayed a manner which was at once affable and reserved," not only taught him the principles of a refined style but also imparted to him the secret that only by hearkening "to the voice of Nature herself" would he learn to understand Virgil. And the apt pupil learned his lesson well, for he interpreted the classics in the terms of life; they were to him no mere dry-as-dust studies. The grateful Anatole was never to forget his master whom, intellectually, he deemed the greatest man he had ever known. That such a man left no works to perpetuate his name has given him cause to suspect "that the highest human worth has often perished without leaving a trace behind it." Yet, surely, that is not absolutely true if we are to take into consideration Anatole France's acknowledged debt to him.

With school at an end—he was not fated to go to the university—the time came for Anatole France to make a decision as to his future vocation. Monsieur Dubois enjoined upon the boy not to become an author; *le père France* had no exaggerated opinion of his son's talents; the mother's love alone spoke in no uncertain tones: "Be a writer, my son; you have brains, and you will make the envious hold their tongues." Yet the fond mother, of Flemish extraction, was a practical woman who looked after her husband's business better than he did himself. But withal she was gentle and charming, and being a devout woman she took it upon herself to recount to her son the lives of the saints; she told him stories and she sang to him. She was attractive in a feminine way, and the boy adored her.

In any case, the question of the boy's future decided itself by a process of elimination. Law, medicine, the army and the civil service all came up for consideration and were dismissed because he had no aptitude for them; there was no prospect of success in any of these. Agriculture sounded attractive, but as he had no land to farm, this too was dismissed. As for commerce, he absolutely had no sense of money; in this he was like his father. As a little boy he once asked his mother whether it was the people who bought or the people who sold that paid the money; this was not the sort of character to embark on a career of buying or selling.

3

There was only one alternative left; to become an author. Are there not enough authors in this world?

There can not be too many if their self-confessed function is as lofty-minded as this:

"It is the artist's part to love life and show us it is beautiful. Without him, we might well doubt the fact!"

Does this mean that the author must lie?

By no means. For the author of *The Garden of Epicurus* says elsewhere:

"If I were called upon to choose between beauty and truth, I should not hesitate; I should hold to beauty, being confident that it bears within it a truth both higher and deeper than truth itself. I will go so far as to say there is nothing true in the world save beauty."

It is science, not art, which has truth for its objective. For he sees that illusion is necessary. "I love the truth. I believe that humanity has need of it; but assuredly it has greater need still of the deception which flatters it and consoles it and gives it infinite hope. Without deception it would perish of despair and boredom."

Strange words, are they not, for a man who has been repeatedly called a skeptic? He espouses reason with such good effect that he is able to see the unreason of reason; so that, in the final analysis, he is driven to say a word for ignorance: "Ignorance is the necessary condition, I do not say of happiness, but of existence itself. If we knew everything we could not bear life an hour."

He pursues the thought relentlessly to its ultimate conclusion. He, the son of a bookseller, who had lived his life among books, is forced to inveigh against books. He compares those who read many books to opium-eaters, declares that they live in a dream, "insensible to the real world and prey to terrible or beautiful fantasies," so subtle is the poison which penetrates their brains. "Books," he goes on to assert, "are killing us. We have too many of them, of too many kinds. Men lived for ages without reading anything, and those were the days . . . in which they passed from barbarism to civilization. They were without books, but not without poetry or philosophy; they knew by heart their songs and little catechisms." Wealth of knowledge is killing incentive and paralyzing our original faculties.

4

The opinions of Anatole France are important, since they, more than his life (which, until the Dreyfus affair, was a quiescent matter), convey a portrait of the man. And, that in the logical processes he passes from one extreme to the other and walks the dangerous rope of contradiction, is an essential feature, since a man who is able to see both sides is on his way to tolerance, in which irony and pity are inevitable ingredients. In a sense, both sides are leading a pitiful, tragic existence, and all that prevents the genial spectator from having an active share in it is that "gift of seeing the comic side of things," which had stood him in such good stead in his school-days. "I noticed," says Anatole France, in recalling those days, "that my comrades' passions were violent, whilst mine were gentle; that they suffered from theirs, whilst I enjoyed mine."

This gentleness is at the root of his tolerance, and far from wishing to rob the faithful of their faith, he behooves them to cling to the one thing which makes life livable. "Religions are strong and beneficent because they teach man his *raison d'être,* the final causes of his existence. . . . In a society where all faith is blotted out in darkness, sin and sorrow lose all their meaning, and only strike us as odious jests, ill-omened farcical impertinences." Strange words, are they not, for one who has been called a skeptic and whose works, *en bloc,* were to be placed on the *Index* of the Vatican? But, then, France was no friend of official religions.

"Suffering, pain—how divine it is, how misunderstood! To it we owe all that is good in us, all that makes life worth living; to it we owe pity, and courage, and all the virtues. . . . It is through pity we remain truly men."

The man who wrote these words has been called not only a skeptic but also a mocker!

To be sure, he could mock when he wanted to, as when, in a characteristic manner, he says:

"The law, in its majestic equality, forbids the rich as well as the poor to sleep under bridges, to beg in the streets, and to steal bread."

Or:

"The rich give a little that they may keep much."

Is not his sympathy with the poor and the downtrodden expressed in these words?

To be sure, in his middle period, he could be thoroughly pagan in his attitude toward life, and by "pagan" is implied that attitude of mind which seeks poise and harmony and does not exclude pleasure from the scheme of existence. In such a life violence in one direction or another is eschewed. The real danger is one extreme or the other toward which the spirit or the senses may tend. *Thais,* a recreated picture of an ancient world, juxtaposes two panels, two truths, both right and both wrong. Though they contradict one another, they must be called truths, because those that live them are equally sincere, and both mean well. Thus, Nicias, the skeptical, Epicurean philosopher, into whose mouth Anatole France has put his own philosophy, speaks to Paphnutius, once his friend, now a Christian monk:

"My dear Paphnutius, do not imagine that I think you

extremely absurd, or even altogether unreasonable. And if I were to compare your life with mine, I could not say which is preferable in itself. I shall presently go and take the bath which Crobyle and Myrtale have prepared for me; I shall eat the wing of a Phasian pheasant; then I shall read—for the hundredth time—some fable by Apuleius, or some treatise by Porphyry. You will return to your cell, where, leaning like a tame camel, you will ruminate on I know not what formulas of incantations you have long chewed and rechewed, and in the evening you will swallow some radishes without any oil. Well, dear friend, in accomplishing these acts so different in appearance, we are both obeying the same sentiment, the same and only motive of all human actions; we are both seeking our own pleasure and striving to attain the same end—happiness, impossible happiness. It would be folly on my part to say you were wrong, dear friend, even though I think myself in the right."

To the converted courtesan, he says:

"And you, my Thais, go and enjoy yourself, and be happier still, if it be possible, in abstinence and austerity, than you have been in riches and pleasure."

This is Anatole France in his most characteristic vein; it is he himself who speaks through the mouth of Nicias. For an objective writer, he puts a lot of himself into his books. To read all of Anatole France is to obtain a full portrait of the man.

This two-sidedness of the man has brought charges against him from the younger school. It has been complained that France is a pessimist, that his ideas lead into a blind alley. In a sense, this is true; yet the main plea holds good: live and let live. Cling to your faith, by all means; but let reason have its rightful share in the guidance of your life. We can do with a little more tolerance, and if happiness be denied us, we may at least find a measure of content.

Beauty, in itself, is something worth cherishing. Language is a means of making life more livable. He followed this rule in his style. "Form," he says, "is the golden Vase wherein Thought, that fleeting essence, is preserved to Posterity." Again: "It were as witless to separate words from matter as a perfume from the vial that contains it." Even more emphatically he exclaims: "Woe betide him who despises form, for a work endures by that alone!" Yet, as a warning against style too aware of itself, he can say at the same time: "Let us beware of writing too well; it is the worst possible manner of writing." He holds for individuality even in criticism, and he argues that objective criticism can no more exist than objective art. A belief that objectivity exists is an illusion. "The good critic is he who relates the adventures of his own soul among masterpieces." And this is the rule that he has followed in his own critical papers.

All this rightly belongs to his period of existence in the Ivory Tower.

5

The moment arrives when he sees the folly of books. It is a book-ridden age, and books no longer have the influence they once had. Voltaire and Rousseau, between them, helped to create the French Revolution. What writer nowadays can sway the multitudes to action? Forced, perhaps, to this conclusion, our artist-philosopher inveighs against books in the manner already quoted. He is, really, restive in his Ivory Tower; he is eager to come down and talk to men.

And the Dreyfus affair comes opportunely; he enters

the fray. No longer he is content to remain an abstract champion of right. The year 1898 finds him in the arena with Zola fighting to set right the flagrant miscarriage of justice. He tells the story of the case in *L'Histoire Contemporaine,* and again, in his inimitable fashion, in *Penguin Island.*

Never again does he retire permanently to the Ivory Tower. Next he is interested in the proletariat and becomes a Socialist. In that guise Anatole France, the lover of classics, is truly inexplicable, except as a reaction from his former self. Henceforth he abandons his "poise," and definitely ranges himself with the under dogs. He does a thousand things hitherto unthinkable, from attending workingmen's socials to parading with the communists flaunting the red flag. He denounces the Versailles Treaty. He receives at his house, filled with exquisite art works, dubious personages of Russian extraction, much to the disgust of his old servant, Josephine, to whom it is a mystery "why Monsieur receives such dirty people. . . . These Russians do nothing but dirty the whole house. And of a certainty they have bombs on them. If Monsieur would only listen to me, he would make a better choice of his acquaintances." Other, more important personages are even more mystified and incensed to boot for the expression of his radical political opinions. Anatole France has become a different man; they can not and do not want to understand his complete *volte-face* performance. They say he is not the real France, they refuse to take him seriously, they say, "It's just his hobby."

His English biographer, Mr. J. Lewis May, anxious to have Anatole France's own explanation of the change in him, of his adherence to a definite political party, asked him pointblank about it. The master's reply was cryptic:

"If your friends are asking that, then tell them when you get home, to go and read their *Don Quixote*."

Pressed further, he offered no explanation.

Did he not mean to imply that he had had enough of books and wanted to take a turn at tilting at windmills?

6

So much for the mental portrait of the man. How did he appear to the eye?

He was tall and thin, and slightly round-shouldered. His forehead high, his nose aquiline, his profile was very long, and this length was further accentuated by his small beard. There was refinement in the outlines of his face, which impressed one with gentleness rather than with vigor. The eyes, their gleam intensified by the silvery whiteness of his hair, were intensely black and penetrating, and contradicted the serenity of the face. "This roguish look in an almost impassive face is France completely," says Monsieur Gsell, who saw the master often and noted his moods. His taste in dress, at all events at home, was ecclesiastical. He was usually attired in a long clerical dressing-gown, delicate in color and soft in texture. His head-gear was a skull-cap, which seemed never to leave him. It was a bright red.

This cap, we are told, played a great part in his conversation and manners.

"Unconsciously he makes it reflect his thoughts.

"When he is joyful, his cap has a provocative air. . . .

"When listening to an interlocutor, he pushes it back on to his neck, as though to allow the ideas greater ease of penetration to his brain; whilst reflecting, he pulls it back again, almost on to his nose, as though to concentrate his thoughts under this vizor. . . . "

7

In 1920 he married, in 1921 he received the Nobel Prize (which he gave away to charity), in 1924 he died.

Anatole France, who bequeathed laughter, is in his books. All of him that matters is there; when one speaks of timeless men mere dates are of little concern.

THE COMPARISON OF TWAIN WITH FRANCE

Mark Twain and Anatole France—can a greater contrast be imagined?

The one was produced by a poineer race, puritan in mood; the other by an old nation with long tradition, half pagan in spite of Christianity.

The one was born and brought up in a hovel situated in a wilderness; the other in (or over) a bookshop in the most cultured of all modern cities.

The one had practically no schooling and had learned all he knew in the world of hard experience; the other studied the classics and even in boyhood listened to the talk of very cultured men.

The one was urged by his Calvinist mother "to be good"; the other was encouraged by his equally devout Catholic mother to be a writer: "you will make the envious hold their tongues."

The one, at all events in the early years, lived life to the full (not in the pagan sense), and encountered joy and sorrow; the other lost himself in books and intensest kind of mental life aloof from men, and lived in an Ivory Tower.

The one had ultimately a hankering for the Ivory Tower, which he was never to enter; the other got weary of his Ivory Tower and wanted to join in the life of men, without quite succeeding.

Both one and the other were men of genius; the one characteristically American, the very embodiment of energy, almost a symbol of his country; the other typically French, an apostle of reason and balance, a perfect product of Latin culture. Both put a great deal of themselves into their books.

Yet there were many points at which, for all their differences, the two men met. There were more points at which they diverged.

They met, in the ultimate sense, in their recognition of the folly of men and of the absurd short-sightedness of human nature; they diverged in their methods of attack, conditioned in both instances by differences of racial psychology and environment.

Mark Twain, nurtured on ideas of "good," was disappointed to find human nature and activity, on the whole, bad. He felt himself cheated, and the discovery made him wroth; so wroth, indeed, that he forgot his habitual smile by which his admirers knew him. He began to despise men, and he despised himself for not daring to say frankly how much he despised them. He spoke his mind only "as from the grave," in his *Autobiography* published after his death.

Anatole France, nurtured on ideas of mind and beauty,—both things illimitable and eternal,—early in life learned not to expect too much from human nature; even at school he was saved from disgust by his gift of seeing "the comic side of things." Later he was to say: "I have no illusion about mankind, and, so as not to hate them, I despise them. I despise and pity them. Mutual contempt means peace on earth, and if men would only thoroughly despise one another they would do themselves no further harm and live together in an amiable tranquility."

In a word, this means tolerance, good-natured tolerance; let us laugh, since otherwise we should weep.

He flies to the defense of the French so-called skeptics, men guided by reason rather than sentiment. "When the most skeptical thinkers have long meditated face to face with the uselessness of the eternal flux of the Universe, face to face with the little thing sad humanity is, face to face with the absurd sufferings men inflict on each other during the brief dream of their existence, they are filled with deep commiseration for their fellow-creatures . . . From this compassion to brotherly love, it is but a step—quickly taken. Pity becomes active, and he who thought he was for ever detached from everything, passionately throws himself into the fight to aid his unfortunate brothers." Hence, he thinks skeptics the most idealistic of mortals, only "disappointed idealists." They deserve more appreciation. "As they dream of a very beautiful humanity, they grieve to see men so different from what they ought to be. And their habitual irony is but the expression of their discouragement. They laugh, but their gaiety always masks terrible bitterness. They laugh so as not to weep." Skepticism, to France, suggests the most humane feelings; "in any case, it forbids crimes!"

In defending the skeptics, France defends himself, he defends Voltaire, he defends what is most impressive in the French genius: Reason, which hides a warm heart, and is brave to the point of fighting for poor misguided humanity.

Now listen to Mark Twain:

". . . Of all the creatures that were made he [man] is the most detestable. Of the entire brood he is the only one—the solitary one—that possesses malice. That is the basest of all instincts, passons, vices—the most hateful. That one thing puts him below the rats, the grubs, the trichinæ. . . . Also . . . he is the only creature that has a nasty mind. . . ."

So he continues for several pages in his study, *The Character of Man.* Only contempt, and not a single word of pity.

This is all the more strange because here was a man who

had had his share of good fortune, of prosperity, of happiness in marriage (why should we doubt his own words?); he had world-wide fame; he had been welcomed everywhere as America's unofficial ambassador; he was surely born in the lap of the gods. Above all, he had had a good time himself and he had given a good time to others; he had laughed and he had made others laugh; it was true that at times he had made a clown of himself, what of that? That, too, required its own gift.

Why suddenly (not so suddenly, perhaps) this change? Where the former humor, the familiar gibes, in these late fulminations against the pitiful biped, Man? Man, he says, "tarries his little day, does his little dirt, commends himself to God, and then goes out into the darkness, to return no more, and send no messages back—selfish even in death."

And now listen to Anatole France, the skeptic, of whom we have reason to expect less:

"We shall all be swallowed up one day, every one of us, and we know it; the wisest thing is to forget about it."

A plea for tolerance. Is life bad, not what it ought to be? Agreed. Well, let us make the most of it. This is the pagan's credo. The pagan is a Latin.

What of Mark Twain? Where the optimism, the optimism which is the daily food of his people, the food they had been used to, the food they must have, the food they had been led to expect? Mark Twain had been an excellent provider of it. It was as if suddenly he had snatched the manna of heaven from the plates of his admirers and handed them a cup of wormwood. At first, they thought it was another of his little jokes. Should they take him seriously?

But he was serious; very serious, indeed.

His case provides pathos on a large scale. Though they,

ANATOLE FRANCE

From *Franciana* by Joseph L. Dirick
Raoul Simonson, Brussels

MARK TWAIN

Courtesy of Harper & Brothers, photograph by A. F. Brady

his admirers, knew it not, he was the very symbol of America's tragedy. And still is.

The American people, in spite of their practicality, are a people of sentiment and illusions. A pioneer race, which has had to struggle for sheer existence, it has learned to judge spiritual success by material values; literature, as well as commerce, came to be regulated by the law of supply and demand. A good author was one who successfully surmounted the law of the average; a poor author was one who could not make ends meet. To succeed one went out for "definite things." Now, what is a definite thing? Money, a motor-car, a house, anything tangible to the senses; indeed, the whole world of reality. But if you had asked Anatole France, he would have said: "No, these things are not real." That they are thought real is an illusion. What is real is a thought, a fancy, a generous inclination, beauty. The real world is the world created by the imagination, since it is the only world capable of producing great happiness; "definite things" have a place in the harmony but not the whole place.

Mark Twain, a great man, was a victim of his background and generation. He had an excess of energy; he was a veritable Niagara of power, he had found it easy to harness this power to supply the demand made upon it; he became rich and popular, the doors of the great were open to him; he should have been the happiest of men. Yet, as his posthumous confession shows, he was far from happy in those last years when he faced the final reckoning and found himself wanting, and found all of mankind wanting. He felt that things were not what they seemed, that something was wrong somewhere. What it was, he felt dimly in the deeps of himself, and he realized that he might have been different, that what he was had been created by his audience; no longer he felt like laughing, but turned upon his audience, which looked to him for laugh-provoking gibes, to castigate it in terms of detestation. He was suffering a reaction; and an American in reaction is a person who goes to the other extreme; witness to-day the once law-abiding citizen deliberately breaking the law of prohibition. But the law of balance is the law of contented life; and because she has not abused this law, the country of Anatole France has still her wines. This must not be thought extraneous to the comparison: Anatole France is France, Mark Twain, America; both men were stamped with the virtues and the faults of their countries; one had balance, the other exuberance; who will say which is the greater virtue? If a choice had to be made, many would choose exuberance, which properly directed could work miracles of ecstasy. Childlike exuberance was the supreme quality of Mark Twain's genius, as it is of his country.

The difference in the genius of the two men and of the two races which produced them could not be better marked than in their treatment of the same theme: both men wrote the *Life of Joan of Arc.*

It is enough to say that Anatole France has sought to convey above everything else a rational explanation of the Maid's activities; and that the realistic character of France's history greatly incensed Mark Twain.

As for Mark Twain's account, that is an altogether different affair. His chief burden has been to show the spotless purity of the French heroine, her "unique . . . flawless . . . ideally perfect" character. The long catalogue of her marvelous virtues is given in the preface to the book which is the author's own favorite production on which he had worked lovingly for years. The suspicion has been expressed that Mark Twain has created a purely imaginary character out of his latent sentiment fed on America's worship of perfect and innocent womanhood.

The relative merits of the two conceptions need not enter here: what is important is that the one is as surely Anatole France and French as the other is Mark Twain and American.

It comes down to this: one might conceivably bemoan the fact that America is not Europe, but surely not that Mark Twain is not Anatole France.

PAUL GAUGUIN—"THE SAVAGE"

Paul Gauguin, whom contemporaries were to call "the savage" and whom posterity was to know as a great rebel and a great painter, came home that evening to his elegant flat in Rue du Tourneaux in a singularly distressing state of mind. He had had a particularly successful day at the bourse, his speculations having netted him several thousand francs. It was good to have this money in the pocket. It was good to be healthy, well-fed and comfortable. It was good to have the things one wanted. He stretched out from where he sat in a large cozy chair before a large table with its shaded lamp, which had been just lighted by his wife, and took a bottle of old cognac and helped himself to a glass. He sipped the cognac slowly, and felt every drop pass between his teeth, like a sybarite.

Yet, inwardly, he felt discontented, even bitter.

He was of medium stature, stockily built, strong yet sensitive-featured. He had a long vigorous nose, aquiline like an eagle's; small, heavy-lidded, gray-green eyes, under arched eyebrows; a thin drooping mustache hanging over large coarse lips; a pointed chin, and chestnut-red hair, which fell in straggling masses over a broad but rather low forehead; presenting in the *ensemble* a portrait of intense physical virility combined with sensitiveness.

Despite his health and strength and the visible well-being of his surroundings, discontented shadows passed across his face, and inwardly he felt strange unaccustomed tremors as of a sleeping volcano awakening.

That day, not for the first time, he had witnessed on the floor of the exchange the familiar sight of men, so-called civilized beings, like so many beasts, scrambling and fighting in the effort to sell or buy shares. Their faces, which he now recalled with singular vividness, were distorted, greedy, desperate. With wild eyes and frantic gestures, they jostled one another, while their almost unintelligible cries, mingling, filled the place with a mad restless clamor. Even as his own person jostled with the rest and joined in their inarticulate cries, as of birds descending on crumbs of food, he had at one instant caught himself laughing at this unseemly spectacle and had murmured under his breath, "The pigs!" And these men went to church and called themselves Christians! God, how sick he was of the whole business!

But it wasn't altogether that which distressed him now. Something deeper, more insidious, went on working within him, and threatened to explode. A strange idea. An unaccountable emotion. It was a dream of sun, color, peace, ecstatic peace; of a land where money was unknown and men lived in brotherly amity. A dream of a new Garden of Eden. A dream of happiness, of god-like serenity.

He rose from his chair, and resolutely went to the portrait of his mother, which hung on the wall. He regarded it with a fixed intent gaze. What a strange, elusive small head had Aline Marie Gauguin, with its enigmatic expression, like one of those archaic Greek heads, passionate yet serene, with the changeless smile of eternity! How proud she looked! Proud with the blood of Spain (and he had more than a suspicion of its blend with the blood of the Incas), which flowed in her veins. And there was beside her a sketch done of that strange woman, her mother, the once celebrated Flora Tristan, born in Peru of a Spaniard of noble descent, Mariano Tristan y Moscoso. Flora had married a certain Chazal, a passionate man but nobody in particular; she had eloped with him and had thereby incurred the wrath of her stately parents, who straightwith disowned their self-willed daughter and refused to take her back even after the birth of Aline when she left Chazal. Flora became a Socialist pamphleteer in Paris and had quite a following. Paul smiled at the thought. He strongly suspected that it was her beauty that they followed rather than her ideas of human liberation. "And who would not follow beauty?" he mused to himself. Indeed, Flora's own husband, having, years later, the misfortune to meet his wife again in Paris, in a fit of jealousy stabbed her and was condemned to twenty years' penal servitude for the offense. Paul again smiled. He understood Chazal. There were men like that. If they could not possess beauty they must slay it. And it enabled him to understand the curious blend of bloods flowing in his own veins, that tragic violence of the Chazal-Tristan union, of which Aline was born; and he the son of his mother! Long asleep, something was stirring within him, filling him with an active distress and a growing aspiration.

He looked at these two beautiful faces, and he spoke aloud their names, which now sounded for him as songs calling to battle.

"Oh, Flora Tristan! Oh, Aline Marie Gauguin!"

He was becoming conscious of their blood flowing through his veins. "And should not Paul Gauguin do something, be something?" Must he for ever remain a banker, and die a *bourgeois?*

Life, hitherto dormant, roused in the deeps of him with a great stirring, filled him with as yet an unutterable longing to play the part for which he had been cast by nature.

How had he ever come to be married, to unite himself

to an ordinary woman, and to have five children by her, now millstones around his neck? And he an issue of such blood, born in Paris on a fateful June day in 1848, at a moment when the shots of the revolutionaries were flying from behind barricades! It seemed inconceivable. He had had, even as a mere youngster, the *wanderlust,* and more than once had traversed the wide seas as an ordinary sailor. How had he got into this?

"I'm really a savage!" he murmured to himself, and as he looked around the room with all its comfortable arrangements he was seized with a sudden impulse to break things. Then he laughed. "I suppose I have enough of the civilized man in me not to do it. Every civilized thought in me seems to paralyze my will. Civilization is paralysis."

At the same time his glance fell on the paintings on his walls. He had, during the last five years, since he was thirty, been collecting paintings. But his greatest pleasure, of late, had been to do some painting himself, and this he could manage only on Sundays! Irony of ironies! On the day which all good Christians regarded as a day of rest he was able to indulge in the only work he really loved. Work? Yes. But also a joy. All work should be a joy, so he thought. That was the trouble with our civilization, he went on reflecting. Work was one thing, joy another. The hand no longer took pleasure in what it did. People shut up everything in separate compartments. The very men he had seen scrambling that day for filthy lucre were devout Christians on Sunday. Bah!

His eyes lingered lovingly on the paintings. He had some choice things. Two Daumiers, a Manet, some Renoirs and Monets, two Cézannes, and a Pissarro, among others; mostly men who were being laughed at just then. What was it to him what fools did? These things were beautiful, and they soothed him into a calm and filled him with ecstasy, which time and time again turned into despair because he was only a dabbler, a dilettante, in a position to paint only on Sundays. How ridiculous to have only one day a week for that which he loved best!

His glance rested for a long time and with particular affection on the Pissarro, an early one; and on the Guillamin. It was not that he thought them better than the others. But he had especial tenderness for them because it was just five years ago that he stopped before a dealer's shop and saw them in the window; the paintings of these men had brought back memories of the warm light and color he had seen in the tropics. He had looked up these men, the authors of these pictures, and had been seduced by them into the practise of painting. He felt grateful to them for bringing an interest and a pleasure into his life. But it proved also a vexation and a pain on the six days of the week in which he could not paint. His business in Bertin's banking-house, in Rue Lafitte, demanded all his time but Sundays. He was a prosperous man, but lately his position had begun to gall him.

If only it weren't for his wife and his five youngsters—including his own, seven mouths to feed! The code of civilization demanded that he support his helpmeet and their progeny, and he was an honorable man. It was a real dilemma, and it irked and fretted him. And now his whole being, volcanic in mood and growing more so each day, threatened to explode.

He asked himself again: How had he come to marry this woman of the north, this puritan, this Mette Sophia Gad, a Protestant clergyman's daughter, of Copenhagen? Hers was a good family, to be sure, which enjoyed an honored position in the Danish capital. That had meant something to him earlier when he had wanted to settle down. But now that his dream had come to him and incessantly troubled him, it presented a dilemma from which there seemed to be no way out.

Yet that very day he had made an irrevocable decision.

He knew it would be a cause of great pain and perturbation to his wife, and he had yet to tell her about it. He knew it might involve him in sacrifices too; these, if need be, he was willing to stand. All the same, it was not pleasant to hurt other people, even if there was no help for it.

"I'm a poor sort of savage!" he thought. "Damn this civilization which puts weakening ideas into one's head!" At the same time, he mused on, no man of genius ever let family obstacles stand in his way. Was he a genius? That hardly mattered. How was he ever to know if he did not try? To be sure, he did try on Sundays! He laughed aloud. Art was a "jealous mistress," so everybody said. That was true enough, and a commonplace. Well, then, what mistress would put up with seeing her lover once a week while he devoted the rest of the time to his wife? What, after all, did his devotion to his art amount to? "Bah!" he almost shouted, and gave an expressive grunt.

He heard his wife's footsteps in the corridor approaching his door. There was a knock, and, in response to his determined "Come in!" she entered.

"I've heard that you've had a good day on the bourse!" she greeted him. She looked maternal, as befitted one who was the mother of five children, and had that touch of northern austerity which marked her as the daughter of a Lutheran clergyman.

"Yes. And we'll need it!" he said rather brusquely, plunging at once to the crux of the matter.

She looked at him questioningly, as if she understood that his manner portended something more than lay revealed on the surface.

"I'm going to leave Bertin's!" he announced.

"Leave Bertin's? What do you mean, Paul?" There was alarm in her voice. "You are not going into business for yourself?"

"Yes, I am! But it will be a different sort of business. I am going to paint pictures!"

"Paint pictures?" she repeated vaguely after him, with visible agitation. "You already paint on Sundays!"

"On Sundays!" he cried with exasperation. "You talk as if I were wasting one day a week. What's the good of painting on Sundays? I am going to paint every day hereafter! Yes, every day!"

"And how are we going to live?"

"How? Other painters sell their pictures. Why shouldn't I?" His voice softened. "There's a fortune in it when you get going!"

"That's just it!" persisted his wife. "It takes years to get going in art. How often do we not hear of geniuses starving in garrets?"

"Nonsense!" cried Gauguin. "I'm different. I'm a practical man. I haven't spent all these years on the stock exchange for nothing. I will see to it that the rich swine pay, and pay handsomely! And Madame Gauguin will have a more honored place as the wife of a great painter than as the wife of a moderately successful stock-broker!"

Mette stopped protesting. She had a great faith in her husband. And his last words had the effect of opening up an alluring vista for the future. The idea of being the wife of a successful artist and of mingling in the society of celebrities pleased her, and she made no further demur. In any case, she saw that his mind was made up, and she knew that he was not the man to be swerved from his purpose.

And henceforth he kept to his resolution: the stock exchange knew him no more, he painted every day.

In eight months the Gauguin family found themselves in straitened circumstances, and Paul's relations with Mette grew more difficult.

"Let us go to Brittany," he said. "Everything is cheaper there. Beefsteak is actually ten sous less per pound than it is in Paris."

The man who had but lately the income of forty thousand francs a year and been lavish with it developed a spirit of strict economy. He entertained the notion that ten sous saved on this and that would enable him to keep his large family going.

He had already sold at a loss his small choice collection of paintings, though it nearly broke his heart to do it. He had kept three, a still life and a landscape by Cézanne and an interior by Pissarro, which he could not bear to part with. And he had a sentimental regard for the Pissarro, for, with a childlike gratitude, he could not forget that it was Pissarro who first opened his eyes to the paradise of color. He had also left his comfortable flat in the Rue du Tourneaux and moved to the Rue Carcel at Vaugirard. Most of the proceeds derived from his collection dissipated, he moved once more, this time to Brittany.

For several months the little tribe stayed at Rouen and suffered all manner of privations. Poor Madame Gauguin, in moments of vexation at their changed fortunes, could not desist from reminding him of the flesh-pots of the Rue du Tourneaux. Paul listened in silence and went on painting. He was hungry himself, but he was becoming used to hunger. Suffering sharpened his genius. He dreaded one thing, and that was that his suffering might go so far as to kill him before he had accomplished his dream in color.

Madame Gauguin could stand it no longer. "Let's go to Copenhagen," she said. "There my people have a position, and perhaps they can bring enough influence to bear to secure you some easy job which will still enable you to indulge in your art!"

And once more the family, like a gypsy camp, raised its tents, and moved to Copenhagen. This brought only new troubles. Paul persisted in his free Bohemian ways in an atmosphere wholly alien to them. Mette, in her home of rigid Lutheran piety, found herself at loggerheads with her husband. As for Paul, the only thing he liked about the place were the excellent culinary creations of his mother-in-law. "By gad," thought Paul, "that woman can cook almost as well as I can paint!" He could not pay her a higher compliment. That was the whole secret of life: sticking to one's job! Many excellent cooks were spoiled by going into the arts. So thought Paul, and, in spite of the unfriendly atmosphere, went on painting.

"They think me a savage!" he once said to himself in the midst of his creating, and added, laughing: "They are quite right. I am!"

His contempt for civilization and its conventions produced, one fine day, a first-rate scandal. He happened to be walking on the road which overlooks the bay of the Sund, and he was silently bemoaning the difficulty of securing necessary models in the nude. He was dreaming of a terrestrial Eden where men and women walked about as God made them and were not ashamed. Just then he chanced to look down. There, below him, he saw a naked woman leave a small cabin and approach the water. She was the wife of a Protestant minister (not that that mattered!), and she was on her own estate, one of several bordering the beach, where the sexes were in the habit of bathing separately and wholly naked. Here eyes trained to modesty did not pry; for, of a truth, since Adam was driven out of the Garden of Eden he was not meant to look upon the nakedness of women. So were these people taught, and the quiet Danish women bathed in the seclusion of their estates without thought of man being so brazen as to venture to look upon them. But Paul had no consciousness of being brazen. The whiteness of the flesh, the soft rounded contours of the body, the natural grace of a woman walking; indeed, all the rhythms of the human mechanism, interested him, and his only thought was how he might render nature's wonders with pigments used with taste and skill. Thus absorbed, he watched the woman slowly walking, and a composition was taking form in his mind. Just as the woman was about to put one of her feet in the water, a frantic feminine voice from the bathing cabin called to her:

"Mother! Mother! Come back! There's a man looking!"

The elder woman looked up, met Paul's gaze, and, with a shriek, rushed back to her cabin.

The next day there was the devil to pay. Voices were raised against this impudent vile stranger who had dared to infringe on the decency of the good people. And Paul was forced to fly. He went first to Paris, then to Brittany. He thought grimly to himself:

"All the people who know me will now say: 'Paul Gauguin is a wicked man. He has deserted his wife and children, and has left them to shift for themselves!' "

So it was to be. Society raised its hand against Paul and declared him its enemy. He did not deny it. He *was* an avowed enemy of society as society was constituted, and his hand was raised against it, as society's hand was raised against him. He was yet to issue his challenge but the creation of color symphonies embodying his dream of Eden, full of serene rapture and of love—love which was simple and natural and did not flaunt itself in the familiar frantic gestures of the civilized European, to him an insidious, degenerate and neurotic creature.

If only he could sell his paintings! He would send some of the proceeds to his wife. After all, the poor woman was not to blame. He had given her five children. And Europe, civilization, did not look after its children. Poor things, he did not care much for them, except for Aline, but he did not want to see them starving. He had lately sent nineteen paintings to the Impressionist exhibition. The practical results were nothing to boast about. The idea of starving before he had put his dream on canvas filled him with horror, and it was becoming an obsession.

He was reduced to pasting up bills at Gare du Nord at three francs and fifty centimes a day!

Here in Paris they were saying horrible things about him. They were saying that he was ruthless, selfish, rude—in short, "a savage." He was proud, reserved, and did not suffer fools gladly. He divided the artistic world into two classes, geniuses and hangers-on. The hangers-on did not like being put where they belonged.

Seeing him starving, one Schuffenecker, who had, like himself, given up the exchange for painting, had taken him in. And the malicious were circulating stories of how Gauguin, imposing on his host, made himself thoroughly at home in Schuffenecker's place. "One would think," said one of them, "that Gauguin was the host and poor Schuffenecker a mere intruder!" As for Gauguin, he thought: "What of it? After all, I have the genius, and Schuffenecker is my moneyed patron." Shall the world lose his dream because he was squeamish? Life had deprived him of the means necessary to the expression of himself. If he was what he thought he was, he must take his means where he found it. Schuffenecker's studio was useful, and food was not less essential if he was to go on painting.

Unknown to others, he was being consumed with an

inner turbulence, with a fearful unrest, with a fire which threatened to split him. This fire was being fanned by the externals of his life, by what he saw about him. He was sick of all this hubbub, of this interminable gossip, of petty envy, of useless strife. The lives of these men, bitten with the poison of Europe, were hardly better than those of the men he had seen scrambling and fighting at the bourse. There was no frankness, no honesty, no amity; not anywhere. There was something rotten about it all. He longed for the peace of some isle, where life roamed free under the sun, where the folk lived without regret for yesterday or thought for to-morrow, where the sunlit seas lapped gently the serene shore. It was a portion of his dream.

Memories of his early voyages returned to him. And stirred by them and by his dream, he made a dash for Martinique. A friend went with him, a Charles Laval, almost a mere boy. The sun and the wild verdure and the warm sea and the swarthy half-breeds, like beings cast in bronze, found their way into Paul's paintings. It was not the same sun which he saw in Brittany, where sadness called to him, and the Martinique sun and all the rest he found there were a portion of his dream. But young Laval could not stand the sun's heat, and, brooding under it, tried to take his own life. Paul saved his young friend and they returned to France, but not before he had caught a glimpse of what he sought.

About this time, in response to an appeal from his friend, Vincent Van Gogh, he went to Arles, where the two friends painted their color symphonies almost side by side. In ways they formed a contrast, these two: the one a "savage," the other a naive child and a Christian in spirit; and they loved and respected each other. But it was not very long before Gauguin returned to Paris, outwardly as be-

fore, exhibiting a pride which caused him to be hated, inwardly torn with a tragic grief.

What had happened? As he looked back on it, the whole thing took on the semblance of a frightening nightmare. And it was the culmination of his European experience, of his sadness and disgust.

He remembered vaguely the growing moodiness and irritability of his friend. One day Vincent turned to Paul who was working on his own portrait.

"Yes, the likeness is there," said Vincent slowly. "It is I—after I have gone mad."

And that very evening—that unforgettable evening!—while they were sitting in a café, Vincent really went mad. He had thrown his glass at Paul's head, and the latter had to take him home and quiet him.

Next day—God, what a day!—Paul made preparations for returning to Paris. While passing through the Place Victor Hugo he heard quick, sharp little steps, which sounded very familiar to him. He turned in time to see Vincent making a dash for him with an open razor. Paul looked at him with an intent gaze, the sort with which men have been known to quiet a beast. Vincent paused, lowered his head, then started running back to the house.

Broken with grief, and in the deeps of despair, Paul turned his steps to a hotel, and engaged a bed there. Tired out, he at last fell asleep, and slept until evening.

He went out-of-doors and found a crowd gathered in the square. There were policemen at the house where the two friends lived.

This is what had happened.

Vincent, after his threat against Paul, returned home and shaved one ear clear off. As soon as he contrived to stop the bleeding he did up his head tightly in a Basque cap and left the house. He went direct to a house of ill-repute and handed the ear, which had been well washed, to the porter. "Here," he said, "is a present from me." Then he hurried home and, after closing the blinds and leaving a lighted lamp near the window, flung himself on to a bed and fell asleep.

Ten minutes later the street given over to the *filles de joie* was in a clamor and filled with chatter about the extraordinary happening.

The report went around that Vincent was dead.

Paul found Vincent lying in bed. He touched the body gently. Its warmth reassured him. "Thank God, he's alive!" thought Paul. This certainty appeared to restore his energy and his presence of mind. He turned softly to the Police Inspector:

"Sir, I beg you to awaken this man with the greatest care, and if he asks for me say that I have returned to Paris. The sight of me might be fatal to him."

Unknown to Vincent, Paul was still in the house when the sick man awoke. He at once asked for his comrade, then for his pipe and tobacco, and ended by demanding his money-box which was down-stairs. So he actually thought that Paul might rob him! Paul, loving his friend, winced, but immediately recovered himself. He was now ready, armed against suffering. Or thought he was. For when one dives into the deeps of the sea of suffering one may bear up under its weight without perceiving it.

He seemed later to remember an illuminating moment while painting a portrait of Vincent, when he saw a vision of "Jesus preaching goodness and humility." And, in the final moment of his leave-taking, when he had stood before the sleeping Vincent, he saw another vision which became associated in his mind with Golgotha.

It was a different man who returned to Paris than left it. But no one knew it but himself.

In Paris he was to receive a letter from his friend who, then living at an asylum, was able, in lucid intervals, not only to paint, but to remember the wrong he had done Paul. "Dear Master," he wrote, "it is better, after having known you and wronged you, that I die in a clear mind rather than in a degraded state." And later, he heard that Vincent "shot himself in the stomach with a pistol and died in a few hours, lying in bed, smoking a pipe, his mind as clear as ever, loving his art and hating no one."

Here people were saying malicious things about the Paul-Vincent episode. "Gauguin is a savage, and has an evil eye." Such was the legend which was growing up around his name. And Paul did not deny it. "Yes, undoubtedly, I am a savage, and many men with whom I have associated have gone mad." And again and again he asked himself: "Am I a criminal?" Nor had the old story about his having deserted his wife and his offspring died down. Paul bore it all with stoicism, and went on painting every day—every day.—He had kept to his word!

One woman loved him. Her name was Juliette, but few who knew him ever saw her. He kept her from vulgar eyes. She gave him all, and asked nothing in return. She was a simple creature, no blue-stocking, and loved him with no thought of the morrow. Intuitively she felt his greatness, knew him to be different from the others, and he sometimes spoke to her of his dream. "A land, my dear, where there are no shopkeepers, no money, no false shame . . . where men live without thought of injuring one another . . ." He came to her from the turmoil of the life around him as a traveler in the desert comes to his oasis. . . . But his dream was always with him as a beckoning mirage and would not allow him to rest. The Vincent affair had been the last straw. He must get away from this dangerous evil jungle of civilized life to some place where things were different, where he might try not only to paint his dream in peace but live it! How tired he was of this perpetual clamor, of this vain noisy world, which incessantly jangled on his nerves!

Was there one spot left on earth where he might rest, where he might paint his earthly paradise in reality as well as in the spirit? How was one to paint the visible calm and peace of soul when one was surrounded by strife, the puerility of hangers-on, the traffic of shopkeepers, the petty bickerings of critics, the inanity of society, the idiotic ridicule of the public? Serenity belonged to God and to eternity, and here was neither God nor faith, neither worship nor worshipers. Only the golden idol, Money, and round it the *danse macabre* of men who did not know that they were dancing to their ultimate doom. Disdain for everything about him filled him, and only peasants and children he respected and loved. Before them his shyness would disappear, his customary rudeness give way to a gentle courtesy.

How long, oh, how long, must he suffer? Where, oh, where, should he go?

Chance one day brought about a solution. He read the report of a lecture. A certain Van der Veere, on the previous day, had tickled the jaded palates of a fashionable audience by describing the beauties of Tahiti. He pictured this island as a terrestrial paradise, where money was unknown. "Under a sky without winter, upon an earth of marvelous fertility, the Tahitian has only to lift his hands to gather his food; so he never works. For him life means singing and making love."

This newspaper item filled him with intense excitement. The mere word, "Tahiti," became to him the open-sesame flinging open the gates to the sought-for paradise.

On to Tahiti! He made another irrevocable decision, second only in gravity to his decision to take up painting.

He went just as his pictures began to sell. He auctioned his unsold pictures and received several thousand francs. Before his departure he was fêted a great deal. He smiled to himself at his friends' solicitude—no doubt, there were some among them who were delighted to see him go! As a final honor, a joint benefit performance was arranged for him and the poet Verlaine, which brought Gauguin nothing and Verlaine only a little. This event saw the first production of Maeterlinck's *The Intruder*. Paul alone, perhaps, saw the irony of this. He saw Death itself stalk on the stage like a premonition of what awaited him in his paradise. He knew what awaited any one who sought paradise, God's kingdom on earth. "Where there is greatness, there is Golgotha!" These words of Heine's came to his mind, and lingered there with a curious persistence. He knew, yet he did not flinch.

What happened to Paul Gauguin in Tahiti?

That is a long story, but it can be told briefly, like a parable. Here he found not paradise but remnants of what must have been once paradise, and he made haste to gather up the remnants lest they be lost. Here by day the sunlit seas gently lapped the serene shore, and the immense, lovely, clear dome of the sky really might be called heaven. And in the night there were the dense silences between the last glow of the descended sun behind the inland hills and the white glow of the dawn, and in this darkness Christ might have walked as He walked in Gethsemane. And sometimes Paul thought he heard the communings of ancient South Sea spirits, now in exile.

But the European blight had set in—strictly speaking, the French blight. Like a virulent poison, civilization had already left some ugly spots on the primitive beauty of the island; Progress made for the progressive degeneration of the islanders. And on the very day of Paul's arrival, he met with the significant omen: the last Tahitian king was lying in state!

This was in Papeete. Farther inland, glimpses of the terrestrial paradise remained. Here Paul settled, took to himself a native wife, and dressed and talked like a native. Here he went on painting his color symphonies of the life which, under pressure of Europe, was passing; and these canvases, serene challenges, went to Europe to taunt jaded men. He became a legend there, and more than ever a "savage." As for him, he might have remained happy where he was, but for one thing, and the one thing which he came here to escape—money! Hardly a letter he wrote to his great friend, Georges Daniel de Monfreid, but expressed his dire straits, his need of money. He needed money for canvas, for paint, for a habitation, for food. This was in accordance with the regulations of civilization, which had conquered the island. Nothing was to be had without money. And if you wanted money, there was a French bank here. Thus, even in this terrestrial paradise, he felt the grip of civilization at his throat.

Paul's paintings were selling in Paris and in Copenhagen in a small way. Some of the money went into the purses of dealers, some found its way to his wife's purse. Some came to him too, but it never sufficed to "keep him going."

He went to France, and returned disgusted.

He finally went to one of the islands of the Marquesas group, hoping to find a more primitive form of existence there than in Tahiti. Here he took the part of the natives against the French, and suffered indescribably. He died alone, sick and discouraged, mourned only by the natives.

Now "the savage" is held in great regard by Europe; the civilization he despised holds him in honor. And one of his paintings fetches enough money to have kept him painting a lifetime! A hungry, haunted spirit, he lived for posterity; therefore, posterity alone knows how to honor him.

If an epitaph were needed, nothing could serve better than the title of his Tahitian masterpiece, *D'ou venons-nous—Que sommes-nous—Ou allons-nous?*—"Where do we come from—What are we?—Where are we going?" And that picture is all the answer we may have. If humanity were to understand it, then indeed the stock-brokers would stop "stock-broking" and the terrestrial paradise might be in sight.

HENRY THOREAU—HATER OF SHAMS

ONE evening—it was during the early 'forties—a man carrying under his arm a boot which needed mending was walking toward the cobbler's in the village of Concord, Massachusetts. He was advancing with the firm step of a man used to walking long distances across country, and there was something in his stride which bespoke resolution of character and independence of mind—something almost pugnacious, one might say. Under thirty years of age, with a large aquiline nose and queer mouth which its owner would have done well to hide under a deciduous hirsute growth over the upper lip, he was decidedly unprepossessing as to looks. But his eyes, which had the appearance of being used to gaze into long distances, were clear and honest and intelligent and virile; a stranger might have also considered them hard. The same stranger might have found himself at a loss if he had tried to determine to what stratum of society the man with the boot under his arm belonged, to what trade he was bound, and what justification could be found for him in life. The man looked as if he did not give a tinker's dam as to what any one thought. Now and then, as he walked, a farmer or a work-hand he happened to meet greeted him laconically, and it was clear from the greeting that he enjoyed their respect and even their affection.

The man was nearing the cobbler's, when a big jovial fellow clapped him on the shoulder, an action which did not seem natural when one considered the proud aloof bearing of the man whose shoulder suffered the indignity. The good-natured man was Sam Staples, the local jailer and tax-collector, and the man on whose shoulder his hand descended so affectionately was none other than Henry Thoreau, a graduate of Harvard and now a local celebrity, a philosopher whose aim in life was to be natural, himself, and to meddle in no man's business.

Staples, though a jailer, was a kindly soul, and had a fondness for Thoreau, and his first remark was friendly enough.

"I'll pay your tax, Henry, if you're hard up."

But Henry was not hard up, and said so. To be frank, he thought the State poll-tax unjust, and he hadn't the least intention of paying it.

That being the case, poor Staples, being the authorized tax-collector of the place, had no alternative but to do his duty, which was to conduct his friend to jail. He did this with not a little reluctance and regret.

Henry made no demur. A lover of solitudes, he was mindful of the fact that in jail as well as anywhere, he would have the longed-for opportunity to meditate to his heart's content without hindrance from intruding, well-meaning people. He was self-contained; he bore his world, such as it was, within himself. They might deprive him of his physical liberty, even of his possessions; they could not take from him the only capital he had which was of any value,—his thoughts,—the only capital which does not diminish with full use. And where is there a better place than the inside of a jail to contemplate the beauties and benefits of official institutions? He had given much thought to the subject, and here he was to have a practical demonstration of his opinions. He was nothing if not practical.

Was it so tedious, so boring, then, to sit in a little cell, with his thoughts for companions? Not when the thoughts, despite their being shut in between the walls of the skull as one's body is by the walls of the jail, are yet free to journey at will through the universe. Eastern sages, he was aware, can think of infinity while for days and weeks contemplating a crack in the wall; and there was something of the Eastern sage about Henry. The world itself, as he saw it, was for most men but a larger prison in which they walked about wrapped in the illusion that they were free while actually bound by a thousand habits and fictitious needs and conventions, hiding their real selves atrophied by that larger ignorance which was far from being bliss. Not much space is needed for the body if one's thoughts are free. His mind wandered, now to the Pharaohs, now to Pericles, now to the eternal Ganges, then into the starry space; and neither the Chinese Wall nor the multitudinous nebluæ of the Milky Way hindered their progress, faster than the light of stars. It was marvelous thus to sit still and survey time and space. Thus also, thousands of years hence, future ages might look back upon Thoreau's outer world and pronounce it a prison, wherein ignorance and barbarism reigned. And the prison cell in which he sat in punishment for his virtue was the living symbol of that world.

So Henry was thinking, while his observant glance paused on a spider weaving his web. Back and forth, back and forth, from point to point, from point to point, journeys the deft insect, weaving its silken thread to catch the stupid fly which wings through space and might go on winging through space, an infinitude of space, yet allows itself to be caught in the silken meshes of tenuous illusion. Is not this a picture of dual man, man the spider and man the fly, one weaving the web, the other flying into it—meshes the prisoner may not break for all the fineness of the silken tissue? Foolish man, to be caught thus to his undoing!

Henry was having a marvelous, an exulting time.

Foolish, foolish man, to live and struggle under laws and regulations binding him to shop, counter or office desk, to think ever and ever of security, to fill his house with a thousand useless things matching the furniture of his mind, to toil and moil, to indulge in petty joys and petty lusts, in the end to die without having lived. Six days a week a man did toil, and on the seventh he rested. Foolish man not to have a week of one working-day and six Sabbaths!

His mind went wandering to his college days. He had gone to Harvard. For what? Harvard had not taught him anything. He saw no way of using Harvard knowledge in life. He had cast off all that knowledge which spurred men to careers, "to get on" in the world, as the saying goes. He deemed as useless much of what other men called useful. What he had said on the day of his "commencement" he stood by now, years later. He had then said: Men were active, energetic, restless, they thought faster and freer than ever before. The winds and the waves, and all the provision of nature, were not enough for men; they must needs dig deep into the bowels of the earth that they might travel faster on its surface. The earth had become a vast beehive. Yet, in the midst of all this bustle, how many men lived their lives wisely and well? Hardly one in a hundred. How many were happy? One might count the happy ones on one's fingers, and they were by no means among the bustlers. As often as not, they were like the happy beggar of the fairy tale whose shirt the king sought for his happiness only to find that the beggar had no shirt. The happiest traveler was he who carried the least baggage. Possessions hindered men from taking wing.

What a wonderful place the earth was with its profuse beauty, with its diversity of climes, variety of vegetation and of animal life, and changes of season. It was the Garden of Eden, if men wanted it so. Yet what were men doing? They were abusing the wealth of nature, they thought of nature wholly in terms of utility, they made nature a beast of burden, and made themselves beasts of burden. The commercial spirit was rampant in the land, everything was done to foster and sustain it. It developed "a blind and unmanly love of wealth." The ruling spirit, "it infused into all our thoughts and affections a degree of its own selfishness; we become selfish in our patriotism, selfish in our domestic relations, selfish in our religion."

So Henry had thought when he was twenty. So he thought now, years later. He was a man who had his mind made up when he was born. He would die thinking the same thoughts. To him there was this vexing thing about most men: they were too confused by the conflict between their nature and their education to know what they wanted. They were one thing one hour, another the next. Impulse pulled them one way, civilized artifice another. One never knew where to find them. But he, Henry, never had the least doubt as to the sort of life he ought to lead; for that matter, he had more than an inkling that it would be well for the world if it could share his modest desires. People thought too much of making their lives useful; they saw everything in terms of utility. Yet he, Henry, knew with a knowledge which would brook of no contradiction that "this curious world which we inhabit is more wonderful than it is convenient; more beautiful than it is useful; it is more to be admired and enjoyed than used." And again and again he thought, it would be well if the order of things were reversed; "the seventh should be man's day of toil, wherein to earn his living by the sweat of his brow; the other six his Sabbath of the affections and the soul—in which to range this wide-spread garden and drink in the soft influences and sublime revelations of Nature."

He himself was the happiest of men. He communed with the trees of the forest and heard delicious mysteries in the mere rustling of leaves in the wind; he spoke with the birds and the snakes and knew their secret wisdom; it was fine to walk on the soft moss yielding under his feet; every blade of grass lived for him its own enchanted life. It was a joy to pick a berry on the way. Was this monotonous? The seasons gave him diversity. And, oh, the splendors of the sun in the spring! It warmed your back with a soft tenderness; it thawed out the sleepy winter in your soul; you felt that first slow awakening as when the tiny rivulets begin to flow from under the yet clinging snow. And, oh, the splendor of water as it mirrors blue skies, and the joy of being in a canoe as it gracefully skims the pellucid surfaces, and the attendant joy of pausing somewhere, leaping on to shore wooded with pines, of building a fire in a remote glade, of spreading on the ground your modest repast tastier than any dish out of the king's kitchen, of gulping it all down with a cupful or two of the freshest, coolest of spring water which you had gone out to find and had found!

He was a savage, some had said, and he had not said nay. There was something to be said for savages. He felt a closer kinship with the red Indian than with the white man who had driven him out. Poor deluded white man, with his bagful of illusions, and flasks of fire-water to sustain them! Men had been swept along by ambition—for conquest, for wealth, for power. Of what avail these energetic efforts which were always stopped by the grave, always ended by tumbling into a small hole three by six, the mightiest ambitions being but food for worms? They could not take with them the kingdoms they had conquered, the wealth they had accrued. Folly and vanity!

And yet, he thought, there was one thing surely worth while; and that was Love—when it was Love! Not love founded on sham or illusion; nor yet that love, like other things in men's lives, inspired by the commercial spirit, based on lust, convenience or blindness. Far from being blind, Love, if it was Love, was the most seeing thing on earth; it could not be simulated, nor could it be a victim of deception. True love was the highest wisdom; a double harness, if you like, but a double harmony too; one was at harmony with oneself and one was in harmony with the other. It was the supreme friendship of two imaginations as well as of two hearts. It was always the lover's imagination that was hurt before his or her heart was hurt. A thing of infinitely delicate perceptions, it saw and it felt, and its fingers played on the heart as on a stringed instrument luring from it a tune of passionate ecstasy or a dirge of aches and wails. Love was the greatest reality, for it could least endure sham. And nothing lived on sham so much as that unreality which so often passed with men under the name of Love. Did not a hidden lust hide under a mask of polite pretentions to purity? Certainly, there was a great deal of sham in society's attitude, which was to swathe the subject in silence and mystery. But this silence was not the silence which took natural things for granted, and it was born of the effort to hide false shame; and this mystery was not the mystery which is as a screening veil to a sacred religious rite, but an implication of something downright nasty and ugly. Thus was the most sacred function in life, the function of producing more life, so intimately allied with the deepest religious mood, dragged in the mud. What was more beautiful than man and woman in harmony, in body and spirit? What miracle surpassed this, while Love remained? The flame of a perfect union consumed false shame and elevated passion to the realm of religious experience. Did not Herodotus relate how the Assyrian husband and wife, after experiencing the mutual ecstasy, had sat up until dawn round the bowl of burning incense as a tribute to the creative spirit of their God? Only that which was sham countenanced false shame and extolled it as a virtue, masking from the world unclean flames hurtful to the race. And the hope of the race, thought Henry, lay precisely in Love, in harmonious unions born of Love. Men could not be improved, as some men thought, by being bred in the way cattle are bred. "Let Love be purified, and all the rest will follow." Yes, he thought, "a pure love is the panacea for all the ills of the world."

There was, to be sure, no woman as yet to fill Henry's life for him. Why did not the preacher practise his own doctrine? Henry's life was full as it was. He was in love with Nature; he sat at Nature's feet and let her caressing breezes run through his hair. He strove to be at one with her, to imbibe of her eternal wisdom, and dreamed of creating children in the form of books which should teach men to return to forgotten ways. He was a man of one mind, of one heart, and his mind and heart were one. That was the secret of life, he was sure: to create a harmony within oneself and to relate that harmony with the natural world. He was a part of Nature, and he must find his place in Nature. He must not, as other men do, think one thing and act another. He must make his life fit his philosophy; he had better chuck it if he couldn't! How many artists and philosophers advocated the ideal life and themselves lived in discord with their thoughts! How many men gave lip-service to God, while leading ungodly lives! The man and his art should be one, as the lover and his beloved are one. Henry smiled to himself. Was it not for this that he was in jail? He paid his road-tax, which was reasonable; but he would not pay his poll-tax, which was unreasonable. It was but a frail gesture for one man to make, but was not his manhood worth something to himself? He would not encourage injustice. Rogues were at liberty, but he, a man careful of great virtues, was in jail. Was not that the measure of the Government's folly? Why should the State go to the expense of lodging him for no crime save the possession of that precious contraband, principles? It was, in its way, a trivial enough matter, but to yield was to give his principles a strength no greater than that of their weakest link. His life, such as it was, was a harmony, or it was nothing; either he lived up to his professions, or he did not. It was essential for that world which was himself to resist the outer world which tried to impose its unprincipled life upon his principled nature. No, he would not give in.

Man needed but little here below for happiness. Henry, with not a little pride, allowed himself to indulge in dreams of a humble dwelling he would one day build with his own hands. He took a slip of paper from his pocket and a pencil,—one he had made in his pencil-making days in his father's factory and as good a pencil as could be obtained in those days,—and began to make a reckoning of what the house would cost. He would build it of refuse shingles, of old brick, of such odds and ends as he could buy or find. Twenty-five to thirty dollars he thought would cover the cost. His furniture would be of the scantest. He would have three chairs in his house, "one for solitude, two for friendship, three for society." There would be no locks on the doors; there was no material possession that Henry valued so much as to bemoan its loss.

He felt as if he would like to go farther and farther from civilization. He had no particular longing for the society of friends. Not because he felt he was better than they, but because he felt as if he were nothing. He was nothing, and there was no place for him. Young as he was, he felt infinitely old; he was tired of institutions and customs and conventionalities. There was little hope of breathing new life into old forms; if a new life were to come for men, it would have to come from both within and without. He was at best able to offer a feeble protest, and let it go at that.

There was his friend Waldo, known to the world as Ralph Waldo Emerson, a philosopher, whom some have called "the sage." Waldo had turned out a heap of wisdom bound between book covers. He was a good man, a transcendentalist, a high thinker like himself. What fine thoughts that man uttered, how finely he uttered them! Yet, somewhere deep within himself, Henry had faint glimmerings, that even he, the great, the gentle Waldo, had in some way failed him. No, not in any intimate sense, for how can any man fail another? A man can fail only himself. Let us then say that Waldo, somehow, failed himself. To Henry's mind no man should rest content with the utterance of thoughts. The greater their power and beauty the greater the responsibility devolved upon him who uttered them to express them in life, to act upon them. To make life conform with the best thoughts was a passion with him and a necessity as well. On the other hand, Waldo——

Henry did not finish his thought. At this very instant, gentle Waldo himself appeared in person, and his kind human eyes peered through the doorway.

"Henry! Why are you here?" came the half-reproachful greeting from the visitor.

"Waldo! And why are you not here?" replied Henry, with an inward chuckle.

The next morning, to Henry's discomfiture, the smiling, good-natured Sam Staples appeared, with an invitation for him to leave jail. Henry demurred. He rather liked the place, and certainly he would not pay his tax. There was no necessity, Staples informed him. Some one had been there and paid it, and he really could not keep his friend in jail unless he chose to go and rob or kill somebody. The philosophic Henry left the place and wended his way to the bootmaker's to get his mended boot.

THE COMPARISON OF GAUGUIN WITH THOREAU

HENRY THOREAU the American and Paul Gauguin the Frenchman have as many points of unlikeness as of likeness. They meet in a common desire for a new Eden on earth, but as will be seen their ideas of the hypothetical garden are at considerable variance, conditioned as such ideas are by race, climate and environment, and not a little by the fact that the one is a philosopher and a puritan, the other a painter and a full-blooded man. Each has been called a "savage"; this epithet could hardly, with any fairness, be applied to two such complex, sensitive beings as Thoreau and Gauguin. It would be more true to say that they were so saturated with civilization that in sheer despair they turned their mood to savagery as a cure for a growing malady which was beyond cure.

First, as regards the points at which they meet. They are both rebels against the existing order with all its mechanical artifices and appliances, which, though apparently intended to make us all more comfortable, actually create for mankind a multitude of unnecessary "necessities"; these, besides making useless labor, serve to swamp the fundamental impulses and functions of life and, presumably, take from man that natural enjoyment which is his right. Hence, it is not surprising to find Thoreau and Gauguin believing in simplicity, but the difference between the simplicity of one and that of the other is nothing short of abysmal. Before this difference is defined, it should be emphasized that from his first conscious moment, Thoreau was a stable character whose urge to simplicity was as first nature. To him may be applied Goethe's words: "Well it is for a man who can make the end of his life tally with the beginning."

As for Gauguin, his need finally came to him as a reaction from the life he was living. In short, he came to it as a convert who felt he had been duped, and he came with all the ardor of one who had intense vigor and fine perceptions. He had, until then, lived a life in its own way full and even rich, in a positive sense; beside it, Thoreau's life was colorless and negative. At all events, when Gauguin made his final decision to abandon bourgeois Europe for Tahiti he was hating civilization with that full-blown hatred which comes with discovery; he was one who suddenly had his eyes opened to the realization that everything around him was sham and deceit and that he himself had all his life been the dupe of those shameless forces whose true nature had only now been revealed to him.

Thoreau very early saw the futility of the vast energy expended by man for material ends; perhaps the frugality of his own nature—he was a mixture of Norman and Scotch stocks—gave him the power to see more clearly than other men how, as humanity worked harder, its wants piled up and its once humble habitations became relative mansions, repositories of numerous useless furniture and gewgaws; thus the human mind floundered in the confusion of its possessions. A puritan philosopher, wishing to see the race improved and holding noble conduct to be the supreme goal, he saw but one way out of the maze of false cumulations: a return to Nature, the source of things; for at the source all things are clear and simple, as yet unpolluted by the perverse indulgences of human activity gone wrong. Was it so hard to leave a crowded junk-shop, in which one's every movement was hampered and every free thought lost under the dust? Well, he for one, a detached spectator, seeing from the first how things stood within, simply refused to enter. He wanted to belong to himself, and not to the things which you thought you possessed but which really possessed you. The men he discerned in the dark recesses of crowded interiors belonged to them as inevitably as the pieces of furniture which formed such an intrinsic part of them. To enter would be to lose himself, to leave every hope behind of being a free natural man.

Gauguin, a husband, a father of five children, a stock-broker by trade (a stock-broker of all things!) lived in such a junk-shop. A dream of color having come to him somewhat late in life, his eyes were opened to the true state of affairs. And what an awakening it was! It played havoc with the lives of his family, but above all with his own life, and left its mark on the world's art.

It was rather curious that the two "savages" should meet on ground which may be deemed Christian, on the principle of "Take no thought for the morrow. . . . Sufficient unto the day is the evil thereof."

Listen to Thoreau:

"Why should we live with such hurry and waste of life? We are determined to be starved before we are hungry. Men say that a stitch in time saves nine, and so they take a thousand stitches to save nine to-morrow."

And now hear Gauguin:

"If only people did not spend so much time in useless and unrelated work! One stitch a day—that's the great point."

What both men clearly saw was that in civilization men lived in such constant fear of poverty and were so concerned about future security that they forgot to live in the present.

Thoreau, with the practical nature of a puritan philosopher, at the very beginning divested himself of all wants, so-called "needs," which might weigh as ballast on his soul,

Henry Thoreau

Courtesy of Houghton Mifflin Company

Paul Gauguin

From *Letters of Paul Gauguin*, copyright by Dodd, Mead & Company, Inc.

and he worked out a scheme of life which enabled him to reverse the usual order of things and really to put into practise the idea he had expressed in his "commencement" talk: that of having one working-day a week and making the other six "his Sabbath of the affections and the soul." He had calculated with a truly New England practicality that it would require but thirty to forty working-days a year to support himself, and he built himself a shanty in Walden (Waldo-Eden) which cost him the munificent sum of $28.12½! Gauguin had also, with his own hands, built himself a house in Tahiti, but being an artist and having a prodigal nature, he made it beautiful with stained-glass windows and wood-carvings of his own device. He wanted more than Thoreau, and his desires broke him where the more modest ones saved the New Englander his peace.

It must be admitted, Thoreau did without things. Nor was this a sacrifice on his part. He neither needed nor wanted things. He was a nay-sayer. He had said No to so many things. He once said No to a lady who had offered him her hand in marriage! One suspects that sometimes he rather annoyed his friends by his attitude of negation. He must have now and then proved something of a damper on their spirits, while children loved him as he loved them, which was also true of Gauguin. One thinks of the witty saying of a friend: "I love Henry, but I cannot like him." And it was Emerson who said of him:

"He was bred to no profession; he never married; he lived alone; he never went to church; he never voted; he refused to pay a tax to the State; he ate no flesh, he drank no wine, he never knew the use of tobacco; and though a naturalist, he used neither trap nor gun. When asked at dinner what dish he preferred, he answered, 'the nearest.' "

It is easy to enjoy life when one's wants are small. What pleasure was his came from within, and that which was within responded to a few things without and created its own small yet perfect harmonies. And so he swam and skated and climbed and boated. For a livelihood he did occasional surveying or manual labor. And, as he had once said, he "had traveled far in Concord." This life provided for him an Eden of sorts, within the reach of all, and he undoubtedly thought that what sufficed him should suffice all. But he made no effort to convert anybody. He had no intention of meddling, and all he asked was to be left alone.

It was different with Gauguin. A volcanic temperament, rage possessed him when he realized the lie of the life around him. Energetic, he carried war into the enemy's camp. Civilization accepted his challenge, pursued him to the bitter end. That was partly, perhaps, because he was again and again in dire straits and needed money. And money was civilization's great weapon; lack of it to provide his wants and paints for his pictures was his weakness. Once or twice it came to him, to pass between his fingers like water. He had the fault of his virtue. He was prodigal in his art, and he was prodigal in life. It was a harmony of sorts, but it was disastrous. Could he have saved the whole of his prodigality for his art, he might have saved himself the bitter fate which awaited him. To reproach him with this is also folly.

Beauty rather than conduct being his ultimate goal, his idea of beauty implied its own code of conduct, just as Thoreau's idea of conduct implied its own code of beauty—austere beauty, to be sure, but still, beauty. So here, beginning from different starting points, the two men again meet—in a measure: just as two men, one traveling east, the other west, are inevitably bound to meet. In this meeting they may find that they seek the same thing, with personal modifications. As has already been pointed out, there was French blood in both. But the admixture in one was

Scotch, in the other Peruvian Spanish. Was it not because of this difference that they diverged so violently one from the other? They both diagnosed, with a clarity peculiarly French, the malady which infected civilization. Does not Gauguin, if in different words, echo Thoreau's thought? Gauguin says:

"Artists have lost their savagery, and no longer able to rely on instinct, one might better say imagination, have strayed off on many different paths to find the productive elements they have no longer the strength to create, and now they can not work except in disorderly crowds, feeling frightened, almost lost if left to themselves. . . . All that I have learned from others has only hampered me. So I can say: no one has given me anything. It is true I know better. But I prefer that little which is my own."

It has been charged against both men that they have been too solitary, too unsociable, too indifferent to others. Gauguin is fully aware of the charge, for he says somewhere: "That is how unsociable I am. I admit my words are sometimes sarcastic, I do not flatter, bend my back, and sneak about begging in official salons." Thoreau's relations with men were easier because he mingled less with them, and his social errors were mostly those of omission rather than of commission. He did not anger the existing order as Gauguin did, because he kept out of its way; nor had he wholly turned his contemptuous back on it as Gauguin had when, with a gesture truly heroic, he abandoned Europe for Tahiti. But the painter's anger was great when he saw the devastating effects produced on the South Sea islanders by the encroaching Europeans; equally great was the suffering he experienced on realizing that he was half-civilized, half-savage, which created a conflict within himself hard to resolve. He saw in the isle of Tahiti vestiges of a passing Eden, in which men lived in amity, lazed their lives away in serene indolence, walked about naked without false shame; he saw in all this a potent criticism of hypocritical Europe, a land which preached a beautiful religion without any effort to practise it, and made of money a god, and lived in the continual strife of a material competition which brought pleasure to the few and suffering to the many. Energetic, volcanic, distressed with numerous fears, skeptical with irreligion; that was the one half of him, his heritage from Europe, working like an insidious poison to destroy him; there was the other half which longed for faith, the only thing which might create true art, and for a serenity of mind and soul which comes with faith. He sought it here, in his new surroundings, and snatched at glimpses which were passing. And for all his inner distress and material wants, he managed to imprison, on canvas, in bright colors, these glimpses of paradise vouchsafed him before he died.

His pictures went to Europe which admired Gauguin from afar and made a kind of legend of him without understanding the import of his creation. Is not this reminiscent of Swift, who wrote a bitter satire in *Gulliver's Travels,* now mostly read as a children's fairy tale? But the miracle is that Gauguin's pictures are by no means bitter. In his way Gauguin has conquered. "Is the Indian vanquished who smiles at his torture? Decidedly, the savage is nobler than we." So Gauguin had once said, and it is equally true that those who to-day look on his smiling evocations in paint can not miss his magnificent serenity, but they are not apt to see the inner torture of their author. Is it not a miracle that a man suffering such terrible torture should have created such serene dreams? And so the spirit has, after all, conquered matter, and humanity, willy-nilly, is a sharer in the victory.

There is a difference between the "nether Eden" that

Thoreau so often spoke of in his books and the Eden which Gauguin painted. It is a difference largely of temperament. If Thoreau had painted, his figures undoubtedly would have been clothed, by no means luxuriously, but still, clothed. He lived in a climate in which clothing was necessary. There would have been other differences typical of Northern temperament and thought. It is logical to suppose that every race, if it could be induced to create Eden, would create it in its own image, according to its own peculiar needs and concepts. But in essentials, the serene joys which both Thoreau and Gauguin had sought, all Edens are bound to have common features.

We are far from Eden. But though men die their aspirations live. The words of Thoreau, the pictures of Gauguin are not lost. Bad as things are, they might be worse but for dreamers and their dreams. In what they leave behind there lives the undying aspiration for that Eden which man once had had and lost.

HERMAN MELVILLE—THE SEEKER

One summer afternoon in 1851, before the motor-car made necessary those straight, broad, superb roads which now intersect the New England countryside, a tall, erect, splendid-looking man might have been seen making his way on horseback along a narrow winding lane undulating among the Berkshire Hills. At close scrutiny it might have been seen that the man, who was in the early thirties, had a magnificent head adorned with an abundance of hair and a longish beard; he sat well; his bearing was regal; the man and his horse might have been one, a centaur, if such a thing could be said to exist in a New England landscape. It could be seen, too, that here was a man of irrepressible energy accustomed to the out-of-doors; but his eyes were incredibly small for so large a head and they had an abstract remote look which seemed incongruous in otherwise so active a face. He glanced ahead with a repressed eagerness, and now and then there was in his eyes a flicker expressive of some hidden joy. He loved his horse, that much was evident from the way he stopped to pat his head and to feed him sugar; at the horse's side ran a huge Newfoundland dog which, at the sudden spurring of the horse, would bay in friendly manner at the horse and rider.

The man was Herman Melville, whose life had been as rich in adventure as that of Odysseus, and who had descended into sinister depths of existence denied to the legendary Greek. Odysseus had had his goddess Athene to guide him from his troubles to safety, but here was a man abandoned both of men and gods. Yet a flicker of hope illuminated that heart, for man is a hoping animal and as long as he has energy and a healthy appetite he will challenge the fates and trust to the remote chance of emerging victor.

But the rider had on that morning a more precise reason for his hope, a more specific cause for the spark of hidden joy which flashed in upon the vast caverns of despair in his innermost being. For he had just left his home in Pittsfield, with its faithful Calypso and issues of that union, his hostages to fortune, and was on his way to see one whom he hoped to make his friend of friends, the one and only Nathaniel Hawthorne, who lived at Lenox, six miles away. Some inner consuming fire urged him on, as if the realization of this dream were a matter of life or death. And though he did not know it, it was.

Could men be more different than these two? Hardly. Let us look at them, let us examine the texture and furnishings of their minds, the emotions by which they are moved.

Nathaniel had been brought up in quiet surroundings by a fond mother and an equally fond sister. In his youth he had been solitary, with no heart for visitors or visiting. In his dreams he had longed for life, but outwardly, by day, he showed no perceptible symptom of any desire, but steeped himself in the ineffable New England melancholy which served as a kind of anodyne to whatever inner distress may have been his to endure. When his heart began to long for Sophia Peabody, transcendentalist, blue-stocking and semi-invalid, like himself a discourager of neighborly intimacies, he ventured forth toward her with a furtive air; and when his sister, Elizabeth, learned the state of affairs, she suffered pangs of jealousy, to say nothing of the shock at the unexpected discovery that her brother was, after all, a man after the manner of other men. After an adoring, ecstatic courtship, Nathaniel married Sophia; even before nuptials he had called himself "her husband"; and in marriage he continued to adore her; perfect Puritans both, yet they were Adam and Eve, and they had their Eden on earth. They were happy, ecstatically happy, and Sophia's rare absence from the home hearth left Nathaniel wandering about the house like a lost soul. At the time of his meeting Nathaniel he had just had his first great success. *The Scarlet Letter* had been published the previous year, and his name had traveled wide as the light of a new star. Up to now, both Nathaniel and Sophia lived the life of recluses; together they were a world sufficient unto itself. To be sure, when they had lived at Brook Farm, Concord life made its effort to draw him into its Transcendental circle, but Nathaniel had resisted; even Emerson's repeated visits had failed to impress him. He had listened to the Sage of Concord's metaphysical discourses with not a little skepticism; he had scorned Margaret Fuller; some of the others he had frankly considered bores. Thoreau alone he had respected for his concrete virtues and saw with pleasure at his house. Then Melville came, a man fifteen years his junior, and enthralled him with his energy, with his vivid tales of the South Seas.

What was Melville? Here was a man who had not been content to sit still and remain a spectator. He had seethed with life; he had been a ship buffeted about in almost one continuous tempest, with rare intervals of calm which only presage the renewal of the storm. Born thirty-two years before in New York City, of a sturdy proud stock—his grandfather on his mother's side was the famous General Peter Gansevoort, of Dutch blood; his father, Allan, one of the pre-Revolutionary Scotch-Irish emigrants, could trace his ancestry back to one Sir Richard de Melville, del Compte de Fife, a worthy of the thirteenth century—he had adventure in his blood and hardihood in his fiber. He had loved his cold stately mother with an almost fierce love though she had shown no tenderness, and he had adored his grandfather Peter, an impressive figure of six feet four, with a heroic regard, still further nurtured by the circumstance that the fates had removed him from among the living when Herman was but seven years old. This Peter Gansevoort he was to remember as one who in his youth and manhood had accomplished feats of valor, and who had later become "a pure, cheerful, childlike, blue-eyed, divine old man; in whose meek, majestic soul the lion and the lamb embraced—fit image of his God." He saw the portrait "a glorious gospel framed and hung upon the wall, and declaring to all people, as from the Mount, that man is a noble, god-like being, full of the choicest juices; made up of strength and beauty." It had been there since childhood, a model of heroic stature, expressly created for his emulation. Herman was thirteen years old when his father died; his fantasy had also hoisted his parent on to a pedestal, an image for worship. Later, as Herman grew to maturity and his body and soul went through hells of experience, he was to modify his filial ecstasy; for disillusion was to dog his steps, and disillusion casts a shadow upon the past as well as upon the present, creates a doubt as to whether what had seemed true is really true, making of memory a storehouse of sorrow instead of joy.

When Herman was seven his father sent him for a time to his uncle, Peter Gansevoort, living in Albany, and in a note to his brother-in-law Allan Melville described his son as "very backward in speech and somewhat slow in comprehension." The memory was laughable now: was he not already the author of several celebrated works: *Typee, Omoo, Mardi, Redburn, White-Jacket?* and he was now in the throes of the sixth, *Moby Dick; or the White Whale.*

He laughed inwardly at the irony hot on his heels: he would go down to posterity, as but the other day he had said to Hawthorne, as a "man who lived among cannibals!" Had not the same fate overtaken the author of *Gulliver's Travels,* a book full of mordant bitterness now given to children as a kind of fairy tale? Here, from the depths of himself, he was pouring out life at white heat, living secrets to awe men with the frightening mystery of existence; and men only shrugged their shoulders or laughed or said that here were nice tales for boys! They would say so more than ever after he had died. *Typee* would be given, in all likelihood, to babes, "perhaps with their gingerbread." Scornfully, before Hawthorne, he had uttered his prophecy. What a man, Hawthorne! He alone, of all men he knew, was aware of the true inwardness of things. What a piece of colossal luck his meeting with the man! Just as he was writing his terrific yarn about the Whale, a furious drama revealing the conflict of man with malignant natural forces; did ever a dramatist before essay the whole deep ocean as a stage for his actors? Oh, that he "had Vesuvius' crater for an inkstand!" he had written that day. And, again, "To produce a mighty book, you must choose a mighty theme!" What puny efforts the world dubbed art!

He felt exultant. All the tragic experience he had had, all the life he had lived, seethed in his breast, and he was intoxicated with the pride of one who had been through hell and come out of it alive to tell the tale. The most terrible suffering, the most bitter disillusion, had for the moment become a fierce joy, like the joy of one who by some miracle lifted himself across the enchanted line which separated gods from men. Oh, how had his intense bitterness become this joy? Oh, how had he, a thing of earthly dust, become transmuted into ethereal spirit winging its way among gods, listening to forbidden secrets for which payment would be afterward exacted? Such was his mood, until he returned again to earth, spurring his horse Hawthorneward.

Yet his mind went on reveling in his past. What a host of tales he had told Hawthorne and had yet to tell him! Was there a better listener? Was it because Hawthorne himself had lived so little that he listened to the younger man's exploits with an attention he had paid no other man? Did the older man, while enthralled, secrete a regret in his heart? Generous Hawthorne, not he the man to envy unhappy Melville?

It was true: at the age when Hawthorne had been leading a quiet life at Bowdoin College, eager for life yet apprehensive of experience, he, Melville, having arrived at his seventeenth year, had cut loose from his numerous family and kin, and, rendered desperate by some inner need to experience life at its deepest and highest, went to sea as a common sailorboy. "When I go to sea, I go as a simple sailor, right before the mast, plumb down into the forecastle, aloft there to the royal mast-head. True, they order me about some, and make me jump from spar to spar, like a grasshopper in a May meadow. And at first, this sort of thing is unpleasant enough. It touches one's sense of honor, particularly if you come of an old-established family in the land, the Van Rensselaers, or Randolphs, or Hardicanutes." And it needed "a strong decoction of Seneca and the Stoics to enable you to grin and bear it." His bunk had been in a dark, damp, smelly hole; his food had been vile. "My heart was like lead, and I felt bad enough, Heaven knows; but I soon learnt that sailors breathe nothing about such things, but strive their best to appear all alive and hearty." And "there was plenty of work to be done, which kept my thoughts from becoming too much for me." But when he had learned something of the trade, there was delight in furling the topgallantsails and royals in a hard wind, and in hopping about in the riggings like a Saint Jago's monkey. "There was a wild delirium about it, a fine rushing of the blood about the heart; and a glad thrilling and throbbing of the whole system, to find yourself tossed up at every pitch into the clouds of a stormy sky, and hovering like a judgment angel between heaven and earth; both hands free, with one foot in the rigging, and one somewhere behind you in the wind."

There it was, this eternal contradiction of things, the deepest miseries so indissolubly merged with heaven-aspiring ecstasies, a twin emotion of which a sail-ship was the most expressive symbol! And even the miseries, the sufferings—had he not found that "the scene of suffering is a scene of joy when the suffering is past?"

He loved ships as he loved men. What a host of marvelous fellows he had met at sea passed before his eyes! Men of low estate but worthier than kings. His good friend, Toby, with whom he had passed his exile among the cannibals in the Marquesas; Doctor Long Ghost, who mocked the captain with a mockery worthy of a master of the art and who could quote Virgil on occasion and talk of Malmsbury and repeat poetry by the canto, especially *Hudibras*; Jack Chase, "a Briton and a true-blue; tall and well-knit, with a clear open eye, a fine broad brow, and an abounding nut-brown beard." Never had he loved a human being as he loved this Jack Chase. He had met him on the man-of-war, the *United States*. "No man told such stories, sang such songs, or with greater alacrity sprang to his duty. The main-top, over which he presided, was a sort of oracle of Delphi; to which many pilgrims ascended, to have their perplexities or difficulties settled. . . . He had a polite, courteous way of saluting you, if it were only to borrow a knife. He had read all the verses of Byron, all the romances of Scott; he talked of Macbeth and Ulysses; but above all things, he was an ardent admirer of Camoens' *Lusiad,* part of which he could recite in the original." Jack and he were fast friends. "Wherever you may be now rolling over the blue billows, dear Jack, take my best love along with you; and God bless you, wherever you go."

There was a day, oh! unforgettable day, on board of that ship when he, Melville, might have ended as a murderer and a suicide. He had been summoned by his captain to appear at the mast. Melville's heart had jumped to his throat at the summons, and he hurriedly asked Fluke, the boatswain's mate at the fore-hatchway, what was wanted of him.

"Captain wants you at the mast," Fluke replied. "Going to flog ye, I guess."

"For what?"

"My eyes! you've been chalking your face, hain't ye?"

On the complaint of a lieutenant he had been charged with neglecting some trifling duty to which he had not known he was assigned. The horror of the moment returned to him. To be flogged ignominiously for a crime of which he was utterly innocent! He could see it all vividly, the little group gathered round to officiate at the punishment, and a crowd of sailors forming a circle to witness the castigation of one of their fellows. A design, born of some natural instinct, had formed quickly in his mind. He stood a little to the windward of the captain, and though the latter was a large powerful man, it was certain that a sudden rush against him, along the slanting deck, would infallibly pitch him headforemost into the ocean, though he who so rushed must needs go over with him. His blood seemed clotting in his veins; he felt icy cold at the tips of his fingers, and a dimness was before his eyes. But through that dimness the boatswain's mate, scourge in hand, loomed like a giant, and Captain Claret, and the blue sea seen through the opening at the gangway, showed with an awful vividness. . . . It was not the thought of the degradation that swayed him to his purpose, but some instinct diffused through all animated nature, which, as he explained afterward, prompts even a worm to turn under the heel. . . . Captain Claret ordered Melville to the grating, just as the culprit was preparing to carry out his own desperate design.

"Captain Claret, I know that man, and I know that he would not be found absent from his station if he knew where it was."

The unexpected intercession had come from a corporal of the marines, and Jack Chase, good Jack Chase, gathering courage, had also stepped forward. And Melville had been saved from exercising the "inalienable right to kill," justified, he thought, in circumstances, though he did not believe in war. He was a militant conscientious objector, "a pacifist with a vengeance."

If he had come near being a murderer, he also, more than once, had faced death. . . . How often he had stood on the brink of it and looked across the deep abyss into the unknown! And not he alone, but all his comrades on the high seas. Assuredly, courage was "the most common and vulgar of the virtues," as he had once said. And a constant facing of death bred a contempt for life. This again was covered by the law of the eternal contradiction of things.

There were the cannibals. . . . It was the cannibals who had renewed his faith in human nature. The cannibals of the South Seas were in their way noble fellows until the missionaries had begun meddling there. . . . Well, he had told the truth as he saw it, and was called a liar or otherwise abused for his pains. All the same, he saw no good reason for changing his opinion that the civilized man was the most ferocious being on earth.

When he had wearied of cannibals and ships and the high seas and hunting whales, he returned to civilization to live as well as he could the life of his own kind. After all, "Life's a voyage that's homeward-bound!" He was twenty-five when he leaped ashore for good, a hero returned. But a hero can't live on his heroics, and he began to bethink himself of something to do. Why not write books about places in which he had been and about things he had seen? came the suggestion from many quarters. And he sat down to write. As he meditated over the past and, in contemplation over experience gathered and lived, began to digest his storehouse of facts, it dawned on him that his inner life was only beginning. "Until I was twenty-five I had no development," he had written Hawthorne. But the transition from a life of action to a life of contemplation was hard; the folk he had left behind when he started on his long wandering were the same, but he was different; his own kin had seemed strangers.

The success of *Typee,* his first book, on both sides of the Atlantic, had predisposed him to meet the new life halfway, and his thoughts turned to marriage as to an anchorage of a life whose wandering was done. He had found an object for his affections in Elizabeth, the only daughter of Chief Justice Lemuel Shaw of Massachusetts, and lavished upon her all the frustrate adoration he had had for his cold proud mother. Hard as his life had been, he kept the realities and the abstractions apart, and he could not and would not reconcile them. And, as in his wanderings he was ever moved by "an itch for things remote," so now, in his practical life, he pedestaled his bride-to-be, high above him like a sanctified image, that he might perform genuflexions before it and worship it. They were married. Things had, somehow, not panned out according to his need and desire. Elizabeth was a New Englander. As for him, he was a citizen of the world, with the world grown too small for him! Passionately he turned to his work. Book after book came from his pen. He had a family to support; and writing offered him his only chance for an income, which, while far from coming up to his expectations, was better than none. An active energetic man, he cultivated his farm at Pittsfield. And Elizabeth's father made up the difference.

Such was Melville, when he first met his neighbor Hawthorne, living six miles away in the sanctified felicity of an adoring wife and adored children, and in the delectable aura of his first real fame. Mrs. Hawthorne busied herself making the Red House a sheltered Eden. She had a mind and was a woman of accomplishments; she knew Latin, Greek and Hebrew; and, dreaming of lasting fame for her husband, she kept a journal in which she recorded a host of trifles concerning his life. In short, she was a great man's helpmate, and she guarded her Nathaniel with the jealous eyes of one who knows that she possesses great treasure. And Nathaniel fully returned her ardor; he found her sufficient. Theirs was an undying honeymoon, which too often excluded the too friendly stranger.

Matters went differently at Arrowhead. Had Melville, in his new estate, expected too much? Did his quest of the absolute undo him now as it had undone him before? Was a man with the burden of such a tempestuous past hard to live with? Melville locked the secret into the deeps of himself. At any rate, the first flush of married life was over. In his heart a pedestal, bereft of figure, remained. He plunged fiercely into work, and upon a foundation of numberless realities he superimposed fantasies, alien and remote to a world which kept its feet on the ground and was in no mood for being seduced by clouds or subterranean mysteries. Men thought the author of *Mardi* mad.

Yet here was a man who longed for human contact. But in his own fashion. He could not and would not compromise with mere acquaintance. Since he could not have love, he wanted friendship, which, with him, was another and grander name for love. And here was the man Hawthorne, who presented a worthy object for his love; was there a worthier? Blind man, not to have seen that there was a Mrs. Hawthorne guarding Nathaniel with the jealous eyes of one who knows that she possesses great treasure; Mrs. Hawthorne, who, with the realistic eyes of a woman, discerned the greatness and the power of the intruder, who was one, perhaps, in time to overshadow the gentle Nathaniel. That was shrewd of her, because Melville had appeared as an admirer and had bestowed almost embarrassingly fervid praise on Nathaniel's creations; not unlike a lover who sees in his adored a being unlike any other being on earth. He did not apprehend danger; many a lover has lost his New England love by being too fervid.

Never had Hawthorne liked another man as he liked this Melville. Never had he taken any one so close into his intimacy, and in so short a time. They were at first shy of one another, as sensitive men, endowed with gifts of genius, often are. But one day when they went picnicking together, like the good neighbors they were, a thunderstorm forced them to take shelter in a narrow recess of mountain rocks, and this chance afforded them two hours of talk. They found they had much in common; they emerged friends.

Thereafter Red House saw Melville often. Here he regaled his friend with enthralling, vivid tales of things he had heard and seen; while Sophia, watchful, sewed, and the children listened enthralled; so marvelous was the telling that when he finished it was hard to break the spell and make the listeners understand that they were in reality by a New England fireside, and not in some remote Pacific isle. One evening, when Melville left after telling the most graphic yarn about a fight he had witnessed on an island in the Pacific, Mrs. Hawthorne suddenly asked: "Where is that club with which Mr. Melville was laying about him so?" They searched everywhere for it, and, not finding it, concluded that he must have taken it away with him. They decided to ask him about it the next time he came.

And here he was: the man himself on his horse, the friendly Newfoundland at his side. Melville jumped from his horse.

"Where's that club, Melville?" Hawthorne greeted him.

"What club?" The visitor looked perplexed.

"The club you brandished last night when you told us that yarn of yours! Mrs. Hawthorne was sure you had one. We looked high and low for it, without any luck."

"Ha! Ha!" guffawed Melville. "I guess it's still in the Pacific isle, if anywhere!"

"Really?" asked Mrs. Hawthorne incredulously, coming on the scene.

Melville stayed to tea, and after supper Hawthorne put Julian to bed, and Melville and he had a great talk "about time and eternity, things of this world and of the next, and books and publishers, and all the possible and impossible matters," one of many talks that lasted deep into the night.

"Have ready a bottle of brandy," Melville once wrote him, "for I always feel like drinking that heroic drink when we talk ontological heroics together." As their talks proceeded, Melville, for all his hard experience, showed little interest in those every-day realities which so interested Hawthorne. He was concerned only with ultimate things, with metaphysics and mysticism. He was pouring his perplexities into *Moby Dick* which he was writing then. . . . Even then he understood that he was fighting a losing battle. "My dear Sir," he wrote Hawthorne, "a presentiment is on me,—I shall at last be worn out and perish, like an old nutmeg grater, grated to pieces by the constant attrition of the wood, that is, the nutmeg. What I feel most moved to write, that is banned—it will not pay. Yet, altogether, write the *other* way I cannot."

Melville lived for these confidences, written and spoken, with Hawthorne, and as time went on he abandoned himself to them with that sense of the absolute with which he did all he undertook. Hawthorne was a reticent man. And there was Mrs. Hawthorne. . . .

They began to grow uneasy in the Hawthorne household about Melville's growing ardency. It was pleasant enough to have such a distinguished visitor admire one's books, but to have a passionate heart poured out without reserve and not to be attuned in spirit to respond to it was a vexation and a pain. Melville must have, at last, become aware of it, and the knowledge was to him a source of agony. He had depended so much on this friendship; he needed it; he had always been a lonely man, and he felt the ultimate loneliness creep in upon him. And as he grew more desperate, his despondency stole into his letters, which throbbed with an obscure pain, a secret perturbation, as of one in the throes of a great fear and on the eve of surrender to something which, from the first, had been inevitable. At the same time, it seemed as if the writer of these letters were unwilling to yield, to confess his failure; there was an insistent note in them, as of a lover making a last desperate effort to convince his beloved who should but would not understand. He knew what folly it was, since his epistles could only distress the recipient. But what were the odds? Deliberate folly was the last refuge of an uncompromising man on the eve of losing his last illusion. "I stand for the heart. To the dogs with the head!" And so there was one final outburst, one final flare of the fire before it burned itself out.

It happened when Melville sent a copy of *Moby Dick,* fresh from the press, to Hawthorne, to whom it was dedicated. Nathaniel, on reading it, responded at once with a letter. He had apparently liked bits of the book, but the fundamental thought, the plaint that ran through it like the *leit-motif* through a colossal symphony, must have distressed him as the throbbing passion of the man Melville had distressed him. What Nathaniel wrote might be gathered from Herman's reply:

"Your letter was handed me last night on the road going to Mr. Moorewood's, and I read it there. Had I been at home, I would have sat down at once and answered it. In me divine magnanimities are spontaneous and instantaneous—catch them while you can. The world goes round, and the other side comes up. So now I can't write what I felt. But I felt pantheistic then—your heart beat in my ribs and mine in yours, and both in God's. A sense of unspeakable security is in me at this moment, on account of your having understood the book. I have written a wicked book, and I feel spotless as the lamb. Ineffable socialities are in me. I would sit down and dine with you and all the gods in old Rome's Pantheon. It is a strange feeling—no hopefulness is in it, no despair. Content—that is it; and irresponsibility; but without licentious inclination. I speak now of my profoundest sense of being, not of an incidental being.

"Whence come you, Hawthorne? By what right do you drink from my flagon of life? And when I put it to my lips—lo, they are yours and not mine. I feel that the Godhead is broken up like the bread at the Supper, and that we are the pieces. Hence this infinite fraternity of feeling. Now, sympathizing with my paper, my angel turns over another page. You did not care a penny for the book.

But, now and then as you read, you understood the pervading thought that impelled the book—and that you praised. Was it not so? You were archangel enough to despise the imperfect body, and embrace the soul. Once you hugged the ugly Socrates because you saw the flame in the mouth, and heard the rushing of the demon,—the familiar,—and recognized the sound; for you have heard it in your own solitudes.

"My dear Hawthorne, the atmospheric skepticisms steal into me now, and make me doubtful of my sanity in writing to you thus. But, believe me, I am not mad, most noble Festus! But truth is ever incoherent, and when the big hearts strike together, the concussion is a little stunning. Farewell. Don't write a word about the book. That would be robbing me of my miserly delight. I am heartily sorry I ever wrote anything about you—it was paltry. . . .

"This is a long letter, but you are not at all bound to answer it. Possibly if you do answer it, and direct it to Herman Melville, you will missend it—for the very fingers that now guide this pen are not precisely the same that just took it up and put it on this paper. Lord, when shall we be done changing? Ah, it's a long stage, and no inn in sight, and night is coming, and the body cold. But with you for a passenger, I am content and can be happy. I shall leave the world, I feel, with more satisfaction for having come to know you. Knowing you persuades me more than the Bible of our immortality.

"What a pity, that, for your plain, bluff letter, you should get such gibberish! Mention me to Mrs. Hawthorne and to the children, and so, good-by to you, with my blessing!"

And, having signed his name, Melville knew that all was ended. The fires of his joy died in him. Love and friendship were not for him; not he to content himself with anything short of all. No half-emotions for him, neither in one thing nor another. And he understood that he was like Captain Ahab in this. Captain Ahab, on one of his earlier voyages, had his leg snatched by the White Whale,

Moby Dick, and he equipped a ship to pursue the leviathan to bring about his destruction. In the end, after the long chase, he and his ship were destroyed by the object of his pursuit. Thus it was now: he felt himself undone, destroyed. By whom, by what? By his own demon, who would not let him rest, who urged him on toward an ideal, an ultimate world, in which complacency was dead, and faith and ecstasy were alive. His quest ended in disaster, and what faith and ecstasy he had had were lost irretrievably.

With a heavy heart he sat down to write *Pierre,* the story of his failure, the story of the failure of man. For man was made in God's image; in the vain endeavor to live up to it, he destroyed himself; if he made no effort to live up to it he destroyed God in himself. And he faltered over this terrible contradiction, this horrible dilemma, like a rope-walker crossing an abyss, to whom either brink was equally untenable. Man had pretentions to religion; but, he asked himself, which way did virtue lead on earth; and he was forced to conclude that "the heavenly wisdom of God is an earthly folly to man," and that true virtue was punished rather than rewarded. "God's truth is one thing, and man's truth another." Men professed Christ; but they were by no means Christians.

Such conclusions were not palatable to a complacent world. And as Melville renounced the world, it revenged itself by renouncing him. *Moby Dick* was followed by six years of literary activity, but there was no token that the world wanted his creations, and as he had a family and one must needs keep body and soul together, Melville found a place as Custom-House Inspector, which he kept for twenty years. He was sixty-seven when he retired. His wife's inheritance allowed him to spend his final years without material worry. He stopped writing for publication, and as he did nothing by halves, he retired completely into the shell of his obscurity. His death in 1891 passed almost unnoticed. If a fit epitaph were needed, the opening lines of *Moby Dick* will serve excellently. "Call me Ishmael." For Ishmael he was upon the earth. And, like the Ishmael of his book, he escaped into life again only by means of a coffin. That is the miracle of resurrection. Melville nowadays passes for a great man, even for a very great man. For there is a thing we call poetic justice. For whom, indeed, should poetic justice be reserved if not for a poet? Herman Melville, temperamentally, was a poet, and a major one.

ARTHUR RIMBAUD—POET AND MERCHANT

1

Madame Rimbaud, a middle-aged, determined-faced woman of the class commonly termed by the French *la petite bourgeoisie,* which covers a multitude of sins, all of them eminently "sensible" and "practical," was conducting her two little girls across the meadows which lead from Charleville to Mézières. At their side there walked a boy of about sixteen, a gawky, growing boy, with large red hands; he was dressed in a square-cut, double-breasted jacket, a little, flat, pancake hat, and he had long, silky hair which hid the back of his collar and nearly touched his shoulders. There was nothing remarkable in all this, which suggested little more than an unruly schoolboy, but his eyes, when he lifted them from contemplating the ground, provided a revelation; they were "insolent and splendid," as some one was to describe them, and his mouth was "sulky and hostile." There was about him a curious mixture of childlikeness and maturity, of backwardness and decision. He did not appear to enjoy his perambulation by his mother's side. She was chattering away at her children like a magpie when he turned to her and said:

"I am going back home!"

"Why are you going home, Arthur?"

"I 'm going to get a book. If you walk slowly, I'll catch up with you."

"Very well. Only don't stay too long. We'll be looking for you!"

Without another word, the boy turned on his heels, leaving his mother dubiously shaking her head after him.

She was worried about Arthur. He was a strange, secretive boy, one hard to deal with. She had had to keep him down. There was never any telling what he would be up to. She was afraid he would take after his father, an army officer, disgusting with his easy ways and roving disposition, not at all the sort of man to bring a family up properly; ten years ago they had parted company; they couldn't go on living together; it was best for the children's sake. And ever since she had been strict with them. She would have no vagabonds in her family. Vagabonds were enemies of society. The mere word "vagabond" roused her ire. Men and women ought to grow up respectable. She would see to it that when her sons and daughters grew up they would marry and lead proper family lives. Then, by and by, there would be grandchildren. That would be nice and proper; she herself would give time to them. . . .

As for Arthur, she couldn't make him out at all. He had been sulky lately, keeping to himself, or going off on jaunts. Not that he hadn't always been queer, so different from other boys. To be sure, he was quiet and well behaved. But, *mon Dieu,* he wrote poetry! And he had opinions! Fancy a mere child having opinions. Why, when he was but nine he was already trying to dictate as to what he was and wasn't going to learn. He had then the cheek to ask, why should he trouble to learn Latin? Even if it meant a degree and if a degree were the only means of getting a good position—well, he didn't want one. He would be a *rentier.* "As for Greek, the vile language is not spoken by any one, any one in the world. *Ah saperlipote de saperlipopette! sapristi!* I will be a capitalist. The positions they give you if you pass are either those of a shoeblack or a pig driver, or a herdsman."

The idea of a nine-year-old youngster daring to question the education in the best schools, and running down college degrees and the rewards which fell to the lucky owners of them! Of course, she didn't disapprove his idea of becoming a capitalist. There was some sense to that. Still, an education was bound to help one, even in becoming a capitalist, *ne c'est pas*? Well, she wouldn't let him get away with his ideas. She saw to it that he kept his nose to the school grindstone. If he misbehaved, she made him learn a hundred lines of Latin by heart, and if he didn't do the job properly he was out of a meal! And she had enlisted the aid of her two daughters to keep a watch on him. They were good little girls, she was proud of them, and they had religion too! Well, she had been rewarded for her pains. Her boy did awfully well at school. From what she had heard from his form-master, George Izambard, no other boy could touch him as far as studies went. All the same, she wished that fellow Izambard didn't lend him all those newfangled books from that awful place, Paris. He actually encouraged him to read Victor Hugo! She must have a talk with Izambard, and tell him that that sort of thing wasn't good for her boy. There was her Arthur always running off in his spare time to the river, and lying down there for hours on the bank reading books or writing poetry. She didn't want her boy writing poetry and daydreaming his life away. What did he see in the Meuse, anyhow?

She paused in her perambulations and looked back. There was no sign of Arthur. Why wasn't he coming back? At least half an hour must have elapsed. She hoped he wasn't getting into a scrape. He sometimes got into a scrape when she wasn't around. She sat down in the grass with her little girls and waited. She waited a long time. And still no sign of Arthur. She rose and with her young ones began walking back to Charleville. They reached the house. Arthur wasn't there. She was vexed. Then angry. As the hours passed, and he did not appear she was alarmed. She took her two little girls by their hands and took the meadows again toward Mézières.

The poor woman hunted high and low for her boy, first at Charleville, then at Mézières; far into the night, dragging her two little girls by their hands, she hunted for him, but in vain. There was one aspect in his disappearance which was of particular anxiety to her: that was the boy's dangerous Republican sympathies, coupled with the news that the Germans were approaching Sedan. People were leaving their houses before rumors of disaster. These things happened in 1870.

In her anxiety she appealed to Izambard, who was spending his summer holiday at Douai. If any one could help her, it would be the young instructor.

2

While Madame Rimbaud was experiencing her anxieties, what was happening to the boy Arthur?

When he left his mother he walked rapidly back to the house, took a few necessary things, felt the few francs in his pocket,—he had come by them by selling a few books he had got as school prizes,—and started for Paris. He had come to this momentous decision some days ago, but had not thought it wise to divulge it even to Izambard, with whom he had kept up a correspondence. Izambard had kept him supplied with books and papers from Paris, and now that his one comrade was gone and he had exhausted all the books he had left behind at his lodgings, Arthur spent hours of agony in boredom. Banville, Verlaine, Gautier and all the rest of his heroes lived in Paris;

there, too, the Republican leaders were plotting at the risk of their lives. In short, all that he loved was in Paris; here in Charleville there was nothing but spiritual desolation. The war made communication difficult; Charleville was close to the frontier, and Mézières which adjoined it was a fortified town, rumors and alarms came aplenty, but not a single book from Paris to throw a ray of joy on his life.

The life at Charleville as lived in war-time seemed to him utterly absurd. There was the public square of the town, where the life of the place centered. A military band would play while the timid bourgeois fiercely discussed the war; it made him laugh and he was impelled to ridicule the scene in a poem. And he wrote a letter to Izambard, congratulating him on living no longer in "the most idiotic of all the country towns. . . . Because it is next door to Mézières and because two or three hundred soldiers march through its streets, the people gesticulate with the notable ferocity of non-combatants. It is frightful, all the retired grocers dressed up in uniform! It is staggering and detestable how the solicitors, the glaziers, the tax-collectors, the carpenters, and all these pot-bellies, a rifle across the chest, display their patriotism at the gates of Mézières. My country is rising up! . . . I would rather see her sitting down. Don't shift your feet! that's my principle." His one consolation had been his reading of Verlaine's *Fêtes galantes,* which had given him infinite delight.

What was there for him to do in Charleville? Simply nothing. His elder brother—lucky devil to be rid of his managing mother!—had joined up with the army, and there was no companion his own age fit to associate with. Why, they were mere children! He had shocked a group of schoolboys once by telling them that what made him superior to them was that he had no heart. They couldn't see any sense in that, although all he had meant was that reason was better than silly sentiment. There was only one boy, younger than himself, who had the sense to follow him, that was Delahaye, and Arthur showed his appreciation by allowing him to accompany him on his long and frequent walks into the country. "What a job," he confessed once to his young friend, "everything in my head must be blotted out. Lucky the child who is abandoned on the roadside, brought up at random, reaching manhood without any of those ideas inculcated by schoolmasters or by one's family; new, clean, without principles or notions—since everything we are taught is false—and free, free of everything."

What good were the prizes he had got at school for Latin and other subjects, without half trying? When the war broke out those silly fellow schoolboys framed a petition to the Minister of Education asking that the cost of their annual prizes might be devoted to the prosecution of the war. Would he, Arthur Rimbaud, sign it? they asked, bringing the paper to him. No, not he! He rubbed it in by pointing out to them that those who had already signed it had no prizes to lose. And he needed his prizes for a good purpose, though he wasn't going to tell them about it; in short, he had already conceived the idea of escape to Paris, and the few francs for which he could dispose of his prizes wouldn't go amiss!

And here he was actually starting for the city of cities, his adored Paris. He spat vigorously in the direction of the many ugly industrial structures which composed hated Charleville, cast a loving glance at the flowing Meuse, and, falling into a vigorous stride, walked on. He boarded a train; he was burning with one thought: Charleville was behind—Paris ahead. He would be with the brave Republican rebels and with the poets. Life held nothing else.

Arthur reached Paris with not a sou in his purse, and in debt to the railway company for thirteen francs. He had, indeed, hoped that the exciting events around Paris would abet him, and that there would be a welcome to an ardent Republican. Instead, the unsympathetic railway officials handed him over to the police. It was hardly to be expected that he would show any more respect for the guardians of the law than he would for other institutions; he showed such contempt for the source of their authority that they decided to detain him until inquiries had been made into his identity, which he persistently refused to reveal. Besides, the city was in a state of ferment. A Republican outbreak might be expected any moment, and the presence of German spies was also feared. The poems found in his pocket did not help his case; on the contrary, they were regarded as suspicious documents. Thus it came to pass that Arthur spent his first night of freedom among the human dregs of Paris.

He maintained silence when brought before the magistrate in the morning. What was the use? Could he, by any chance, appease an official of the empire by the revelation that he was in Paris to assist the Republican rebels in proclaiming a Republic? As for admitting to that pig of a magistrate that he was a poet, he was not such a fool as to invite mockery. And he refused to give his address; he hadn't come to Paris to be ignominiously returned to his mother. The magistrate promptly sent him to Mazas jail as a vagabond and political suspect. Those days and nights of squalor among degrading companions he was to remember long after, and a poem was to come of it. But Arthur Rimbaud was not one to throw off sorrow by means of a poem.

The news that a Republic was proclaimed on September fourth gave him such pleasure that he was moved to give the address of his home. Besides, his suffering had been keen; he had had time to reflect; his surroundings gave him the opportunity to grasp the nature of the conflict which men must wage before they were free. There was also the news that Sedan had been lost and Charleville was cut off by rail from Paris. In his distress he wrote to Izambard and pleaded for help. "Your poor Arthur," he signed himself, and contritely begged his friend to write to his "poor mother," to console her. But he took good care to ask the sympathetic schoolmaster to take him to Douai, and not to Charleville.

Izambard did not fail the boy, but furnished the money owed to the railway, and took Arthur into his own home. He appeared at Douai serene, fully recovered in spirits. And his conduct satisfied the aunts with whom Izambard lived.

Madame Rimbaud was not content with this state of affairs, and Izambard made every effort to return the boy to his mother, which was no easy matter just then when the war interrupted the usual communications. He finally succeeded.

Arthur returned home to find his mother's rule stricter than ever. But, having tasted the sweets of snatched freedom, he endured his mother's authority for a week, and, early in October, again fled.

3

As the first time, he had gone out for a walk. Bitter experience had taught him not to take a train without a ticket. And he kept on walking. He had got as far as Brussels, tramping all the way, begging his food where begging was likely to get it for him, and using his wits where wits were the more efficient measure. He slept now in barns, now in a lodging demanded from the mayor of a village, and now and then he walked into a house and tumbled into bed when the owner was not looking. Once a farm-hand saw him entering a house, and he tumbled out of bed much quicker than he had tumbled into it. At Charleroi he extracted an invitation to dinner from the proprietor of the *Journal de Charleroi* who, charmed with the eloquence of the boy, was on the point of offering him a job on his paper, but by the time the dessert was reached Arthur was expressing himself so injudiciously, if still eloquently, concerning certain statesmen, his anticlericalism and socialism, that the host straightway changed his mind. There was that unruliness about him which always put people off.

Once in Brussels, he made for the house of one of his schoolmasters, who did not know of his escapades and had in the past admired the boy's scholarly attainment. He told a great yarn which made him to be a kind of John the Baptist. And he received a bounteous welcome. He left the house clean, with a fresh collar, and his purse filled with silver.

A little later Izambard, apprised by Arthur's mother of her son's new escapade, arrived at the schoolmaster's house to find the culprit fled. He was astonished, on returning to Douai, to find his young friend installed with his aunts. "It is I. I have returned!" was his way of greeting them. And in the shelter of this hospitality he was putting his late adventures into verse. There was plenty of good paper in the house, and he was so neat that at the least blemish he recopied the poem. "Why don't you write on both sides of the paper?" one of the aunts asked him, thinking it a waste. "For the printer," he replied with confident audacity, "one never writes on the back."

Izambard found him in no hurry to return. But there

were the persistent demands from Arthur's mother. Besides, for all their good nature, the aunts were beginning to grumble. There was no alternative but to send the young man packing. Izambard did it all in the kindliest manner possible. On the way to the train he gave him sensible advice on all sorts of matters, and especially on the respect which was due to one's parents. "You must exercise patience and perseverance," he said. "You'll win your mother over in time." Izambard felt pleased with himself. It seemed to him that the boy was impressed, that he understood him, that he was inwardly moved, that his heart was touched. Still, there was a doubt in his mind. Perhaps he deceived himself. . . . The boy was so impenetrable!

A few days later he was reassured by a grateful letter from Arthur. At the same time, he wanted Izambard to know how hard it was for him to stay at home—so much harder than before he had tasted freedom. "I am dying, I am decaying in platitude, evil-mindedness, and sameness." He was minded to fly again, "to-day even." He had new clothes, he could have sold his watch, and freedom was a fine thing! "But I stayed! I stayed! and so many times I wanted to go off again. . . . But I will stay, I will stay. I did not promise that, but I will do it to deserve your affection. . . . It is a matter of doing something for you and I would die to do it. . . ." And he signed himself, *"Ce 'sans-coeur' de A. Rimbaud."*

With the resolve thus expressed in his letter, he tried to reconcile himself to his lot in Charleville. Except for the bombardment of Mézières by the Germans and the death of several civilians, confirming him in his conviction of the futility and barbarism of war, life was dull for him. One day he and Delahaye watched a procession of the victorious troops. His young friend expressed his admiration of the marvelous efficiency of the Germans. In reply, Arthur fairly bristled with contempt. "What does it mean?" he said. "Nothing more than that the Germans will be turned into a nation of slaves serving a vast military machine! That they are amenable to discipline is only a reflection of their inferiority to us. Because of that, in relation to us, the vanquished, they are backward, outdistanced, positively inferior!" Prophecy is but another name for clear sight, and at sixteen Arthur was endowed with a clear sight denied to elders. It was not an unmixed blessing, and it explains much that followed.

The winter months of 1870-71, months for him of inaction, filled him with loathing for Charleville, which returned the compliment. The siege of Paris was in progress; the heroic defense did not fill him with elation, since he could regard everything only in relation to himself; and here he was, fretting his life away in Charleville, which was heavily populated with imbeciles. Then the pleasing news came: the siege of Paris had been raised. At once he sold his watch, and bought a ticket for Paris.

It was his third flight.

4

He arrived in the capital toward the end of February. He knew no one and was without money, but full of Communist faith in brother Communists who, he thought, were sure to welcome him and provide for him out of the common hoard.

But how to approach his brothers? He bethought himself of one André Gill, a caricaturist with Republican sympathies, whose work he admired. He had no introduction, but what could you want with an introduction to a man who was your spiritual brother? That was nonsense, of course, and he could well do without it. He called on Gill, and did not find him at home. And, seeing the door-key within reach, he helped himself, entered Gill's studio and, without much ceremony, tumbled on to a bench in the lobby and was soon asleep.

He was wakened by Gill. "Who are you, and what is your business here?" he was asked gruffly, while the host shook him.

Arthur rubbed his eyes with his large red hands, and muttered: "Too bad you woke me just as I was having a marvelous dream!"

The astonished host waited for his uninvited guest to come to. When he did, he explained that he had come to share in the struggle of liberation; that he was a poet; that out of his communion with the noble rebels he would create song for the glory of man.

Gill laughed. "Don't you know, young man," he said, "we've just been through a siege. We have been hungry. We are still hungry. You'll find everybody more worried about filling their stomach than about their soul or their mind! Take my advice. Go home! You'll be well off there! Here's ten francs, and be off with you!"

"Silly duffer!" thought Arthur, but he took the money, which would come in handy. As for the advice, advice was cheap. He would have none of it. But inwardly Gill's words disturbed him; he had expected a different kind of welcome.

For a whole fortnight he had the very deuce of a time. It was winter. He slept under bridges and in coal barges; for food, he gathered scraps from the garbage. He walked about the streets of the city he both loved and hated, and collected impressions which before long would be transmuted into exquisite verse. . . . But one can't live on dreams. . . . For the time being he must confess himself beaten. Hungry and footsore he trekked home. With strength which comes from the spirit, he dragged through the journey of one hundred and sixty miles. . . .

5

He was still only sixteen, but no longer the same gay boy who had left home the first time. He had tasted bitterness where he expected sweetness, he had seen inferno where he had expected to glimpse paradise. His clear brain told him he must rid himself of futile ideals, foolish prejudices; he must base his future on firmer ground. The pleasures of men did not please him, and he avoided them; not for him the frivolous love of women, the silly sensuality which might bring him down to the level of the abominable Musset; not for him the heartless fripperies committed in the name of heart. He cast these from him as things which degraded the civilized man, and began to cram his head with all manner of knowledge from books: Eastern legends, magic, science and philosophy, interested him among other things. He abused the aged librarian roundly for not meeting his wants quickly enough, until the old fellow began to hide from the avid bookworm. What others thought of him did not matter to him in the least. He responded to the demands of his inner life, and excluded the outer world from the sensations he experienced.

And he went on writing verses.

6

He was itching to go to Paris, where on March eighteenth the bourgeois Republican government was overthrown and replaced by that of the Communists. Soldiers weary of war, workers in revolt, declared an era of equality, and young Arthur, in the midst of his inward preoccupations, was awakened to something of his former enthusiasm. But his mother held the purse-strings, and pestered him to get something to do. Then he heard that he could get thirty sous a day as a member of the National Guard; so once more he set forth and reached Paris on foot in six days. This time he was received with great ardor. Here was a mere boy, with a spark of fire in his blue eyes, who had come to them with the simple greeting: "I have walked sixty leagues to be with you." They at once made a collection for him, and he, as promptly, spent it in standing them drinks. The Communists were ill equipped, and he served without a uniform, which was to turn out a great piece of luck for him, as on the government's recapture of the city every one in Communist uniform was promptly shot.

When Arthur entered Paris he had hoped for great things. At last the social revolution for which he had yearned had come; humanity was on its way to establishing heaven on earth. Of course, there would be violence; that would be necessary at first to teach pigs the value of pearls; at any rate, there would be nobility in this violence, and none of that pettiness and paltriness which, as he had seen, so indelibly stamped the enemy of progress. Alas for Arthur, who was yet to find out that human nature, whether bourgeois or Communist, was a thing of the same texture. Sensitive to the life of those around him, his youthful delicacy and ardent idealism suffered a shock in the grossness of gregarious barracks life; there were dirt and moral stench and downright ugliness where he had expected heroic virtues; nobility and sacrifice and fraternity, supposed to have animated and inspired his comrades, were empty words. He who had dreamed of the emancipation of man felt himself duped, and the sadness and the rage which took possession of him were unutterable. His deepest emotions thus thwarted became destructive fires. There was something irreconcilable in the thought: what man might have been was one thing; what he chose to be was another. It formed a conflict in his mind and soul, and out of this conflict his most terrible poems were to come.

And in this frame of mind he returned to Charleville, a boy still in appearance but a full man in his bitter comprehension. He was one who had sought love and understanding, and had found neither. He turned more than ever into the deeps of himself, and his solitariness was a vast desert in which the only oases he found were the moments in which he wrote his poems.

7

Something prompted him in those days to send a small sheaf of poems to Verlaine. Was it that he expected to find in poets what he had failed to find in soldiers and in workers?

It proved a shaft that hit its mark. Verlaine was impressed. Rimbaud should come to Paris, he wrote him. That was the place for a poet such as he. Arthur wrote frankly; he was young, inexperienced, ill-mannered, and he had no money. Verlaine, having consulted a number of brother poets and secured their aid, invited Arthur to his home; he had a young wife, and the couple, to save the expense, lived with the parents of Madame Verlaine.

To his friend Delahaye, on the eve of his projected journey, Arthur, then not yet seventeen, unbosomed himself. After reading his latest poem, he said: "Ah, yes, no one has written anything like it. I know that well. . . . And yet . . . This world of writers and artists . . . Salons, fashion . . . I do not know how to behave. I am awkward, nervous, I do not know how to talk. . . . As for thought, I am not afraid of anyone . . . but what am I going to do down there?"

8

The women of Verlaine's household were astonished to see a tall gawky boy enter the house. They had expected a young man, but here was a bony boy with a plump, rosy, childlike face, large rough hands, and speaking with a provincial twang. They were astonished to see him coming in alone; as Verlaine and Charles Gros had gone to the station to meet him and had not returned. Arthur, in the company of these women, was self-conscious, and, before their steady survey and questions, stammered broken replies. Altogether, the women were not impressed with the guest they would have to feed and entertain in the weeks to come. And Arthur was not the man to set out to please people. His awkwardness, indeed, was so great that it sometimes gave the impression of deliberate arrogance; the ladies were loath to put up with it. To make matters worse, he was fiercely hungry on his arrival, and the ravenousness with which he devoured his food gave the ladies, who had to make the ends meet, something to think about.

Verlaine himself welcomed his guest, in whom he felt the existence of untapped creative resources, vastly stimulating. The first days together were happy days.

The winter found Rimbaud once more in the Paris streets, hungry and destitute.

Remorseful, Verlaine sought him in the streets and in the cafés and at last found him, ragged, cold, hungry and covered with vermin. His round childlike face had grown lean, but handsome with the more rigid contours of manhood. He had about made up his mind to return to Charleville, but the tender solicitude of the older poet overcame his scruples of pride and he consented to remain. To the appeal for "one of us," Theodore de Banville, Prince of Poets, furnished him with a lodging in the attic of his house and with other necessities.

Then began the chapter of the intimacy of Rimbaud and Verlaine which was to lead to the ultimate tragedy in the lives of the two poets.

9

Verlaine's attitude toward Rimbaud was one of adoration. He admired his lucid intellect, his audacity, his diabolic disdain, his robust masculine soul, his Faustian craving for a world beyond his reach. He discerned in the youth a being superior to any he had known, and he did not hesitate to say so before the company of goodly poets as often as they met. To have this rude, ill-mannered boy thus pedestaled for them to worship hurt their self-esteem, and Verlaine's persistent adulation became something of a bore. This drove Rimbaud and Verlaine more and more into each other's company, away from the rest. Verlaine could not now do without the young master whose alert, swift mind, by mysterious enchantments, fecundated the secret creative chaos in Verlaine, bringing poems to birth the more exquisite for their paternity. In this interplay of complementary temperaments lay Rimbaud's hold over Verlaine.

Rimbaud's visionary sensations were at this time intensified by the deliberate and systematic use of alcohol and hashish. He walked and sometimes sat as in sleep and gave himself up to clairvoyant visions. Afterward he analyzed his own hallucinations. "I believe in all the enchantments," he wrote. "I invented the color of the vowels: A, black; E, white; I, red; O, blue; U, green. I regulated the form and the movement of every consonant, and, with instinctive rhythms, I flattered myself that I had invented a poetic language accessible, one day or another, to every shade of meaning. I reserved to myself the right of translation. . . . I accustomed myself to simple hallucination:

I saw, quite frankly, a mosque in place of a factory, a school of drums kept by the angels, post-chaises on the roads of heaven, a drawing-room at the bottom of a lake; monsters, mysteries; the title of a vaudeville raised up horrors before me. Then I explained my magical sophisms by the hallucination of words! I ended by finding something sacred in the disorder of my mind." And he made discovery after discovery, leading to the ultimate renunciation of all that he had achieved, perhaps, too easily. The intensification of his inner life did not improve his courtesy and manners, and brother poets, all but Verlaine, did not regard him over-friendly.

In the meantime, as was to be expected, the increasing intimacy between Rimbaud and Verlaine was not without its effects on the Verlaine household. Verlaine, even without Rimbaud, was by no means an ideal husband. His wife soon lost her affection for him, and his excesses had become nauseating to her. With Rimbaud on the scene, her father saw an opportunity of ridding himself of an undesirable son-in-law. And the household united in making Verlaine's life at home a burden for him.

At this juncture the two friends set out on a journey together.

10

All that happened on that journey would make a story in itself. For this account, passing over the curious minor adventures, the main points will suffice. After excursions into Brussels and London, the two friends, the worse for their unbroken companionship, returned to Brussels.

This was how things stood with them: Rimbaud, who was ever changing with growth, despised everything he had done before; and Verlaine, less alert, was no longer able to keep up with his young friend. Disagreements arose; the fretful moments increased. All that kept them together was Rimbaud's material dependence on Verlaine. A hankering arose in Verlaine for his young wife.

An effort at reconciliation with Madame Verlaine having failed, he had but one desire, and that was that Rimbaud should stay with him. The knowledge that Rimbaud was determined to leave him put Verlaine into an irresponsible state, presaging a catastrophe. Possessed by despair, which now and then passed into rage, Verlaine drank heavily. He bought a revolver which he showed Rimbaud. "It's for you, for me, for everybody!" he said.

Rimbaud would have gone long ago, but he had no money, and he was trying to borrow the fare to Paris from Verlaine's mother.

After one of his periodic exits toward the dram-shop Verlaine returned, locked the door and sat down facing Rimbaud, who was at the opposite end of the room. To all his entreaties, Rimbaud answered that he would not stay. Verlaine fired. The shot struck Rimbaud in the wrist. The second shot was fired at random and hit the floor. Then Verlaine fell into a mood of remorse, and begged Rimbaud to shoot him.

Rimbaud appeared to bear no ill will. He went to a hospital to have the wound dressed. As he would not stay, Verlaine's mother gave him twenty francs so that he might return to Charleville. They were all walking to the station together when Rimbaud, taking alarm at an unexpected motion on the part of Verlaine, began to run. Verlaine pursued him, and Rimbaud turned to a policeman for protection. The details of the case were investigated, and Verlaine received a sentence of two years' imprisonment. Rimbaud must have been as fully disgusted with the judges as with Verlaine. But during a visit to a familiar café in

Paris, he was sneered at by former associates who had heard garbled versions of the affair at Brussels. What did he now care what they thought or said? The solitary youth sat there, silent in his pride, impervious to a world for which he had a deep, inscrutable loathing.

He had been with social rebels, he had been with poets; everything was so paltry. He had found pettiness where he expected to find epic virtues. He was making his final decision which was to take him away from literature—and from Europe. "Priests, professors and masters," he announced in his last work, "you do wrong in surrendering me to justice. I have never belonged to these people. . . . I am a beast, a savage. But I may yet be saved. . . . The wisest course is to quit the continent." There were a few others who were thinking the same thoughts, but for them words in themselves provided an escape; their poems were their Promised Land. But Rimbaud was not one to do lip service to a conviction; to think was to act.

With a soberness as deliberate and systematic as his intoxication had been, he set out on the long road of preparation. He traveled much, absorbing science and languages; he did not disdain to work with his hands, and he rid himself of all scruple and illusion. For a while he lived by his wits, eventually landing at Alexandria, where he secured a job as overseer of a quarry in Cyprus. He was twenty-five when he returned home with typhoid fever. He was sunburned, his cheeks were sunken and deeply lined, and he had a beard. But there was a new earnestness, and an air of self-reliance about him. His early friend Delahaye once ventured to ask him if literature still interested him. He shook his head, and, with a half-amused smile, replied quietly: "I no longer concern myself with that."

What would Delahaye have thought if he had known the kind of thoughts that were occupying Rimbaud's mind?

His attitude had grown bourgeois. He had said at nine, "I will be a capitalist." And he was now thinking out ways and means of putting his thought into action. He had tried the paternal side of his temperament and it had failed him; now his life and intentions coincided more with his mother's ways of life. He had made up his mind. He would become a merchant in Africa, he would get together some money and marry some ordinary girl, and have a son, and there would be no nonsense about this son, who would be an engineer, "a man rich and powerful through science."

11

Henceforth, we see Rimbaud in Africa and the East, where he spends eleven long and terrible years, until a swollen knee sends him to Europe for relief only to meet it in death.

We find him first at Aden, on the Red Sea, an employee of a French trading house. What a terrible place it is! "There is not a single tree, not even a shrivelled one," he writes in one of his letters, "not a single blade of grass, not a rod of earth, not a drop of fresh water." Aden, indeed, lives in the crater of an extinct volcano—is not this symbolic of Rimbaud?—and the sea has filled this crater with sand. "The sides of the crater prevent the entry of any wind, and we bake at the bottom of the hole as if in a lime kiln. One must be indeed a victim of circumstance to seek employment in such hells!"

Next we see him transferred to the Abyssinian branch of the house at Harar, which is a pleasanter place. He penetrates into hitherto unexplored places, and trades in ivory, musk, coffee, gold and ostrich plumes. As he moves among natives, he is "obliged to talk their gibberish languages, to eat their filthy dishes, and undergo a thousand worries from their laziness, treachery and stupidity. And this is not the worst of it; there is the fear of becoming animalized oneself, removed as one is from intellectual companionship."

He then goes into partnership with one Pierre Labulut and, thinking to make a fortune, tries gun-running. Old Menelik of Abyssinia wants guns, and is willing to pay good prices for them. It is a risky business, and the caravan must often spend fifty days in the desert among unfriendly tribes. Political complications ensue, and, to make matters worse, Rimbaud's partner dies, leaving Rimbaud burdened with debts. With great persistence and courage, he not only pays off the debts but presents his partner's son with a sum of money. He is not very distinguished for his charitable actions, so this ought to be remembered.

With what money he has, he goes to Cairo, to try his fortune there. He can not return to Europe; he is afraid of dying of the cold winters there, and he is accustomed to "a wandering, free and open life." Besides, he has "no position" there! No position! Is not that the mind of his mother speaking, the mind of the petty French bourgeois? It is as if he had rounded a complete circle of natal influences, and ultimately returned to the stronger force of his origins.

In the course of his mercantile wanderings he receives a letter from a Paris journalist. A book of his poems has been collected. Writers are agog over his genius. He is influencing the verse of the younger men. He has become a legend. What is he doing now? asks the journalist. Everybody wants to know. It is a matter of interest to the public.

Rimbaud only snarls, flies into a rage.

Nothing interests him but the problem of "getting on," and living out his existence. "Like the Mussulmans," he writes, "I know that what is to come comes, and that is all."

He returns to Europe only because of his knee. His leg is amputated, but that does not relieve him. He spends months of agony in bed, nursed by his sister, and, drugged to ease his pains, he experiences hallucinations and relives his life. He dies "prophesying" and repeating, "Allah Kerim! Allah Kerim!"

CHARLES M. DOUGHTY—THE SUPREME TRAVELER

THERE are rare men in this world about whom it is hard to write, about whom it is presumptuous to write. It should be confessed at the very start that to this class belongs Charles M. Doughty, whose *Arabia Deserta* is admitted by the discerning to be the greatest work of prose written in English during the nineteenth century. Doughty was essentially an Englishman: he had character,—an abundance of it,—and he was a man of action. He had, besides, the power of expressing himself in words; he translated the great adventure of his life in terms of great language. His life and his books are, indeed, inseparable; they are of the same texture and design, and because this written record is as superb a piece of self-portraiture as it is a panorama of life in the Arabian desert, it is meet that those who really want to know about Doughty should read his book; for sheer power and art, the carefully wrought narrative can not be bettered or even equaled. This short essay must needs be brief and wholly inadequate; its only excuse is that the man Doughty belongs to the great figures which distinguished the late century; at best it may serve as a sign-post. "This way lies *Doughty*,"—the discriminating traveler will take the road of exploration, he will plunge right into the *Arabia Deserta,* and alongside of him will walk, or ride on a camel, the man Doughty, who will be so essential and integral a portion of the desert landscape in which the reader will find himself.

"A new voice hailed me of an old friend when, first returned from the Peninsula, I paced again in that long street of Damascus which is called Straight; and suddenly taking me wondering by the hand 'Tell me (said he), since thou art here again in the peace and assurance of Ullah, and whilst we walk, as in the former years, towards the blossoming orchards, full of the sweet spring of God, what moved thee, or how could'st thou take such journeys into the fanatic Arabia?"

In these words does Doughty's extraordinary narrative begin, and they are the key-note to the man and the book. Is there something alien about them to our modern ear, accustomed as it is to uncouth careless speech, staccato phrasing, the jangle of the telephone and the harsh phonetics of the garrulous radio?

These words are melodious, they are poetry, they are as simple as the first speech of men, and are they not a fit gateway to the world we are about to enter, a world of primitive men speaking what seems to us quaint speech marked by accents and hyperbole peculiar to the Orient? Here men, as poor as mice, live on a few dates or on a little camel's milk, and they walk on arid soil with nothing to shield them from the broiling sun; but they commune with the heavens and they have a contact with the one thing that matters: God, whom they call Ullah. And they talk and act like men whose communion with the All-Powerful is direct and intimate and not as in our overcomfortable civilization in which religion is nowadays a worn texture dubiously shot through with well-defined threads of doubt. Here is great material poverty, here also is great spiritual wealth. Hence, "fanatic Arabia," a phrase that spells danger for the *Nasrany,* the Christian intruder, hated as the enemy of the God of the Faithful.

But the speech quoted has another aspect, equally important, since it sheds a light on the personality of Doughty himself. To the last day Doughty shunned the, to him, temperamental inadequacies of the modern world. When he sat down to write *Arabia Deserta,* he made up his mind to use no books that contained words which were not in Chaucer and Spenser. The work that he studied most assiduously was Hakluyt's voyages. This accounts for his antique style, which has been a stumbling block to so many but gives his book its peculiar charm. And, characteristically enough, his companion in the desert was part of a folio copy of his favorite Chaucer; it accompanied him through the whole of his hazardous journey of nearly two years and returned with him as part of the contents of his camel-bags. To what degree he kept aloof from the movements and literature of the day is best illustrated by a story the writer has chanced to hear. He can not vouch for the truth of it, but every legend undoubtedly has a basis of truth, and this one must also have one. The story goes that in his old age Doughty happened to be in a publisher's office when the name of the most distinguished of his contemporaries, Thomas Hardy, came up. "Who is Hardy?" asked the patriarchal old man to the amazement of those present.

Arabia Deserta is Doughty. Never has a book so amply demonstrated that well-expressed truth: style is the man.

There is need to stress the superb detachment of Doughty, since it furnishes the key to the nature of his achievement. He was in Arabia no ordinary traveler; he traveled as a Christian, he did not deign to assume a disguise where a disguise might have proved the better part of valor; yet he lived with the Arabs, drank with them and ate with them and received proposals of marriage from their women; he was with them, but not of them. It was right to kill a Christian, and, indeed, more than once he was in danger of death; yet here was one Christian who made himself respected, one Christian whose courage more than once stayed the hand of the fanatic. It is hard to tell why he deliberately announced himself a *Nasrany* wherever he went; such a course seemed foolhardy; yet he did, and escaped to tell the tale. And what a tale! What power was there in the man that carried him through the long hazardous adventure? He impressed men with his sincerity, his dignity, and, ever at the mercy of native and Bedouin, his very helplessness always found him defenders when he was in his direst straits. There is this to be said: he was no missionary, and, though he proclaimed himself a Christian, he respected the religion of others and made no effort to argue the superiority of his faith. He carried simple medicines with him and won hearts by curing the sick. Very poor, very helpless, he often had to accept the charity of the passing wanderer, who was nearly as poor as himself. Not a strong man, physically, and in bad health when he started from Damascus, he endured the trying climate, with its extremes of heat and cold, with unfaltering courage. Yet, like the Arabs themselves, among whom he lived like one of them, he managed to subsist on scant rations, and to ride his camel in forced marches across difficult country; thus, often from sunrise to sunset, and sometimes into the depth of night, shelterless under the blazing sun or facing fierce winds.

Seldom has there been a greater triumph of spirit over matter. Doughty started on his journey in 1876; he was thirty-three then, tall, upright, stately, with thick reddish hair and beard,—already something of a patriarch in appearance, which old age was to intensify; his ostensible object in making the journey was to make impressions of ancient sepulchral inscriptions at Medain Salih, three weeks' march from Damascus. It was here, at the very beginning of his journey, that he first encountered that fanatic hostility which he was to meet again and again with increasing intensity as the caravan approached Mecca, until he was safely at Jiddah, where he "was called to the open hospitality of the British Consulate."

At Medain Salih he found the sculptured monuments he had sought and he carefully impressed their superscriptions. Then he decided not to return with the pilgrim caravan to Damascus, but to pursue his journey into the high desert, where he might view "those vast waterless marches of the nomad Arabs; tent-dwellers, inhabiting, from the beginning, as it were beyond the World."

"Unto this endeavour, I was but slenderly provided; yet did not greatly err, when I trusted my existence, (which could long endure, as in Sinai, with little more than heaven's sun and air,) among an unlettered and reputed lawless tribesfolk . . . which amidst a life of never-ending hardships and want, continue to observe a Great Semitic Law, unwritten; namely the ancient Faith of their illimitable empty wastes. . . ."

And despite the friendly Arab voices which warned him, he proceeded with his journey. "The haps that befel me are narrated in these volumes: wherein I have set down, that which I saw with my eyes, and heard with my ears and thought in my mind; neither more nor less."

The result is a marvelous narrative which holds its place with the greatest narratives of the world, both as a record of places and people and as an autobiography.

He carried note-books with him, and in the midst of all manner of difficulties and continued danger he assiduously recorded the aspects of Arabia as well as the conversation, the customs, the virtues and defects of the Arabs. He did this so vividly and so intimately and with such astonishing thoroughness that no writer after him could even hope to equal him, much less surpass him. It is significant that years after the first publication of the book, when the demand arose for a new edition, Doughty could neither add nor take away a word.

For all his superb detachment, possibly because of it, he entered the skin of the Arab and brought away with him the Arab soul. That at the same time he managed to maintain an aloofness, to surrender nothing of himself, gives his achievement a place among the worthier British legends. His feat was peculiarly English; that is to say, it belongs to what is best in the English genius, whose mastery of alien races is no mere accident. Doughty possessed the truly English virtues in abundance; but he was greater than all the English governors and viceroys because he used his power as an artist and not as a politician, and he so distilled the essence of a great foreign people into a magnificent book as to make that people live for us as a principality in the empire of our mind. One wonders whether the Cambridge examiner who, when Doughty was still a student, declares that he "had such a dishevelled mind," lived long enough to revise his judgment.

No disheveled mind could have acted in crises in Arabia as Doughty did when his life was at stake. When, on the last stage of the journey, almost within sight of Jiddah which was to offer him relief and release, a fanatical assailant stayed his hand in which a knife was poised, ready to strike.

"' . . . Thou art not afraid!'—'Is not Ullah (God) in every place?' 'Ay, wellah Khalil.' Such pious words are honeycombs to the Arabs, and their rude hearts are surprised with religion. 'Dreadest thou not to die!'—'I have not so lived, Moslem, that I must fear to die.' "

Is not this magnificent? Even the fanatic can not kill a hated Christian after an answer like that.

There were long stretches of time without such hair-raising episodes but which required another kind of courage—the courage of endurance. During the summer months the times were hard in the famine-stricken sandstone and lava-covered wastes, when the eye was avid for the sight of green and the stomach for a little food. Doughty shared the scant lot of the Bedouin.

"I endured their summer-famine with the nomads. Languor of hunger, the desert disease, was in all the tents. *Maanalon,* we have nothing left, said the people one to another. The days passed by, days in this weakness of famine, in forgetfulness of the distant world, and the wasting life of the body."

This is bad enough, but what of that when other things, less definable, are present to offer consolation, peace and the vision of eternity beyond the ken of complacent humanity.

"The summer night's delightful freshness in the mountains is our daily repast, and lying to rest amidst wild basalt stones under the clear stars, in a land of enemies, I have found more refreshment than upon beds and pillows in our close chambers. Hither lies no way from the city of the world, a thousand years pass as one daylight; we are in the world, and not in the world, where Nature brought forth man, an enigma to himself, and an evil spirit sowed in him the seeds of dissolution. And looking then upon that infinite spectacle, this life of the wasted flesh seemed to me ebbing, and the spirit to wave her eyas wings into that divine obscurity."

The author of *Arabia Deserta* died but two years ago in his eighty-third year. A week before his death he asked to be moved to his study that his eyes might rest on his beloved books. He left behind several poetical works of great merit, but not comparable with his prose. Fully as great as his masterpiece was his personality, which, like the book, belonged to another age. He was, indeed, an Elizabethan living out of his time; not so robustious, perhaps; and sober with the spirit of nineteenth-century Protestantism, the one thing which separated him from the great Englishmen who lived during the reign of the Virgin Queen.

THE COMPARISON OF MELVILLE WITH RIMBAUD AND DOUGHTY

MELVILLE, American of Americans.
Rimbaud, Frenchman of the French.
Doughty, Englishman of the English.

Three great adventurers, the adventure of each colored by the specific genius of his race.

First, Melville. He had sought an escape from the petty realities of a pioneer people in the immensity of ocean adventure, returned to relate his Odyssey, and, not finding listeners, retired to the shelter of bitter obscurity. Like the Ancient Mariner of Coleridge's poem he tried to hold the Wedding Guest by the coat lapel, so as to force the fellow to hear. The wedding guest could understand the wedding but not Melville's story, and Melville was forced to give him up as a bad job. Melville was not the only great American to suffer this experience; there was Poe, who took to drugs and drink; and there was Walt Whitman, who did not care whether any one heard him or not. Poe plunged into visions and dreams; Whitman into a roseate optimism of his own creation; Melville, successively, into life, literature and the unfathomable sea of metaphysics. He was driven to the latter recourse by his having challenged the fates in both life and literature; the fates accepted the challenge and sent him back reeling.

Immensities attracted him, and that, in its way, is peculiarly American; only, from the practical point of view, he committed the indiscretion of admiring big ideas instead of big things. A sky-scraper is a concrete thing, an idea is elusive and useless. Americans, a race of pioneers who for generations have had to face practical problems of existence to the exclusion of abstract matters, have use only for concrete useful things. Even their idealism, with which they are bountifully supplied, is essentially practical in character. Melville found himself very much in the position of talking to the man who could worship only in a structure we call the church and who could not quite grasp the idea that another man's tabernacle might have the sky for roof and all the earth and waters for paving-stone. He was anything but parochial. A great seeker, he was in no mood to respond to the parochialisms of American life, but reacted against them with an intensity that cut him off from all contact with it. Like all who sought for the absolute in life as well as in thought, he was much concerned about the potential greatness of his people, whose growing indifference ultimately robbed him of that warmth which genius needs for its nurture.

"It is for the nation's sake, and not for her authors' sake," said Melville, writing of Hawthorne, "that I would have America be heedful of the increasing greatness among her writers. For how great the shame if other nations should be before her in crowning her heroes of the pen?"

Neither America nor England had much use for Melville while he was alive; history does not present a more wretched instance of neglect. Thus was "the most powerful of all great American writers" rendered impotent by the apprehensive Lilliputians.

There is that Russian fable about the man who went to the zoo and, when questioned afterward, admitted to having seen the little birds and the rodents and all manner of small beasts. As to the elephant—well, he simply "hadn't noticed it"! Was not this the relation of critic and reader to Melville on the American scene?

Melville had the misfortune to write about a Big Whale. That he wrote, to use modern jargon, "a whale of a book," was a sufficient offense for his relative neglect by "home" critics and for his abuse by the English. "To write an immense book one must have an immense subject," wrote Melville, and immense was the penalty he paid for the attempt. He had committed the unforgivable sin of not writing petty books about petty people, a fashionable virtue then as now. But when the flood subsides, as it must, it is the high peaks which are first visible. As for the flotsam and jetsam, they are simply nowhere.

Melville is essentially a subjective, an autobiographical writer. There is no need for him to cry from the housetops, but for those who can read he nevertheless tells his story clearly and unmistakably. He tells it in *Redburn,* in *Typee,* in *Omoo,* in *White Jacket,* and more particularly in *Pierre.* The precise note is less clear in *Mardi* and in *Moby Dick.* That is true in-so-far as no memoir of their author can be based on them; yet surely in *Moby Dick,* as in no other book, does the author show his heart if not his features. Is not its unforgettable essence as precise in its way as the illuminating connection seen between Pierre and Melville? For may not the White Whale be Melville's confession of his own transcendent illusion, of his own quest of the unattainable, driving him to his ultimate despair, his ultimate doom? As Mr. John Freeman, in his illuminating study on Melville, says: "During the first half of his life Herman Melville was investing himself with illusions and discovering them to be but illusions, and during the second half he was trying to make terms with the bareness that remained and avoid an exhausting, cynical conclusion."

That is true; yet I wish that the author of these lines had pursued his line of thought further; that he had explained the symbolism of the dénouement of *Moby Dick*. And the point is this: Melville did more than "make terms with the bareness that remained," did more than "avoid an exhausting cynical conclusion." The moment we observe Tashtego hammering the flag to the mast of the ship *Pequod* a sudden flood of inspirational truth illumes the proceeding, and we know that in the continued life of the spirit the good ship is still here, that Ahab is not dead, that Tashtego and the rest of the brave crew are also alive and transcendently so, and that they can not die until the whole, noble, questing humanity is dead. And then that final supreme touch, the author escaping on a floating coffin to tell his tale! Why a coffin? Here you have the old myth of resurrection, new life through death, in a new form; life cleansed through and by experience. The present revival of Melville is but another illustration of this.

The truth is that Melville, a romantic and mystic of epic stature, in every sense a Promethean character, was far from and above petty human strife. "He remained a cloistered thinker," says Mr. Freeman justly, in regard to his long seclusion, "but I cannot believe that he was cloistered because of petulance; neither niggard vices nor niggard virtues were his. He had withdrawn because he had failed and because he had been driven to accept the world's terms. In his own secret proud way he had challenged the world and the world had defeated him by ignoring the challenge and starving him." And what a cry from the heart, full of compassion, Melville himself utters in one of his stories:

"Humanity, thou strong thing, I worship thee, not in the laureled victor, but in this vanquished one!"

There is little here to please modern worshipers of success; to the "go-getters" and the "make-gooders" he is bound to remain a closed page.

Arthur Rimbaud

From *Rimbaud: The Boy and the Poet* by Edgell Rickword, Heinemann, London

Charles M. Doughty

From *Wanderings in Arabia* by Charles M. Doughty
Duckworth & Co., London

It is to the eternal shame of a generation which neglected so great a figure as Melville. It would be idle in this instance to avail oneself of the conventional argument that men of genius are improved by suffering and that every added enforced torture goes into their work. Melville's sufferings were, in the first instance, of his own choice. No gratuities were needed to assist in the nourishment of his genius. But heaven alone knows how many fine works have been lost to us through his enforced long seclusion and the necessity of earning his bread. Melville himself was thoroughly aware of this, for (as Mr. Freeman points out), he declares, with the consciousness of all the untold within himself, that the immediate products of a great mind are not so great as the undeveloped or even undevelopable greatness; "in Shakespeare's tomb lies infinitely more than Shakespeare ever wrote." Is there not a suspicion in Melville's mind that Shakespeare, no less than himself, not only could not give expression to all that seethed within him, but also that he had not the opportunity. Melville continues: "In this world of lies Truth is forced to fly like a scared white doe in the woodlands; and only by cunning glimpses will she reveal herself, as in Shakespeare and other masters of the great Art of Telling the Truth—even though it be covertly and by snatches."

And with these noble words let us comfort ourselves. No other nation could have produced Melville, yet he is by no means a typical American. But America did produce him by reaction from itself; and in that sense he is a symbol and a reflection of a country whose spiritual self lies prostrate before its material power.

Now as to Rimbaud. He died in the same year as Melville, thirty-six years younger than the American. He was thirty-eight years old when he died. At this age Melville had suffered his literary death, having given in to the fates and become Custom-House Inspector in New York. It would be as idle to speculate as to what might have happened to Melville's literary reputation had he died at thirty-eight as to speculate on what might have happened to Rimbaud's had he gone on writing. What is significant is that both men, at a point of their career, deliberately abandoned the pen and took up vocations belonging to the domain of commerce. Melville, it is true, did this unwillingly, having been driven to the recourse by the need of earning a living. But what drove Rimbaud to it? The reasons are as much more complex in his case as France is more complex than America. Indeed, Arthur Rimbaud's hard French logic drove him to all his actions and reactions.

In the comparison, the ultimate formula may be reduced to this: America would not accept Melville, Rimbaud refused to accept Europe. Here is a distinction with a vast difference. Did not Melville say, "I stand for the heart. To the dogs with the head!" And did not Rimbaud, even as a boy, pride himself on his superiority to the other boys because he had no heart?

It would be hard to present a more clearly defined juxtaposition of two different points of view reflecting two different races.

And now for the inevitable irony: American sentiment rejected Melville for all that he had in common with it, to wit, the heart; Rimbaud's French logic rejected that France which prided itself on its lucid thinking. A paradox, if you will, but inevitable in either case.

Melville had too much heart (witness his intense affection and his demand for its return!); America, proud of its average, could not quite grasp it, not even an exceptional American like Hawthorne. The wolf packs kill their leader if he advances too far ahead of the herd; Melville was killed because he was too far ahead of the human pack—even in the matter of the heart.

Rimbaud had too much mind, which saw, perhaps, too clearly the havoc reason can play with whole nations when the heart is not fully attuned to it. Witness his disillusion, first with his Communist comrades, later with the artists! Unlike Melville, he wanted to get away from the herd because he saw that it could and would kill him if he did not! He ran away from that Europe which preached reason and had murder in its heart. If he had lived until the autumn of 1914 he would have doubtless seen his worst forebodings realized. So fortified was he with reason that he practised even the vices as deliberately as a scientist made his experiments, and for the same cause: to learn the why and the wherefore of things. His logic drove him from one extreme to the other; he had as deliberately adopted the bourgeois mode of existence as he had at the first the artist's; logic is a pendulum between one extreme and another. His wayward life as an artist was not without consequences; he left issue: Verlaine and Mallarmé are the children of his virile mind. As for Melville, his *Moby Dick* should remain for all time the Bible of sea-story writers. Joseph Conrad, a lesser than he, lived to achieve that popularity which he longed for and was denied.

What is there left to say of Doughty? Little and everything. He was an Englishman. His work does not show that he gave much thought to philosophy, and he did not wear his heart on his sleeve. He combined action and contemplation in a peculiarly English way, so that it is impossible to tell which proceeds from the other and where the one ends and the other begins. As some would say, he had, in his English way, "bungled through"! How? What does it matter? The result is magnificent. He had that great attribute, character, in the English sense. This is not to say that Melville and Rimbaud were without character. It takes great courage to accept or renounce, to say Yes or No, and both the American and the Frenchman had this courage to a superlative degree. But they were men of extremes; their virtues were, perhaps, not sufficiently tempered one with the other; this robbed them of the added virtue of endurance which the combination gives. There is an endurance, a timelessness about Doughty, a sense of being beyond action and reaction, bound to affect his triumph. He possessed, in the ultimate degree, the English virtue of "not knowing when one is beaten," and where defeat is not acknowledged ignorance is victory.

He has left behind him a narrative superlatively English both as regards language and method of procedure. No moral is preached, but we are left with the ineffable memory of a dignified personality, a gentle reserved man full of hidden strength, above all, of a humble traveler who has given us contained pleasure in a tale of wanderings well told.

FERDINAND LASSALLE—PRINCE OF THE PEOPLE

THIS is the story of a man who, against all manner of odds and by sheer will, rose to great power and to the leadership of multitudes, by whom he was beloved, and, at last, in a weak moment, by some irony of fate and in his very prime, fell in consequence of his love for a woman. A giant in all but stature, a modern Samson, he allowed a woman to shear his locks and, blinded by the Philistines of his time, he rose up in his wrath and destroyed himself. It was all very unnecessary and sad. Is not that true of all tragic heroes? The name of our tragic hero is Ferdinand Lassalle, of the heroine, Helene von Dönniges. Such were their names in real life, though George Meredith, in *The Tragic Comedians,* loving them both, called the one Alvan, the other Clotilde. "Two wishes make a will!" Meredith puts into the mouth of Alvan in speaking to the lady of his heart. There were indeed two wishes here; there was a will too, and where there's a will there's a way, and yet—and yet—— But listen to the story.

It was toward the end of July, in the year 1864.

Ferdinand Lassalle, the much hated and the much beloved, was at Rigi-Kaltbad. The air here was fresh and invigorating. The green of the great slope below him stretched downward toward the pellucid waters of Lake Lucerne; the view afforded out of the hotel-room window was magnificent. And well that it was so. For the famous Lassalle, fresh from his greatest triumphs, was tired and weary.

His persistent championship of justice, his years and years of exertion on behalf of the poor and the downtrodden, had won for him the admiration and, in some cases, the detestation of men in high places, and the affection of the thousands upon thousands who struggle for mere existence in the low. These multitudes, whose number increased each year, would they not have made him king this very day if they had but a little more strength and power, a little more iron and blood in their fiber? There was indeed some talk of making him king. As it was, he was already their prince; he possessed his principality not in the number of acres but in the countless adoring hearts of his followers.

He was that curious thing: an aristocrat by nature who loved the common people and was beloved by them in return.

But a little while had elapsed since he made his tour of the Rhine provinces. His journey had been one series of popular acclamations. In all the towns and upon all the roads he was greeted with serenades. There were triumphal arches, garlands, inscriptions of welcome, applause, endless cheering—the glad tumult of countless voices. How happy they were to see him, their champion and deliverer! Workingmen, young and old, pressed around his carriage, held up their young ones to catch sight of him, struggled to shake his hand or hear his voice which they loved so well. It was like the birth of a new religion, and Heine's description of him as the Messiah of the nineteenth century seemed on the verge of proving true. As he had approached Ronsdorf he could see even at a distance hosts of people thronging the heights. On the way there, the towns of Solingen and Wermelskirchen poured forth their legions; laughing factory girls threw flowers in profusion at the carriage amid such fervor as was not remembered by any living inhabitant. On the downward curve of the hill, where the road turned, the gathering crowd ran alongside and behind the carriage, filling the June air with their exultant cries. Some ran as far as Ronsdorf. The speeches he then delivered! What applause greeted his every trenchant remark, uttered with hammer-like intensity! "We must weld our wills unanimously," he had at one moment cried, "and put that hammer in the hands of a man whose intelligence, character and good-will we can trust, that he may raise the implement and strike!" And as he heard the applause he knew that the hammer he had so longed to possess was at last in his hand, and that great would be the fall of the oppressors where and when he should strike. And yet—and yet——

The enemy was strong and active. Friends did not always help as they might, workers sometimes failed in their duty. Even now, with all his power, he was under sentence of four months for contempt of court.

He was painfully weary now, in this beautiful Rigi, where nature appeared at her most sublime, and the air was blithe, and everything seemed made to heal souls in distress. He was thirty-nine—and a half, to be exact. At the height of his powers, in his prime, and just as he had achieved the first peak of his desire. In the distance, through the window, the snow-capped Jungfrau, seen but faintly behind other peaks, taunted him with the thought of heights yet to climb. And he was tired, unutterably tired.

A premonition—God knew where it came from—oppressed him. Why should he feel like this just as he had molded the workers into a united body ready to fight for their rights, to establish a workers' brotherhood on earth? And they, these workers, adored him, as happy subjects, their benevolent prince. Those in power feared him and fought him tooth and nail. What of that? They were few, the workers many. And he was no believer in mild tactics.

They would use force if need be, if the end justified it. Yet, after having sacrificed much, devoted what small fortune was his to the cause, the power he sought almost within his grasp, a premonition troubled him. In his last speech to his followers he had already spoken of the possibility of his overthrow: "If I am overthrown, may some successor and avenger arise from my bones! May this great and national movement toward civilization not come to an end with myself!" But a week ago, at a meeting of the Union at Düsseldorf, he had said: "Next year you will be obliged to drape this room with mourning." At the same time, as he was starting for Rigi-Kaltbad, some one said to him, "We shall meet again, Herr Lassalle!" And his reply had been, "Who knows?"

An early memory came back to him. He was but sixteen. He announced to his father that he had decided on his profession. He would devote himself to working for the sacred interests of humanity. He would pursue the objects started by the French Revolution. He would agitate for a better world, he would serve the interests of truth. Truth, he had seen even then, must be supported, if need be, by physical force, "for those in possession of the thrones would have it so."

"Why should you, of all people, become a martyr?" his father had asked.

"Oh, yes," he had said at the time, "he is right. Why should I, of all people, become a martyr? But if every one said as much and withdrew with like cowardice, when would a warrior be forthcoming? Why should I, of all people, become a martyr? Why? Because God has put a voice in my heart that calls me to battle; because God has given me strength and fitted me for battle: I can feel it! Because I can fight and suffer for a noble cause. Because I will not deceive God in the use of my strength which He has given me for a definite purpose. Because, in one word, I can not help it!"

Ever since then he had fought. He had fought in the public tribune and in the legal courts, always championing those whom injustice threatened. And more than once he had been in jail. He had fought a long fight and a hard fight, and now he was tired. Was it so astonishing that he should be tired?

He rose from his chair, from which, through the window, he had been contemplating the remote Jungfrau, and walked to the mirror. Half absently he studied his face in it. There was no denying it: he was handsome, with his high forehead, his face and eyes keen with the experience of a thousand storms and fights. Yet, at this moment, he looked old to himself. And he felt old. Had he burned himself out? Was his last youth fleeting? Where was that young man who, at twenty-three, with an eloquence which astounded the court, defended himself against the charges of "theft" and turned the charges into an accusation against the accuser, and, indeed, against the whole of society as it was constituted? Where was the youth described in the court records as "Ferdinand Lassalle, twenty-three years of age, born at Breslau, five feet six inches high, with brown curly hair, an open forehead, dark blue eyes, a well-proportioned nose and mouth, a round chin, a narrow face and slender figure"?

In that not to be forgotten indictment of August, 1848,—the year of the revolution—he was charged before the Assize Court at Cologne with abetting the theft of a cash-box. A strange charge against so idealistic a spirit. What happened was this. He had become friends with the Countess Sophie von Hatzfeldt. This lady, who was handsome in spite of her thirty-nine years, had been abominably treated by her husband, and young Lassalle took up the cudgels on her behalf against the count. Two years previously, he had induced two other young men of extremely rich and distinguished families to abstract from the count's mistress a cash-box, in which a contract was supposed to have been kept securing to this mistress from the count a handsome annual income. One of the young men was released; his motives could hardly be misconstrued; after all, he was heir to two or three million thalers. The other young man was given five years. And now Lassalle, who had already suffered imprisonment while awaiting trial, came forward to defend his case. Defend? That is hardly the word. Once in the prisoner's dock, he turned accuser, and brought all his guns to bear on the case of the countess and against the mean count, who had referred to him as the "silly Jewish boy." Such ruthless logic, such extraordinary eloquence, from a youth unversed in law had never been heard before, such chivalry on behalf of a woman seldom witnessed. . . .

He then had begun the study of law in earnest and by 1854 the count found the "silly Jewish boy" more than his match and unconditionally accepted the humiliating terms of peace which Lassalle had dictated to him. As a reward the countess gave Lassalle, as her attorney, the stipulated four thousand thalers a year, which relieved him from worry and enabled him to return to his unremunerative scientific studies.

At twenty-four, following the Revolution of 1848, he was already one of the leaders of the Republican party, addressing political gatherings and calling for armed resistance when the Prussian Government, by a breach of the Constitution, declared the National Assembly dissolved. The success of counter-revolutionary forces put him again in jail. His speech before his judges was one of the astounding things of the time. He was all fire, and his words were all fire, which might have melted the hearts of his listeners, had not the Lord hardened them against the cry of justice as He once hardened the hearts of the Pharaohs.

And now Lassalle, heart-sick and weary, was like another of his race who had gone before him, and he stood glimpsing the Promised Land, which, by some curious intuition he knew he might not enter.

He resisted his thoughts. He made an effort to turn to more pleasant ones. He who had been adored by many women suddenly thought of his golden-haired Helene, of her who had put all the women he had ever known in the shade. Never before had he thought of a woman as he thought of Helene. Never before had he taken an "affair" seriously. He had changed his loves as he would change a dwelling. But this was different. He wanted to marry Helene. They had heard of one another before they met. Some one told her, "You are the first woman whom I have ever been able to think of as Lassalle's wife." To Lassalle some one had said, "You are the man to make a husband to Helene von Dönniges!" They had met at the house of a mutual friend. The inevitable happened. They were enchanted with each other. It was love at first sight. There were difficulties. Her parents were Jew-haters, though her mother was herself a Jewess who had abjured her faith to marry the man of her choice; in short, she was the worst kind of Jew-hater. Besides, Helene had already been half promised in marriage to an adoring youth, Herr Yanko von Racowitza, by no means a distinguished personality but one whose love was pure and tender. She felt tenderly toward him, too, but had no great respect for him. She had always dreamed of a man who could command her, whom she could look up to, who could make her feel that she was in the presence of a superior being. And she had heard that Lassalle was very thick with Bismarck and that the great statesman listened to him with respect.

Lassalle was not the man to brood long. He made an energetic gesture, shook himself, walked over to the desk, snatched a sheet of letter paper and began to write rapidly.

There was a knock on the door.

"A lady to see you, sir," said the Swiss hotel attendant.

"A lady?" He thought quickly. He did not know whom to expect.

"Yes, on horseback."

Lassalle issued forth and when he saw his visitor his face lighted up with a glad radiance. His weariness all at once dropped from him like a garment, he was young again, his lively eyes gleamed a lover's welcome. "You, Helene!"

It was Helene von Dönniges. Helene, his golden-haired one.

She, spirited, lovely with the frail loveliness of aristocratic blood, a dream incarnate, returned his smile. She was delighted to see him so glad. He was handsome, and the light in his eyes on beholding his loved one, made him still handsomer. There was something kingly about him. Little wonder men seriously spoke of him as of one who might conceivably displace the Hohenzollerns on the Prussian throne. Woman-like, she was glad of his distinguished appearance, as there were two or three friends with her, and she could not help her suddenly born desire to display her lover, who, it was to be seen, was proud to love her, and who, it could not escape the onlookers' eyes, was not unloved by this gracious, slender, animated girl. The look in his dark blue eyes challenged her with its spark of fire. Could she do less than respond? Spark leaped to spark. Her companions were quietly amused. One of them, an Englishwoman, had more than an inkling of the situation.

Would he join the party? Superfluous to ask. He who commanded thousands and hundreds of thousands was a slave of Helene.

How did she come to be there? he asked as they walked.

What could be simpler? She was with her family at Geneva, and she heard that he was at Rigi.

What was he doing when she called? The question came from her.

Oh, he! He was doing something which concerned a matter most precious to his heart.

Most precious?

Yes. It concerned Helene and himself, their future together. He was writing letters. One was to a friend whom he besought for an introduction to her father. The other was to the countess—Countess von Hatzfeldt.

She laughed her light elfin laugh. "You with your countess!"

"You're not jealous?" This time he laughed.

"Heavens, no! Why should I be?"

"She has been a good friend. I want you to write to her."

"If you wish it!" There was obedience in her voice, but it had a dubious note.

They walked and talked. He was eloquent as always. She listened and urged him to go on talking. He painted their future together in glowing colors. Attuned as they were in spirit, what wonderful things could they not do together!

"Come," he said half seriously, half jestingly—it was not the first time—"Come! What do you say to our leaving this company to-morrow? Why wait? Let us go to Paris, wed there, and nevermore part company?"

"Impatient man!" She paused; then added that he might make at least one effort to win her parents' consent.

"What have your parents against me?"

As if he didn't know! He was a Jew; and, in their eyes, a demagogue to boot. The fact that Bismarck honored him and spent hours in conversation with him did not seem to impress them. She had mentioned his name before them only once, and that quite casually; yet her father flew into a rage at the mere mention of it.

Besides, as she had already written him, she had still a painful duty to perform. She must slay in cold blood the true heart of Yanko von Racowitza, the young man who had given her the purest love, the noblest devotion. But for his, Ferdinand's, sake, she would do even what was wrong!

The next morning they climbed the summit of Rigi, to see a sunrise. What a happier augury for their future than a sunrise? But the morning was foggy and damp. Lassalle raged at the climate and talked to her about his love. For her sake, he would renounce politics, he would give himself to science and literature, he would take her to Egypt or India.

He looked adoringly at the pale trembling girl, who was little more than half his own age, and saw that here at last was a fit mate for him, a woman perfect in every respect, so beautiful, so free, so wholly suitable to him, who loved him so much, and who would merge her will in his, which was to him indispensable. Her one fault, possibly, was a lack of will, but as he wrote to the countess, he should have enough will for both, and she would be "as clay in the hands of the potter."

He would laughingly remind Helene that he was a Jew. Jew or Mohammedan, what did it matter? She liked to think of him as a pagan. He was, above all, "her idol, her Cæsar, her royal eagle." For all that, she loved to command him. All she had to do was to say, "Lie down!" and he would lie down at her feet, like a pet animal.

Three days of passionate wooing passed at Rigi. Everything was forgotten but their love. They played like two innocent children. He sent her two letters each day full of tempestuous adoration, and telegrams to greet her in the morning and telegrams bidding her good night.

A letter from the countess, throwing cold water on his new "affair," could not dissuade him. He followed Helene to Berne.

He made love like a young man who had never been in love before. As he sat on her window-sill, he read poetry to her; he brought her books to read, overwhelmed her with adolescent sentiment. He made her his confessor, told her of his past, laid his future plans before her to the last detail, and, in the beauty of the moonlight, indulged in "window-dreams," rich with ardent imaginings and romantic aspirations, such as belong only to youthful Titans.

"The day may yet come when I shall place the crown of victory upon your brow. Would you like a triumphal entry into Berlin in a carriage drawn by six horses? Our enemies are as numerous as the sands, but we shall drive over their bodies with people rejoicing and cheering about us. 'Ferdinand the defender of the people!' 'Long live the Republic and its golden-haired lady President!' "

Thus the too few evenings passed in the moonlight, now in dream-like revery, now in lyric outburst and passionate whisperings, and the days in idyllic love-play of two children, wise in their way yet ignorant of human malice hiding in ambush prior to its beast-like spring. Nothing had ever been so real, or would be so real again to either lover as this week of weeks. And that which was yet to follow was as a nightmare which follows on a dream of beauty. Play on, children, play on! But in the wings stands an old men's Greek chorus whispering its melancholy asides, lamenting that which is yet to come.

Again and again Ferdinand asked her to run away with him, but she gently expostulated, saying she would be ready to run when all else had failed.

At last they parted company. Their understanding was that he would follow her to Geneva, that he would make an effort to win her parents over. After all, he was somebody. He was the great Lassalle, whom even Bismarck honored. Would a miserable little diplomatist like Herr von Dönniges be able to resist him? He had done greater things in the face of the most violent opposition. He would appear before her parents; they would listen to him, they must listen to him; he had a persuasive personality, and he would persuade them. To be sure, he was well aware that he was hated by the upper circles of German society, but of the depth of that hatred, great man that he was with a great man's simple nature, he had no inkling.

The scene now changed to Geneva. The time was August the third. Helene arrived in the morning, Ferdinand was to follow in the afternoon.

Helene found her relatives happy and excited by the betrothal of her sister Margaret to Count von Keyserling. The count was a great catch! And Helene accepted the prevailing good cheer as a happy augury. Was not this a good time to tell her mother even if Ferdinand had expressly forbidden it?

At last, finding her mother alone, she told her of her love for the Socialist agitator. Her mother turned a withering loathing glance at her.

No! No! It was impossible! Madness itself. The idea of any nice girl wanting to marry that creature! Did not Helene know that he was a dangerous demagogue, a man of loose morals who had carried on with the Countess von Hatzfeldt? And was he not a thief—and a Jew? "Quite, quite impossible!" cried the outraged woman. Why, if such a thing happened, Count von Keyserling would break his engagement with Margaret. And would he not be right? He could hardly be expected to unite himself with a connection of that kind. She was mad to think of it!

Herr von Dönniges, Bavarian diplomat, who was paid by his State for his services of tact and dignity, was still more blunt; he raved like a maniac and swore like a trooper. He reviled Helene, and cursed her, and threatened to disown her. In the meantime, if she persisted, he would confine her to her room. As luck would have it, a friend of the family whom Lassalle had once affronted and who had sworn vengeance, was present, and he added his voice to those of the others.

Helene felt crushed. Oh, what had she done! How foolish she had been! She might be even now safely sheltered in the arms of the man she loved, if only she had listened to him. Her idol, her Cæsar, her royal eagle! If only she had gone with him when he had first proposed flight to Paris!

Well, it was not too late yet. Her lover would arrive in town that afternoon. There was no time to be lost. She knew her father. And nothing was to be gained by allowing an interview between the two men to take place. She must prevent a meeting at all costs.

She hurriedly scribbled a note and managed to get it delivered at the hotel where Ferdinand intended staying. And awaited with impatience the hour of his arrival.

At last the hour came. She eluded the vigilance of her family and ran to his hotel, which was in the neighborhood. She inquired for Herr Lassalle. He had not yet arrived. Heavens, what could make him so late? The train must be late. She went out-of-doors, only to run into Lassalle descending from his carriage. Thank God, she found him! Quickly she poured out the story of the morning's happenings in his ears.

When Lassalle saw her trembling, distraught, he begged

her to follow him into the hotel. He entered a room, and she went in with him. She fell down at his feet.

"I am your wife," she cried in imploring tones, "yours, wholly yours! Take me then from here, if you would keep me! And at once! To Paris—anywhere!"

"My child," he began, "things can not be so bad——"

"Don't you understand? They won't listen! Mother abused me. Father cursed me. They think you terrible. They'll shut the door in your face! I beg you——"

"Why didn't you obey me?" he asked, with a shade of annoyance in his voice. "I told you to leave it all to me. . . . Now, now," he went on cajolingly, seeing that Helene was beside herself with grief and too distraught for censure, "leave it to me. I am Lassalle. Lassalle will not let trifles stand in his way. They will learn who Lassalle is. They——"

His words fell like a cold shower on Helene. She felt herself growing numb. She nerved herself to an effort.

"Don't you understand, my dear? You will only be insulted, and they won't let you see me again. They're dreadfully stubborn. If you want to think of our future together, there's no time to be lost. Not a moment! We must take the next train for France!"

A maid entered. There was a carriage ready to take them to the station. There was a train starting for Paris in a quarter of an hour. He waved her away.

"They must learn who Lassalle is," persisted the blind man, on his dignity, faltering on the path of action for the first time in his life. "I am not a thief in the night to be thus dissuaded from my purpose. I promise you, Helene, they will give you to me, and they will do so in the consciousness that it is an honor and not a disgrace. . . . But you will be compromised if you remain here. Have you a woman friend in town?"

In a voice more dead than alive she named Madame Caroline Rognon.

"Let us go there. I'll leave you with her. Then I shall see your father."

She numbly complied. They left the hotel, Helene leaning on Ferdinand's arm.

The astonished Madame Rognon admitted the lovers. Soon Frau von Dönniges appeared. Margaret was with her.

Lassalle appealed to the mother. They loved each other, he began, but did not proceed further; for the woman, in a manner that bespoke the virago, with a contemptuous gesture waved him away, the man whom thousands honored, whom Bismarck regarded as one of the great men of his time.

Lassalle restrained his anger and asked what the good lady had against him.

What she had against him? What a question! As if every one didn't know the sort of person he was, what with his dealings with women, his notorious politics—— As a final shot, she flung at him: "Cash-box thief!"

This was too much. Helene sprang protectively to her lover's side. She would not allow even her mother to utter such a calumny against so noble a man. He retained an outward calm; he must (so he informed the elder lady) bear in mind that she was Helene's mother and maintain toward her the respect due her in consequence of that virtue. But, after all, he must talk to a reasonable being; he would see Herr von Dönniges.

Helene's mother laughed. Well she knew what treatment he could expect from her husband. Why, he would be driven from the door as if he were a stray dog! She told him as much.

"She's right! There's no hope there!" Helene tried to

persuade him, clinging to his arm. She waited for a word from him, the sort of word she had a right to expect from him, the great Lassalle, the ruthless and unfaltering of will and quick of decision. Why did he talk, argue, hesitate, parley with a woman such as her mother was? She, Helene, was his wife, his very own, an integral part of him. Why, then, didn't he seize her and fly with her? It seemed such utter madness to see him talk with her mother, even greater folly to wait to talk with her father.

He disregarded her, made light of her warning. What had he to fear? He was Lassalle, whom Humboldt called the *Wunkerkind,* whom Heine called a Messiah, whom Bismarck honored. And who was Herr von Dönniges? An inconsequential little diplomatist. A nobody. It was inconceivable that Helene's father could triumph.

He turned to Helene. Would she be willing to do anything he asked her? Yes, anything! She was his, his utterly; she would do his bidding if he asked her to follow him to the ends of the earth. Only one thing he must not ask her, and that was to go back to her parents.

"That is the one thing I ask you to do—for my sake!"

She looked at him dumfounded, not comprehending.

He was calm. She could not understand his quiet manner. How could he so calmly hand her over to her parents?

"Trust me!" he said. "It shall not be said that Lassalle steals his bride and runs away with her like a common horse-thief! . . . Madame," he said, turning to Helene's mother, "Helene is mine. You can see she obeys me. I give her into your care. She will be returned to me in the honorable and accepted fashion."

Helene listened to this with dismay. It stunned her. It was as if he had hit her, cast her off, as if he had put heavy fetters on the love she bore him, hindering her every breath. She had loved him because he was her royal eagle, soaring freely in the heights; because he was one of the rare spirits who asserted his right in life and took what he wanted without asking. Could this, indeed, be her lord, her Cæsar? In humiliation, her girlish heart fluttered.

No sooner was he gone than she heard her mother's taunting voice:

"There! You see. He has abandoned you! A fine lover!"

Presently, her father put in an appearance, and, with imprecations, seized her by her hair and half dragged her, publicly and unashamed, to their house, not many yards distant, where he locked her up in her room and began to subject her to the most humiliating treatment.

Lassalle was not long in realizing the enormity of his mistake. Cut off from all access to Helene, he was driven to despair. He vowed that he would move heaven and earth to recover his golden-haired one, without whom he could not go on living. What a fool he had been! To have had the prize in his grasp and thus to let her go! He now understood that he had not been himself when he had committed the one folly of his life. Now he began to write passionate letters, one after another. But none brought a response. He did not know that his letters did not even reach her. He turned for assistance to his friends and to the great ones of the time, noblemen, generals, scholars, the Bishop of Mayence, the Bavarian Minister of Foreign Affairs—Baron von Schrenk, and even Richard Wagner. Overtures were made to the von Dönniges family from many quarters. Lassalle's friends may have had good intentions, but they acted like Judases. Holthoff, who went presumably to plead Lassalle's case, begged Helene to abandon him and to obey her parents. The historian Rüstow, who also came on Lassalle's behalf, was cold and aloof, if not actually hostile. He inspired her with fear, not to say aversion. What did Ferdinand mean by sending such a man? His whole attitude implied that Lassalle was better off for being rid of her. Then the final capping to her disillusions, the Countess Hatzfeldt's letter demanding a meeting with her "to settle the question of her relations to Lassalle." Horrible! None of these confidants seemed to give a thought to Lassalle's personal happiness. Nor did they appear to understand her or her position; she was under the tyrannic constraint of her father, she had to speak a language forced on her by external circumstances, and not one of Ferdinand's emissaries made an effort to listen to those inaudible voices which came from her distraught heart.

There was the irony: a single meeting with her lover would have brought her back to his arms. As it was, his messengers only furthered the distance between them.

Lassalle's despair deepened. His whole life was at stake. If he lost Helene, his future was worth nothing. The faith which had borne him through many trials would be gone for ever. No more triumphs for him. He might as well lie down and die.

Then one day he received a letter from Helene, beginning with "To Herr Lassalle. Sir——" It informed him that she had again become reconciled to her betrothed, Herr Yanko von Racowitza, whose love she had regained, and that she deeply repented of her earlier action. . . . There could be no more question of marriage between them, and she was now firmly resolved to devote to Herr von Racowitza her "eternal love and fidelity." It was signed with her full name.

The love-blind man did not understand that the letter had been dictated by Helene's father.

In answer, he wrote a heart-rending letter, which, like his other letters, she never received. It was, by turns, tender, passionate and abusive. He could not understand, he said, such a betrayal. He would not survive it. His fate was now in her hands. "But if you destroy me by this wicked treachery . . . then may evil fall upon you, and my curse follow you to the grave!" In any case, he assured her, he would not give her up. He would continue his efforts to win her. He ended: "Helene, our destinies are entwined!"

But the result of all his efforts was an interview with Helene's father. It was not a friendly meeting, and counter-accusations were passed. There was no other consequence.

He was never to see Helene again.

And, for all his achievements, for all his power and will, he had not the strength to face the world as a lover jilted by a chit of a girl. "So I fall with and through her will—a dreadful example of the fact that a man should never tie himself to a woman." Thus he wrote at the time.

Then the man who did not believe in duels did an extraordinary thing. He challenged Helene's successful lover, Herr von Racowitza, to a duel. Enraged and maddened by his failure, of which there was no longer any doubt, he filled the letter carrying his challenge with the coarsest insults against Helene, thus making sure that his challenge would be accepted.

It was tragic and pitiable to see natural nobility and chivalry turned against themselves. King Lear cursing his daughters, King Lear among the elements had not more pathos than this. But energy, like murder, will out, and Lassalle's magnificent energy, which had hitherto been used for recreating the social order, was now bent on self-murder. He had, by his own efforts, after a titanic struggle, wrought his fortune, and now, like a blinded Samson, he was to bring the Philistine edifice over his own head.

The duel was arranged.

Now that the decision was made, he was calm. It was the calm of a man set on his own doom. "Nonsense!" said he to Colonel's Rüstow's plea that he have some practise in shooting. His opponent was less indifferent, and on August twenty-seventh, the day before the duel, fired one hundred and fifty shots in a shooting gallery. Next morning Lassalle was sleeping quietly, and Colonel Rüstow had to awaken him to keep his appointment with Herr von Racowitza.

Within five seconds following the signal given by Herr Rüstow, Herr von Racowitza fired. Scarce a moment afterward Lassalle replied. He missed, for he was already tottering from a mortal wound. He was suffering torments of pain, as he was being driven to the hotel, and he spoke hardly a word. But so great was the life force and the will of the man that he firmly made his own way up the stairs in order not to alarm Countess Hatzfeldt who was waiting for news of the duel.

After three days of the most excruciating pain he died. There is food for speculation in the words found on the breast of the wounded man, the last words he ever wrote:

"I hereby declare that it is I myself who have put an end to my life.

"F. Lassalle."

"August 28, 1864."

Four thousand persons, including men of distinction and rank, followed his hearse in Geneva. He was buried in Breslau. His monument bears the following inscription:

"Here rests what is mortal
of
FERDINAND LASSALLE
the Thinker and the Fighter"

What of Helene?

"Lassalle will certainly kill Yanko," she thought, not without pity for her accepted lover, just before the duel. "When Yanko is dead and his body is brought here, there will be a stirring in the house, and I can then fly to Lassalle."

But Yanko arrived with the news of his triumph. And, oh, how she hated him! But Yanko was patient and kind, devoted and tender, and he slowly won her over. A year after their marriage he died of consumption. The time came when Helene's parents cast her off, and she went on the stage. Later she married a Russian Socialist, S. E. Shevitch, and lived with him for a while in New York before removing to Riga. They made a happy couple.

Before she died, she wrote a book in which she told how it all happened.

CHARLES STEWART PARNELL—IRELAND'S UNCROWNED KING

1

It was on an evening in the year 1880. Captain William O'Shea came to his home in Eltham, bringing with him the O'Gorman Mahon, notorious adventurer, duelist and politician, now an old man with white hair and jolly, blue, boyish eyes, and, despite his age, still a handsome man standing six feet three in his stocking feet. Both men had been returned to Parliament for the County of Clare; and the younger man, good-looking in a vapid way and, as always, fastidiously dressed, brought the elder in tow, that they might together celebrate their victory and have as merry a time as was proper on such an occasion.

It was decided to go to Greenwich for dinner. Captain O'Shea's wife, Katharine, accompanied the men. She was, in spite of middle age, a handsome woman. A close scrutiny would have revealed nothing classic about her features. They were large and uneven, especially her nose and her mouth, but her big eyes were fine and frank and emotional. Yet, undoubtedly, she was handsome, and her robust figure was attractive. She looked more Italian than English.

The three of them sat up late into the night, while the men discussed Irish affairs, told stories and gave amusing accounts of how the election had been won. They had kissed nearly every girl in Clare, and they drank with every man; that had been hard on Willie, who loathed Irish whisky. Willie had had a hard time because of his fastidious dress. The poor didn't like it and looked gloomy when they saw him; but he won their hearts by admiring their babies and live stock and by smiling his best.

Now and then, as was to be expected, the talk turned on Parnell. They admitted he was doing great things for Ireland, but couldn't quite understand the man. He was an Englishman, with all the Englishman's aloofness and reserve, and it was the devil alone that could understand him, said O'Shea. He had voted for Parnell to lead the party, but really feared his advanced views. Still, he couldn't help but admire the man. How he had managed to push the cheery and gentlemanly Mr. Butt out of his job and take lead of the party was still a great wonder; greater still—they couldn't help laughing over it—that he should have learned a trick or two from Mr. Biggar. Biggar was something of a joke, but he was a pretty efficient joke. He was a rough, ugly-looking man; some one had dubbed him Caliban. When Disraeli saw him for the first time he looked at him through his eye-glass and said, "Is he a leprechawn?" And he had made his money out of pigs! As for his private life, it was by no means a model for decent law-abiding citizens. A greater contrast could hardly be imagined than the contrast between this uncouth fellow and Parnell, an English gentleman with a long ancestry of gentlemen. But in Parliament Biggar had one able trick, and Parnell, watching him, had learned it, and learned it well. It was the policy of obstruction. "If you won't let our measures go through, we won't allow yours to go through!" That was the gist of the policy. With the votes at his command, he gave the party in power constant trouble. He was shy, not at all a ready speaker; public speaking was very painful to him. But he "always knew what he wanted to say, and said it." That was Mr. Gladstone's tribute to him. He did not, like Irishmen, spoil things by floweriness or over-elaboration. But he had a beautiful harmonious voice which impressed all who heard it. And he had a strong will, ruthless with all who thwarted him; he used this will for the one thing that mattered to him: Home Rule for Ireland. With that single-heartedness and astuteness for which he had become famous, never had Ireland's prospects for self-government seemed so bright. Because of her new alien leader the country's hopes ran high. The people had suffered much from misgovernment, they were poor, again and again they had suffered eviction from their wretched hovels, and here was a man who really appeared to love them and to think of their welfare. The whole Irish question seemed to center in Parnell.

It was natural that the two newly elected members from Clare and Mrs. O'Shea should talk of the leader. Was it true, Mrs. O'Shea asked, that Parnell's mother had planted in him his hatred of England? That was the common impression, replied one of the men; and both proceeded to relate stories of the strange woman, Delia Parnell, who, though she lived mostly in America, had always come to their Irish home at Avondale that her children might be born in Ireland, returning as soon as possible to America. The O'Gorman Mahon, however, thought that Parnell's hatred might have actually arisen from his study of records of English misgovernment in Ireland and of barbarities inflicted upon her peasantry in the name of England's authority. And many were the reasons given for this conclusion.

Mrs. O'Shea was getting rather bored by this incessant talk of Parnell, when the guest turned to her and said:

"If you meet Parnell, Mrs. O'Shea, be good to him. His begging expedition to America has about finished him, and I don't believe he'll last the session out."

Then he went on to explain how aloof and reserved the

man was, and that he was so sensitive on the subject of his health that any one who broached it was bound to feel that he had been tactless.

Captain O'Shea, at this point, interrupted to say that he and Mrs. O'Shea were going to give some political dinners in London and that they intended to invite Parnell. "But I am sure he won't come," he added, with a laugh.

Mrs. O'Shea showed no interest in the suggestion, but decided in her mind that she ought to ask Parnell to any dinner she and Willie gave to the Irish party.

2

Many Irish political worthies came to the dinners instituted by the O'Sheas, but Parnell, though he accepted the invitations, never appeared, which brought from Willie the customary exclamation, "I told you so!"

The "vacant chair" became a joke among the guests, and many laughing allusions were made to it. They dilated on the subject, and each tried to outdo the other in telling tales of Parnell's inaccessibility. He was so inaccessible, it appeared, and he so disliked social intercourse, that the most important hostesses in London could not get him to come. "And yet," some one said at the table, "Parnell mixed freely with society in America and in Paris before he became a politician for the sake of the Irish poor." "I defy you to fill that chair!" exclaimed another guest, laughing. And all the guests took up the note and defied Mrs. O'Shea "to fill the vacant chair."

Mrs. O'Shea, undaunted, took up the challenge. She said:

"Ireland's uncrowned king shall sit in that chair at the next dinner I give!"

The statement was greeted with laughter and applause.

3

A short time later, on a sunny day, while the House was sitting, Mrs. O'Shea, accompanied by her sister, Mrs. Steele, drove up. She sent in a card asking Parnell to come out and speak to her in the Palace Yard.

Parnell came out. She saw a tall, gaunt, bearded figure; he looked thin and his face was deadly pale. He was smiling, as he looked frankly into her eyes. His own eyes were curiously burning and they seemed to look into hers with an intentness which threw her off her poise. The sudden thought illuminated her brain:

"This man is wonderful—and different!"

She found her tongue.

"Mr. Parnell, why haven't you answered my last invitation to dinner? Is there nothing at all that will induce you to come?" She smiled at her own method of attack.

He gave an answering smile. "I am sorry, Mrs. O'Shea," he said. "But I haven't opened my letters for days. But if you'll let me know the date of your next dinner, directly I return from Paris from my sister's wedding I'll surely come!" And the tone of his voice clearly indicated that, undoubtedly, he would. The voice charmed her.

Then a seemingly ridiculous thing occurred.

She was leaning forward in the cab to say good-by to him, when a rose fell out of her bodice on to her lap. Parnell picked it up, pressed it to his lips and placed it in his buttonhole. The cab drove away, with Mrs. O'Shea's head in a whirl.

That was how things began.

4

He came to dinner a few days later. He looked frightfully ill. The party was a small one, and after dinner Mrs. O'Shea took her guests to the Gaiety Theater. She and Parnell sat together in a corner of the box, and he poured himself out like one starved for a confidant. He told of all his troubles: troubles in politics and troubles of the heart. He told her the story of his one unlucky love-affair. But it did not seem incongruous to either of them. It was to them the most natural thing; they both felt as if they had known each other a lifetime.

There was his affair with Miss Woods. Some years before, this pretty, vivacious American girl, with golden hair, small features and blue eyes, had jilted him. After showing every affection for him, the young lady, romantically inclined, decided she could not marry a man who was "only an Irish gentleman," without distinction or an achievement to his credit. As a distraction from his disappointment he had turned to Irish politics, and had become the celebrity she had wanted him to be. On his late journey to America he had met her again, and renewed his suit. But, ironically enough, in the ensuing years both had changed. She no longer sought celebrity in a husband, but demanded absolute devotion. As for him, he was devoted—to Ireland. Fortune was more fickle than any woman. The pair went to a ball together, and while they were mounting the stairs, the lady of his heart slipped into his hand a scrap of paper, on which was scribbled the verse:

Unless you can muse in a crowd all day
  On the absent face that fixed you,
Unless you can dream that his faith is fast
  Through behoving and unbehoving,
Unless you can die when the dream is past,
  Oh, never call it loving.

As he went on talking in low monotones, she sat there

at his side in complete sympathy and companionship with him, and his eyes seemed like sudden flames as they caught the light of the stage.

"By the way," he asked suddenly, "who wrote those lines?"

"It sounds like one of the Brownings."

"Well," he said simply, "I could not do that, so I went home."

Was he aware of it? He was entering upon a life in which he would not be able to forswear his devotion to a woman for his devotion to Ireland. There was no question here of "going home." Nowhere had he felt so much at home as with this woman, who was already married and a mother. With his whole heart he would serve her, and she—she would give the strength to sustain him in his fight for Irish freedom!

Here the curtain descends on Act One.

5

Henceforth, they became inseparable.

Mrs. O'Shea began to frequent the Ladies Gallery of the House, which became their trysting-place. On Wednesday evenings, when his presence could be dispensed with there, he would ask her to drive with him. They would drive miles together in a hansom cab into the country, during which, like shy lovers, they would discuss a hundred things which did not matter, but not the one thing which was of such concern to them. At first, the chief subject of discussion was the question of Willie's chances of being returned again for Clare in case another election was sprung on the country. At heart, Parnell had never liked Willie much and mistrusted him, but he was willing to do all he could for him for Mrs. O'Shea's sake. After these drives they would return to his private sitting-room in Cannon Street Hotel and talk politics until Mrs. O'Shea was interested and at ease; then lapse into one of those long tense silences which she was beginning to know as dangerous because of the complete sympathy they implied between them. Afterward, he would walk with Mrs. O'Shea right past the members of the Irish party gathered in the hall, without giving a sign that he was aware of their presence, and conduct her into a waiting cab which would take them to St. Thomas's Hotel for dinner.

But his work called him. One day Parnell left for Ireland. Letters came in rapid succession for Mrs. O'Shea from Dublin. Up to November ninth the writer began with "My dear Mrs. O'Shea," but on the eleventh he suddenly plunged in with "My dearest Love," though on December second again, as if he were aware of his indiscretion, he returned to "My dear Mrs. O'Shea." They were rapidly drifting into that state in which he was to call her "Queenie" and she to call him "King." Which, altogether, was not so far different from most love-affairs. In this case there were wider issues involved; "the course of true love" was to have the most dire consequences for a whole nation.

". . . I am still in the land of living," he wrote in his second letter, "notwithstanding the real difficulty of either living or being, which every moment becomes more evident, in the absence of a certain kind and fair face."

She, for her part, as became a wife and a mother, fought against their love, even while succumbing to it. She was alone in her fight. She spoke of her children, of the importance of his work, of the disaster that might ultimately engulf them both. But he answered her: "For good or for ill, I am your husband, your lover, your children, your all. And I will give my life for Ireland, but to you I give my love, whether it be your heaven or hell. It is destiny. When I first looked into your eyes I knew."

But that was many weeks later. In the intervening weeks, between their first meeting and the time these words were spoken, that is, in the autumn of 1880, Parnell came to stay with the O'Sheas, only going to Dublin when he was needed there. He was ill, suffering with the throat. He slept in a kind of stupor, and would awake to complain of the green carpet. He was superstitious about green, and said it was responsible for his sore throat. A bit was cut out and sent to London for analysis, only to be returned with the statement that it was quite harmless. She took care of him, nursed him, saw to it that his sleeps were not disturbed and forced him to take drives into the country for fresh air. As for him, he often sat up late into the night and spoke in his low broken monotone, betokening deep feelings held in check, of Ireland's unhappiness, of the cruelty committed there in the name of justice. It was terrible to hear of the old people, of sick men and women, of mothers with children they had just borne, of little children naked as they had come into the world, all thrown out from the tiny wretched hovels and left to shift without shelter or bread.

Willie was away most of the time.

That same year, 1880, Parnell fearing arrest for sedition, conceived the idea of disappearing for a few weeks. He came down one night to Eltham, and when Mrs. O'Shea answered his signal and let him in he smiled and said that she must hide him. As she watched him eating his supper which she always had ready for him at three A. M., she felt rather hopeless, for he was a big man and it was hard to see how she could hide him from the servants. Then an idea came to her. She would make use of the little room which opened out into her own. It was a little boudoir dressing-room and had a sofa in it, and she always kept it locked and never allowed a servant into it. And so he stayed there and sometimes read *Alice in Wonderland*, which he thought "a curious book." The servants must have thought Mrs. O'Shea's appetite unusually good in those days.

And still Mrs. O'Shea fought helplessly against the love which would surely end in disaster for both.

In the spring of next year Parnell brought his telescope from Avondale, and together, cheek to cheek, like young lovers, they spent many nights watching the stars and following the course of the planets until they faded in the dawn.

Parnell was heavily immersed in politics that year. Never had he worked harder for his adopted country. In April, Gladstone introduced his Land Bill which promised a measure of relief to Ireland, but the bill was full of defects and was drawn up without consulting the Irish. Parnell followed his usual policy of aloofness, and he pressed for amendments. Badly crippled in the House of Commons, the bill became a law.

In the early autumn Mrs. O'Shea went to London on Parnell's business, for she had assumed the position of secretary to her lover. Her mission was to learn the movements of the government. Her health was then delicate, her nerves on edge, and she was obsessed with all manner of fears. A terrible loneliness now began to possess her when her "King" was away from her. His tenderness and consideration always comforted her. She was with child—*his* child. And the worst of news awaited her. She learned that after a Cabinet Council the Secretary for Ireland, Mr. Foster, had left for Dublin with a warrant for her lover's arrest. And Parnell had already warned her:

"Be brave, Queenie. I can not stay outside while all these others are arrested, and it is bound to be soon now."

On her return home who should be there but Willie, looking extremely pleased, as he announced to her that Parnell had been arrested that morning. She knew the news directly she saw his face with its unconcealed joy. She simulated, hid her true feelings, and replied in a languid voice that, after all, Parnell, "couldn't keep out of jail much longer." But her heart was not here at all; it was in Kilmainham Jail with her lover. Placidly she plied her husband with questions about prison life.

Henceforth, she lived wholly in letters which managed to reach her from jail. From the time of his arrest until the birth of his child the following February, she lived a curious existence, like one walking in sleep, and pursued her usual home routine with her aunt, whom she loved dearly. Only when a letter from him arrived was there a flutter in her heart and a flicker in her eyes, which betokened that she was still in the land of living.

The baby, a little girl, was beautiful, and apparently strong and healthy, with the brown eyes of her father. For hours she watched the silent child who, with curiously grave, contemplative eyes, gazed into her mother's, and to Mrs. O'Shea it seemed that there was something in them of the fires which always smoldered in the depths of her lover's eyes.

Within two months she saw the child of her love slowly dying. The doctors could do nothing. She feared that her father would never see her.

In those days Willie was good to her. She told him the child was dying; he respected her wish to be left alone. But, oh, how hard it was for her! For he had no suspicion of the truth, and, for her King's and for Ireland's sake, she must repress her longing to tell him. She felt her equivocal position keenly, but let those judge her who will! Willie suggested immediate baptism, to which she offered no objection. She had previously agreed upon this with her lover who, though a Protestant himself, had no feeling against the Catholic religion.

Then the news arrived that Parnell could come for a few hours! A parole had been granted him for the purpose of visiting Paris to attend his sister Delia's funeral. What unspeakable comfort there was for her in the prospect of his being able to see his child before she died! Parnell came, held the dying child in his arms, then left for Paris.

On returning from Paris he paused *en route* for Kilmainham at Eltham. He sat up all night with Willie working out the "Kilmainham Treaty" which offered a modification of his obstruction policy and gave the government an opportunity to save its face in the dilemma into which it had forced upon itself by the arrest of the Irish leader and his colleagues. Willie was to act as a "go-between." That much was settled before dawn. Mrs. O'Shea could not join them. She kept vigil by the side of her baby, who died just as her lover stole in to kiss them both good-by.

6

Parnell left Kilmainham on terms arranged in that night talk at Eltham. Willie—or *He* as the two lovers constantly referred to Captain O'Shea in their talk and their letters—took a lot of credit to himself for the performance of bringing Parnell and the government together. At the same time, for his own satisfaction, he insisted upon Parnell signing a letter promising a modification of his obstruction policy; this letter he wanted to present to the government. Privately, Willie explained to his wife that he had to do this, as Parnell was "so shifty" and could not be trusted to carry out any agreement that was not in writing.

As a result of the treaty, Forster resigned his position as chief secretary for Ireland; Lord Cowper resigned with him. Coincidently, Redmond's Land Bill, drafted by Parnell at Kilmainham, was introduced in Parliament and started a heated discussion.

Parnell's efforts "to slow down the agitation" were by no means easy. He expressed himself to Queenie as appalled at the intensity of the passion of hate that he had loosed, held in check only by the sheer dominance of his will. He replied to her pleadings:

"Yes, I hold them now with my back to the wall, but if I turn to the government I turn my back to them—and then——?"

At this time three other Irish M. P.'s were released from Kilmainham. Forster attacked the procedure of the government in Parliament, and poured out his wrath on Parnell. "If all England can not govern the Member from Cork, then let us acknowledge he is the greatest power in Ireland to-day."

Then an appalling thing occurred. One Sunday morning Parnell was taking a train for London to see Davitt, lately released from Portland Prison, when, on buying a newspaper, he was startled to read the news of the murder of Lord Cavendish and Mr. Burke in Ireland. There was grave significance in this. It meant that all his overtures to the government went for naught, that he would personally be held responsible. He had long known that the Irish were their own worst enemies; it was discouraging. But here was the accomplished fact: he saw all his work undone; if not undone, then damaged in a way that would require no end of effort to mend.

Mrs. O'Shea was at his side, watching the look of horror which had crept into his eyes. The train was coming in.

"Quick!" she cried. "You must catch this train. See Davitt and others as arranged and as many more as you can find. Go, you will know what to do, but you *must* meet them all at once."

A heavy depression upon him, he turned away. "I shall resign," he said.

"No, you are not a coward!" she replied, running beside him on the platform.

That same evening, Willie, Mrs. O'Shea and Parnell were having dinner at Eltham. Again he reiterated his intention of resigning. "The thing makes me feel hopeless of doing any good," he said.

At one moment, just as the maid was leaving the room after placing the coffee tray on a small side-table, a picture which hung immediately behind Parnell crashed to the floor. The picture was a large engraving of the House of 1880, and among those in the picture were Parnell and Willie. Nervous tension reigned. They all jumped to their feet. Willie's chair was overturned. Parnell held on to his chair in a tense grip, staring at the picture lying on the floor among the broken glass.

"There goes Home Rule, Parnell!" came from Willie, with a laugh, as he picked up the picture.

He cut short his laugh, as he saw the grave look in Parnell's face.

"Perhaps the wire was rotten," Mrs. O'Shea hastened to explain, "or the maid had shaken the picture as she passed!"

But all efforts of Parnell to break one end of the wire proved futile. And Willie added to the agony by saying that the maid was at the other end of the room and couldn't possibly have shaken it. Parnell said nothing. They now spoke of other things.

Later, when Parnell and Mrs. O'Shea were alone, she

said: "You did not really mind about that picture, did you? It was only a rotten wire!"

He replied: "It was an omen, I think, darling. But for whom? Willie or me?"

"Nonsense!" she said, and the subject was dropped.

7

The ensuing years were fraught with many happenings for Parnell, such as inevitably befall men of active temperament engaged in politics—above all, in Irish politics. And Parnell was obviously a fated man, or, as the phrase goes, a man of destiny. The Liberals fell, and rose again. Gladstone was at the helm. The Home Rule Bill was introduced. Never, in some respects, had its prospects been so bright. The Pigott forgeries in *The Times* implicating Parnell had cropped up and been exposed, completely clearing their victim. The Parnell-O'Shea romance proceeded apace. And now there comes on the stage Captain O'Shea—Willie—the commanding, if not the most lovable figure. It is *his* act.

For Willie had conceived an ambition to become the Under-Secretary for Ireland. Moreover, he had an idea that, for his part in negotiating the Kilmainham Treaty, he was entitled to consideration, especially from Parnell. Indeed, he asserted that Parnell owed him that, that the leader had made him a promise.

At this time—this was 1885—Willie was experiencing parliamentary difficulties. Far from contemplating any prospect of achieving his ultimate ambition, there was the question whether he would be returned to Parliament from Clare. He showed a fatuous disdain for his Irish colleagues, refused to sit with the body of the Irish party, and from his vantage point on the Ministerial benches seemed to sneer at them, and, what was still more irritating, gave the appearance of being tolerantly amused at the uncouthnesses, mannerisms, accents and attire of the Irish members. The sounds of "Misther Spaker, Sir!" would bring to his face a smile, naturally galling to those who felt themselves to be its victims. Witty, cynical, a smart raconteur, he was popular among his own set, and was much sought as an after-dinner speaker. But these were not qualities to endear him either to his colleagues or to his constituents.

Nevertheless, in the face of protests from prominent members of his party, Parnell said he would help him. They could not understand his insistence. It could do Ireland no good, it could do Parnell no good. Yes, he had promised Queenie that, if need be, he would "thrust him down their throats." Nor could he do otherwise. Parnell was in a dilemma, and the freedom of Ireland was at stake. It was dangerous at this time to have his private life exposed before men who would never understand that such a love as theirs was could know no barriers of laws and convention. Such an exposure before the public could mean only one thing: a death-knell to Ireland's freedom.

Both Parnell and Mrs. O'Shea used every means to help Willie. At this time Mrs. O'Shea acted as a private mediator between Parnell and Gladstone, and, in that capacity, exercised not a little power of her own. She interested Lord Richard Grosvenor, then Liberal Whip, in her husband, and secured his promise to help him. Embarrassing situations arose, for they all knew the private life of Parnell and Mrs. O'Shea, and, in a manner accepted by English custom, winked at it as long as the affair was not made public. The Grand Old Man himself was not unaware of the situation, and he had always seemed to her, in spite of his gracious courtesy, "a beautiful bird of prey . . .

with piercing, cruel eyes belying the tender courteous smile." But the time had not yet come for him to swoop down. Would the time come? Mrs. O'Shea asked herself. She knew that he would show Parnell no pity.

Parnell's opinion of Gladstone coincided with Mrs. O'Shea's. There was that dinner he was yet to attend at Hawarden with the Grand Old Man, at which he was to answer Miss Gladstone's question, "Who is the greatest actor you have ever seen, Mr. Parnell?" with, "Your father, undoubtedly," an answer which was to delight his questioner.

For all the efforts made in his behalf, Willie showed no gratitude; he thought Parnell was not doing enough, and even charged him with treachery. Parnell's position was made more difficult because Willie absolutely refused to sign the pledge to act with the party in the event of election. But pledge or no pledge, and in spite of all efforts, Clare would not have him. He refused any constituency which was not Irish. And only Galway was now available. True to his promise, Parnell forced him "down the throats" of the Galway constituents.

There was an interval of peace for the romance of Parnell and Mrs. O'Shea. Their love grew. They could not live, one without the other. They now had a house at Brighton, and one day, while working in the garden, he dropped the spade from his hand and scribbled a poem which he handed to her with the remark, "I am a poet. And descended from the poet, Thomas Parnell."

"Not a poet, even though descended from one," she laughed; but was astonished at what he had written.

> The grass shall cease to grow,
> The river's stream to run,
> The stars shall ponder in their course,
> No more shall shine the sun;

The moon shall never wane or grow,
The tide shall cease to ebb and flow,
Ere I shall cease to love you.

He was a poet, after all, she thought, touched by the tribute.

He had curious ideas, which had no relation to his rôle of practical politician. He spoke to her of his belief in a personal destiny and fate, against which it was useless to contend, and how he believed that certain souls had to meet and become one, till in death the second planet life parted them until sheer longing for one another brought them together again in after ages. "But it seems so lonely like that," she protested. It was lonely, he admitted. That was why he was so afraid of death, and hoped with every bit of him that they should die together.

Mrs. O'Shea hardly saw Willie now; they were drifting more and more apart. Before his friends Willie was still talking of Parnell's perfidy.

8

Then the long-deferred blow came. Call it Act Four.

It was in the autumn of 1890 that Parnell was served with a copy of the petition in the divorce case. About the same time papers were served on Mrs. O'Shea at Brighton.

Distraught as she was, and on the verge of a breakdown, she urged him to fight.

What was the use? he asked her. They wanted the divorce, but divorce or not, he should always come to her. He should come to "his home," whatever happened. And was he not altogether in the right? Had Captain O'Shea possessed her any more when Parnell first met her than ten years later when he divorced her? She had been O'Shea's wife in name only. Parnell took nothing from

Captain O'Shea. Only in the eyes of the law had he done wrong.

And now he sat at her bedside for hours, taking the most tender care of her.

Once she broke down and cried, because she had ruined his life-work, but he petted her as if she were a sick child. He told her that his work was still Ireland's, would always remain Ireland's, but that his heart and soul were hers to keep for ever, and had been since that summer morning when his eyes first looked into hers.

"Queenie," he said, "put away all fear and regret for my public life. I have given, and will give Ireland what is in me to give. . . . But my private life shall never belong to any country but to one woman. There will be a howl, but it will be the howling of hypocrites, not altogether, for some of these Irish fools are genuine in their belief that forms and creed can govern life and men . . . they are among the world's children. I am a man, and I have told these children what they want and they clamor for it. If they will let me, I will get it for them. But if they turn from me . . . it matters not in the end. . . ."

But she had hurt his work, she again protested.

"No, you have not. I sometimes think that it is why you came to me, for I was very ill then and you kept the life in me and the will to go on when I was weary of it all; you have stood to me for comfort and strength and my very life. . . . It had to be, and the bad times I have caused you and the stones that have been flung and that will be flung at you are all no matter, because to us there is no one else in all the world that matters at all—when you get to the bottom of things."

The *decree nisi* duly arrived. They spent an elated day, discussing plans for the future. There was infinite relief for them in the thought that they need not wear masks any longer, that they could be happy together without hindrance of any sort. And they were happy. Laughing, Parnell suggested that the decree be framed.

9

Elsewhere, other scenes of not so idyllic a nature were taking place.

The Irish in Ireland declared themselves as behind their leader; the Irish in England were preparing to make a stand with the non-conformists. The latter, after a public meeting at Sheffield, informed the government that they would insist upon Parnell's resignation. Mr. Gladstone became alarmed. If Parnell remained in power the Liberals stood in danger of losing the General Election. The prey was ready. The Grand Old Man showed his claws. . . . He wrote a letter to Mr. Morley stating among other things that "notwithstanding the splendid services rendered by Mr. Parnell to his country, his continuance at the present moment in the leadership would be productive of consequences disastrous in the highest degree to the cause of Ireland."

The gathering storm burst. . . . Its center was Committee Room 15—unforgettable room! One who was present said that Parnell entered it looking "as if we had committed adultery with his wife." Members of the Irish party, wholly ignorant of the letter, reelected Parnell leader without any discussion. Whereupon, Mr. Gladstone, to save his face with his party, sent the letter to the Press. Parnell decided to fight.

The next day Committee Room 15 witnessed another meeting of the party. Parnell entered "looking calm, unconcerned, imperious." Several members asked him to reconsider his decision and to resign. He listened to all they had to say, then rose and left the room without having spoken a single word. He went home and told Queenie that he would have to fight. Could she bear it? It would be tough work. "Yes," she answered, "if you can." At heart she faltered, for he seemed frail, and his face was so white, so delicate, and only his eyes burned with life. She doubted whether his health would stand the prolonged strain.

That night, in spite of illness, he wrote his famous manifesto, addressed "To the People of Ireland." In it he commented upon Gladstone's letter and declared it to be an assault upon the independence of the Irish party. The facts, which he now put before them, he said, "will enable you to understand the measure of the loss with which you are threatened unless you consent to throw me to the English wolves now howling for my destruction. . . ."

Two days later, Parnell read his manifesto to several prominent members of his party. Objections were raised to it, and one member considered the words "English wolves" particularly offensive. "I will not change them," interrupted Parnell. "Whatever goes out, they will remain." He was adamant. The next morning the papers published the manifesto, and the once proud Irish party was broken in two.

Committee Room 15 saw many bitter wrangles. Some of his former faithful followers now began to attack Parnell. The chief of these was Mr. Timothy Healy, who continued to hold the stage throughout the unseemly proceedings. At one moment some one cried, "Away with him! Away with him!" and some one else completed the irony with, "Crucify him!" Uproar followed upon uproar. While some cast accusations for the Irish disaster upon Gladstone, Mr. Healy interrupted with the cry that the Irish cause "perished in the stench of the divorce court."

At another meeting one member called Parnell "a dirty trickster" and Healy, supporting him, cried, "Allow me to depose you!" Some one ironically declared that Gladstone was "the master of the party," which, in the silence that followed, brought the insinuating snarl from Mr. Healy, "Who is to be the mistress of the Party?" Parnell, having endured many insults to himself in silence, could not allow Mrs. O'Shea to be insulted; he retaliated in strong but clean language, adding, "Mr. Healy, I will not stand very much more from you."

But Mr. Healy was to reserve his most offensive language for his speeches in Ireland. This is not the place to recount all that happened on that extraordinary tour. The woman, whose name he had tried to make a byword, survived all the hard epithets flung at her, and no doubt the man who uttered them lived to regret them.

Parnell also went to Ireland, and from all accounts the large populace gave their leader a reception overwhelming in friendliness. "We will die for him!" they cried. He took heart; he would go on fighting.

Although he did not know it, he was fighting against something stronger than Mr. Healy, against something stronger even than the whole British Empire. He was a very ill man.

He journeyed hither and thither, and made many speeches. His energy was terrific.

Toward the end of June—this was in 1891—he married Mrs. O'Shea. Some who still supported him apparently thought this even a worse offense than adultery, for they immediately thereafter forsook him. But he carried on his fight with demonic intensity, which frightened Mrs. Parnell and caused his doctors to warn him. He disregarded the warnings.

He fought almost to the last moment. Then, after four

days in bed of sheer fatigue, weariness and increasing fever, he died.

His death stirred England, and it cast a pall on Ireland. Honor was paid him *en route* for Ireland, and in Dublin, where his body was laid under the shadow of O'Connell's statue, the funeral was a memorable spectacle; thousands, weighted down with a heavy sorrow, followed the hearse, while the band played a *caoine,* with its mournful wail of *Ululu! Ululu!*

Thus, from ancient days to our own, great men and martyrs have often been rewarded with fine funerals. But what many who saw Parnell's funeral did not know was that it was also, in a sense, the funeral of the Home Rule Bill. His work went to the grave with him, but it has had its resurrection in our own day. And no man had been more deeply moved by a faith in the ultimate triumph in a cause he fought for; nor was he dissuaded from his faith by beholding at the last the ruins wrought by a disastrous love which in the first place had given him the strength to build the temple.

10

The play is ended. Yet if an Epilogue were needed, it would be well, in this instance, to put the scene at another time and in another place.

The scene is America—to be precise, Newport, Rhode Island. The time, 1880. Parnell's brother, John, and his sister, Theodosia, finding themselves there, decide to "call on Charley's old sweetheart," as they call Miss Woods. Miss Woods talks rapidly, evidently stirred and rendered nervous by the memories which her visitors have aroused.

Suddenly she says, "Do tell me how is your great brother, Charles. How famous he has become!"

She stops, gives a deep sigh, seems on the verge of tears, then suddenly cries as if from the depths of her heart:

"Oh, why did I not marry him? How happy we should have been together!"

Yes, says an Invisible Chorus, they might. But then there would have been no story to tell. Irony is the gods' sport!

HONORÉ DE BALZAC—ARTIST AND LOVER

1

Honoré de Balzac, of whom a later celebrity was to say that "he invented the nineteenth century," sat in his study in the Rue Cassini, in Paris, navigating rapidly his quill pen across a manuscript folio; other sheets already written upon, the top leaf hardly dry, were scattered on the commodious table. Now and then, the writer picked up the huge jug at his side and poured himself out a cup of coffee as black as the ink on his quill, and, gulping it down in big gulps, proceeded to write even more rapidly; he gave the impression of being in a fever. Thus he dashed off another half-dozen pages, drew a vigorous line across the bottom of the last page, threw down the pen on the table, and rose from his chair to his full height, five feet two inches.

He looked taller. That was, perhaps, because of the straight lines of his white Dominican gown with hood, which he habitually wore while at work. He was really big, thick-set, square-shouldered-and-hipped. There was solidity about his neck, chest, body, thighs and limbs; but, supple with an indefinable fluidity, he appeared to carry his weight lightly. His waist was girt with a rich Venetian-gold chain, from which there hung a paper-knife, a pair of scissors, and a gold penknife, all of them handsomely carved; his feet were encased in embroidered slippers.

There was something elemental about the head as well as the body. It was big. The hair was scattered over the back of his neck and cheeks like a mane. The lips were ample, rising at the corners. His black eyes, soft yet fiery, exhilarated at this moment to creative ecstasy, gleamed with happiness at the thought of another masterpiece done. But even the stress of the moment could not hide the kindliness which beamed from them and cast, as it were, its soft diffuse rays over the large full cheeks, which were usually rosy and strongly colored but now pale from the hard mental exertions of many days and nights.

The room itself is worth describing. It was oblong, about eighteen feet by twelve, very high. Thick window curtains were drawn tight, to shut out the outer light. Two medium-sized candlelabra, each holding two steadily burning candles, lighted the room. One would have hardly suspected the presence of the brilliant sunlight outside. The candles burned at all seasons while the great man was at work, and there was the constant illusion of night here.

The furniture was simple. The chief piece was a magnificent ebony bookcase, with mirrored panels. It held its owner's collection of rare books, mostly on mystic, occult and religious subjects, all bound in red morocco. Facing the bookcase, between the two windows, was a carved ebony cabinet, filled with red morocco box-cases; a plaster statuette of Napoleon I graced its top. A tiny paper was stuck across the sword-sheath. A close examination would have revealed on it these words written by Balzac:

"What he could not achieve with the sword I will accomplish with the pen. Honoré de Balzac."

In front of the mantelpiece mirror there was an alarum in unpolished bronze, and on either side a vase in Crown porcelain. To the right and the left of the mirror there hung all sorts of woman's trifles, such as a crumpled glove or a small satin shoe, and similar articles. Elsewhere, a little rusty iron key hung on a string; this its new owner revered as a talisman. On one of the walls was a tiny framed picture which showed beneath the glass a scrap of brown silk, with an embroidered arrow-pierced heart, inscribed with the English words, "An Unknown Friend." (Women from many countries were for ever sending him letters and gifts, and sometimes, as in this instance, anonymous avowals.) The simple writing-table was covered with green baize; before it stood a large Voltaire armchair upholstered in green morocco; other chairs of ebony were covered with brown cloth.

Balzac stood for a few moments contemplating the heap of manuscript with unfeigned pleasure. Another stone in the colossal edifice he was building! He had a great plan in his mind for a history of all contemporary society; none of your dry-as-dust chronicles which passed as history, but a story, or a series of stories, of human nature and of manners told excitingly, by which the terrible if fascinating century in which he lived would be remembered by posterity. (The plan had been in his head for some time, but it had not yet reached that coherence which was to enable him later to call it the *Comédie Humaine.*) The work he so fondly contemplated with his eyes was a masterpiece. Yes, another stone in the monument he was erecting. What a host of stones he had already put in place! *The Sceaux Ball, Ferragus, The Chouans, The Country Doctor, The Shagreen Skin,* and dozens of others! And he was only at the beginning.

The two things he longed for were surely coming to him, "to be celebrated and to be loved." Indeed, he had already had more than a little of both. They were his due, the due of genius. Great men deserved great women. Great generals never lacked the women they wanted, and great artists were at least as good as great generals. The time was coming, surely, he thought, when he would be counted with Rabelais and Molière. He was barely thirty-five now, and he had already done something to be proud of. And, by gad, he meant it. He would do in his own world more than Napoleon did in his.

What, after all, were Napoleon's uniformed armies against the armies of characters he was recruiting in his mind and letting loose on paper? What a host they were in their many-colored variety drawn from every condition of life: clerks, notaries, soldiers, workers, idlers, scholars, artists, philosophers, priests, doctors, lawyers, merchants, fortune-seekers, sharps, pawnbrokers, all manner of women including duchesses—he had a particular predilection for duchesses! He carried this world in his huge brain, and he could marshal out its population in all its accountable and unaccountable antics at will. He was Balzac, Honoré de Balzac.

Some envious ones had questioned his right to use the titular "de,"—the pigs! As if he couldn't prove to their satisfaction that he was not of humble ancestry but the real thing. It was true, he had started with nothing, but give him only time, and the house of Balzac would arise on the solid foundations of his fame and the accruals of that fame. He was making good money now, but that was nothing! He had no talent for piling it up. A coin was round as well as flat, and it had a knack of rolling away, once in his hands. He was always running from his creditors. He wanted real money, lots of it! And he would get it, in one fashion or another. He had lots of schemes in his head for making it.

That wasn't a bad one he had told the other day, the one he had mentioned to his friend Henri Monnier. It ought to be good for half a million francs at least. He would rent a shop on the Boulevard des Italiens. All Paris was bound to pass by there. Next he would establish a store for colonial produce. Over the window he would have printed in letters of gold, "Honoré de Balzac, Grocer." This would create a scandal. Everybody would want to see him serving the customers, with the classical counter-skipper's smock on. . . . Suppose each person spent only a sou. Half of it would be clear profit. Well, he would gain so much a day, so much a week, so much a month. In a month he would have his half-million francs!

Better still, he would marry a duchess, or at least a countess, with money. What was there wrong with that? Wasn't he good enough for a countess? He would confer an honor on her by marrying her. Any one ought to be proud to marry Balzac. There were his mother and his sister Laure always trying to make a rich match for him, and his mother, in particular, constantly got incensed with him for not biting at the bait. But what could he do with an ordinary piece of baggage? He was Honoré de Balzac, and he had bigger game in view. It was natural, to be sure, that his mother should want him to marry any girl with a fair *dot*; he owed his mother fifty thousand francs which she had put into one of his ventures to save him from bankruptcy; that had been generous of her, all the more as it was practically her last money, and he appreciated it; well, he was contributing to her support, and the day would come when he would pay the whole debt. As he had repeatedly told her, "Sooner or later, politics, journalism, a marriage, or a big piece of business luck will make me a Crœsus. We must suffer a little longer."

The truth was, he had a lady of his own in mind—a countess at that! But the lady was married. That was a real drawback, though——

It all happened in this way. About two years before—that was toward the end of February of 1832—his publisher Gosselin handed him a letter with a foreign postmark. The writer of it said that she had admired his

Scenes of Private Life and thought that the delicacy of sentiment which these early novels contained was lacking in the *Shagreen Skin,* and she begged him to forsake his ironic skeptical manner and return to the more noble aspects of his genius. She signed herself merely "The Stranger," and entreated him to make no effort to discover her identity, as she had very good reasons to remain anonymous. Nevertheless, his curiosity aroused, Balzac made some vain attempts to find his correspondent.

Seven months later, a more romantic letter arrived. It was full of mysterious allusions, and concluded with the words, "You no doubt love and are loved; the union of angels must be your lot. Your souls must have unknown felicities. The Stranger loves you both, and desires to be your friend. . . . She likewise knows how to love, but that is all. . . . Ah! you understand me."

If this were not enough, a third letter soon followed, asking Balzac to acknowledge its receipt in a certain newspaper, which he did, and in the course of the advertisement he expressed his regret at not having his correspondent's address for a direct reply.

At last, the lady revealed herself. She was the Countess Evelina Hanska and she lived in the Ukraine. She further made it known that she was young, handsome, immensely rich, and that, alas, she had a husband, with whom she was not so happy as she might be. (The gentleman, indeed, was twenty-five years older than she, and she had married him only because of the impoverished condition of her own family of ancient lineage.)

How excited he had been on the receipt of this letter, which set his imagination aflame with all the possibilities inherent in the situation. He, Balzac, all at once felt himself to be on the eve of achieving his heart's desire. Lovely, a countess, and heaps of money. He'd provide the fame.

There was the husband, of course! But what was a mere husband between two such people who loved each other? He devoutly believed in his star. Without further ado, he pedestaled his lady, and performed genuflexions such as no previous lady earned from his knees. He began to write her letters, to pour out his heart to her, to tell her of his struggles and ambitions. In his mind she was already his, and they two lived together in a palace of his imagining.

The countess, for her part, was eager to meet him, the great Balzac, who, to judge from his writings, knew women's hearts as no other man before him. She must see him, who drew her so powerfully, who fascinated her even before she had met him. What must he be like in the flesh? And it was agreed upon that they should meet at Neufchâtel, in Switzerland. Her husband, Count Hanski, and her child, Anna, together with Anna's Swiss governess, who acted as intermediary, accompanied her.

Balzac, without letting any one know the reason for his hasty departure, set off for the trysting-place. They had previously agreed that they should meet on the main promenade. Madame Hanska sat there, on a bench; one of Balzac's books was on her lap; her husband sat at her side. Undaunted by this most inauspicious prospect, Balzac came up and greeted the lady already enshrined in his heart. Did she feel disappointment in observing the little stocky man who stood looking at her? Did she hope that it might be some one else? How could she? He, the great Balzac, was certain that he was in appearance all the beautiful lady expected him to be. He, at all events, need not defer to any one. And, on one point, there was no doubt at all in his mind; Madame Hanska was charming beyond his fondest expectations.

He saw before him a beautiful woman of twenty-seven; she had splendid black hair, the smooth and deliciously fine skin of a brunette, lovely small hands, and she was naive and imprudent "to the point of embracing him before every one." Thus, he had written to his sister Laure, from whom he couldn't keep the delicious secret, adding: "I say nothing about her colossal wealth. What is it in comparison with beauty? I am intoxicated with love."

Yet there had been a fly in the ointment; there always is. The particular fly was Count Hanski, who never quitted the pair for a single second. What a bore! A great man such as he is not used to restraint. Well, the fellow was old, and not in the best of health; in spite of his presence, the beautiful young woman managed to convey to her adorer some hope. And Balzac was happy, very happy. He returned to Paris, ecstatic over his good fortune. . . .

As the novelist stood before his writing-table, looking down on the sheets of his new work, his mind temporarily freed from its herculean labors, he rapidly recalled his happiness and thought of the greater happiness yet to come. Other women he had known became as nothing in comparison with his adored Eve. He thought ironically of Maria, to whom he had but lately dedicated *Eugenie Grandet.* She had been among his recent loves. She "fell like a flower from heaven, exacted neither correspondence nor attentions, and said, 'Love me a year and I will love you all my life.' " He gave her this dedication, as something he owed to so simple and generous a spirit. Not so Madame de Berney, his earliest and most persistent companion. She was many years older than he, and she had helped him and taught him much, and she had given him all a woman can give to a man; they had been happy together in their day,—if only she did not protest so much when he took on younger and fresher loves! Hadn't he given her as much as he had taken from her? Hadn't he at one time made her happy? Wasn't he even now giving her of his pure friendship?

What a hullabaloo she had raised when she had first heard of this Hanska affair! Why, she hadn't even seen the woman. The protest against the imperious Madame de Castries and the simple Maria was nothing to this. She was getting to be something of a bore. Was it nothing to her that she had known the great Balzac, shared his spiritual counsels and his bed? Would not posterity remember her precisely for that? Decidedly, women could be unreasonable. Now, Eve was different. The one woman who was different. At the thought of Eve, his face broke into a happy smile. He was willing to forgive all women for Eve's sake.

He went over to the mirror and looked at himself with satisfaction. His short neck, in particular, gave him pleasure. "All great men have short necks," he mused and suddenly bethought himself of his hunger. Latterly he had been working eighteen hours at a stretch, drinking plenty of black coffee but eating sparingly; his one consolation had been to take a bath, in which he would lie for an hour, plunged in meditation. And he had hardly seen a human soul. Now he must dress, go out among beings, above all satisfy his sudden-born appetite.

That evening he went out with his publisher. This is what he ate: A hundred oysters, twelve chops, a young duck, a pair of roast partridges, a sole, hors d'œuvre, sweets, fruit (a dozen pears or so), choice wines, coffee, liqueurs. Those who sat near looked on astonished. It was the sort of thing one read about in Rabelais, and never expected to see in real life. He was making up for lost time; there was a time to eat and a time to produce masterpieces; he would show them that he could do one as handsomely as the other. His companion, who was on diet, ate only soup and a small chicken. Here were the relative values of author and publisher, thought Balzac.

2

Let us make a jump of sixteen years. The year is 1850, the year of Balzac's marriage, and the year of his death.

Count Hanski died eight years before, removing the most formidable obstacle to his formal union with Madame Hanska; yet, to his exasperation, the lady showed no inclination to hurry matters. She had her daughter Anna to look after, she explained, and there were questions of inheritance to be settled before she could take the irrevocable step. Crestfallen and chagrined, he expostulated, entreated, filled his letters with reproaches. He could not understand her hesitation. Love such as theirs should not brook delays, his pride was hurt. And he took the opportunity to pass some strictures on the character of women. Later he was to employ more persuasive tactics tending to excite her sympathy and her pity.

Those sixteen years, except for his few visits to her Ukrainian estate and to Vienna, were devoted to passionate epistolary wooing. The man who knew women, and apotheosized the woman of thirty (and over!) lost all restraint and poured himself out in torrents of passion which spoke of his complete submission. "Why shouldn't you have a poet?" he wrote to her, referring to himself, "as other people have a dog, a monkey, a parrot—the more so as I have in me something of these three creatures: I always repeat the same phrase, I imitate society, I am faithful." And, again, moved by his longing for her, he said: "Adieu, loved friend, to whom I belong like the sound to the bell, the dog to his master, the artist to his ideal, prayer to God, pleasure to cause, color to the painter, life to the sun. Love me, for I need your affection, so vivifying, so colored, so agreeable, so celestial, so ideally good, of such sweet dominance, and so constantly vibrating."

His passion for Madame Hanska did not prevent him from carrying on amatory correspondence with other ladies. There was one, in particular, "Louise," who wrote him in English. He had never met her. She had read his books, and felt an affinity with him. His mind and heart, susceptible to the feminine mystery, responded to the call of the siren, and there was a growing warmth in his letters to the unknown, as if he were on the verge of the ultimate espousal. Louise, however, stopped writing, and the episode was concluded without Madame Hanska's discovery of her potential rival.

He suffered no scruple for his seeming unfaithfulness. Was he not a great man whose brain was peopled with legions of characters, and was not his heart equally spacious and capable of harboring a host of loves? Where was the harm? Had he not once argued in favor of love-letters as a commendable exercise which "formed a writer's style"? And it was something of a feat to be able to write to more than one lady at the same time. Different ladies, different techniques.

Anyhow, his lady was far away, and he worked hard enough to deserve a little recreation. What man worked harder than he? Eighteen hours a day at a stretch, and sometimes twenty. He had made himself ill with coffee, he had fasted, he had toiled, he had denied himself much. He had given birth to a world, and what an exciting world! The *Comédie Humaine,* which had first come as an impossible dream, was fast becoming a reality; he had piled volume on volume; the realm he called into being was without physical limits. Walter Scott, from whom he had learned something, had never dreamed of it. He had recreated all of society on paper; he had made manifest the world of his day in all its infinite variety. He had marshaled his actors on a vast stage, not a mere dozen or two, but hundreds, even thousands, five thousand at the very least, and no two alike. Men and women, and more men and women. He was far from done, they were still pouring out, this vast multitude. He had created much, but he was not done creating. In his desk he had a list of over three hundred titles of novels and stories he had still to write, and he was constantly adding to the list. Could he live long enough to accomplish it all? The doctor had told him—but never mind the doctor! He was Balzac, and he, with his inexhaustible energy, would outlive them all. So he thought.

Besides, he had been to a fortune-teller lately, and had been told that things would be coming his way before long. A man who had things coming his way was going to be there to enjoy them. The fellow could have hardly been a fakir. He had told him ever so many things which were true. He had told him that he had had many struggles and many victories; could any one doubt it? And he had described the lady of his heart. There simply could be no mistake about it.

There was a house near Rue Fortunée which, out of the joint funds of himself and Madame Hanska, was being fitted up as the future home for Balzac and his bride-to-be. Seventeen years had passed since their first acquaintance, eight since her husband's death. It was time. There could be no more plausible delays. Madame Hanska's daughter, Anna, had lately married. Even then, the lady held off after giving her consent. He must take one more journey to Russia, and carry off his adored by force. The house was ready; he had furnished it piece by piece; it was made up of many choice pieces he had picked up, one here, one there: lovely, cunningly wrought objects to delight his bride. He knew genuineness when he saw it, and how to pick up bargains, which he sometimes did by a ruse. He was particularly proud of his pictures. His last additions were a Greuze, two Canalettos, a Van Dyck; the gem of his collection was a Holbein. The house was like his fame, slowly but solidly collected; it was unreasonable that his fame should not now bring him great fortune or that the house should not receive its mistress.

He now wished he hadn't squandered so much money in the past, for he had money in his day, and it had always slipped through his fingers. Money, money, money! He could never get this matter of money out of his brain. He thought he should have it when old Hanski died; but the widow never offered it, and he could not bluntly say to her that her fortune was his, though he had always told her that his was hers. And now, on the eve of marriage, the fates visited two destructive fires on Madame Hanska's estate, causing great losses. How often he had come near securing fortune by the efforts of his own resourceful brain, so often on the verge of having millions in his grasp! But it takes money to make money, and he never had quite enough to make the turn. Once an indiscretion of his tongue put money in other people's pockets. That was his scheme of extracting silver from mines in Sardinia once worked by the Romans. The scheme, on investigation, proved feasible, but before Balzac could avail himself of the opportunity, a hint he had thrown out was seized upon by another who made a fortune. His schemes for making money had been legion, but all his efforts invariably ended in losses, debts and in running from creditors. He despised the world he strove to conquer.

He managed to seclude himself, to work in conditions impossible to other men. Even now, he was pestered by the importunities of his aged mother. He had never paid her debt, but then he had offered her a share in his home. And what did she do when she came there? Nervous, fretful, not always in harmony with his moods, she made life a burden by complaints and wailings. She violated his peace, and, driven to desperation by the constant petty tiffs and annoyances, he was forced to tell her to go. He had tried to recompense her with an allowance, which was not so regular that it left him free from her reproaches. Unnerved himself, under the blows from a none too appreciative world, and more ill than he knew, he complained to Madame Hanska of his treatment by his mother, whom he placed among his numerous enemies.

He now lived for the one felicity, that of having Madame Hanska as his wife. He saw in his imagination his drawing-room, presided over by a woman illustrious by birth, polished and imposing as a queen, cultured, witty, beautiful, attracting the *élite* of society, thus establishing domination to the envy of persons of power. He chafed under delays.

At last she consented, and Balzac, ill from overwork and years of drinking coffee, undertook his last journey to the Ukraine to collect his bride.

3

On March fourteenth they married, and the bridegroom was overjoyed. He thought he had never known happiness before. "I have had no flowery spring," he wrote to a friend in Paris. "But I shall have the most brilliant of summers, the mildest of autumns. . . . I am almost crazy with delight."

With equally naive delight he informed his physician, Doctor Nacquart, that he was now the husband of the grandniece of Marie Leczinska of royal blood and the brother-in-law of an aide-de-camp general of His Majesty the Emperor of All the Russias, the Count Adam Rzewuski, stepfather of Count Orloff; the nephew of the Countess

Rosalia Rzewuski, first lady of honor to Her Majesty the Empress; the brother-in-law of Count Henri Rzewuski, the Walter Scott of Poland; the father-in-law of Count Mniszech, of one of the most illustrious houses of the north, and so forth, and so forth!

His dream of joining himself to the highest aristocracy was realized. But within three months he was to be dead. Seventeen years of a consuming passion and a lifetime of the most strenuous labor and abuse of coffee do not go for nothing. The giant who had once startled Paris by his Gargantuan appetite was a very sick man. And the Russian winter was no ally.

The return journey, a month after the marriage, was no triumphal affair. He suffered from heart trouble, she from rheumatism. It was heart-breaking. It took a whole month to go a distance usually done in six days. Not once, but a hundred times a day (he wrote later), their lives were in danger. They were often obliged to have fifteen or sixteen men, with levers, to get them out of the bottomless mudholes into which they had sunk up to the carriage-doors. . . . At last they arrived in Dresden, alive, but ill and tired. Such a journey aged one ten years. . . .

An ill-omen marked their arrival on the night of May twentieth in Paris. Balzac's imagination could not have invented anything more sinister, more grim.

The two travelers drove up before the mansion in Rue Fortunée, which had been so long ready to receive them. The house was lighted to welcome them. Balzac's mother must have seen to that. Indescribably weary, they left the cab, and rang the bell. They rang it again, and yet again. Where was the valet, François Munck, who should have opened the door to them? No one answered the repeated rings. Balzac now rang, now shouted, now thumped at the gates. The lights in the house mocked him. An occasional pedestrian stopped and joined in the shouting and knocking; the cabman dumped the luggage on the narrow sidewalk.

The refined aristocratic Madame Balzac, cold and disgruntled, unused to such a reception, was on the verge of hysteria. Poor Balzac, ill himself, was distraught with anxiety and grief. A crowd had gathered around the pair.

At last a locksmith was fetched. The whole party, including the bystanders, passed through the gate, and, on entering the house, was greeted with an extraordinary spectacle. The valet had gone out of his wits, had smashed the crockery, turned the furniture upside-down, spilled wine on the carpet, and torn up the flowers. They found him wandering about the house, madly gesticulating. He was seized and secured by the visitors, who then helped to bring in the luggage, which accomplished, they left the house.

Thoroughly unnerved, the unhappy Balzac went straight to bed.

4

Sadder for both of them than the home-coming were the days and the weeks to follow, not so many for him.

It was not what either looked forward to. What precisely happened in that house intended for joy and dedicated to sorrow no one knew, but suspicions were rife. Could anything else have been expected? Balzac was heavily in debt when he had led her to believe that he had discharged his obligations, and he was ill, very ill. He had worn himself out. Did it change matters any that he had worn himself out for her sake, that these long years of frustrated passion had helped to wreak the havoc on his once robust frame? She, used to better things, to ease, to luxury, to a social life, and expecting to dominate over a salon, found it hard to conquer her disappointment. Did she sometimes show her pain, her irritation, her inability to accustom herself to her new life? She could not help it. The house was silent. A heavy pall had settled on its objects gathered with such loving care. The rare old pieces, the bric-à-brac and gewgaws, the pictures by the masters, did not console her. She often retired to her room, where desperately her thoughts roved in the world she had had and so foolishly had lost. Once or twice she had burst into anger. What good was anger here? It came in sudden flames, leaving painful smolders to rack her continually with their diffuse pain.

She often looked in the glass. She was still handsome despite her forty years. She remembered, not without irony, the middle-aged women her famous husband celebrated in his books, and felt constrained to laugh. What did life hold for her now? Again, she thought: how foolish she had been not to have seized her chance sooner, before this had come to pass. She had been an idiot. He was not wholly to blame. He, undoubtedly, loved her. It was harder for him than for her. And she caught herself pitying the invalid lying helpless in another room, facing his own self-reproaches for bringing sorrow upon her whom he had loved all these years only to have this sorry reward.

Balzac lay in his bed in an agony of physical and mental pain, which not all the drugs could assuage. His bronchial trouble was gone, to-morrow they would treat him for the heart. Two things worried him: his work and his wife, two things in his mind indissolubly connected. It was the ecstasy inspired by her which had enabled him all these years to animate his created world; his mind was meditating on future creations. When would he be able to work again? was the question he again, and yet again, flung at the doctor. Just now he was unable even to hold a pen. "I can neither read nor write," were the last tragic words he had been able to pen to his friend Theophile Gautier as a postscript to a letter he had been forced to dictate to his wife. He looked regretfully at her, and expressed sorrow for taking her away from the life which had been her portion.

But his diseased heart and kidneys, between them, were contriving his death, now fast approaching. Every one but the patient knew the end was near. Balzac, his brain as alert as ever, was planning a larger population for his unfinished *Comédie Humaine,* which already included some fifty volumes. Could such a brain die, its work undone? No, that was impossible. The thought that it would die soon did not even enter his mind.

At last, even he began to have qualms about his brain's eternity.

It was the middle of August. Doctor Nacquart was in his room. "Doctor," he said, "I want you to tell me the truth. . . . I see I am worse than I believed. . . . Tell me, will I recover?"

The doctor hesitated.

"You are courageous," he began at last. "I will not hide the truth from you. There is no hope."

The sick man's face contracted. His fingers clutched the sheet.

"How long have I to live?"

"You will hardly last the night."

There was a silence. Then the dying man murmured half to himself: "If only Bianchon were here! He would save me."

In respect for his patient, Doctor Nacquart restrained a smile. For Bianchon was a fictitious personage, a doctor, who appeared in Balzac's pages. At the last moment the world he had created had become more real in his mind than the world in which he lived. What true creator does not have this experience?

On the evening of August eighteenth—this was two days later—Victor Hugo having heard that Balzac was dying, called in Rue Fortunée. Except for an old woman and a man whom he took to be Monsieur Surville, the dying man's brother-in-law, the house seemed devoid of human beings. Madame Balzac had retired to her apartments; the poor woman may have been tired, but her absence from the dying man's chamber has given rise to aspersions which to this day have many adherents. Others again say that his last days with her were unalloyed bliss. These rival assertions, in the absence of definite information, will not get us anywhere near the truth. Fortunate is the man Shakespeare in that we know no more about him than that he was born, was married and died (and there are some who say that he was not even born!).

However that may be, the story goes that when Hugo ascended the splendid, red-carpeted stairway, decorated with numerous statues, vases and paintings, his nostrils were assailed with a most horrible odor. Gangrene had set in, the body was decomposing even before it had become a corpse. Could irony go farther with a creator? Sounds of hoarse stertorous breathing came from the chamber. Bolstered up among the cushions of the mahogany bed, lay the body of the author of *Comédie Humaine,* changed strangely in form and feature.

One thing impressed itself on the visitor's mind: the profile of the dying man was startlingly like Napoleon's. Balzac was unconscious.

Greatly saddened, Hugo went home, where several visitors awaited him. "Europe is on the point of losing a great mind," he said to them.

That night Balzac died. Three days later, over his

coffin, at the Père Lachaise Cemetery, Victor Hugo delivered the funeral oration. He said in the course of it:

"The name of Balzac will mingle with the luminous track projected by our epoch into the future. . . . Monsieur de Balzac was the first among the great. . . . All his volumes form but a single book, wherein our contemporary civilization is seen to move with a certain terrible weirdness and reality—a marvelous book which the maker of it entitled a comedy and which he might have entitled a history. It assumes all forms and all styles; it goes beyond Tacitus and reaches Suetonius; it traverses Beaumarchais and attains even Rabelais; it is both observation and imagination, it lavishes the true, the intimate, the bourgeois, the trivial, the material, and, through every reality suddenly rent asunder, it allows the most sombre, tragic ideal to be seen. . . ."

5

A word about the widow. Without obligation on her part, she lived to pay her husband's debts, and she saw to it that a decent annuity went to his mother. This should be remembered to her credit.

Why, soon after her husband's death, she should have formed a liaison with the artist, Jean Gigoux, must remain as much a mystery as her true relations with Balzac in the days when the great shadow was falling athwart his life. In any event, it must be the ultimate irony of the whole Balzac history. Who knows? Perhaps she should not be judged too harshly.

THE COMPARISON OF LASSALLE WITH PARNELL AND BALZAC

LASSALLE and Parnell were both political genuises of a superlative order; hence, it is possible to compare them, but some, not without cause, are bound to ask: Why drag in Balzac?

If he cared to stretch a point, the writer would answer that even on political grounds it would be possible to compare the three men. Lassalle was a Socialist, the first man to organize workers into unions and to preach the doctrine of "blood and iron," which Bismarck was later to make use of. Parnell organized Ireland for Home Rule and preached not a dissimilar doctrine which, as the English spirit of compromise was about to enter the councils of the governing power, he was to modify. As for Balzac, he was an ardent Monarchist, and he declared that Monarchism was one of the two principles upon which he built his *Comédie Humaine,* Religion—more strictly speaking, Catholicism—being the other. Early in his career he unsuccessfully ran as a candidate for political office; Balzac, who was a world in himself, might have made a good politician, just, as in other circumstances, he might have made a great man of business.

But there is no intention to base this comparison on political grounds. Its stress will be laid on the fact that here are three men of widely diverse temperaments, all of whom the fatal love for a woman has helped to lay low. Let us range the protagonists into two categories: the sentimental German and the sentimental Englishman in one, the clear-seeing, analytical Frenchman, who made a practise of dissecting women's hearts, in the other. The three women, to be sure, also belong to three distinct races, but that need not enter the argument. Passion in women obliterates all racial frontiers. In general, the distinctions of passion are not so great as those of mentality, and the racial mentality of great men is bound to color the processes of their conduct under stress of passion.

There is hardly a being on earth so adaptable as the Jew. He has the faculty of taking on the coloration of the country of his birth or of adoption. He can out-German the German, out-English the Englishman. Lassalle was a Jew, but he was also a German. His German virtues, his interest in philosophy to mention one, are preeminent. He was, in German fashion, sentimental. For a man of his age and experience, his whole manner of the wooing of Helene von Dönniges smacked of German adolescence. What other judgment may be passed on a man of action who, forgetting to act, pauses to sit on a window-sill of his lady's room, in the moonlight, to recite love lyrics? And this is but a prelude to greater sentimentalities, culminating in the greatest sentimentality of all, the duel (which, intellectually, he thought a silly institution). His final surrender to the national temperament wrought his ruin; no other explanation may be offered as to why this man of iron will should have allowed a beautiful but weak-willed girl to interrupt his life-work.

He had had "affairs" before, and once he had come near marriage with a Russian actress of mediocre talent who deceived him into believing that she was of royal blood. She was nineteen, and though, in the words of George Brandes, "she was far from beautiful, and by no means wealthy or distinguished, she seems to have been a lively and enthusiastic character. To her Lassalle offered his hand with astonishing precipitation." The character of the lady may be adduced from the fact that some years later she revealed to the world in three languages that Lassalle had loved her and been rejected. From all accounts Lassalle had made a perfect fool of himself with this girl who was about half his age. "So far as we can judge this incident from matter published," comments Brandes, "it is a strong proof of Lassalle's weakness of judgment where women were concerned." The old adage about a chain being no stronger than its weakest link may well be applied here; all of Lassalle's strength went for naught because of that note of sentimentality in his character. And, discovered in his weakness, he could no longer face the world in that leonine pride which marked him in his political career.

The Parnell-O'Shea romance, a more substantial affair, as the years through which it dragged would indicate, is marked by one feature conspicuously Anglo-Saxon. It is the spirit of compromise, and it would be idle to reproach the protagonists of the drama which ensued, since they were the victims of this spirit and not its authors. Here were two beings who genuinely loved each other; fate had tied the woman to a man whom she did not love. The cause of a whole nation was at stake, and social custom being what it was, discovery meant ruin to it. Parnell and Mrs. O'Shea were driven to conceal their love; nevertheless, every one knew and winked at it, including Gladstone. Such is the spirit of moral compromise which prevailed in Victorian England. Only when the affair became a public scandal, when the culprits were "caught," did it assume the proportions of a crime, and the men who knew all the time turned on the leader and his companion, and tried to drive the one from politics and to make of the other a byword of shame.

This could not have happened in the Latin countries. The Parnell-O'Shea affair was wholly conditioned by the code which prevailed in the country in which it was enacted

HONORÉ DE BALZAC

From a drawing by David d'Angers, 1843

FERDINAND LASSALLE

From a portrait by Jakob Steinhardt (1923) in *Lassalle—Mensch und Politiker* by Konrad Haenisch Franz Schneider, Verlag, Berlin

Charles Stewart Parnell

From the painting by Sydney P. Hall
in the National Portrait Gallery of Ireland

In the eyes of the law they were guilty; in spirit they had not sinned. Parnell was a reserved English gentleman, whom accident gave a home in Ireland; Mrs. O'Shea responded to the deepest in herself and in him; she could not rob her husband, Captain O'Shea, of something which had never been his. Both lovers paid the penalty in a truly Anglo-Saxon way, and nothing more need be said.

From the Parnell-O'Shea to the Balzac-Hanska affair is more like the crossing of oceans than that of a mere channel. Or it is like the swing of the pendulum from one extreme to the other. They represent, morally, two different worlds. The first would be rank hypocrisy to French eyes. The second, considering particulars, would be sheer immorality to the English. For though Balzac loved Madame Hanska (above other women!) he was not above having an affair or two on the side. This is not so reprehensible in French eyes, however rumors may have disturbed the Polish countess. Did he love her as Lassalle loved Helene von Dönniges and Parnell loved Mrs. O'Shea? His letters which he poured out in the course of seventeen years are full of protestations of passion; seventeen years is a long time for mere whim to have its way; yet some biographers maintain that the author of the *Comédie Humaine* was full of calculation and that, allowing for the lady's beauty and intellectual attraction, he was allured by the title and by the lady's immense wealth.

If that is true, then, indeed, the irony of the Balzac-Hanska affair is great, for when Madame Hanska came to him, she was no longer young, and her wealth was gone, and Balzac himself had one foot in the grave. There are not a few who assert that she had helped to put it there.

These facts are worth mentioning; but to the main argument they are beside the point.

What is important is that for seventeen years Balzac received a mental stimulus from a real or imagined love which helped him to create. To the man of imagination of Balzac's type marriage in itself was not all-in-all; it is more than likely that the long waiting delayed disaster, that it sustained him through his creative labors, that marriage provided a release of the tension, causing his will to snap.

Love, then, rather than marriage has a place in the creative processes of Balzac; he owed something to women even before he began his correspondence with Madame Hanska. It is natural for a man of Balzac's type to imagine that his latest love is his first real love, as when he writes to Madame Hanska after a few weeks' acquaintance, "It is only the last love of a woman that can satisfy the first love of a man," the implication is that he had never loved before and that she would never love again; whereas, the actual truth is that not only had he loved before, if not so ardently, but that shortly after perpetrating this aphorism he carried on an amatory correspondence with another "Stranger" called Louise, while Madame Hanska, but a short time after his death entered into a liaison with the artist, Gigoux.

Several factors enter into the composition of the alliance with Madame Hanska projected in Balzac's mind. She was, in the first place, a countess of the best Polish blood, handsome to boot; she was immensely rich; and she had a superior intelligence, with a penchant toward mysticism for which he had a weakness, which met with no response in the other women he had known; in giving counsel regarding his books she exercised an authority which aided him in his work; emotionally, she did not yield as readily as other women, wherefore the affair was prolonged through the years. A certain amount of calculation on Balzac's part may be granted; but without a genuine infatuation their relations could hardly have lasted. He had a mind which was capable of projecting whole populations, but he was ever in need of stimulus to animate them, and this he obtained from women—and coffee! As late as 1846, he writes to Madame Hanska:

"For me, the sixteen volumes done in the last five years are an inexplicable miracle. . . . Were it not for some new courage in my heart—a courage of a kind that will uphold a shipwrecked man, all one long day, in struggle with the billows—were it not for some new courage, why, just in port, I should succumb to the lightest of all waves. Into a fighter's wound you have poured marvelous oil—a perfect woman, a devoted mother, a good and compassionate friend."

This was clear sight in view of what happened later: was it not precisely in the year of his marriage, when, so to speak, he had just got into port, that he wholly collapsed? This French analyst dissected women's hearts as no man had done before him. Nor was he always kind to them. Listen to this: "The most Jesuitical Jesuit among the Jesuits is a thousand times less Jesuitical than the least Jesuitical woman." He let this pass as a jest, but is not many a jest spoken from the heart? Most of the women with whom he had had intimacies had been his slaves. This was not true of Madame Hanska, who made a slave of him. They were, in all likelihood, happier in their correspondence than in their direct relations. His journeys to Russia helped to pull him down physically; evidence seems to point to the fact that the intermittent brain fever he suffered on his last journey there was largely due to the lady's too frequent changes of mind; there is little doubt that that and the journey home, in conditions to which the aristocratic wife was not accustomed, hastened his demise.

In the final analysis, we are forced to the conclusion that Madame Hanska, in her apotheosis, is largely a creature of Balzac's imagination, as much as Père Goriot is, or Balthasar, or Vautrin. Such a character as he saw in her was necessary to him, and with the inexorable logic of the imaginative Frenchman he created her in the image of a goddess whom he might worship and who might bless his labors. What could he not do if she were with him—and always? That sounds logical enough. He never finished his *Comédie Humaine;* nor did he live his life out in the manner he had planned. As a remote goddess, she helped him to build his monument; as a woman, a being all-too-human, she brought him and his work to a premature close.

Thus, in a sense, does logic, even French logic, ultimately defeat its own ends.

JOHN BROWN—TRAITOR AND PATRIOT

IT WAS night; it was Sabbath; it was mid-October—to be exact, the sixteenth—the year 1859. It was dark; it was dismal; it was chill as only a fall night could be chill. But for the measured tramping of men, two by two, eighteen in all, and the creaking of the wagon at the head, not a sound stirred in the bleak night; the narrow country lane down which the little army wended its way was deserted and the surrounding landscape heavy with the autumnal mood. A curious solemnity possessed the eighteen as they walked in almost abstract order, wrapped in long gray shawls to keep them warm, somber and silent like a despair which has passed beyond the bounds of words. The heavy starless sky hung above them like a pall, and they walked under its enveloping gloom, as it were, prisoners of night around whom the dark was slowly tightening as the shroud tightens around a man that is doomed. And they walked with that characteristic resolution of men who had chosen their own fate and who, once having chosen, had no power to retract. The eighteen were armed with rifles, and these rifles were light compared to the dread which filled their hearts, as it fills the hearts of the bravest on approaching the brink of the unknown.

There was no moving pillar of fire such as led the Israelites to the Promised Land, but, immediately ahead, in that creaking wagon, filled with pikes, fagots, a sledge-hammer and a crowbar, sat the austere leader, notorious as the reputed author of the murders at Pottawatomie, and now commander-in-chief, John Brown, "Ossawatomie Brown," alias Shubel Morgan. His heart in that darkness was as a pillar of white fire leading the eighteen on.

And, before the wagon, like spies of Israel, marched the advance-guard, Captains Cook and Tidd, brave men both, armed like the rest with rifles, and, in their pockets, official sealed orders allotting to them their preliminary tasks.

Twenty men in all. *And* John Brown.

But a little while before the whole company, in a mood of exultation, had their last supper together, and swore fealty to their chief. His words, "Men, get on your arms! We will proceed to the Ferry!" had released the pent-up emotion of his followers, who had been subdued by prolonged inaction. Drunken without strong drink, the men let loose a pandemonium of rejoicing which, like a fitful, fretful wind was to die down to silence as suddenly as it had begun.

They had been sitting long enough and at last they were to move. At last they were to strike. A blow for freedom would be struck that very night. It was to be a mere beginning in the long battle to free slaves. Twenty men went with John Brown. Three remained behind to guard Kennedy Farm, headquarters and depot of supplies.

A little scene was enacted here which was to linger in the men's minds—a wordless little scene fraught with pathos. This was the parting of the Coppoc brothers. One of them went with Brown, the other made one of the three who stayed behind. They shook hands and embraced, and lingered a moment over their embrace like men fully aware that they would not embrace again.

Now they were on the march, the brave advance-guard of two, the doughty commander-in-chief in his creaking wagon, and the silent eighteen with feelings and thoughts too grim to be spoken. Could one hiding behind a bush or behind a tree have seen the shadowy procession, he might have, with some reason, regarded it as a funeral cortège headed by a hearse. Who knows? Perhaps, the eighteen felt that too; they must have dimly felt that they were following a hearse. More than that, they must have in some way felt that they were not following it as mourners, but as disciples who were to have a share in the Golgotha of their lord and were not to deny him even after the cocks crowed.

At this moment some of them must have been possessed by doubts, by dim questionings and misgivings, stirring deep in that world within them which men call the soul. Whither, after all, were they going like thieves in the night? What was the object they hoped to achieve? What grim fate was urging them on a mysterious mission, from which, from the very beginning, there was no drawing back? The general had chosen his soldiers well, no bullies, but to the last one of them men of principle, and Christian enough neither to swear nor to drink. As for killing, that was another thing. They were ready to kill in the name of the Lord, ready to swing the sword of Gideon to show the world that under God's law men were equal, whether they were white or black.

They were going to Harper's Ferry, where government property, an arsenal, was situated. That much they knew.

But what would they do at Harper's Ferry? Attack government property, the arsenal? To attack government property, above all an arsenal, was treason—treason! Treason was punishable with death. Death was . . . But here thought stopped. Death was as unthinkable as space, as ungraspable as the wind. All rivers flowed into the sea, and all souls flowed into God. John Brown, who knew his Bible, had taught them that. He knew that Book from the words, "In the beginning" to the word "Amen!" and He who had inspired all the burning words of the Book inspired John Brown. So John Brown had said, so John Brown believed, John Brown was man enough to persuade others to believe with John Brown. His army was small, but it marched like one man, like one soul.

That is, John Brown's followers believed their cause to be just. Did justice betoken success? Injustice had reigned too long for any man to be sure. And what man wanted to die a cruel, perhaps futile, death in a cause which promised to be a lost, a hopeless cause? No mercy would be shown them by men who believed in slavery.

Twenty-three men, counting the three left behind. *And* John Brown. Always "and John Brown." But what could twenty-three men, even with John Brown, do against the countless hosts of the great South, who as firmly believed that slavery was right as this tiny host believed it wrong? Here was folly, sheer folly, folly on a grand scale, which, rising to the height of mountains, awakens a commensurate faith capable of moving mountains, and is beyond the fear of ridicule. A grim Don Quixote sat in a creaking wagon, and eighteen grim Sancho Panzas blindly followed him, none lured hither by any promise of a hypothetical isle, and all facing the prospect of almost sure death, that "ultimate isle" which sooner or later falls to the lot of one and all.

Why this haste to consummate marriage with death?

Grimly the eighteen marched behind John Brown, without knowledge of what their tasks might be, of what foe they were on their way to smite. Harper's Ferry was not famous as a slave settlement, what slaves were here were treated well by their masters. But they would soon know. The march from Kennedy Farm to the Ferry was but six miles all told. But time and space had no meaning here, the moments dragged on like miles through an endless eternity.

What of the commander-in-chief? John Brown sat on the seat of the wagon, a rigid, bronze-like figure, with patriarchal beard, his inflexible mouth set, his heart hardened by God, his small fighting head with its graying hair under his old battle-worn Kansas cap, his clear blue-gray eyes piercing the darkness to some remote beyond.

And, as in days gone by, he retired, as it were, away from his men, and wrestled with his God in secret prayer. He loved peace, did John Brown, not war, and he prayed for some directing vision, such as had come to him now and again, but no answer came, only an inner urging strengthening his will for the fighting of God's battles for His children's sake.

To be sure, he had a plan of sorts, which was hardly more clear to himself than to his men. In years past he had studied in books campaigns of guerrilla warfare, and remembered the wise counsel about "deep and narrow defiles when three hundred men would suffice to check an army." That was all very well if an army came to attack you. But no army came, and John Brown had to look for a foe which was everywhere and yet nowhere. It was not a bad idea, that of making dashes against slave settlements and returning unscathed to mountain fastnesses. But why deliberately march on Harper's Ferry, which was in appearance and in fact a perfect trap, entered by a narrow bridge, which, once crossed, put a river between yourself and your source of supplies, making escape well-nigh impossible? Why such a shrewd Connecticut Yankee as John Brown, ex-shepherd, ex-merchant, with experience as a Kansas raider, should have made an open-eyed effort to walk into the trap, puzzles sane men to this day. Yet it is for his folly and madness that John Brown lives, for even folly and madness are justified by success, and his success, if not the sort he deliberately aimed at, was prodigious and even greater than he had planned. And words, potent words, were to be its result and its crown, inspiring, in time to come, hosts of men to deeds valorous and bloody.

Deep within John Brown's heart a white flame burned, the flame of righteousness, the flame of God, and he knew with that inscrutable knowledge which comes from a faith by no means blind, that his cause would triumph and that he was to be an humble instrument of that ultimate victory.

Yes, he had a plan of sorts. He proposed to attack the arsenal as a demonstration against a government he could not respect, a government which allowed slavery and bore the brunt of the guilt for the existence of the abomination. He would, incidentally, capture a few slave-owners, and release their slaves; some of the rescued slaves would, undoubtedly, of their own will swell his ranks. He would alarm the town, the alarm would reverberate through the South; yes, and through the North too. As for him, he would escape with his reinforced army to his base of supplies—Kennedy Farm, where, after arming his black allies, the whole contingent would take to the hills to sally forth again to other and still other raids.

He would not fail. He could not fail. And he had past experience to encourage him. Had he not faced the ruffians and the cutthroats in Kansas on their own terms and beaten them and won Kansas to free-soil? Bloody Pottawatomie came to his mind, when, with several cronies, he, John Brown, had struck terror into the hearts of the proslave camp by murdering or instigating the murder of several of its most despicable members. It was true the deed was done in the dead of night, and some of the victims had been, so to speak, dragged from their beds. What of that? He had long since decided that the devil could be fought only with his own weapons, the only weapons the devil could understand. But the other side used the same argument. And it thought that John Brown was the devil's own emissary. Again and again a price had been offered on his head, and he, John Brown, had walked contemptuously by the bills exposing his own likeness and the price thereon.

The Lord was on his side. The Lord had saved him for this task. John Brown had failed in business, he could not fail in this. At a time of life when men begin to think of feathering their nests against approaching age, he, John Brown, had ceased thinking of self and his loved ones, but only of carrying out the will of his Maker, who chose certain men and women for tasks which they could not help but perform. By sheer will he had crushed what tenderness there was in him lest it hinder him, and, leaving his wife and the comforts of home, he offered his body and his soul to the cause of liberation and recruited sons of his own sinew in the same cause. Of their own will they had suffered hunger, cold, and all manner of hardship, and more than once faced the rabid fury of mobs and death itself without flinching. The women of the family stayed by the home hearth and, with faith in their patriarch, bore the trials of long anxious waiting with fortitude.

"Take more care to end life well than to live long," he once had said, and, with an eye on Death, which might at any moment embrace him, he had grown old. A long beard and mustache now served to hide something of the fighter's face, which had previously revealed its fierce implacable mouth and forceful chin; they gave him a venerable appearance. But his small gray-blue eyes, "full of light and fire," and the handsome aquiline nose, gave witness to the name of "Eagle," an appellation more than once used by those who chanced to meet him. He was quiet and calm, his self-control astonishing; "a volcano with an ordinary chimney flue," Thoreau had said of him.

As he sat in the wagon, firm and still and unruffled, he heard the footbeats of his men, as it were the beats of his own heart, that determined rhythm imposed by the Lord on his picked warriors. They were in the minority now, he reflected, but . . . For all his Yankee humor, never did he condescend to a rueful smile at the reflection that twenty-four men were a minority with a vengeance, where millions were antagonistic, thought differently, or, worse still, did not think at all. Instead, his heart rejoiced, even exulted at the thought. A minority however infinitesimal but conscious of its rights, based on moral principles, and with the Lord on its side, would sooner or later confound the majority, however great.

Was this madness? Lunacy? He did not think so. But then no lunatic is aware of his own lunacy, a faculty he shares with prophets and poets and all those who are not afraid of ridicule, because, after all, they are not aware of being ridiculous. The day would come, he felt with an impelling intuition, and with a faith almost fanatical, when men would justify him. Of how near that time was he had no inkling.

But whatever were the reflections of the men and of John Brown himself, they were suddenly cut short by the approach to Harper's Ferry. The Knight of Abolition, all expectant, was girding his loins for the fray.

It was in the early hours of the eighteenth that John Brown, battered and laid flat but still alive, was made prisoner by a force under the command of Robert E. Lee, then colonel, and who, by a curious irony, but two years hence, was fated to lead the armies of the South and to hear the echoes of "John Brown's body" over bivouac fires.

What happened in those two nights and the intervening day, between his entry into Harper's Ferry at ten thirty and the moment of his being laid low? They can be told briefly: the things which happened the first night, the day after, and the night yet to follow.

At the entrance to Maryland Bridge, a civilian watchman, who imagined that he was living in times of peace, could hardly believe his senses when asked by the advance-guard to hold up his hands. If, at first, he thought it a joke, he was soon undeceived. He was made prisoner. The watchman at the other end of the bridge, in spite of his fright, refused to surrender the key to the armory. Prepared for a refusal, the invaders availed themselves of the crowbar in the wagon; soon the armory gate stood agape.

This done, John Brown and his men crossed the street and took possession of the arsenal. An army of two was left to garrison it, while John Brown and the others went on, making prisoners of what men came their way.

Beyond Bolivar Heights, five miles from Harper's Ferry, there lived a gentleman-farmer and slave-owner, Colonel Lewis W. Washington, a great-grandnephew of the Father of His Country, who had been likewise a gentleman-farmer and slave-owner. And this Washington had a pistol in his possession which had been presented to his great-granduncle by General Lafayette. He also had a sword, and the myth-makers said that this sword had been a gift to the great general by no less a personage than Frederick the Great. And John Brown, who thought that the Declaration of Independence, with its "Whereas all men are born free and equal," should under that term include the black man as well as the white, conceived the preposterous idea that a new revolution was in order, and that being the case, he ought to use the weapons which did duty in the first one. Did he hope to find some potent charm in them which would work miracles?

It is more reasonable to suppose that, like all great men, John Brown had a healthy instinct for the dramatic, was keenly aware of the value of a gesture. The great mass of people were swayed by gestures. Dramatic imagination was the most unpuritanic of virtues, and John Brown was the most puritanic of men, but he was not the man to draw back from using the devil's weapons where the enemy was the devil himself. After all, violence itself was of the devil, and he knew it; he was no believer in force. Yet he had used force, he would go on using force. He, a tender-hearted man, once having admitted its need, must perforce admit the need of a whole bagful of devilish tricks. He had been a non-resister himself once, like the rest of that tongue-wagging crew who called themselves Abolitionists. Well, how far did it get them? Simply nowhere. He was heartily sick of talk, talk, talk. Talk was only good if it made a man want to fight, and fight hard. That's where a grand gesture came in; the theater in life, for which, without being aware of it, he had a sneaking admiration, was not the less authentic for being expressed under a mask of puritanic austerity. He remembered about Napoleon, the day that worthy returned to France from Elba and met the Bourbon army sent to take him, living or dead. And what did this Napoleon do? He bared his breast to the army, and said, "Fire away, my men!" or words to that effect. And did they shoot? No; the whole army, to a man, went over to his side. That was the medicine to give them, reflected John Brown, his soul exulting at the thought, and he wanted weapons which had already fought for liberty, American liberty. There was a charm in the pistol which both Lafayette and Washington had shot with. What better talisman than a sword used by Frederick the Great and the great Washington? Was it silly, sentimental? Perhaps. Men have judged the whole affair as downright nonsense. Why did he not use the sword of Gideon he had so much talked about? John Brown was a Yankee, a practical man. And he knew that people were impressed only by definite concrete things. Gideon's sword was but a fancy, but Washington's power and Lafayette's pistol were definite things, things to conjure with.

Whether for one reason or another, he was possessed to have these weapons, and, at the risk of losing much valuable time, dispatched an expedition to fetch them. By way of adding to the gesture, he gave orders that Colonel Washington be made to hand them over to the negro Anderson, a member of the raiding party. This was done.

Colonel Washington was made prisoner. His slaves were set free, or rather they were invited to join the raiders and battle their way to freedom. For weapons, pikes were handed out to them. The little party, consisting of Colonel Washington and his slaves, was accommodated in a four-horse wagon on the premises, and the singular procession set off for the Ferry, not without going through a similar performance on the way.

They arrived at the Ferry to find the small town awake, seething with excitement. There had been firing, and, irony of ironies, the first person to be shot by one of John Brown's men was a free, harmless, well-to-do negro, in enjoyment of his freedom, and, moreover, one who had not offended and offered no resistance. He was the baggage-master at the station, he was ordered to halt, and in the performance of his duty he would not. A bad omen . . . Yet Brown himself had in the last order exhorted his men to remember that "the lives of others are as dear to them as yours are to you: do not, therefore, take the life of any one if you can possibly avoid it; but if it is necessary to take life in order to save your own, then make sure work of it."

Other things happened. And they happened haphazard, without any concerted plan. John Brown had relied too much on God, who, in military matters, gives preference to good generals.

A train had come in, and was held up for the night. Why did John Brown finally allow it to back across the bridge? Sheer folly again. The conductor lost no time in dispatching the news of the "insurrection" with the alarming information of the rebels being "a hundred and fifty strong." And, thanks to the institution of the telegraph, the news flew fast, east and west, south and north. The wires had been cut at Harper's Ferry, but those beyond were available. By eleven in the morning, the president of the United States, Governor Wise of Virginia, and Major-General George H. Stewart, of the First Light Division, Maryland Volunteers, were in possession of the essential facts, hours before John Brown had counted on their being known.

Again, the shooting of the baggage-master had stimulated Doctor John Starry, the physician of the town, to take to horse and spread the alarm nearer home. Here, once more, an error had been committed. Doctor Starry had kept in touch with the raiders nearly all night long, yet escaped arrest; the arrests were made haphazard. Doctor Starry spurred his horse; it did not take him long to arrive at Charlestown, but eight miles away.

At Charlestown the news created consternation. For years men hereabouts had lived in constant fear of the revolt of black men, who one night might rise to murder their masters in their beds. For this harsh fear they had to thank the accursed Abolitionists. What the South, then, had feared, had come to pass. Alarm bells were rung, and ununiformed militiamen, gathering their kit in the twinkling of an eye, were up and on the march. Other companies from elsewhere, both uniformed and ununiformed, eagerly moved forward about the same time.

Where was the protecting angel, to cry in John Brown's ear: "Make haste, John Brown, while there's time!

You've stirred things up enough, and even as it is, there'll be the very devil to pay. You've done enough for one night! Gather up your own while you may and run!"

But John Brown lingered in the engine-house with some of his army and all his prisoners, about thirty in number, while his too few ways of retreat were being cut off, one by one. John Brown, solicitous for his men and prisoners—the party did not consist of quite fifty men all told—was having breakfast prepared for them. His own men fought that day without a morsel. After all, the poor fellows must eat; nor could he forget that the prisoners were human. During the morning, John Brown's lieutenant, brave Kagi, sent messages to his commander-in-chief, urging him to leave. Escape was still possible. Why did he linger, letting the golden hours slip? What did he hope for? What could he expect to achieve? He was concerned about his prisoners. He had no thought of letting them go. Did he hold them as hostages against a possible attack? One thing was certain: he still counted on negroes leaving their masters and swelling his forces so as to make them well-nigh irresistible. He had faith in human nature, which was no monopoly of the white man. Would they, the blacks, not rally to their savior and deliverer? They would do so, he thought, as soon as they had grasped the fact that John Brown and his men had come to risk their lives for their sake. That anticipation of active gratitude proved vain.

John Brown was putting all the eggs in one basket, thought Kagi, who held the rifle-works.

In the meantime troops were pouring into Harper's Ferry. They began their work by cutting off John Brown's main line of retreat, the way he and his men had come. It was no longer possible to regain Kennedy Farm. Here and there, where Brown's men kept guard, skirmishes were being fought, and men fell on both sides fighting furiously.

Atrocious acts took place, and Brown's men, living or dead, did not escape the wrath of the enraged natives. The fighting went on, confusion reigned until at last the battle began more and more to center around the engine-house where the commander-in-chief was sheltered with what remained of his men, and with his handful of men held off the hundreds who assailed him. All day the small host defended themselves, while more and more reinforcements poured in for the enemy. As day merged into twilight they still fought, and only when twilight slowly lapsed into night did the hostilities cease. But Kagi and other brave men who had composed the outposts were no more.

In the engine-house, John Brown had stood all day, collected and serene, directing operations, Emperor Frederick's sword dangling at his side. If he was tired, he did not show it, and, with a word now and then calmly uttered he bolstered up the others, while he never ceased to treat the prisoners with the greatest courtesy.

A citizen with a white flag tied to an umbrella came with a summons to surrender. John Brown expressed a willingness to negotiate; he hastily scribbled his terms. The gist of the note was that in consideration of all his men, whether living or dead or wounded, being delivered to him with all their arms and ammunition, he would take his prisoners and cross the Potomac Bridge, a little beyond which he would set them at liberty; "after which we can negotiate about the government property as may be best." It concluded: "Also we require the delivery of our horse and harness at the hotel."

This last delicious bit, is it not worthy of the Knight of La Mancha? Well might the excellent steed he demanded have been called Rosinante, and well did our Yankee Quixote need her and her harness for future exhibitions of his prowess!

How did the quaint message, stated in terms of commanding dignity, as of one military chief to another, strike the opponent with his multitude of well-armed men at his back? Did he break into guffaws, present so much as a smile at the naive presumption? History but records his brief reply, stated in terms altogether official, to wit: under no conditions would he consent to a removal of the citizens across the river.

John Brown, who bore the ordeal with equanimity, was bitter about one thing: his own messengers bearing the white flag of truce had been shot down like dogs. "What else did you expect when you took up arms that way?" was the retort of Captain Sinn, a friendly enemy who deigned to enter and to speak with him. "I have weighed the responsibility and shall not shrink from it," was John Brown's reply. Besides, he had been considerate. He might, if he had so desired, have slaughtered all the inhabitants in the town, but he had been considerate; he was entitled to honorable terms. Captain Sinn reproached him: why, the very first man John Brown's forces had killed was a poor defenseless negro, a free man at that. John Brown said he was deeply sorry. Such things, with the best intentions in the world, were bound to happen. Captain Sinn departed, and, with a chivalry not to be outdone by Brown, sent a surgeon under his charge to the engine-house to attend to a wound which had been inflicted on Watson Brown, one of Brown's two sons who had fought at his side.

As the dusk deepened, the engine-house grew quiet; it had no light, the cold was intense. Both prisoners and raiders lay on the brick floor and tried to rest. Only young Oliver Brown, in the agony of his wound, groaned pitifully, and begged:

"Shoot me, father! Shoot me!"

"Oh, you'll get over it!" was the brusque reply.

"Shoot me, father! Shoot me!" came the desperate, persistent cry.

John Brown showed exasperation. "If you must die," he called, "die like a man!"

Not by so much as a quaver in his voice did the stoic father reveal that inner agony which ravaged his soul. In silence, in his heart, he prayed to God his Father to strengthen his son and to harden his own resolution to enable him to bear up under the ultimate travail the approach of which he felt was near. Outwardly, more than ever, he was a rigid bronze statue, serene and changeless.

He heard his son's groans slowly die away. At last Oliver, in his corner, lay quietly.

"Oliver!" his father called from the spot where he was conversing with Colonel Washington.

There was no answer.

"I guess he's dead," said John Brown. Those who heard him could detect no tremor in his voice

Near the dead Oliver lay, silent, his brother, Watson, his life's spirit ebbing away. And not many paces away lay a dead Canadian who, like Oliver, had been shot while standing in the doorway of the engine-house.

Four men were all that were left here of John Brown's original force who were still alive and unwounded. Four men—"and John Brown." All who saw him then, even in their weariness, could not help but admire the tall, wiry, staunch figure of the patriarch, divine in his serenity.

"Is it true we have committed treason by being here?" one of the four asked him, having overhead a fragment of conversation.

"Certainly."

"If that is so," answered the man for himself and a comrade, "we don't want to fight any more. We thought we came to liberate the slaves, and we didn't know that we were committing treason." It was too late. At dawn both men were to meet death on the bayonets of the marines.

With the arrival of regular troops and the marines, the end was clearly in sight.

The direction of the final act to the Harper's Ferry tragi-comedy was left to Colonel Robert E. Lee. After making the necessary preparations for taking the fort, he sent John Brown a summons for surrender, with a guarantee for the personal safety of Ossawatomie and his men. The offer was rejected, as the only terms upon which he would agree to capitulate practically amounted to being allowed to escape. Whereupon, with thought for the prisoners, Lee called on volunteers for "taking these men out." To insure their safety, only bayonets were to be used.

Lieutenant Green, at the head of the marines, took charge of the attack. In his haste, he left his quarters armed only with a light dress-sword. Had he brought a sturdier weapon, the final and most pregnant chapter of the history of John Brown would have remained unwritten, and John Brown would have died acknowledged by some as a traitor, by others as a lunatic, by the charitable as a well-intentioned if misguided fanatic, and not as the singularly noble and heroic figure who illuminates the stage of American history with a light casting other contemporary figures into a penumbral twilight and enduing it with all the spiritual value of a Rembrandt masterpiece.

Green's light dress-sword—let us call it the magic wand, which was to produce the miracle of the resurrection of John Brown, the John Brown shackled in chains and no longer free to contend with temporal weapons, but with a serene speech full of potent, unforgettable words. Yet the use of arms had served a purpose. It put John Brown in the limelight, gave him an audience which otherwise might not have paused to look and to listen.

The attack on the engine-house began with three marines battering the heavy doors with sledge-hammers. Those within, the defenders as well as the prisoners, knew that the crucial moment had arrived. Nothing happened. There was a pause. Close by the dead corpse of Oliver, John Brown, with one hand, was feeling the pulse of his dying son, Watson; with the other he was grasping his rifle ready for firing. Now and then, in composed tones, he turned to give orders to his men. Presently a different sort of noise sounded against the door. It was evidently made by some heavy object used as a battering-ram, as it happened, a ladder. From within, the noise was terrific. A second blow followed on the first. There was a crash. A stream of daylight poured through a hole low in the left-hand door. John Brown, without showing the least agitation, released the hand he was holding, dropped on his knee, took aim and fired. The bullet skimmed through the hole, hitting no one. A moment later Lieutenant Green, holding his light sword, deftly climbed through the hole. He quickly got on his feet, ran to the right of the engine, which was situated behind the door, passed quickly to the rear of the house, and came up between the two engines. He exchanged a quiet greeting with Colonel Washington, whom he knew; the southerner was standing near the hose-cart at the front of the engine-house. On a knee, a few feet to the left, knelt a man with a rifle in his hand, pulling the lever to reload. Colonel Washington pointed to Brown and said:

"This is Ossawatomie."

The young lieutenant sprang at Brown, lunged at the bending figure with his light sword, which brought the commander to his knees. Whether the sword struck the belt or a bone, it was uncertain, but the weapon bent double at the first stroke. Lieutenant Green then seized the bent sword in both his hands and showered blows on Brown's head, drawing blood and laying him flat. It was thought he was dead.

Fast on the heels of Green, followed several marines. A scuffle ensued, with casualties on both sides. It lasted only a few minutes. Soon the body of John Brown was borne out; two thousand spectators looked on.

When John Brown came to, he was lying on "a miserable shakedown, covered with some bedding," in the office of the paymaster of the armory.

His head ached painfully, and, indeed, could he have seen himself he would have been shocked at his appearance. His hair was clotted and tangled, his face, hands and clothing were powder-stained and blood-smeared. Beside him, in the same condition, lay his faithful lieutenant, A. D. Stevens.

His eyes still shut, he wondered. Where was he? Who was he? A strange sense of unreality pervaded his whole being, as slowly the events of the past two days returned to him and gradually restored his identity. He heard voices dimly, as through a wall, and these voices now and then spoke his name. He half opened his eyes, and closed them again, but not before he had glimpsed dimly, as through a compact veil, several human shapes hovering as in a dream. His thoughts went on returning to him like scattered pigeons returning to their nest.

He felt strange. He was John Brown, and not John Brown. It was as if something imponderable had gone from him and left him light-headed, and, now, new different thoughts were crowding in his brain, thoughts of a strange, incredible clarity, of an almost winged exultance. It was as if God had sent a new light upon the earth, and, he, John Brown, soared in this light, and was intoxicated with its purity. Moments passed in sweet forgetfulness . . . moments of eternity. In his physical lassitude,

John Brown felt curious infusions of strength, reassurances of the truth of his cause, and of God being with him.

Once more his eyes opened, and, in spite of the physical pain the slightest movement gave him, he felt an increasing serenity as if something had been lifted from him; the human figures in the room assumed definite shapes as he caught the sound of voices and now and then clear fragments of utterance. There was not the slightest vestige of fear in him. It was as if he were aware that his effort had not been lost, that what was yet to come would justify him as the conscious instrument of God's will.

His eyes fully open now, he faced the men in the room cheerfully and with a flashing alertness in his eyes which must have astonished them. And calm, clear, fearless words hovered about his lips.

For audience, he had men chosen for him, as it were by the foreseeing fates; for nearly all who were there were destined to play great rôles in the heroic drama, of which the scenes with John Brown as the central figure were but a fitting prologue. And Robert E. Lee, J. E. B. Stuart, Senator J. M. Mason, Governor Wise, Congressman Vallandigham, Andrew Hunter and Congressman Charles James Faulkner were among its *dramatis personæ*.

With his customary courtesy, that nature's nobleman, Colonel Lee, began by offering to clear the room of all visitors who annoyed or pained the two wounded men.

"No!" came the prompt response from John Brown. It was the last thing he wanted. "I am glad to make myself and my motives clearly understood!"

And all the answers which followed were so obviously charged with the man's integrity and spiritual ardor that honest men differing from him in opinion were forced to acknowledge these virtues and attendant courage. Not once did he hesitate or falter, and not even the reputed utterances of Joan of Arc before her inquisitors excelled the answers flung by John Brown.

Quite early a passage of words had occurred. Some one had called John Brown by an opprobrious name, to which he retorted, "If you have your opinions about me, I have my opinions about you."

"Mr. Brown," said Governor Wise, "the silver of your hair is reddened by the blood of crime, and it is meet that you should eschew these hard allusions and think upon eternity. . . ."

"Governor," came in clear firm tones from John Brown, "I have from all appearances, not more than fifteen or twenty years the start of you in the journey to that eternity of which you kindly warn me, and whether my tenure here shall be fifteen months, or fifteen days, or fifteen hours, I am equally prepared to go. There is an eternity behind and eternity before, and the little speck in the center, however long, is but comparatively a minute. The difference between your tenure and mine is trifling and I want to therefore tell you to be prepared; I am prepared. You all have a heavy responsibility, and it behooves you to prepare more than it does me."

After a few such passages, the governor formed a flattering opinion of John Brown, who became in his eyes, "the gamest man he ever saw," albeit he also saw in him "a fanatic, vain, garrulous, but firm, truthful, intelligent." Above all, he considered him a "bundle of the best nerves" he ever saw in a man of his condition and in attendant circumstances.

Who furnished the money for the expedition, Mr. Mason bluntly asked John Brown. The wounded man replied that he furnished most of it himself, and that he was not willing to implicate others. He admitted his folly in allowing himself to be captured. He could have easily saved himself if he had exercised better judgment and not yielded to his feelings.

Why did he tarry in getting away? The answer was simple. He had some thirty-odd prisoners, whose wives were in tears for their safety, and he felt for them. He wanted to allay the fears of those who believed he came here to burn and to kill. He had allowed the train to recross the bridge. That should have assured every one that he did this to spare the feelings of the passengers and their families and to allay the apprehensions of the natives that they had in their midst a band of marauders without any regard for life and property, nor any feelings for humanity.

But, averred Mason, some people were killed while passing in the streets quietly. John Brown promptly denied any knowledge of this. Indeed, he asserted, the prisoners themselves were witness to every precaution having been taken to prevent it. Why, his men even allowed themselves to be repeatedly fired at without returning fire.

Mr. Mason returned to his first line of questioning. "If you would tell us who sent you here—who provided the means—that would be information of some value." Undoubtedly it would.

But John Brown was not the man to give away his friends. "I will answer fully and faithfully about what concerns myself—I will answer anything I can with honor, but not about others."

Mr. Vallandigham, member of Congress from Ohio, entering at this moment, flung the question:

"Mr. Brown, who sent you here?"

And Mr. Vallandigham got his answer:

"No man sent me here; it was my own prompting and that of my Maker, or that of the devil, whichever you please to ascribe it to. I acknowledge no man in human form."

His object in coming? "To free the slaves, and only that."

What in the world did he suppose he could do with such a handful of men? He didn't want to discuss that question.

"You could not do anything." This from a young man brought forth the retort:

"Perhaps your ideas and mine on military matters differ materially."

"Do you consider this a religious movement?"

"It is, in my opinion," answered Brown, "the greatest service a man can render God."

"Do you consider yourself an instrument in the hands of Providence?"

"I do."

"Upon what principle do you justify your acts?"

"Upon the golden rule. I pity the poor in bondage that have none to help them; that is why I am here; not to gratify any personal animosity, revenge or vindictive spirit. It is my sympathy with the oppressed and wronged, that are as good as you and as precious in the sight of God."

"Certainly. But why take the slaves against their will?"

"I never did."

"You did in one instance as least."

Stevens here intervened in firm clear voice: "You are right. In one case, I know the negro wanted to go back."

Did John Brown have anything more to say for the benefit of the people? The question came from a reporter of the *New York Herald*.

"I have nothing to say," was the answer, "only that I claim to be here carrying out a measure I believe perfectly justifiable, and not to act the part of an incendiary or a ruffian but to aid those suffering great wrong. I wish to say, furthermore, that you had better—all you people of the South—prepare yourselves for a settlement of that question that must come up for settlement sooner than you are prepared for it. The sooner you are prepared the better. You may dispose of me easily; I am nearly disposed of now; but this question is to be settled—this negro question I mean—the end of that is not yet."

"Lynch them! Lynch them!" cried the multitude a few days later as John Brown and his surviving companions were put on the train bound for Charlestown.

"It would be cowardly to do so!" the governor pacified them.

And not expedient, he might have added. The case had attracted enough attention to make an issue. They must show the North that Virginia could take care of her own affairs and knew how to punish traitors according to their deserts. A quick trial was as good as a lynching and had the merit of being deliberate and legal. The man was a traitor and deserved hanging. There was no reason for delay. Here was no reluctant Pilate washing his hands of the affair, but a Herod eager to present the hirsute head of the prophet to his beloved South, that she might dance with the gory relic for the edification of her citizens and to the mortification of the North. How was he to know that barely two years would elapse before he should call up his fellow citizens to emulate John Brown's treachery and to seize Harper's Ferry before the Federal troops could take possession?

It was on October twenty-sixth, exactly a week after his capture, that John Brown, in the Court-House at Charlestown, before Judge Richard Parker, was on trial for his life.

He looked as proud as ever, drawn to his full six feet of slender wiry manhood, and there was challenge in his bearing, though his eyes were still swollen and the bruises from his last fight were in evidence. Stevens, terribly wounded and hardly able to stand up, and Coppoc and the other survivors, were also here, but as each chose to fight separately, the stage, for the time being, belonged to John Brown.

Judge Parker was a just man, according to legal rights. The court was hostile, there was no pity in any eye in all that court-room. The eight examining magistrates having decided that the prisoners were guilty, the trial proceeded. The court, with a show of fairness, assigned to them legal counsel, Messrs. Faulkner and Botts, whom later John Brown was to dispense with. But John Brown would have no sham justice without the world being aware that it was sham. His mind, clear and alert, alive on springs of challenge, he addressed himself to the court in tones firm and defiant, cognizant that the world was listening.

"Virginians," he began, "I did not ask for quarter at the time I was taken. I did not ask to have my life spared. The Governor of the State of Virginia tendered me his assurance that I should have a fair trial, but under no circumstances whatever will I be able to have a fair trial. If you seek my blood, you can have it at any moment, without the mockery of a trial."

He had no real defense, his memory was poor, his health bad. There were mitigating circumstances, he said, which could be urged in the prisoners' favor.

"But if we are to be forced with a mere form—a trial for execution—you might spare yourself that trouble. I am ready for my fate. I do not ask a trial. I beg for no mockery of a trial—no insult—nothing but that which conscience gives, or cowardice would drive you to practise. I have now little further to ask, other than that I may not be foolishly insulted only as cowardly barbarians insult those who fall into their power."

But his fight for delay, his fight for the arrival of his own counsel from the North, proved unavailing. He did or did not know that no counsel could avail him; in the meanwhile, while contesting every inch of ground, his every word was heard east and west, north and south, and fell like a seed in fertile ground to germinate there.

As his trial proceeded, he gained heart. Serene in his chains, in his cell, an illumination came revealing that when he shall have passed the threshold of life and death he will have left behind not alone his rotting corpse, but a deathless spirit for animating the hearts of men for battle and for victory. He was, at last, "fully persuaded that I am worth inconceivably more to *hang* than for any other purpose." The secret of life and the meaning of sacrifice thus revealed to him, he awaited the end with a calm joy which mystified some of his foes, won the admiration of others, and perhaps maddened those whose purposes would have been better served if he were a ruffian instead of a martyred hero. His one and only fear was that the plea of insanity which some of his friends had put forward should succeed and his words and acts declared fit to have come from bedlam. No, it must not succeed. He, John Brown, was sound of mind and body, and he pleaded the cause of God, and of man made in God's image, a likeness distorted and betrayed.

On November second, in the Charlestown court-room, the inevitable sentence was about to be passed on John Brown. The world looked on. John Brown *knew* that it was looking on. He also knew that his body would shortly pass away, but that his words uttered in the spirit of his Teacher, could not and should not pass away. The usual question was asked: Had he anything to say why sentence should not be pronounced upon him? He drew himself up to his full height, his eagle blue-gray eyes flashed fire, he spoke in tones as clear as a bell. John Brown was looking beyond the court-room. He was addressing the world.

His one purpose had been to free slaves. . . . He had freed slaves in Missouri without the snapping of a gun on either side, and he had intended doing this on a large scale. He never did intend to murder, or to commit treason, or destroy property, or to excite or incite slaves to rebellion, or to make insurrection.

There was another reason, he said, why it was unjust that he should suffer such a penalty.

"Had I interfered in the manner which I admit . . . had I so interfered in behalf of the rich, the intelligent, the so-called great, or in behalf of any of their friends, whether father, mother, brother, sister, wife or children, or any of that class, and suffered and sacrificed what I have in this interference, it would have been all right. Every man in this court would have deemed it an act worthy of reward rather than punishment.

"This court acknowledges, too, as I suppose, the validity of the law of God. I see a book kissed, which I suppose to be the Bible, or at least the New Testament, which teaches me that all things whatsoever I would that men should do to me, I should do even so to them. It teaches me, further, to remember them that are in bonds as bound with them. I endeavored to act up to that instruction. I say I am yet too young to understand that God is any respecter of persons. I believe that to have interfered as I have done, in behalf of His despised poor, I did no wrong but right. Now, if it is deemed necessary that I should forfeit my life for the furtherance of the ends of justice, and mingle my blood further with the blood of my children and with the blood of millions in this slave country whose rights are disregarded by wicked, cruel and unjust enactments, I say, let it be done. . . ."

The date of his execution having been fixed for December second, he used the interval to speak to his wife and children and friends, and in speaking to them he was speaking to the world. The world listened, and was stirred. Not a single word was lost. But death alone would ignite them, his words, like so many matches ready to start a conflagration.

On December second, as John Brown was leaving his cell for the last time, he handed a written passage to a friendly bystander. It was his last message; should it not be called his last will and testament?

"I John Brown am now quite *certain* that the crimes of this *guilty* land: will never be purged away; but with Blood. I had *as* I now think: vainly flattered myself that without *very much* bloodshed it might be done."

Soldiers, soldiers, soldiers to every side of him, as the wagon drawn by two white horses, with John Brown sitting within on his own coffin, drew near the gibbet upon which he was to swing into eternity. "This is a beautiful country," said he, "I never had the pleasure of seeing it before." There was not a quaver in his voice, his body sat firm on the casket in which his dead bones would shortly lie. "Stonewall" Jackson stood near the gibbet. A believer in God, he looked upon the calm man and "sent up a fervent petition to Heaven" to save John Brown's soul from perdition. And as John Brown was hanging "between heaven and earth" Colonel Preston pronounced: "So perish all such enemies of Virginia! all such enemies of the Union! all such foes of the human race!"

But neither "Stonewall" Jackson nor Colonel Preston yet knew that at the moment the sheriff smote hard with his hatchet, and John Brown's body swung into space, his soul was released, and was, according to its appointed destiny, already "marching on."

GIUSEPPE GARIBALDI—DEMIGOD

GIUSEPPE GARIBALDI. Was there ever a man like him? A heart more brave, more tender? More heroic after the fashion of heroes of legend? To so great a degree fire and pity blended? The name alone suggests the rattle and resonance of drums, and the blast of trumpets, and, indeed, its deep-sounding beauty struck deep into the hearts of men, consuming fear, inspiring leonine virtues. The nineteenth century knew no figure which was more romantic, more picturesque. He was the particular, the brightest star in the campaign of Italian liberation, and to this day every generous heart responds to the name as to some divinity, which was as human as it was divine. And demigods are always loved more than either gods or men.

Born in 1807 at Nice, the son of a sailor whose father was also a sailor, there was wandering in his blood, and he began his life of adventure early. He had a deep affection for both parents, simple honest folk, who gave their son an education according to their means. To his mother, a beneficent, charitable woman, he owed his love of his country, and although far from superstitious, he was never to pass through a storm at sea or a battle on land without feeling conscious of her presence.

His tenderness and his bravery showed themselves even in childhood. There was that slight episode which was to make a deep impression on his memory. He had caught a grasshopper, taken it into the house, and, in handling it, had broken its leg. As he thought of the injury he had done the insect, he was so overcome with grief that he retired to his room and wept bitterly for hours. While he was still a little boy he saw a poor woman who was washing clothes in a deep ditch fall into the water. Without hesitation or thought of danger to himself, he jumped in after her and saved her life. This gave him great joy, a mere foretaste to the joys of danger and well-doing he was many times to experience later.

His education was desultory. He loved to read Roman and Italian history; and he studied his native tongue with a fervor worthy of one who regarded it as the "most beautiful of languages." This was in days when Italy was not Italy, but a series of provinces ruled by alien powers. School bored him; his generous nature early comprehended the evils of a system which encouraged selfishness and mercenariness by offering no other reward but that of money. Whereupon, weary of it all, he proposed to some of his companions that they escape with him and seek their fortune. They fell in readily with the proposal and, taking possession of a boat, and providing themselves with food and fishing tackle, they sailed for the Levant. They were near Monaco when they were overtaken by a "corsair," commanded by none other than young Giuseppe's father, who, capturing the young crew, conveyed them, much to their disgust, to their homes.

Imagine, then, his delight at fifteen when for the first time he stepped, a full-fledged sailor, aboard ship. Everything enchanted him here: the graceful lines of the craft, the tall slender masts, the bust of Our Lady adorning the bow, the rhythmic movements of the young sailors, fine specimens of the intrepid Ligurians! Above all, he loved the songs they sang in their melodious voices. Did they sing of love—he was moved to rapture. Did they sing of Italy—his ardent heart was stirred to ecstasy. For there was no Italy, there was no fatherland in the sense that happy men with a country use the word. Yet they sang of that fabulous country which existed solely in their hearts. How came it there? Vague dreams came to Giuseppe as he listened to these songs; as time passed they assumed more definite shapes. Italy, held by despots, must be redeemed; Italians, to be free men, must fight.

From cabin-boy at fifteen to sea-captain on his father's ship at twenty-five, ten years pregnant with adventure and experience, made a fine man of Giuseppe. Sailing the high seas in those days was a different thing from what it is to-day. Cruising upon the Levant was arduous and beset with many real dangers. The Greeks were waging a fierce war for independence against the Turks; pirates lay in wait in every bay and attacked vessels; hand to hand fights took place with axes and long knives. It was the Mediterranean which Byron did not exaggerate in his verse, and it taught Giuseppe what it had taught Byron: that it was better to die a free man than to live a slave. More than once he was taken prisoner by pirates, and managed to regain his freedom. Such experiences strengthened and hardened him, prepared him for the tasks to come, to face danger with a fearless heart, if need be, tired and sleepless and hungry.

On his second voyage he visited Rome; the sight of the old city, once the capital of the world, now of a sect, moved him to dream of a future Rome, Rome the center and capital of a redeemed Italy, once more a proud city holding up her head among the great capitals of the world. And he ardently prayed to the Almighty to be allowed to see Rome once more, and to see in it the Rome of his dreams.

While Garibaldi was still in his early twenties, the spirit of the French Revolution of 1830-32, traveling westward and southward, seized one young patriot, Ciro Menotti, who stirred central Italy to revolt. The movement proved abortive, Menotti was hanged by the Austrians. Soon thereafter, while in harbor on the Black Sea, Garibaldi heard that the Carbonari movement in Piedmont had come to an end with the summary treatment of hundreds of young patriots, and that a young Genoese student, Mazzini by name, had organized a new conspiracy, under the name of "Young Italy." Garibaldi needed no urging to join it and expressed himself more elated than Columbus could have been on discovering America. The vision of the Rome he saw in his dream rose before him, and he knew where to dedicate his strength, effort and will. From that moment he gave his entire devotion to making his dream come true.

He had been in Italy but a few days helping the Mazzini conspiracy when his activities were discovered, and he was forced to flee Genoa in a ship, disguised as a peasant; for he had seen his name for the first time in a newspaper, and it was in *a sentence of death!* This was in 1834; he was twenty-seven then.

After that he was absent for fourteen years from Italy. The last twelve of these years he spent in South America; they were years of preparation for the redemption of his country. During these years he served as a guerrilla leader for the republics of Rio Grande do Sul and Uruguay.

No ordinary man could have survived the innumerable adventures and trials he experienced here. Even torture fell to his lot. On one occasion after galloping on a horse through half the night, and covering fifty-four miles, he was captured by horsemen with drawn sabers when but within half a mile of his destination. His hands tied behind him, he was placed on a miserable horse, and had his feet bound under him. He was helpless against the mosquitoes which assailed him. In this condition he was taken back to Gualeguay, where even more cruel treatment awaited him. The commandant of Gualeguay beat him brutally with a club because he would not divulge how he had managed to escape, and as this failed to extract the information, the captor put a rope over a beam in the prison, and hung Garibaldi up in the air by his hands, bound together as they were. For two hours he remained suspended in this manner. He felt himself to be in a high fever, and though he was often allowed water he was unable to quench his raging thirst. The suffering he endured after being unbound was terrible, but he did not complain. He should have lost his life but for a lady, Señora Aleman, "generous angel of goodness," who, spurning all fear, came to his assistance.

His marriage not to this lady, but to another, came about in a curious way. It was in 1839—he was thirty-two years old then—when, following a shipwreck, he was cast ashore in the Brazilian province of Santa Catharina. Here an insurrection against the empire was in progress, so Garibaldi and his friends received a warm welcome, which they well repaid by assisting in the capture of Laguna. He was appointed to the command of the sloop *Itaparica,* one of the captured imperial war-ships. He was aboard the ship thinking of the comrades he had lost, and felt very desolate. And for the first time in life his thoughts turned to marriage. Was it desirable for him, with his life devoted to one cause, to burden himself with wife and children? Even as he paced the deck of the *Itaparica,* reflecting, he decided that he would seek for some lady who possessed the character he desired. One day, he chanced to cast a casual glance through a spy-glass at a house on the shore, and observed a girl standing alone. Her appearance struck him as having something extraordinary. So powerful was the impression made upon him at the moment that, without any plausible reason, he ordered a boat to be lowered and he was soon rowed ashore. By soliciting the aid of an acquaintance he secured an invitation to take coffee with the young lady's family; to his delight, the first person to enter the room was the girl herself, Anita Riberas, then eighteen years old.

They had but to look into each other's eyes to feel the irresistible longing for each other. She knew who he was. He understood no Portuguese, so he addressed her in Italian in words which could not be simpler: "You should be mine." She understood him. Pledged by her father to another against her wishes, she fled a few days later with Garibaldi, who bore her away in his ship.

There is no record of a union between man and woman more ideal. For years Anita rode at Garibaldi's side in the South American plains and fought in the same battles in the war of liberation. Her bravery equaled his. In one battle she was taken captive by the royal troops, and, believing her husband to be dead on the battle-field, she obtained leave to seek out his corpse that she might bury it. She profited by the drunkenness of her captors to make her escape, and, mounted on a fiery horse, galloped in the stormy night, over broken rocky ground, by the flashes of lightning. It was hostile country, but all made way before the extraordinary vision and fled in alarm. Coming to a broad mountain stream, which ran dangerously, swollen as it was by rains, she forced her horse into the fierce torrent and, seizing fast hold of the tail, she urged the beast on until they safely reached the other side five hundred paces distant. Eventually, after a separation of eight days, she reached her husband. A glass of coffee was the only nourishment taken by the lonely traveler in four days. It was in such circumstances beset with constant danger that Anita bore her first son, whom Garibaldi named Menotti, after the martyred Italian patriot. Between battles Anita carried the poor infant tied to her by a handkerchief round her neck over rough steep mountain-ways and across torrential streams.

In 1842, on the eve of giving up his strenuous life, Garibaldi received an invitation from the government of Uruguay to form an Italian legion in the war against the tyrant Rosas, of the Argentine Republic. He accepted. This legion, which saved Montevideo during the sieges of 1843 and 1846, gave rise to the red shirt which Garibaldi's soldiers were to make famous in Europe. It happened by mere accident. A Montevideo house had a big stock of red woolen shirts which, owing to the blockade of Buenos Aires, it was unable to dispose of, and it offered them at a low price to the government for the equipment of the legion. Although he commanded the legion, Garibaldi took only the rations of a common soldier, and as candles were not included in the rations, he sat evenings in the dark. This was reported to the government, which presented him with a small amount of money, but even half of this he gave to a poor widow.

After two relatively uneventful years in Montevideo, where he was greatly beloved by all, Garibaldi, who kept in touch with events in Europe, suddenly decided that the time had arrived for him to return. His long season of preparation was ended. He was ready for the great fray which was to make his name known all over Europe.

He left Montevideo with eighty-five of his followers. They knew nothing of some of the happenings at home, of the revolution in Milan and Venice, and of King Carlo Alberto having taken the field. But on reaching Gibraltar, they beheld for the first time, hoisted to the top of a Sardinian ship, a flag new to them—the Italian tricolor. They ultimately arrived within sight of Nice, Garibaldi's native city.

Before the law Garibaldi was still "a brigand of the first category," the sentence on his head having never been revoked. Nevertheless, he and his friends proceeded at once to the field of battle in Lombardy to offer Carlo Alberto the services of a legion, "not unused to war." The offer was received with no great ardor; actually some weeks passed before the provisional government of Milan gave him the command of a few thousand volunteers, but it was the end of the campaign. Garibaldi saw the folly of the temporary peace, but as he could do nothing he led his band into Switzerland and bade them wait until a more appropriate day which could not be so far distant.

Early in the following year matters came to a head. The conditions in the Papal States were terrible; there was a revolution; a republic had been declared, with Mazzini, Saffi and Armellini as the governing triumvirate. And Garibaldi was given his chance. It was a poor chance, to be sure, with incompetent Roselli as commander-in-chief; for Garibaldi was a man to strike like lightning, and Roselli was not the man to help a mere underling pursue a gained advantage.

The Roman Republic was fighting for its life. King Bomba, as Ferdinand II was significantly known, was advancing from the south, and Marshal Oudinot, at the behest of Napoleon III, was marching on Rome, at the head of a French army. The pope, to save his own temporal power, was promulgating all sorts of repressive measures against all who dared to think for themselves. The Inquisition was in full swing. The dungeons, particularly those of Naples, were full of thinkers and honest men chained to walls.

May of that year saw fierce fighting in Rome. Garibaldi, defending the approach near the Corsini Terrace, did valiantly against the French troops under Marshal Oudinot. His own troops consisted chiefly of poorly armed students, artists and volunteers, led for the most part by the veterans from South America, the "Tigers of Montevideo," and so bravely they fought that they put the regular French troops to flight. Seated on his white horse, a handsome figure with a beautiful face and luxurious gold-brown hair, Garibaldi led the bravest and was always where the bullets flew thickest. Despite a wound in his side, he wished to pursue his advantage, but was deterred by the mistaken political maneuvers of Mazzini and the military incompetence of Roselli, his chief. His wounds kept him to his bed, from whence he continued to direct operations, and on hearing that Villa Corsini had been retaken by the enemy, he urged the triumvirate to appoint him dictator. That was the one thing the triumvirate feared to do. Once more on his horse, he continued his intrepid fight, but in vain. After a few weeks of stubborn resistance, the French troops entered Rome, while Garibaldi, escaping with his followers, was pursued by detachments of the French, Austrian and Neapolitan armies.

He beat a masterly retreat to San Marino, using tactics he had learned in South America. Again and again he threw off the pursuing enemy on a false scent. Even in the most dire straits he maintained the strictest discipline founded on honor. Tender-hearted, opposed on principle to the death penalty, he yet meted out death with startling promptness for any act which savored of meanness. Thievery and rapine were thus punished, and once he had a soldier shot for stealing a chicken.

The retreat took place in the heat of the Italian summer. Prior to its start, Garibaldi had called his followers together in the square of the Vatican, and told them that he intended to continue the fight against the foreigner in his own fashion. He held out no reward. Let those follow him who would. "I can not offer you honors or pay; I offer you hunger, thirst, forced marches, battles, death!" Undeterred by the prospect, between three and four thousand men responded to the call. But only two thousand reached San Marino, many having deserted by the way.

Anita rode by Garibaldi's side, though she was about to have another child. At San Marino, after many hardships endured, the little army was able to rest. Though the hospitable little republic, situated on the high islanded rock, was completely surrounded by the enemy, Garibaldi was quite safe from further pursuit. He succeeded in obtaining immunity for his followers who had laid down their arms; then, in the night, escaped with Anita and some of his most intimate and bravest companions. A few were captured and suffered summary treatment. Anita succumbed to privation, and, her strength given out, Garibaldi carried her to a peasant's hut, where she breathed her last. Grief-stricken as he was, he had to flee at once to escape the ubiquitous Austrians everywhere on the lookout for him. The whole route was overrun with the enemy; yet in his flight to the Mediterranean, he managed to evade their gauntlet, and at last reached Piedmontese territory where, after a short respite, he once more left Europe and ultimately reached the United States.

For a while he worked in a candle factory in New York. His duties consisted in bringing the barrels of tallow to the vats in which the tallow was cooked. He suffered here much from rheumatism, a result of his early privations. Later he shipped as a sailor, and afterward obtained command of a vessel, cruising in the East, in the South Atlantic, and finally, in 1854, landing in Newcastle to obtain a cargo of coal for Genoa. At Newcastle, a committee of English coal-miners boarded his vessel and presented him with a sword in token of his services for liberation. "This sword," said their spokesman, "has been purchased with the pennies of hundreds of workingmen, given, not only willingly, but enthusiastically, and each penny represents a heart that beats for the cause of freedom in Europe."

The same year Garibaldi returned to Italy. His brother

having died, he used the inheritance in purchasing a part of the rocky little island of Caprera which until his death was to remain his home.

The year 1860, the greatest year of Garibaldi's life, placed his name with those of the great adventuring heroes of the world. But, first, an episode of another nature should be recorded.

It happened in 1859. Garibaldi, riding with a staff-officer at the head of his troops, met a carriage which bore the beautiful young Countess of Raimondi carrying a letter to him, to which a reply was expected. Smitten with the girl's beauty, Garibaldi, to the great delight of the marquis, her father, made an offer of marriage and was accepted. She had already given her favor to a young man, and apparently still retained her affection for him. At all events, on the nuptial night, Garibaldi, finding her cold toward him, promptly left her with the words that she need not fear him, that he did not want a woman who could not give him her love. This episode had its tragic consequences, which need not be detailed here.

In 1859 Cavour was guiding the destinies of Italy with an astute hand. The situation in southern Italy and in Sicily was auspicious for his plans. The island, in particular, was fermenting with revolt, and secret agents were arousing the inhabitants to fury against the despots. The devout patriot, Rosalino Pilo, saw that Sicily was ripe for a revolution; he also saw that in the existing circumstances the revolution would be rapidly crushed. What, after all, could the poorly armed Sicilians do against the forty thousand regular Neapolitan troops equipped with artillery? He was firmly assured that only one man could handle the situation successfully, and that man Garibaldi. Unable to convince the general of the feasibility of the scheme, he embarked with a companion on a foolhardy expedition for the island and entered into the work of preparation, sure that eventually Garibaldi would come. So sure was he of this that he managed to keep the spirit of revolt alive by going about the island announcing that Garibaldi was coming. Cavour quietly encouraged all this. He saw the importance of Garibaldi in the scheme of things, but neither he nor Victor Emmanuel could give official sanction to a scheme which was tantamount to a declaration of war on a friendly power. Garibaldi at this moment, smarting under the cession to France of his birthplace, Nice, and considering this a personal affront, hated Cavour. Cavour, however, valued Garibaldi for what he was, "one of the greatest forces of which Italy can avail herself," and secretly encouraged any campaign which Garibaldi might be ready to take on his own initiative and which would absolve the government from all responsibility. It will be seen that Cavour was a true countryman of Machiavelli.

Pilo's letters at last overcame Garibaldi's hesitation and decided him to embark on the expedition which must have seemed sheer folly to all who followed it in its early days. But folly often wins where wisdom bids us hesitate. And our Don Quixote happened to be a good general, to boot. History can show no greater achievement than his conquest of Sicily and Naples. It was a feat he accomplished with a little over a thousand men, "The One Thousand," as men shall remember them as long as human memory lasts.

Not only was the raiding party outnumbered forty to one, but, poorly armed as it was, it had to face an enemy well fortified and entrenched and equipped with artillery. Those from whom he had a right to expect assistance acted disgracefully and put all sorts of obstacles in his way. There were several thousand effective rifles in Milan which the people contributed to help Garibaldi. Yet Marchese Massimo d'Azeglio, the Governor of Milan, who had himself fought against Austria, found it on his conscience impossible to deliver the needed rifles, although Cavour desired it done. Elsewhere he was meted out treatment which was little short of actual hostility. At last, toward the end of April, 1860, a consignment of weapons arrived labeled as books. They were old, rusty, obsolete. "Old iron!" was Garibaldi's exclamation when he saw them. Yet what marvels he lived to accomplish with these muskets, whose range was less than half of those of the enemy! Garibaldi's men, it must be said, fought mainly with the bayonet.

There was no hesitation once the decision was made. Garibaldi went on like a demon with his preparations. On the night of May fifth the Thousand embarked at Genoa on the two merchant vessels, the *Piedmonte* and *Lombardo,* and set sail. To keep up appearances, Cavour, immediately after the departure of the vessels, issued orders to Admiral Persano to arrest the expedition if the steamers entered any Sardinian port, but to let it pass if they were encountered on the high seas; whereupon Persano asked for instructions as to what to do in the event of storms forcing Garibaldi into port. The answer was Machiavellian: it was "the Ministry's" decision that Garibaldi should be arrested. The admiral was not one to misinterpret its meaning; he rightly understood that Cavour was not of the same mind as "the Ministry." As the weather was ideal for the enterprise the occasion did not arise, and within six days the two ships arrived at Marsala, simultaneously with two Neapolitan war-ships. It might have gone badly with the raiders but for a miraculous stroke of good fortune. On the previous day, as if by arrangement, two British warships took up positions in the harbor. Was it pure accident that they were there? Lord John Russell, in the House of Commons, strenuously denied the charge that they had been deliberately sent to cover the landing. Deliberately or not, they effectually did cover the landing of Garibaldi's men; every Redshirt was out of harm's way before those in command of the enemy war-ships had time to recover their wits.

Garibaldi's first objective was the mountain city, Salemi, which had already taken up arms against the Bourbon king. Here he issued a decree assuming the dictatorship of Sicily in the name of Victor Emmanuel. A passionate Republican, he did not hesitate to put aside his political opinions for the sake of United Italy.

All along the way he was being joined by Sicilian bands, consisting chiefly of peasants, dressed in goatskins and armed with antiquated rusty weapons. Everywhere he was greeted with rapture. They believed him to be a Messiah. In one place a Franciscan friar threw himself on his knees, and begged to be allowed to follow him. The volunteers regarded the friar suspiciously, but their chief accepted Fra Pantoleo, who helped the expedition valiantly.

The host, like a medieval pageant, marched on, and met the enemy commanding the heights at Pianto dei Romani, under General Landi: three thousand men and four pieces of artillery. The royal troops, confident, came down half-way to meet the Redshirts, but were driven up the mountain again, inch by inch, until they were back on the uppermost heights. Garibaldi's right-hand man, Bixio, brave as any man, hard pressed, thought retreat inevitable, only to meet his chief's retort, "Here we die!" And, against immense odds, they won their first victory. The enemy fled in disorder to Calatafimi.

There were over thirty thousand royal troops in the Island, eighteen thousand of whom held Palermo, toward which Garibaldi directed his volunteers. Another hundred and twenty thousand or more Neapolitan troops were on the peninsula. But the Neapolitans felt confident. There would be no need of reinforcements. The island troops could surely handle the miserable rabble who seemed to them to be walking straight into a trap. Garibaldi's position was precarious, but by adroit tactics he threw the enemy off on a false scent, while he moved his men by night along difficult, precipitous ways, in a raging storm. At the same time he ordered part of his force to make a retrograde movement and to leave evidence everywhere of the whole Garibaldian army being in disorderly retreat. So well he succeeded with this ruse that the Neapolitan general, Colonna, much elated, sent the news to Naples that Garibaldi had been in full flight before him for four days, and this intelligence was soon flashed on the world. What a surprised gentleman he must have been when he heard that on the fifth day Garibaldi had entered that stronghold of strongholds, Palermo itself!

Many fat volumes have been written on the military and political aspects of the campaign of the Thousand and on the heroic conduct of Garibaldi through the arduous days of war and revolution which went to the welding of a free Italy. It is beyond the scope of this brief study to record the innumerable deeds of one whose whole life was spent in action, whose favorite word has ever been "*Avanti!*"—"Forward!" It is enough to say that after he had conquered Sicily he conquered Naples and for ever destroyed the power of the Bourbons in the south.

And what happened after Naples? There were fears that the Republican Garibaldi, his army swelled by reinforcements, would not yield allegiance to a king, even to a king of Italy; and the royalists awaited the prospective meeting of the two Italian armies with apprehensive hearts. General Fanti, suspicious of all Republican elements, was marching toward Naples, and with him was King Victor Emmanuel, over whom he exerted an influence.

On October 26, 1860, Garibaldi, stationed with a few of his regiments in the broad valley between Cajanello and Vairano, saw the Italian army approaching. Garibaldi and his staff dismounted, stood at a village corner and saw battalion after battalion of royalist troops file past them. They were again mounted when the king and his staff approached them. Garibaldi and his officers were dressed in their red shirts, the worse for many battles. Garibaldi had a handkerchief tied around his head, and wore his customary cape. The royalist officers in their gold-laced uniforms looked at them as at strangers.

Garibaldi cried: "I hail Italy's first king!"

The embarrassing moment was over. Victor Emmanuel rode toward him with extended hand, and said: "How are you, my dear Garibaldi?"

"Well, your Majesty. And yourself?"

"Very well," replied the king.

They rode on side by side, and the two staffs tried to fraternize without any success. Garibaldi asked the king if his volunteers might have the honor of occupying the front line in the battle then imminent, but received the reply, "Your troops are tired, mine are fresh; it is my turn now." This answer has been variously interpreted, but Garibaldi surely did not regard it as friendly, for that evening, meeting an English friend, he said sadly: "They have sent us to the rear."

Garibaldi's troops were eventually mustered out without so much as a vote of thanks.

November seventh was designated as the date for the king's formal entry into Naples. Reports indicated that if the king did not have Garbaldi in his carriage, his welcome would be rather cool. On the evening of the sixth, messengers were sent to persuade Garibaldi to sit with the king. Garibaldi's feelings had been badly hurt by the king that very day, but for the sake of the greater cause he had served he consented. Not a word passed between the king and Garibaldi as on the next day, in the midst of a driving rain, their carriage went through the streets of the city, greeted with wild enthusiasm by the people who did not know the state of affairs.

The following day, Garibaldi quietly boarded a small ship which took him to his craggy island home at Caprera. He had borrowed a little money, and took with him some grain to sow on his land.

On the advice of Cavour, the king offered Garibaldi a dukedom and the Collar of the Annunziata, which confers the rank of cousin to the king, also wealth to support these honors. But he refused everything and returned to Caprera a very poor man.

The death in 1861 of Cavour, left Italy without a competent guiding hand. The surrender of the Papal States to the pope and of Rome to the French aroused the indignation of Garibaldi, who raised the cry, "Rome or Death!" In 1862 he put himself at the head of three thousand volunteers, mostly men who had served him before and, if need be, would serve him again. He had started in Sicily and his march to Catania was one series of popular acclamations. At Catania, Garibaldi took possession of a couple of merchant ships and with about a thousand men sailed away by night for the Calabrian coast. The problem which faced Garibaldi was to reach the Papal frontiers without encountering the armies sent on foot by Victor Emmanuel's government to prevent him. He had no desire to fight his own countrymen. And so, for a while, the volunteers sought concealment in the southern Apennines, among whose wild ridges and dense forests they wandered for three days, hungry and fatigued. Toward the end of August they reached Aspromonte, a position of great height and easy to defend. But Garibaldi made no effort to defend it. He issued orders to his men not to fire, but some young Sicilians, fired upon by government troops, could not resist replying. It was while Garibaldi was walking among his troops enjoining them to obey that a bullet of the foe entered his right foot; he was carried to shelter.

What were Garibaldi's thoughts as he lay in a shepherd's hut that night wounded in the name of the king to whom he had given this land? At his side lay his son Menotti, also wounded by an Italian bullet.

Could anything be more ironic? Little wonder that Colonel Pallavicini, instructed "to crush Garibaldi completely, and only accept from him unconditional surrender," should approach the wounded man bareheaded, and express the regret that he should have made his acquaintance on the most unfortunate day of his own life. "This man is not a soldier, but a saint," said one of the surgeons who attended him during the months of acute suffering before the bullet was extracted.

The government saved its face by the issue of a general amnesty on the occasion of the marriage of the king's second daughter to the king of Portugal; in this way a trial of Garibaldi was avoided. It was generally admitted that Garibaldi had tried to carry out the desire of the whole people. And, indeed, in 1864, the French Government had to make concessions providing for the gradual removal of its garrison from the Papal frontier. Three years later this agreement created another uncomfortable situation; Garibaldi, who scorned diplomacy and always followed a line of action, was again making preparations for marching on Rome, when the government foolishly had him arrested. Then followed his escape and a whole series of truly Garibaldian adventures, culminating in defeat, despair and confinement in a prison-fortress. Napoleon III and Victor

Emmanuel between them won a victory over the old lion who had never acknowledged defeat before. But Garibaldi lived to see Napoleon fly like a dog, and Rome free. The year 1870 was significant for Italy as it was for France. "And to think," exclaimed Victor Emmanuel when he heard the news of the empire's fall, "that this good man was always wanting to give me advice!" What he failed to add was that he was nearly always taking it.

If only kings and politicians listened sometimes to the poets—for Garibaldi was a poet, "a Shelley of action," as George Brandes called him—surely, much might have been saved Italy, and her final liberation need not have waited until 1870. Others besides Plato would not have poets in their Republic. Men of imagination, with their direct clear sight, "ahead of their time," are naturally regarded as dangerous by slow stolid lawmakers who abandon truth to the perspective of posterity. In this sense, the least successful actions of Garibaldi were prophetic, and all he had fought for was realized in his own lifetime.

In England Garibaldi was a prophet from the very start. In 1864 his visit to that country was attended by a demonstration in his honor unexampled in the history of a reserved people. From the Prince of Wales to the chimney-sweep, the country joined to do him honor; never had a foreigner been greeted with such shouts of welcome in London. It was reported that some of the Powers were annoyed. And well they might be.

THE COMPARISON OF BROWN WITH GARIBALDI

JOHN BROWN and Giuseppe Garibaldi were contemporaries not solely in the matter of time; their endeavors as liberators link their names where other likeness is absent; and the peaks of their careers were reached almost simultaneously: the Harper's Ferry Raid occurred in 1859, the raid on Sicily in the following year. Both events, however differing in character, were equally quixotic. All nations produce Don Quixotes, and each Don Quixote bears the characteristics of the race that produced him. By the nature of his tradition, John Brown is the typical Anglo-Saxon Don Quixote, with the added flavor peculiarly American; Garibaldi is as surely the Latin variety of the type, marked by significant differences which distinguish him not only from the American specimen but also, if in a lesser degree, from the Don Quixotes of other Latin nations.

That Garibaldi was a natural master of guerrilla warfare, while Brown was a bungler of his job, is, after all, of little consequence here. Even if Brown were more successful in carrying out his plans as a guerrilla leader the essential differences between him and Garibaldi would still remain. These differences are differences between man and man, and more particularly differences between the man of America and the man of Italy. It would be interesting to indicate in a precise way what these are, all the more because they happen to be fundamental. Two conceptions of religion, art and life are involved here, two separate trinities as wide apart as such things can be.

The spiritual fount of the Latin races is Homer; that

of the Anglo-Saxon races, the Bible. The Bible has never touched the southern races in the same way that it has the northern. This truth is strikingly illustrated by the presence of pagan elements in the art and ritual of the Catholicism of southern countries as distinguished from the austere character of the Christianity of northern countries. Two irreconcilable worlds are adumbrated, and between them is an uncrossable gaping chasm; to each the other is wholly damned.

What are the principles which guide these two worlds, the worlds of Garibaldi and John Brown, the one Homeric, the other Christian?

That Garibaldi loathed the Roman Church and its priests (though many priests served valorously in his ranks) and preached a Christian gospel which denied the Church but accepted Jesus as one who came to free the world from slavery does not affect the issue. What does matter is that Garibaldi is a product of the same civilization which produced the pagan spirit still in evidence in the Latin lands.

The Homeric, that is, the pagan world, of which Garibaldi is a fine modern example, is that world which aims at achieving the most perfect human harmony, the complete human being, one who loves and fights and worships and sees virtue in the arts, and in whom, in a sense, everything has perfection as its end and assumes the condition of art. Now, what is a harmony? It is, surely, an agreeable arrangement of parts, the welding often of conflicting parts into a design harmonious to any or all of the senses. Music is a harmony of sounds, life a harmony of existing facts in nature, producing as its supreme design the natural man who accepts all and beats it into a pattern as the craftsman in bronze beats his metal into shapes which charm. The Greek hierarchy of gods, with its symbolical recognition of natural phenomena, was the greatest effort on record to achieve divine and human harmony; and the *Odyssey* is its literary witness. Garibaldi is a kind of modern Odysseus: he achieved in his person and in his life a quality of all-aroundness, akin to a harmony in art. But in one respect he added something conspicuously absent from Homer's creation, a note of infinite tenderness, which to us moderns makes him superior to the Greek hero, who is too cruel for us to swallow whole. "A sort of union of the Zeus and Christ types," as George Brandes, in considering his head, described him; and he was loved for his blend of strength and sweetness, and his chivalry made him the adored of both men and women. "Beyond doubt," says the poet Carducci, "he is worthy to be compared to the best of the ancient Romans, were it not that in him the sense of humanity was more profound and tender than, for many reasons, it could be in them." There is the more complete tribute which George Macaulay Trevelyan, author of *Garibaldi and the Thousand,* pays him:

"The fond simplicity of a child, the sensitive, tender humanity of a woman, the steady valour of a soldier, the good-heartedness and hardihood of a sailor, the imposing majesty of a king like Charlemagne, the brotherliness and universal sympathy of a democrat like Walt Whitman, the spiritual depth and fire of a poet, and an Olympian calm that was personal to himself—all plainly marked in his port and presence, his voice and his eyes—made him, not the greatest, but the unique figure of the age."

Mark the harmony of these several elements rarely found in one man; then let us turn our eyes away to the world across the chasm.

The Biblical, that is, the Christian world, of which John Brown is such a conspicuous example, is that world which aims at achieving the triumph of man over nature, at narrowing his physical horizon, at deepening his spiritual nature. It aims at the rejection of the harmony he has accomplished, since this harmony contains parts unacceptable to the so-called moral man, who desires the strengthening of those parts which he can accept. This man has shut his eyes to the external world, and, having delved deep into himself, and found treasure there, has sought to make the outer world conform to the inner man. In short, he has found it necessary to create One God, the God of the Avenging Conscience. The discovery of Conscience is the Jew's contribution to the world; the Christian came and weighed it down with amendments, sometimes, it is true, contradictory to the tone of the original document. The Gospels are the literary witness to the final rejection of the pagan harmony. In John Brown this Christian conscience found deep lodgment. He was a Jew-like patriarch in relation to his own family, ruling it as the old patriarch ruled his small tribe; toward the world he turned his face like a proselytizing Saint Paul and he saw in this world only a large tribe ruled by One God, the God of the Avenging Conscience. There were no gods, and no nations, and no blacks and no whites, and all men lived amicably like one family, a noble conception, surely, broad in its all-embracingness, but narrow in its acceptance of facts, since it did not allow for the inequalities of nature and the conflicting needs of races and nations living under a variety of conditions and climes.

We arrive at the extraordinary contradiction: John Brown, for all his humanitarian principles derived from the Biblical tradition of the brotherhood of man, was more narrow and less human than Garibaldi, poet, artist in life, and above all, patriot. The Latin races have ever been the patriotic races, and *la patrie* has a significance of which there is no equivalent in Anglo-Saxondom. Brown was not only an Anglo-Saxon, he was also an American, above all, he was a New Englander. He was a nay-sayer, and he had arrived at the ultimate point where nay-saying becomes a positive thing finding expression in action. He was, to use up-to-date vernacular, a man possessed by his repressions, the repressions of his race, and bound to explode in action. Thoreau had said of him that he was "a volcano with an ordinary chimney-flue," an apt description; but Thoreau did not live to see the magnificence of the final eruption. To the end he kept up the traditional character of the fanatical non-conformist, and when he crystallized in those culminating days of his life, charged with drama and prophetic fervor, he spoke simply and austerely, in the language of the Bible. He had in those moments outgrown his provincialism; he was more than New Englander, more than American, more even than Anglo-Saxon; he returned to the fount which nourished him and the Anglo-Saxon race: the Bible. "I am worth now infinitely more to die than to live"—there you have the ultimate recognition of the significance of Golgotha and of the glory of Resurrection. Of romance there is none, of color there is none, the whole thing is enacted in sharp contrasts of light and shade, against a background of austere wavering shadows, until a deepening penumbra descends upon life and absorbs the mystery. Certainly there is drama here, early Christian in mood.

How different the spectacle offered by Garibaldi's romantic figure against the ardent Italian background; consider him, a Zeus-like figure, picturesquely attired, on his white horse, Anita riding at his side, and behind them a moving pageant of animated color, of jovial young Italians lifting their melodious voices and singing songs of love and country which their leader loved so well.

Consider the manner of his carrying off Anita from her father; then the manner of Brown's marriage as related

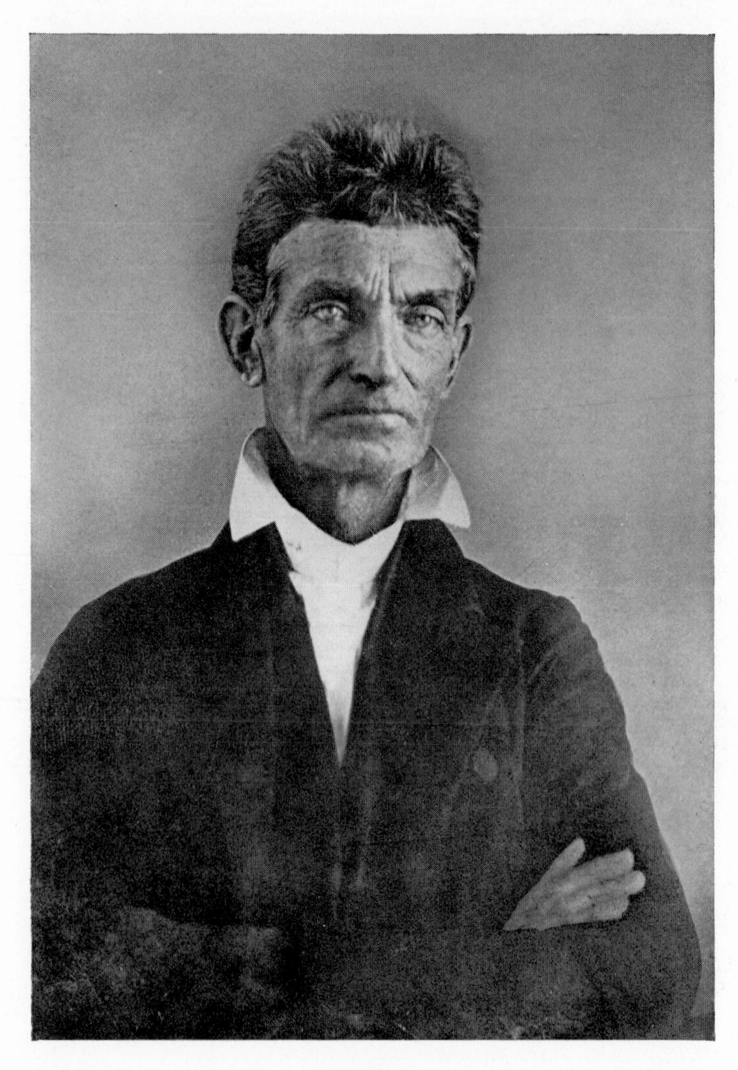

John Brown

Courtesy of Houghton Mifflin Company

GIUSEPPE GARIBALDI

From an engraving in the British Museum based on a photograph
Reproduced from
Garibaldi and the Thousand by George Macaulay Trevelyan
Longmans, Green and Co., London

by himself in his short *Autobiography,* told in the third person:

"At a little past Twenty years led by his own inclination & *prompted* also by his Father, he married a *remarkably plain*; but neat industrious & economical girl; of excellent character; earnest piety; and good practical common sense; about one year younger than himself. This woman by her mild, frank, & *more than all else*; by her very consistent conduct; acquired & ever while she lived maintained a most powerful; & good influence over him. Her plain but kind admonitions generally had the right effect; without arousing his haughty obstinate temper. . . ."

This in an excellent example of his speech and expresses well his homely mood, all simplicity—no dramatics. And how differently Garibaldi talks and writes; all life is poetry to him; you feel in his words the dramatic intonations, the expressive gestures which stamp the Latin. Thus he recalls the night on which he ventured forth on his ship as the leader of the Thousand:

"O night of the fifth of May, lit up with the fire of a thousand lamps with which the Omnipotent has adorned the infinite. Beautiful, tranquil, solemn with that solemnity which swells the hearts of generous men when they go forth to free the slave. Such were the Thousand . . . my young veterans of the war of Italian liberty, and I, proud of their trust in me, felt myself capable of attempting anything. . . . I have felt this same harmony of soul on all nights like those of Quarto, Reggio, of Palermo, of Volturno."

If this be deemed exceptional, the expression of an individual and not of a race, let us turn to Nino Bixio, "the second of the Thousand," almost as brave as Garibaldi himself, yet a Sancho Panza by comparison. It happened on board the *Lombardo* which he commanded. A corporal was impertinent to him, whereupon Bixio threw a plate at the man's head, and summoning every one on deck, addressed them with a fierceness that cowed and captivated his audience. "I command here. I am everything. I am Czar, Sultan, Pope. I am Nino Bixio. I must be obeyed like God. If you dare shrug your shoulders or think of mutinying, I will come in my uniform, sabre in hand, and cut you to pieces." Every one knew that he meant it, yet to a man they entered into the spirit of the speech and applauded the speaker, who walked away in disgust.

Consider, too, the picture of Garibaldi rushing out of his cabin on the *Piedmonte* with a poem he had just written and asking his men to compose music to it that they might sing it as they charged on the battle-fields of Italy.

Consider, again, Garibaldi, handsome in strength, feature and spirituality, beauty enhanced by picturesque dress, adored by women all over Europe. When he was wounded in the battle of Aspromonte women of three countries, Russia, France and England, vied with one another in sending their greatest surgeons to wait attendance on him. "How beautiful you are!" cried the women of Naples and Sicily when he showed himself, in his red blouse and white cape, magnificent on his horse. Women of title and distinction fought in the ranks under him, proud in their obedience to his orders.

There is a Homeric note about it all, a sense of play such as the ancient peoples knew. A measure of morals there might have been; certainly there is no indication of any preoccupation with them. As for profanity, it was undoubtedly a part of the daily routine, though of this too there is little record.

How differently the pages of John Brown's life and its achievements read. The monumental volume compiled by Mr. Oswald Garrison Villard (which for its painstaking thoroughness has never been surpassed) shows one steady conflict between John Brown and the devil, a very real conflict with a very real person, as John Brown sees him. The idea of sin obsessed him. His *Autobiography* (already mentioned), written for the benefit of a thirteen-year-old boy, gives many indications of this. There was his fear of women, or shall we say the wrong sort of women.

"At eight years old John was left a Motherless boy which loss was complete and permanent for notwithstanding his father again married a sensible, intelligent, and on many accounts a very estimable woman; yet he never *adopted her in feeling*; but continued to pine after his own Mother for years. This operated very unfavorably upon him; as he was both naturally fond of females; & withall, extremely diffident; & deprived him of a suitable connecting link between the different sexes; the want of which might under some circumstances have proved his ruin."

Again, there is this confession:

"I must not neglect to tell you of a verry *bad* & *foolish* habbit to which John was somewhat addicted. I mean *telling lies;* generally to screen himself to blame; or from punishment. He could not well endure to be reproached; & I now think had he been oftener encouraged to *be entirely frank*; he would not have been so often guilty in after life of this fault; nor have been obliged to struggle *so long* with *so mean* a habit *by making frankness a kind of atonement* for some of his faults. . . ."

He carried his religion, the religion of a Puritan, into every walk of life; and where he could he forced his ritual on others. This is to be said for him: he tried to live up to its spirit as well as to the letter. His wife deferred to him, and his children looked to him as to a patriarch, though at times they must have sorely vexed him; for he once said of his younger sons: "After a *thorough and can-*

did investigation they have discovered the Bible to be *all* fiction!" At another time he wrote to them: " . . . God grant you *thorough* conversion from sin, and full purpose of heart to continue steadfast in His ways through the *very short* season of trial you will have to pass. . . ." He observed the New England Sabbath, discouraged visits on that day, and forced his apprentices and journeymen to attend church every Sunday. In his little army no profane language was allowed. He insisted on prayers morning and evening, and on thanks to the Bountiful Giver after every meal. One suspects that his sons did not accept their father with undivided allegiance, if one is to judge by an occasional observation on their part of which there is a record. "I think your father looks like an eagle," remarked a visitor in the presence of some of the members of the Brown family. "Yes," came the dry Yankee retort from Watson Brown, "or some other carnivorous bird." There was more than a grain of truth in this. John Brown, kind man and humanitarian, could insist on hard unrelenting measures where, in his opinion, occasion demanded them. There are his words written to his wife in 1850: "I of course keep encouraging my colored friends to trust in God and keep their powder dry." Again he advocates "making clean work" with one's enemies. He is ruthless like the ancient Israelites where he believes himself to be in the right. Had he lived in Florence in the Renaissance he would have been a Savonarola. He had as many virtues as faults.

No one can deny that he played his final rôle magnificently, and that all his mistakes were wiped out by his last days during which he lived and acted and spoke like one inspired. Though Brown did not know it, and would have denied it had any one told him so, he was, during those days, a master in the art of living. It was as if all his previous life he had been preparing for this, as if all the mistakes of those years had been made to make these last days perfect. A pagan would have admitted this much.

Here is enough to make the difference between Brown and Garibaldi clear. In one respect they were alike, for to each Carlyle's words concerning Cromwell may be applied:

"In the dark perils of war, in the high places in the field, hope shone in him like a pillar of fire, when it had gone out in all the others."

Brown stands for conscience, as Garibaldi stands for fire, but in a measure one partakes of the other in truly great men. There are moments suspended in eternity, when across the chasm of two irreconcilable worlds demigods and men will salute one another in respect of courage and of readiness to meet worthy death. Wise men will reject neither Christ nor Prometheus.

HENRI FRÉDÉRIC AMIEL—"THE FAILURE"

THERE are men in this life, exceedingly rare in their way, who in the ordinary sense can hardly be said to live at all, yet who inwardly, in imagination and in thought, have a life as animated and intense as ever was lived by men of action. Such a man was Henri Frédéric Amiel, whose existence was one long unobtrusive reverie, yet which, by some process secret in its workings, as it were, chemical in nature, has left behind it a record of a sublimated personality palpably alive after bodily death. If Amiel did not live in his own lifetime, he lives in a special sense in his now famous *Journal Intime*, discovered and published after his death. Into this book, as into a sculptor's mold which receives the molten bronze, Amiel poured his life, an imperfect transient thing longing for perfection and eternity. His life was thought, but it was not pure thought; to be thought and nothing else is to be inhuman, just as to be action and nothing else is to be a beast. The texture of his thought was shot through with threads of humanness and frailty, and because of this his dreams live on for us.

The Russian, Turgenev, divided humanity into two types: the Don Quixotes and the Hamlets. Lashed by thought, the Don Quixotes act and go on acting; thought gets into their blood, setting their bodies in motion, and to be in motion is their joy and salvation. The Hamlets are those whose blood is frozen into inaction by thought; they are moved to accept action only as a desperate measure, and as such it is bound to prove agony and damnation. Or else, like Amiel, they are moved to resignation; never has there been such an instance of genuine creative impulse stifled by thought; never has the phrase, "sicklied o'er with the pale cast of thought," gained a meaning so significant.

Here was one who started out in life with every prospect of a brilliant literary career, yet doomed to suffer from what Renan called "the sterility of genius." Born in 1821, of Protestant French *émigrés* in Geneva, when the prosperity of the Swiss city, then ruled by an aristocracy, was at its height, he had every advantage of birth and education to fit him for a life of a man of letters. Even in his youth he showed gifts of a high order, and the distinguished circle in which he moved set high store by his future. He was in those early years, despite a natural tendency to pride, timidity and melancholy, by no means a recluse, and he spent many years in travel. Before he was twenty-seven, he had visited Paris, Berlin, Scandinavia, Holland, Vienna, Munich and Tübingen. Later he was to know London. He seemed to know everything. He was acquainted not only with the thought of the time but knew intimately the social and intellectual life of several European countries; he was in personal contact with some of the leading spirits of his generation. It was reasonable to expect much from a personality possessed of such obvious natural gifts, of a mind peculiarly French in qualities of precision and clarity, a mind sensitive and impressionable to an exceptional degree. After his wanderings he reappeared in Geneva in the fateful year of 1848, when, like other great European cities, it was in the throes of a political upheaval. His friend, Edmond Schérer, who met him in the following year, thus describes him:

"He was twenty-eight, and he had just come from Germany laden with science, but he wore his knowledge lightly, his looks were attractive, his conversation animated, and no affectation spoilt the favorable impression he made on the bystander,—the whole effect, indeed, was of something brilliant and striking. In his young alertness Amiel seemed to be entering upon life as a conqueror; one would have said the future was all his own."

He had, moreover, secured an immediate scholastic success, winning in open competition the Professorship of Æsthetics and French Literature at the academy of Geneva, which post, after four years, he was to exchange for the Professorship of Moral Philosophy. It is true that, in one sense, this success cost him dearly, since it isolated him from the aristocratic circles to which he belonged; they unfavorably regarded the young scholar who dared to accept a post under the Radical régime with which they were in conflict. He took no political sides and sacrificed no convictions, but men who feel politics strongly are little influenced by detached natures, and the ostracism to which he was subjected shut him once and for all from a natural social life and drove him into himself. Moreover, his four years' education in Germany with its immersions in metaphysics filled him with a longing for the absolute, a quest which was to occupy him all his life; this shut against him the gates of reality. His was a French mind crossed by German training, a fatal combination in the case of so impressionable a personality. For it is fatal to try "to write German in French"; that he succeeded did not render it the less fatal, since he achieved his success in fusing two mutually antagonistic natures only by doing violence to his own happiness and well-being. In his *Journal*, he is continually poised between the contradictions of his nature; the mental torment which arises from the conflict paralyzes his producing faculties and at best helps in the creation of profound parodoxes, curiously Teutonic in substance and Gallic in form.

But this *Journal* is a posthumous event; it tells all about the man, and was not written for publication. During his life he was commonly regarded as a man who had not lived up to his promise, one indeed who was a complete failure. Amiel himself approved the general verdict. "My friends," he says, "see what I might have been; I see what I am." They watch his inexplicable conduct; he, the man of whom great literature is expected, spends his time composing ingenious verses, in working on all sorts of elaborate metrical experiments, literary trifling, they call it; time passes, the book they have reason to await from him does not come. But there is the posthumous confession:

"I am afraid of greatness. I am not afraid of ingenuity; all my published literary essays are little else than studies, games, exercises, for the purpose of testing myself. I play scales, as it were; I run up and down my instrument. I train my hand and make sure of its capacity and skill. But the work itself remains unachieved. I am always preparing and never accomplishing, and my energy is swallowed up in a kind of barren curiosity."

He makes effort after effort to shake off the enchantment of thought which paralyzes his centers of action, to realize the expectations of his friends, but without avail. And all the while, secretly, he writes his *Journal Intime*, his *Apologia*, the study of his failure, above all, the record of his most intimate feelings and thoughts. In more ways than one the account, published in 1882, shortly after his death, must have surprised those of his friends who remained among the living; for here at last was a work of surpassing merit, such as might have been expected from a man of Amiel's knowledge and talents. But this was something more than a book; this was the man himself, the whole man, in all his strength and weakness, with all his virtues and faults, with all his perplexities and doubts, and with all the aspiration toward the perfection which he could not find in life, in reality.

Now, when a man writes the truth about himself, he is bound also to tell the truth about the world, because however much he may be a definite individual, he must needs place himself in relation to that world. Is not Amiel's very failure a criterion by which worldly success may be judged? "What interests me in myself," he writes, "is that I find in my own case a genuine example of human nature, and therefore a specimen of general value." This, surely, is a reasonable assertion. The value of the *Journal* lies precisely in the picture it presents of man in pursuit of an ideal, an ideal which is high and inaccessible. Externally, men differ, but, in the depths, they meet, and since none can deny that Amiel's ideal is humanity's ideal, it follows that what is most intimate in Amiel forms also the most intimate portion of all men. In short, an intimate truth is also a universal truth.

The real difference between Amiel and other men is in the attitude they adopt toward the ideal. Some men make no effort to approach it because its inaccessibility is so patent to them; others guide their lives by it as mariners guide their ships by the North Star; as for Amiel, he is consumed with longing for it, and there are no half-measures, no compromises, it is all or nothing! Add to this a keen knowledge-gleaning mind, a clear vision and a penetrating analysis; is not failure inevitable? "The point I have reached seems to be explained by a too restless search for perfection, by the abuse of the critical faculty, and by an unreasonable distrust of first impulses, first thoughts, first words. . . . Confidence and spontaneity of life are drifting out of my reach, and this is why I can no longer act." He confesses to not being able to be content with second-best or to discover anything which satisfies his aspiration. "The real disgusts me, and I can not find the ideal."

These words, it must be remembered, are not uttered by

a soured man, a misanthrope, but by a kindly, amiable, unduly sensitive man, who loves humankind and would have it live a perfect life. Now and then marriage occurs to him; there is something attractive to him in family life. "I can not escape from the ideal of it. A companion of my life, of my work, of my thoughts, of my hopes; within a common worship—toward the world outside kindness and beneficence; education to undertake; the thousand and one moral relations which develope round the first—all these ideas intoxicate me sometimes." But thought, like an opiate, can intoxicate us and "yet leave us broad awake." It numbs his sense of action, and forces him to put away any idea which requires willing, the making of a decision. "Reality, the present, the irreparable, the necessary, repel and even terrify me. I have too much imagination, conscience, and penetration, and not enough character. The life of thought alone seems to me to have enough elasticity and immensity, to be free enough from the irreparable; practical life makes me afraid. I am distrustful of myself and of happiness because I know myself. The ideal poisons for me all imperfect possession. And I abhor useless regrets and repentances."

He has an intense horror of ambition, of struggle, of hatred, of all things which are to him "external" and dissipate that essence which we call the soul. "To love, to dream, to feel, to learn, to understand—all these are possible to me if only I may be dispensed from willing," he says in his *Journal*. This admission, which he again and again repeats, is significant. Energy, it will be seen, which is father to striving and willing, itself becomes a kind of evil and partakes of the nature of sin. And the question of sin interests Amiel, the Calvinist, not a little. He is drifting into a kind of Buddhism, which comes easily to an Easterner, but which is unnatural to an European, and at that a Frenchman. In the midst of his surrender, he sees, with a clarity usually ascribed to the Latins, that discouragement itself can be a sin, has been his sin. "Discouragement is an act of unbelief. Growing weakness has been the consequence of it; the principle of death in me and the influence of the Prince of Darkness have waxed strongly together. My will in abdicating has yielded up the scepter to instinct; and as the corruption of the best results in what is worst, love of the ideal, tenderness, unworldliness, have led me to a state in which I shrink from hope and crave for annihilation." And he concludes his statement with this pregnant sentence: "Action is my cross."

This is self-analysis with a vengeance. As he looks upon himself with the perfect detachment of a spectator, he finds himself saying: "The man who insists upon seeing with perfect clearness before he decides, never decides. Accept life, and you must accept regret." But that is what Amiel will not do, and he seeks shelter under the great canopy of thought, a state approximating Nirvana. In the real world we are prevented from being happy precisely by our highest aspirations. For, if we have an ideal, action becomes *but coarsened thought*, and if we hold to this ideal strictly, compromise with reality becomes impossible. "I am always waiting for the woman and the work which shall be capable of taking entire possession of my soul, and of becoming my end and aim. . . ." He has not given away his heart, hence he is restless. He will not let it be taken captive by that which can not fill and satisfy it; he is in the throes of a perpetual quest, which he calls "the malady of the ideal." Must life, then, always be "a compromise between common sense and the ideal"? And he exclaims: "But marriage by common sense!—arrived at by bargain! Can it be anything but a profanation?" On the other hand, ever ready to see the other side, he asks, "Is that not a vicious ideal which hinders life from completing itself, and destroys the family in the germ? Is there not too much pride in my ideal,—pride which will not accept the common destiny? . . ." This faculty of seeing both sides is at once Amiel's great gift and damnation. For a pessimist, he is a very cheerful person, a charming companion, and he loves and is beloved by children.

The *Journal Intime*, which is the living soul of Amiel, is even more important for its implications regarding the world in which Amiel lived than for its portrait of the author. For it is a criticism of the world and a reflection on it. It is a mirror of that reality outside himself to which he can not accustom himself. Humanity leavens its life with ideals, but Amiel finds even the leaven running short. Humanity prides itself on its progress, which has created comfort and has in no sense advanced its ideals. "We are still barbarians—barbarians in education, in eloquence, in public life, in poetry, in matters of art, etc. We must have millions of men in order to produce a few elect spirits: a thousand was enough in Greece. If the measure of civilization is to be the number of perfected men that it produces, we are still far from this model people. The slaves are no longer with us, but they are among us. Barbarism is no longer at our frontiers; it lives side by side with us. We carry within us much greater things than they, but we ourselves are smaller. It is a strange result. Objective civilization produced great men while making no conscious effort toward such a result; subjective civilization produces a miserable and imperfect race, contrary to its mission and its earnest desire. The world grows more majestic but man diminishes. Why is this?"

His answer is that we have too much barbarian blood in our veins, and we lack measure, harmony and grace. "Christianity, in breaking man up into outer and inner, the world into earth and heaven, hell and paradise, has decomposed the human unity, in order, it is true, to reconstruct it more profoundly and more truly. But Christianity has not yet digested this powerful leaven."

The result has been disastrous. Instead of unity we have division, in everything. There is specialization in labor, in education; one-sided development is an enemy to harmony. Analysis disintegrates man, and there is no way for him to achieve a synthesis. Is this not even more true now than when Amiel lived, half a century ago? He sees man as a balance between science and love. "Science is the power of man, and love his strength; man *becomes* man only by the intelligence, but he is man only by the heart. Knowledge, love, power,—there is the complete life."

But the trouble is that science has outstripped love as a factor in "progress." And, as Amiel watches this unequal race, he enters into the mood of prophecy. "Manufacturing Americanism and Cæsarian democracy," he writes in 1865, "tend equally to the multiplying of crowds, governed by appetite, applauding charlatanism, vowed to the worship of mammon and of pleasure, and adoring no other God than force. . . . Materialistic naturalism has the wind in its sails, and a general moral deterioration is preparing. . . ." Yet Amiel's faith in the ideal does not altogether forsake him. "The great democratic deluge," he says, "will not after all be able to effect what the invasion of the barbarians was powerless to bring about; it will not drown altogether the results of the higher culture; but we must resign ourselves to the fact that it tends in the beginning to deform and vulgarize everything. It is clear that æsthetic delicacy, elegance, distinction, and nobleness,—that atticism, urbanity, whatever is suave and exquisite, fine and subtle,—all that makes the charm of the higher kinds of literature and of aristocratic cultivation,—vanishes simultaneously with the society which corresponds to it." To what end, he asks, is all the prevailing "devouring and incessant activity" of the Western nations, and especially of Americans? "They are excited, ardent, positive, because they are superficial. Why so much effort, noise, struggle, and greed?—it is all a mere stunning and deafening of the self." The approach of death alone makes them realize the folly of it all—"why not then admit it sooner?" And lest we espouse science as true reason, Amiel responds with the magnificent phrase, "Science is a lucid madness occupied in tabulating its own necessary hallucinations."

What, then, is the way out of this tangle of existence? The first sentence of the *Journal Intime* strikes the key-note of the whole, and gives the answer—the only possible answer.

"There is but one thing needful—to possess God. All our senses, all our powers of mind and soul, all our external resources, are so many ways of approaching the Divinity, so many modes of tasting and adoring God. We must learn to detach ourselves from all that is capable of being lost, to bind ourselves absolutely only to what is absolute and eternal, and to enjoy the rest as a loan, a usufruct. . . . To adore, to understand, to receive, to feel, to give, to act: there is my law, my duty, my happiness, my heaven. . . . Every life has its potentiality of greatness, and as it is impossible to be outside God, the best is consciously to dwell in Him. . . ."

It is not an answer that will please the pragmatists, the behavorists and the mechanicians: the men most typical of the age which has produced them. Yet it is true: all is confusion to-day, man is chaos. Until there is order, the Face of God will remain invisible; it can be mirrored only in the tranquil waters of life.

Such would seem to be the conclusion arrived at by Amiel.

His own life was a crucifixion on a cross whose arms were Action and Thought. He died in 1881. The last words in the *Journal Intime* are: "A terrible sense of oppression. My flesh and my heart fail me."

But his words carry their living enchantment to this day, and a personality of great tenderness and charm rises out of his book to haunt us.

HENRY ADAMS—ANOTHER "FAILURE"

THE time was the last decade of the nineteenth century, the place the halls of the Great Exposition at Chicago.

Two solemn-looking men, both in their sixties were rambling among the mechanical exhibits. They had just left the display of automobiles; there were several samples of the new monster, which lately had been rapidly coming into vogue and threatening even then wholly to displace the humble four-footed beast which had served men from the beginning of time.

The man who was slightly older talked, the other listened. The talker had been explaining the mechanism of the vehicle, and dilating on its possibilities in the future. He apparently knew everything about it, the listener almost nothing. But he was a good listener, and he took in all his mentor had to say with rapt attention. He gently stroked his pointed beard, while his small but penetrating eyes, deep in the aristocratic head, grew thoughtful; he seemed to revolve a problem in his mind. And now they paused before the new Daimler motor, which the elder man explained minutely; it was a miracle of mechanism, astonishingly complex. The listener was obviously impressed; he put questions to his mentor, but made no comments.

"And now, Adams!" exclaimed the elder man, "let me show you the greatest miracle of all, just to complete your education!"

The other laughed. "The very thing!" he said. Then, after a pause: "To tell you the truth, Langley, what I need is to begin my education. One can't complete something one hasn't begun! Now, can one?"

"Still harping on your pet hobby!" The man called Langley chuckled. "Why, you're the most overeducated man I have ever met. If there's one thing you need, it's to be deeducated!"

"Quite right! Quite right!" responded his companion. "As a matter of fact, it amounts to the same thing."

"You with your eternal paradoxes!"

"By no means. It's very simple. We are on the eve of the twentieth century, yet the educations most of us receive belong to the eighteenth. . . . What connection have I with these marvels you are showing me? Harvard has not taught me to admire them. I am supposed to admire art and the classics. And a horse pleases me. Certainly I have no intention of driving one of the machines you've just shown me. When I see them in the streets, going hither and thither at top speed, they suggest to me nothing more than a nightmare. As for your motor, I can't help admiring it. Yet, if you want the truth, I can do very well without it! And so you see I am not fitted to live in this progressive age."

"What an incorrigible man!" laughed Langley. "I hardly expect the wonders in the next room to convert you. . . . Anyhow, let's have a look at them!"

The two men passed through the broad doorway. One of them was Samuel Pierpont Langley, famous astronomer and pioneer in aviation experiments. The other was Henry Adams: great-grandson of John Adams, the second president of the United States; grandson of John Quincy Adams, the sixth president of the United States; son of Charles Francis Adams, the ambassador to Great Britain at the time of the Civil War; and in his own right, a "failure."

In the great hall which they entered, an astonishing spectacle greeted Adams' eyes: an army of huge dynamos whirling at top speed.

Adams paused. A strange look crept into his eyes. Was it one of admiration or of fear? It was hard to tell. Perhaps both. Unconsciously he took off his hat, as one would in a church, and languidly stroked his nearly bald head. His famous mentor scrutinized it, this thinker's head, long and aristocratic, yet massive, suggesting all the refinements of a distinguished lineage. He caught the look in the eyes, and, respecting the other's silence, remained silent himself. He waited for his pupil to take it all in, have his fill of the miraculous spectacle.

"Well?" he said finally.

As if plunged in a dream, Adams replied:

"It's a case of 'The Virgin is dead! Long live the Dynamo!' "

"What do you mean?" asked his mentor, unable to make head or tail of his companion's strange observation.

But Adams, plunged again into a reverie, made no reply. Indeed, what could he say? The words had slipped out of his mouth without premeditation. He had spoken his secret thought aloud.

And he went on thinking his own thoughts while taking in all Langley had to say concerning the mysteries of the forces at work here. Even Langley, scientist though he was, knew little about electricity or force of any kind. He was aware that the great sun emanated huge heat, but how long this heat might last, and of its possible fluctuations he knew no more than the next man.

"To him [Langley]," Adams was to record later, remembering this visit together, "the dynamo itself was but an ingenious channel for conveying somewhere the heat latent in a few tons of poor coal hidden in a dirty engine-house carefully kept out of sight; but to Adams [he wrote in the third person the better to eliminate the ego and achieve objectivity] the dynamo became a symbol of infinity. As he grew accustomed to the great gallery of machines, he began to feel the forty-foot dynamos as a moral force, much as the early Christians felt the Cross. The planet itself seemed less impressive, in its old-fashioned, deliberate, annual or daily revolution, than this huge wheel, revolving within arm's-length at some vertiginous speed, and barely murmuring—scarcely humming an audible warning to stand a hair's-breath further for respect of power—while it would not wake the baby lying close against its frame. Before the end, one began to pray to it; inherited instinct taught the natural expression of man before silent and infinite force. Among the thousand symbols of ultimate energy, the dynamo was not so human as some, but it was the most expressive."

These thoughts, which he was to put on paper, he kept to himself in the presence of his mentor. Indeed, even this writing he had no intention of giving to the large public, which would never understand. Yet to him, his thought, arrived at through complex ways, seemed infinitely simple. Did he not know that the infinitely simple things were hard to understand unless you took the same labyrinthine journey, ultimately to arrive in the light?

He saw it all too clearly: the two forces, old and new, governing humanity. They were the Virgin and the dynamo. Before the Virgin there was Venus, a force in the ancient world. She was succeeded by the Virgin who moved the medieval world; her power was still felt at Lourdes, and "seemed to be as potent as X-rays; but in America neither Venus nor Virgin ever had value as force—at most as sentiment. No American had ever been truly afraid of either." There was a time when the Virgin set men in motion; thousands of them, tirelessly, through the long decades, would set to work building cathedrals, and would pour their souls into multiple noble and grotesque shapes, which collectively made for unity: Love of the Virgin. Or else, she sent them to fight for her; magnificent animated pageants, every man attired in shining mail and armed with lance and saber, set forth on Holy Crusades, to die or conquer in the name of faith. Like a powerful magnet, radiating her force in all directions, she attracted countless pilgrims to her shrine. . . . Centuries passed, her power slowly waned; here and there, on small patches of the continent, as at Lourdes, she was still remembered and worshiped. . . . And now a new power has arisen . . . the Dynamo. Animate with untold force, beautiful in its own fashion, fierce in its silent pride, it whirled on so fast that it seemed still. Men marveled, whispered of its miracles, performed and yet to come. Henceforth, they would serve it. The Machine would be their God, their master.

And yet . . . and yet . . . Adams could not help reflecting, would its power be as great, as beneficent, as that graceful woman's figure pedestaled and enshrined, stimulating men to ecstasy, to creating art, to loving? No, not all the steam-engines and dynamos ever dreamed of could inspire men with that happiness which raised them above the beasts and but a little below the gods. The Virgin was a woman; the Machine, in spite of its force, a sexless thing,—there was the difference! Stupid men, and blind, not to see it!

And Adams, reflecting on the startling change in men's perceptions, and observing its significance for his country, which fathered the monster, was moved to write:

"The Woman had once been supreme; in France she still seemed potent, not merely as a sentiment, but as a force. Why was she unknown in America? For evidently America was ashamed of her, and she was ashamed of herself, otherwise they would not have strewn fig-leaves so profusely all over her. When she was a true force, she was ignorant of fig-leaves, but the monthly-magazine-made American female had not a feature that would have been recognized by Adam. The trait was notorious, and often humorous, but any one brought up among Puritans knew that sex was sin. In any previous age, sex was strength. Neither art nor beauty was needed. Every one, even among Puritans, knew that neither Diana of the Ephesians nor any of the Oriental goddesses was worshiped for her beauty. She was goddess because of her force; she was the animated dynamo; she was reproduction—the greatest and most mysterious of all energies; all she needed was to be fecund. . . ."

These thoughts were disquieting to Adams, whose mind lived in an age gone by. Man, he saw clearly, had lost his birthright; he had surrendered his right to create to the Machine. As for Woman, poor thing, by this surrender she was deprived of that power over man which in the past had been her function and her glory. She had mothered his art as she had mothered his children. Her energy had been supreme. It was strange that this energy, the energy of sex, should be so foreign to the American mind. "An American Virgin," he added to his notes, "would never dare command; an American Venus would never dare exist."

The thought obsessed him, for he held women in high esteem and regarded men as the inferior sex. For a time he talked of nothing else. It became a standing joke in the circle of acquaintances and friends in which he moved. Sure of sympathy from women, he would, on different occasions, fling the question: "Why is the American woman a failure?" The answer he received from almost any woman was sure to be spontaneous and the same: "Because the American man is a failure!" And she always meant it.

It was quite true. American men were failures. In enthroning the Machine, they deposed not only Woman but themselves. When Woman was a real Force (not the mere ornament and confection she was becoming) Man was animate with the energy she was able to impart to him, and with this energy he wrote and painted and sang and loved (he did this all for her), and now——

Adams' mind, playing with irony, descended to a baser image of this change in the attitude of man toward creation. There was the noble beast, the horse, a little less than human (some averred more), who had served man well for so long that human memory had no record of the beginnings of his servitude, and now the faithful servant was being abandoned—for a machine!

And Man was giving up Woman for the Dynamo.

The time might come when Man would write poems to the Dynamo. But would the Dynamo, in return, reanimate him with its energy? What even if it could! Its mood was monotonous and changeless. It would make of him another machine. In response to its force, men and women, in the thousands, would come to serve it in factories, so many mere cogs. What a dull existence!

Adams' eighteenth-century education had not prepared him to accept this.

That it was all inevitable, he was willing to grant. As a historian, who had tried to fathom the laws of history rather than recount the battles of the nations, he saw other aspects running parallel to the degradation of Woman. After all, the Dynamo was no mere accident but a real symptom of the general condition. Man's surrender, indeed, implied a degradation of all human energy. Only one who is ill can so lightly surrender his creative functions to soulless steel.

There were the implications. The human unity was gone. The family unit was no more. There were cracks in the cement, there were fissures in the walls of man's universe. Democracy, whose aim had been to make life livable for the average man, created a fiercer competition than ever existed under less pretentious régimes. There was no God any longer, no authority in matters either high or low. There was anarchy in the arts. Science, if anything, was in a still worse chaos. The eternal mystery of Force was still unaccounted for, and Science, whose business it was to account for it, jumped from one hypothesis to another. Scientists ranged themselves in schools; they who had once prided themselves on being exact, now frankly confessed that their ignorance increased with increase of knowledge. There was *ennui*; men moved because they were bored. This was a force, if you like; but force created by sheer restlessness is aimless and tends toward disaster.

"*Ennui,* like Natural Selection, accounted for change, but failed to account for direction of change. For that, an attractive force was essential; a force from outside; a shaping influence. Pascal and all the old philosophies called this outside force God or Gods. . . ."

Adams had sought for it in the Virgin at Chartres, "and asked her to show him God, face to face, as she did for St. Bernard." Her gentle reply had been: "My dear outcast, what is it you seek? This is the Church of Christ! If you seek Him through me, you are welcome, sinner or saint, but He and I are one. We are Love! We have nothing to do with God's other energies which are infinite, and concern us the less because our interest is only in man, and the infinite is not knowable to man. . . ."

He had known it. It was the only possible answer she could give him. And it was true. Man maintained his unity only as long as he believed in God, only as long as he maintained an interest in the limits God had allotted him. Once he trespassed these limits, he entered that illimitable chaos, which scientists were beginning to call "the larger synthesis." As if it mattered what they called it! This penetration into chaos brought chaos into the heart of man. Man could no longer think in terms of unity. "Without thought in the unit, there could be no unity; without unity no orderly sequence or ordered society. Thought alone was Form. Mind and Unity flourished or perished together."

And as Chaos meant multiplicity, so Man assuredly, in reaching out for other worlds, was losing his own, like the proverbial dog his water-reflected bone. He now lived in a universe of many shadows; they eluded him as he clutched at them; desperately he held on to keep his footing.

"This education startled even a man who had dabbled in fifty educations all over the world." For he saw clearly that there could be no compromise. One had either to accept the unified universe of religion, or the multiple universe of modern science. "The student seemed to feel himself, like all his predecessors, caught, trapped, meshed in this eternal drag-net of religion."

Or one was caught in the meshes of modern science. What, precisely, did that mean? "By that path of newest science, one saw no unity ahead—nothing but a dissolving mind—and the historian felt himself driven back on thought as one continuous Force, without Race, Sex, School, Country, or Church."

He saw that man as a force "must be measured by motion, from a fixed point." He saw there was an advantage in a study begun with the century 1150-1250, when the unity of an epoch was expressed in Amiens Cathedral and *The Works of Thomas Aquinas*. He proposed to follow the historic line of thought—in philosophy and mechanics—which ultimately led up to the position he proposed to fix for himself, which he could label: *The Education of Henry Adams: A study of Twentieth Century*

Multiplicity. "With the help of these two points of relation, he hoped to project his lines forward and backward indefinitely, subject to correction from any one who should know better."

After years of study, he had arrived at a conclusion: "The motion of thought had the same value as the motion of a cannon-ball seen approaching the observer on a direct line through the air. One could watch its curve for five thousand years. Its first violent acceleration in historical times had ended in the catastrophe of 310. The next swerve of direction occurred toward 1500. Galileo and Bacon gave still a newer curve to it, which altered its values; but all these changes had never altered the continuity. Only in 1900, the continuity snapped."

Then he made the startling discovery: if the same acceleration of progress continued, exceeding man's power to keep up with it, a terrible catastrophe was in prospect; and that before many years had passed.

His discovery filled him with no pride; his victory only distressed him. He was sorry for the child who came into this hit-or-miss world in the year 1900. "All that the historian won was a vehement wish to escape. He saw his education complete, and was sorry he ever began it. As a matter of taste, he greatly preferred his eighteenth-century education when God was a father and nature a mother, and all was for the best in a scientific universe. He repudiated all share in the world as it was to be, and yet he could not detect the point where his responsibility began or ended."

Henry Adams died in March, 1918, having lived long enough to see the worst of the catastrophe he had so accurately presaged almost to the date.

THE COMPARISON OF AMIEL WITH ADAMS

HENRI FRÉDÉRIC AMIEL was regarded as a "failure" by his friends; his posthumous *Journal Intime* is, in spite of talents displayed, a confirmation of that failure.

The friends of Henry Adams were more polite; yet, in its way, his *Education of Henry Adams,* posthumous as far as the large public is concerned, is a confession of failure.

The implications, however, in the writings of both go beyond individual failure and concern the failure of humanity as a whole.

Man lives his most transcendent life in thought and in love, and he who dares indulge in the luxury of an ideal, finding reality falls short, despairs of the world and, naturally, of himself, since he can not possibly find a place for himself in it. Amiel's difficulty arose, on the one hand, from his French gift of thinking clearly, on the other, from his longing for perfection inculcated by German philosophy. He could not reconcile the world of his desire with the real world; this paralyzed his will. The world as he saw it was a failure, and the world seeing in him a misfit, quite properly, felt justified (from its own point of view) in returning the compliment. In such a manner do the many protect themselves against the one. His mind, tranquillized from inaction, mirrored the imperfections of a world too restless to pause to look at the reflection of its distraught face.

With rare prescience Amiel noted the factors of progressive disintegration: the tendency to analysis, specialization in all walks of life, the chaos of competitive democracy, and so forth. He observed the sterile Machine displacing creative Love as a motive force in "progress." And the first sentence of his book already stated his conclusions: "There is but one thing needful—to possess God."

Does not Henry Adams reiterate Amiel, if in different words? Amiel writes more simply; Adams in more forceful images, as when he juxtaposes the Dynamo and the Virgin, animating his idea unforgettably. Adams is more complex, living as he does in a more complex age, but he is also more precise and indulges in less rhetoric. This is because he is subtle and uses Science's own methods in order to dissect Science. He analyzes Analysis, and shows it to be a symptom of a disintegrating age and coming chaos. As a historian, he has attempted to establish certain laws, and so precise are they that he is able accurately to prophesy the approaching catastrophe of 1914.

What Amiel says with exuberance and passion, Adams confirms with coolness and dispassionateness. He is strong in the sense of the universal and of the particular, and his whole *Education* is illustrative of Goethe's aphorism: "The particular is ever subordinate to the universal, and the universal must ever adapt itself to the particular." Thus, by means of woman's changing position in the world he is able to illustrate the changing condition of the world itself, and he can reverse the idea to show how the world has degraded woman to its own condition.

In abstract thought, racial and national frontiers are less definable than in action or in the arts, but there is the greater austerity of style and a general "coming down to brass tacks" attitude which distinguishes the New Englander from the French Swiss thinker; besides these, there is his tilting at the Puritans, which is enough to date and place him.

In the ultimate sense Amiel and Adams meet, since both admit that a synthesis is only possible by a return to God.

Henri Frédéric Amiel

From *Henri Frédéric Amiel, Étude Biographique* by Berthe Vadier. Libraire Fischbacher, 1886, Paris

HENRY ADAMS

Courtesy of Houghton Mifflin Company

In some things Amiel had forestalled Adams, but Adams, in his turn, had forestalled Oswald Spengler. Adams, in his *Education* and *Degradation of the Democratic Dogma,* has left two perfectly terrifying books of profound significance, especially for America; they have a measure of greatness which yet waits to be recognized. Adams, like many another great man, has suffered from middlemen. I know nothing more misleading, for example, than Mr. Gamaliel Bradford's essay; he can find it in his heart to say, "Yet, after all his [Adams'] labor and all his effort, I at least can not escape the impression that he was an author 'for fun.'" And, I at least can not escape the impression that this is sheer nonsense.

GEORGE SAND — SEEKER OF LOVE

1

Pietro Pagello, a dark and handsome man, lately come to Venice as assistant surgeon at the Ospedale Civile, was sauntering with a friend from Genoa, traveler and man of letters, along the Riva dei Schiavone near the Hotel Danieli. Looking up to the first-floor hotel balcony, his eyes were attracted by a woman who sat there. She was small, young, with very black hair, pale olive skin, and large melancholy eyes which, in spite of their somnolence, betokened virility and strength of character. A bright scarlet scarf, bound around her head like a turban, set off the pallor of her face and the blackness of her hair. The effect was heightened by a snow-white collar, to which was attached a cravat. She was smoking a long cigar "with the assurance of a soldier," and chatted with a frail, fair-haired young man, who looked rather bored.

There was something about her which held the young Italian's attention.

"Ah!" said his companion. "You seem to be fascinated by the charming smoker. Do you happen to know her?"

"No. But I would give a good deal to do so. She must be different from the common run of women. Tell me, you who have traveled so much, what do you think of her?"

"I can form no reasonable theory," said the other. "Perhaps she is a romantic Englishwoman, or else an exiled Pole. She looks like a person of high station, and she strikes me as strange and haughty."

The friends parted in the Piazza of Saint Mark, having talked on the way about the lady on the Danieli balcony.

The next day, Pagello was able to assure his friend that the lady was neither an Englishwoman nor a Pole, but a woman of pure French blood. He knew it, too, from a personal interview; for she had called him in to cure a bad headache.

In bidding him good-by, she had asked him to call again unless he heard to the contrary. Her companion, the young fair-haired man, escorted him politely to the foot of the staircase. That was all that happened that morning, but he had a presentiment—whether good or bad he could not say—which whispered to him, "You will see that woman again, and she will make a conquest of you."

Was he in love? "No, no, not yet!" But who was this enchanting stranger? He did not know. Why didn't he ask the hotel-keeper who she was and where she came from? "Why? Because I was afraid to know." "Ah, ah!" cried his friend and his friend's wife, "he is in love!"

It was very natural to think so, in the circumstances.

Some days later, Pagello called on his friends again, this time with a letter in his hand. It was from the lady at the Danieli. It begged Doctor Pagello to call at once at the hotel and to bring along with him a good consulting physician to diagnose the strange malady of her companion, "a man of energetic character and powerful imagination—a poet much admired in France." She did not know what was the matter with him. As nearly as she could tell, "the excitement of brain-work, wine, dissipation, women and the gaming table have much fatigued him and have wrought upon his nerves. He gets agitated over the smallest trifles as if they were matters of importance." It was not the first time. Some three months before, she wrote, he was "like a raving maniac all night long in consequence of some trouble he had on his mind. He thought he saw phantoms round his bed, and he shrieked with fear and horror. . . ." There were other details.

As the friends turned the page and saw the signature, they exclaimed in one voice: *"George Sand!"*

They turned to each other with significant looks, as if to say: "Well, this is no ordinary game!"

They turned on Pagello with questions. Had he visited his French patient? What was the matter with him? How was he getting on?

He replied that his young patient was in bed with a very grave illness which he and his colleague had diagnosed as a serious nervous disorder, the result of drink. And he added: "His name is Alfred de Musset."

"Really?" cried his host. "That is the romantic singer of the moon. Do you know his poems?"

"Yes," replied Pagello. "I have read two or three of them. He has a wonderful imagination—a little extravagant, but very delicate, all the same."

There was little need to discuss George Sand, whose novels even then, practically at the beginning of a career which was to produce one hundred and ten volumes, had penetrated everywhere on the Continent that men and women read French.

His friends chaffed Doctor Pagello.

2

Alfred de Musset was suffering from a grave illness; doctors have given it the beautiful name of *delirium tremens*.

Poor George Sand was beside herself. One night in particular "was awful," she wrote to a friend. "Six hours of such frenzy that, in spite of the efforts of two strong men, he ran about his room in a state of nudity. Shouts, songs, yells, convulsions! Oh, my God! What a spectacle it was!"

But Doctor Pagello was attentive and kind. For hours he sat there with George Sand by Musset's bedside; two better nurses a man never had; he was to acknowledge that they had saved his life.

As she sat there, sad thoughts possessed the woman. There was every reason for sadness. But a few short weeks had elapsed since she had brought him here, her lover. She was romantically minded; romance was in her blood as it was in her books. She had abandoned her former life as housewife because her husband was a miserable stick who could not and would not see that she had an intelligence and yearned for a life of which he had no conception. Besides, he had an excessive fondness for housemaids. It was disgusting. She could not and would not stand that life any more. Secretly she wrote a novel, and at her home in Nohant she had kept in touch with the Romantics who were showing the world just then a new way of life which scandalized the bourgeois. All she loved in her home were her children, Maurice and Solange. She was strong with the maternal mood, but the time came when even this could not hold her there quiescent. Ebullient life surged in her veins; she was surfeited with energy, and energy is will. Paris had long called to her, and when the fateful moment came, she shook the dust of Nohant from her feet and went. She gave thought to her children, and left instructions for their care. She would return periodically to Nohant to see them. They must not suffer, whatever happened. She made an amicable arrangement with her husband: he was to live his life in his own way, and she was to live hers. Why should men live under one rule, women under another? It seemed unreasonable. Surely, what was sauce for the gander, was sauce for the goose.

Once her mind was clear, she was fully capable of action. There would be gossip, scandal, of course. What did that matter? In any case, she had always been regarded as queer. There was that strange mixture in her of bloods; one half of her was a Dupin: that was her father, with a strain of royal blood; the other half was a Delaborde: that was her mother, Sophie, a woman whose morals were of a kind to exclude her from circles of the fastidious and of those who kept their virtue to the fore; in short, she was a vulgar, loose woman; the least said of her the better. The issue of the union was Aurore Dupin who, whatever might be said against her, was a straightforward honest girl given to moods, sometimes somnolent and dreamy, sometimes impulsive. When her aristocratic grandmother placed her in a convent, the Mother Superior's judgment was: "That child will make either a devil or a saint. At present she is sleeping water." "Sleeping water" she surely had been at the time; only it had not occurred to the prescient nun that here was a child who would one day be a devil and saint all in one. Yet at another time she had been called a pagan, "a real pagan," which again had more than a germ of truth.

Her stately grandmother, Madame Dupin, was bringing her up to be an heiress to a noble estate, and for years she had been kept from her own mother, the loathed Sophie Delaborde. But when the old lady died, without carrying out her intention of making a suitable match for Aurore, Aurore's mother appeared, and, driven to make a decision between wealth and position suitable to an heiress of royal blood and going with her mother, Aurore did not quail but chose the harder path: she went with her mother. After all, she was as much a Delaborde as a Dupin; never was she to forget it, and in time to come she was to make literary pleas for the proletariat, even though aristocratic lovers were not to be distasteful.

Then came her parting with her mother, and her marriage with a Casimir Dudevant, a good-looking, well-to-do, but obtuse fellow, who could not see what was behind her large, somnolent, velvety eyes. Not that she knew herself at the time, but as she developed he more than lagged behind. . . . They diverged in different paths slowly, but inevitably. The fates were calling her to "her own life."

It all led to Paris. . . .

From Paris she wrote to a friend: "How I wish to impart to you this sense of the intensity and joyousness of life that I have in my veins and in my breast. To live! How sweet it is! and how good, in spite of annoyances, husbands, boredom, debts, relations, scandalmongers, sufferings and irritations! To live! It is intoxicating! To love, and to be loved! It is happiness! It is heaven!"

The recollection, as she sat by Musset's side, brought back memories of Jules Sandeau, her first guide in Bohemian Paris; with him she had shared her modest ménage and collaborated on novels and in other ways which are frowned upon by convention. Good Jules! . . . How she had loved him in those first days. He had been truly her first love, and possibly might have been her last . . . so she had once thought. But one day she had unexpectedly returned from Nohant to their little apartment, and what she saw banished her every illusion on the score of Jules' love. What else was there to do after such treachery but to send him packing? This she did promptly, and as she was no mean soul, and Jules was poor, she put three hundred francs into his hand to facilitate his departure.

So this was love! Romance! In what way did it differ from her life with Monsieur Dudevant? She would have none of it.

But she was not a woman to give up her illusions easily. Surely, among artists and poets, superior beings, there must be some who knew how to love beautifully. Love, as she saw it in her dreams, was a grand ecstatic affair in which the mean and the sordid had no part.

"Papa" Sainte-Beuve, the critic, who, besides being her admirer, was a sort of father confessor to her, was sorry to see her so disconsolate, and, taking pity, threw a gift her way in the shape of Prosper Mérimée, the novelist. It was a short-lived affair of a week. Could love come from an odious cynic? "Instead of any affection that could pity her and relieve her of her distress, she found only a bitter and mocking frivolity." That was all.

Then . . . Alfred de Musset. In the early days of their liaison she had thought she had at last found heaven itself. . . . He had been exquisite. Could a man have been more favored of the gods? He was young—several years her junior—of aristocratic blood, sensitive, fastidious; the poetic Muse had crowned him with laurels. His elegant supple figure, always attired in the latest fashion, attracted attention on the boulevards, and his abundant fair hair, scarlet lips and nonchalant languid moods made him the adored of the most *élite* of women who crowded the salons. He was, in short, the ideal Romantic, a creature of his time. He was a brilliant talker, and he had wit. It was incredible that this darling of the gods, this exquisite Beau Brummel, should fall into the net of a lively robust woman, half a Delaborde, but he did. He was George Sand's soon after their first meeting. He became a part of her ménage, and his books were stacked with hers where Jules Sandeau's once had had their place. At last here was love, here was happiness! So she had thought. Who should have Romance but two such Romantics?

Naturally, there had been much talk, gossip, speculation. . . . To escape it, this journey had been decided on. It would cost some money, but George Sand was a hard worker; she was willing to foot all bills where that precious thing called Love was concerned. She was anything but miserly, and though her books sold extremely well, she always spent her money on her two children at Nohant and, inevitably, on her third—her lover. She was maternal even in her most ecstatic love.

So great was this maternal gift of hers that on Musset's mother refusing to give her consent to the journey, she herself had visited that grand lady to persuade her that her beloved Alfred would be in good hands in hers, and, strange to say, the lady was fully persuaded that this was so.

And thus it happened that after writing affectionate letters to her darlings at Nohant, George Sand departed for the south with dear Alfred in tow. Genoa first, then Leghorn, at last Florence. . . . Happy days. . . . Then Venice. . . .

"George," said Alfred, as they sat, cold and shivering and weary, in the Casino Danieli on the night of their arrival in the romantic city, "I have made a mistake; I beg your pardon for it, but the fact is, I do not love you."

Could anything have been more disillusioning? Could he have dealt her a more telling blow? For an instant she had felt the earth slipping from under her feet . . . the great hopes she had laid on love, and in particular on this love, vanished in the twinkling of an eye, leaving her heart an aching void. Oh, where was the great love she had sought? Was it not to be found, then, on this wretched earth? She reeled inwardly, then braced herself. . . . Should she tell him to clear out? Why didn't he? She hadn't the heart after her solemn promise to Madame de Musset that no harm should come to her darling boy, and here he was, like herself, a lone wayfarer in a strange town, ignorant even of the language, with not a sou to his name. So she did the only thing left to her: she shut the door between their rooms and resumed her chaste life. Henceforth, she would be his mother. . . .

It was on the next day that at her request Doctor Pagello came. Had she noticed him the day before as he stared up at her sitting on the balcony? If she had, she did not mention it to him when he came. . . .

And now Pietro Pagello became her boon companion at the poet's bedside, and across the sleeping form of the patient she shot furtive glances at the handsome tall Italian, who had just turned twenty-seven. He grew to admire this strange woman, who showed such a devotion to a man whose poetry was admittedly delicate and beautiful, but whose life in the nocturnal purlieus of Venice had lately been of a nature which should have aroused scorn instead of sympathy. He was not a little sorry for her. On her part, she grew more confidential; an intimate note, still slight, had crept into their relations. Together they hovered over Alfred with their attentions, until the patient showed signs of convalescence. Now conscious, he sometimes asked to be left alone, as he wanted to sleep quietly. Pagello and George Sand would withdraw to the adjoining room to have tea and talk. Sometimes the woman would sit down and write for an hour while Pagello sat silently and watched her. With growing health, Musset developed jealousy. Once, straining his strength, he rose on all fours on his bed and glanced at the table where a single cup was standing. He promptly concluded that the doctor and George were lovers and that they had drunk from one cup!

One evening Pagello watched George Sand writing by the light of a candle for over an hour. When she had finished, she handed him the manuscript, a matter of some pages. It was entitled *En Morée,* which puzzled him, though after reading what was clearly an avowal he thought she intended it to mean *The Country of the Moors,* a land where high passion ruled. It was a curious epistle, of which an odd phrase here, a fragment there, couched in the best manner of French Romanticism, acted as sparks, setting his tinderlike substance to flame with an ardency for which his race was famous.

"Shall I be thy companion or thy slave. . . . When thy passion shall have been satisfied, shalt thou know how to thank me? When I shall have rendered thee happy, shalt thou know how to tell me so? . . . Dost thou know what is that desire of the soul that time does not assuage, and that no human caress can lull to slumber nor exhaust? . . . Do the pleasures of love leave thee breathless, and brutalized, or do they throw thee into a divine ecstasy? . . . I know neither thy past nor thy character, nor what men that know thee think of thee. Thou art, perhaps, the best, perhaps the worst among them. I love thee without knowing whether I may respect thee. I love thee because I feel drawn to thee; it is possible I shall soon be forced to hate thee. . . . I may not find in thee what I have vainly sought in others, but I shall always believe thou possessest it. . . . When thy looks are tender, I shall fancy that thy soul is speaking to mine. When thou liftest thy eyes to heaven, I shall imagine that thy intelligence is ascending to the eternal home from which it emanates. . . . I should like even to be ignorant of thy name; but thou must at least conceal thy soul from me, that I may always believe it to be beautiful. . . ."

One thing was clear to Pagello: this woman, lovely and famous though she was, was in love with him, a young practitioner, and he did not know whether he ought to be glad or sad. Now that it had come to this, he felt half afraid, and as he had duties and other pledges he spent the night wondering if he ought not to retreat.

But on the next day, the sight of his lady, smartly dressed, dispelled all his doubts, and his scruples went to the four winds. What were parents, patients, other lady-loves, to this? Only one thing mattered now: this wonderful creature who had been wronged because she had loved too well! In the circumstances, he could do nothing less than offer his unprofessional services, as one who could not let her suffer in spirit as already he had not let her suffer in body. She deigned to listen to him, and his passionate pleadings fell pleasantly on her ears.

In the meantime, Alfred was becoming suspicious, and as his health improved his suspicions increased. At last, he could bear it no longer, and, in a deserted café, put his charges bluntly before his erstwhile lover and still his patron.

"If I had known you for what you are," he said, "I would have put my money on the chimneypiece the first time I saw you, for you are no better than a *fille!*"

"Have I ever been dishonest with you while I belonged to you?" she returned, too kind to remind him that it was her earnings which had sustained their ménage. "Can't you see that when you had called me a nun and a day-dreamer and the personification of ennui and told me that you no longer loved me, I ceased to belong to you? What makes a woman vile is a lie. I have never lied to you.

"Besides," she went on, seeing him soften, "I love you still; it is purely maternal love now. As for Pietro, I am not yet sure how I love him, but I think I love him as a father, and you will be the dear child of us both."

This was something new for Alfred, and only his experience as a Romantic, who eschewed the banal, had prepared him for a situation so fraught with possibilities for a grand gesture, pleasing to himself as a poet and bound to startle the most violent doctrinaire of Romanticism. What will the great Paris say on his return in this unprecedented mood? What lover ever blessed his mistress when she took on another? What lovers ever, in their new-found happiness, had the time and a nook in their hearts for one who but a little while ago had had the favored place? Nurtured by a wonderful woman, in whose lofty mind the idea had had its birth, Alfred's delicate imagination dwelt on the idea until it grew to a transcendent beauty surpassing its author's fondest hopes. She had never seen Alfred like this before, and his burning renunciation and chaste ardor reinfected her with their own attraction rendered a hundredfold more potent. She saw that tenderness, pure tenderness, "had vanquished, penetrated, one might say almost invaded him, entirely." The attitude of George Sand seemed to exalt him with a strange ecstasy; he felt himself to have been "radically transformed by a mystic contagion that emanated from her—and showed in the midst of his tears a sort of triumphant joy."

And, still in this mood, he parted company with her in the Giardino Publico; she chastely impressing three kisses on his forehead, while the good-natured Pietro smiled benignly on them both. He had been assigned his part, that of a charitable father, and, under the ægis of his persuasive goddess, he played his part without fault.

She fulfilled her maternal rôle admiringly, and had provided her boy with a servant and funds sufficiently ample to take him to Paris; she had even accompanied him part of the way, exhibiting a tearful tenderness, which filled Alfred's romantic soul with its own unspeakable comfort. And, having accomplished all that was to be expected of her, George Sand departed with Pietro Pagello on a walking trip in the Tyrol, and eventually returned to Venice with an empty purse, a circumstance forcing them to accept quarters more modest than those afforded by the Danieli. Here, with her customary indefatigableness, she wrote her new book; the interludes she devoted to Pietro, an attentive tender lover. She, a famous woman, cooked for him, and knitted his socks, and between whiles, gliding in a gondola, they exchanged tendernesses, and whispered of "our love for Alfred." Her bruised heart forgot its suffering. This was Life, this was Romance!

Not that there weren't moments of subtle irritation, when her Romance seemed punctured with a tiny needle handled by an obtuse man. There was the moment when, passing under the arch of the Bridge of Sighs, she saw at the remote end of the tiny canal a little lamp reflecting a myriad of lights on the shiny marble palace of Bianca Capello, stirring her fancy to visions of a fairy world. Her mood struck no responsive spark in Pietro, who merely shrugged his shoulders and said with a mocking laugh: "I don't care for such fantasies. Germans take to that sort of thing, but we Italians have different conceptions of beauty. Dream away, if you like! I prefer to contemplate." It acted like a cold shower. Alfred, too, had chaffed her when she had pointed out the spot to him and told him that she saw cascades of sparks and spirits of fire dancing in crystal grottoes beneath the old walls. And now, as then, she retreated within herself, and felt the indescribable desolation of her soul.

They corresponded with Alfred, who, in Paris, was still laboring under the spiritual ecstasy in which he had left Venice and the two lovers. "I love you," he wrote. "I know you are beside a man who loves you and yet I am at peace! . . . From what a strange dream I am waking. And you, too, are reborn. You love; you are beautiful; you are young; you walk under the loveliest sky in the world, supported by a man who is worthy of you. Tell him I love him. Respect my *amitié* which is more ardent than love. It is all there is good in me. It is the work of God. You are the thread that binds me to Him."

The susceptible George, melting under transcendent joy evoked by the poet's mood, wept on Pagello's shoulder, and said:

"Oh, why can't I live between you two and make you both happy, without belonging to either of you."

But situations such as this can not maintain themselves for long in a world in which human nature rather than the ideal rules, and Alfred, sick of the adulation which George poured on Pietro, soon gave way to jealousy. The beautiful existence she had envisioned became a legend, nothing more. How could it be otherwise when Alfred wrote to her that he was "drowned in love, dying of love, knees shaking, sight gone! . . . I must be yours, it is my destiny! I love you, oh, my flesh and bones!"

In any event, it was time for her to return home. . . . Paris . . . Nohant and her children called her. There were other reasons, too. . . .

Pietro sold everything he had. . . . The middle of August saw the two in Paris. . . .

Everything went wrong here. She was back in her apartment, Pagello found himself a cheap attic. Paris was laughing at this latest of George Sand's adventures. Romanticism had outdone itself; the supreme absurdity of the Sand-Pagello-Musset affair awakened laughter in Parisians, accustomed as they were to expect ridiculous words and actions from the Romantics. Pagello, instead of being a hero, found himself very much in the position of a clown. . . . And Musset was clamoring at George's door.

Pietro Pagello saw the end coming, and he wept. Indeed, it came soon. The affair developed into a three-cornered duel, with Musset rising in favor. Now it was Pagello's turn to become jealous. In the confusion the noble sentiments of all concerned vanished. George was obviously bent on getting rid of the doctor. Parisian ridicule did not a little to undermine her attachment to the Italian. But she was generous. She realized what material losses the poor man had suffered in loving her. He had been living in his attic on the proceeds of the sale of his valuables, and he had brought some pictures along by the sale of which he had hoped to eke out a living. They were by no means marketable, and George Sand, undertaking to find a purchaser and failing to do so, pretended that she had succeeded and paid him twenty-five hundred francs out of her own pocket. In addition, she gave him some motherly advice, which "touched him to the depths of his soul." Perhaps, she would meet him in three months' time, perhaps not. And in this manner, Pietro Pagello passed out of the picture, clearing the path once more for Alfred.

She again became Alfred's mistress, but their temperamental differences and the knowledge of the past between them acted as constant irritants. Their reunion lasted but a few days. Not many days passed before she was madly searching for Alfred, who was determined not to see her. In her despair, she cut off all her hair, made a parcel of it, and sent it to her lover. He wept over it, but remained steadfast in his resolution; she began her *Journal Intime,* to which she confided her heart's troubles. In it she appealed to God, and even proposed a bargain. If God would only give back her lover, she would go to church regularly in the future; she would wear out the altar steps with her knees.

But as that did not assuage her grief, she called on all her literary and artistic friends, and asked them to explain what love was. Liszt told her that "only God was worthy of being loved." This was not consoling when one was in love with a man. Heine told her that one "only loved with the head and the senses, and that the heart had very little to do with the matter." Sainte-Beuve alone seemed sensible and did not hurt her feelings. He said: "Love resides in tears; you weep, and therefore you love." That was true. Yes, she did love, and she did weep. . . .

The intercessions of friends availed nothing. The struggle continued for some weeks. She thought it was the end of things for her. . . . But she did not know herself. Love was as the very life to her, and Alfred was by no means the end. Far from it.

3

Let us skip the minor "affairs," the most important of which was her association with Michel de Bourges. He had left her not without offspring in the shape of Republican ideas, a heritage she was to make abundant use of in her books; the proletariat was to be the chief gainer.

Let us come to the really major affair of Frédéric Chopin, since it occupied the best portion of eight years of her life, and the so-called baser passions entered but little into it.

Chopin did not like Sand when he first met her. "That woman is horribly antipathetic to me," he said. He was a sensitive, frail, ailing man; he was suffering at the time from a heart-wound inflicted by a Polish girl who, by the will of her ambitious parents, had married some one else. He was a pet of the salons, where his place was beside the ambassadors, the ministers and the princes. . . . He was conservative in religion as in other things, and an incurable aristocrat; salon life was to his liking. She was a radical, courted the proletariat, and loved the simple life of the country. There was such a disparity between them in all manner of ways. How she managed to get him was a mystery to others as well as to herself. She had come to the point where she had given up her quest of love. Love, true love, had seemed unattainable. "I have known many kinds of love; the woman's love, mother-love, sister-love, nun's love, poet's love. Some have been born and died in me the same day, without being revealed to the object that inspired them. Some have martyrized my life. . . . My soul entered these phases as the sun enters the signs of the zodiac." Was it his frailty that appealed to her, his sensitive, beautiful soul of the artist? She responded to some law in herself, which she liked to call the divine law, and it did not allow her to reject love. . . . In what way did she love Chopin, taking into consideration her own catalogue of diverse loves? There was, perhaps, a little of each in the composition of her love, with the maternal predominant. He was by far her superior as an artist; she could hardly be blind to that, and her protective instinct came to the fore. For his part, Chopin must have at last felt this to have given way to her assaults. Moreover, he was not one to play the rôle of man's love, and before entering into relation with her he frankly expressed himself as not wishing to spoil their spiritual love by any intrusion of the physical. To this the lady replied:

"This way of regarding it is repugnant to me; the word physical love is repellent. The divine mystery, the act of life that is the most serious and most sublime, the law to which even animals and plants and minerals are obedient, should not be regarded as a shameful necessity by man, who alone has received the holy gift of perceiving spiritually what they only feel materially. The body and the spirit can not be separated."

But Chopin's was an artist's mind, incapable of comprehending ideas, but if the proposed liaison could rise to the nature of a poem, he was willing to try it. . . . As he was shy and timid, and was not one who liked his private affairs talked about in public, George Sand had to proceed with the greatest delicacy and tact. It was thought best to go to some remote place; the Balearic Isles, then newly discovered by the tourist world, were chosen for the experiment. Some of Chopin's friends objected to the proposed adventure, chiefly on the score of his health. But George Sand overcame all objections. As he was suffering with chronic bronchitis, the dry, sunny, semi-tropical climate would undoubtedly do him good. And she was a thoroughly capable nurse. As for a piano, she would see to it that he had one. Then, still seeing him hesitate, she started from Nohant with her boxes and bags, sending him word: "You may join me at Perpignan if you decide to come!"

He decided he would.

Their life on Majorca, the largest of the isles, was not all roses. To one fresh from the salons of Paris, the discomforts of the almost primitive life of Palma presented a real hardship. It was winter, and the climate was by no means Paradisean. "Little Chopin" caught cold, and began to spit blood. The doctors of Palma expressed dark opinions. And the natives, assuming that their visitor was consumptive, considered him a menace to the island. And so George Sand and Chopin were forced to flee to the abandoned Carthusian monastery at Valdemosa, where, at a cost of thirty-five francs a year, they hired a number of cells as their next habitation. This place was on a mountaintop; the views to all sides of them were beautiful not to say romantic. But food was hard to get, and George had to add cleaning house and cooking to her other duties. Her patient was given to irritations, and she had to cater to his demands, and write her books besides. Luckily, his piano was there, and when he was with his beloved instrument no other world existed. Chopin was not the only one demanding attention. Her children (should one say her other children) were also here: she taught Solange grammar and helped Maurice with his lessons. By night she wrote her novel *Spiridion.* But everything was made subservient to the needs of the great musician.

All this happened in the winter. Spring came, with promise of relief . . . the fields were lovely with flowers . . . but it was too late to retrieve the situation. It was thought best to take advantage of the first quiet sea to return to civilization.

Looking back on it, she was to say:

"I could have been so happy there in spite of everything, alone with my children! I could have stayed there three years in that loveliness, and snapped my fingers at all the rest. Is there, anywhere in the universe, a Being who is my soul-mate?"

They were back at Nohant. They spent eight years there before the final break came. There had been much mutual nursing, much mutual irritation at times. It is likely that no house can contain two artists at the same time, and one so much greater than the other. It was little short of a miracle that the relation had lasted so long. The break came ostensibly because of a petty quarrel on account of Solange. There is no need to go into detail here, but in this private affair Chopin sided with the daughter, and George Sand's feelings were hurt. He was in Paris when this happened, and he never returned to Nohant.

She had sworn that he would die in her arms, and when years later his time came, she called at his chamber and was refused admission, whether by him or those at his bedside, no one knows.

4

Alexandre Manceau is "the last link in the chain." He is a young engraver who has lived in George Sand's house for many years. He has filled all sorts of functions there in his time, and he has kept more or less in the background.

He is delicate and ailing, but he is wholly devoted to the service of George Sand. He is not a great man, like the others; that is, perhaps, his virtue; for the first time she knows a man who is as willing to give as to receive.

He had come into the autumn of her life, and he is there to anticipate her wants and minister to them. His is a constant tenderness without those heights of passion which ultimately wreck intimacies. They both love flowers, and the garden at Nohant becomes a daily interest sufficient to absorb them both. They have other inclinations in common, little things in their way, but enough to give them both pleasure. He is quiet and faithful, and he is with her on all occasions, great and small.

He divines that she would be better off in some other place than Nohant; so out of his own small savings he buys a tiny cottage large enough for two at Gargilesse, an enchanting village, which seems remote from the scene of her hectic past. Dumas, or some other distinguished visitor, occasionally finds his way here, to "the villa Algira," as they name the cottage; then there is great literary talk. Nothing exciting happens; no emotional upsets, no quarrels. If there is no intense happiness, there is at least contentment. And that has its own reality.

Sand's success as a dramatist forces them to seek a place nearer Paris. And so they put their funds together and buy a small villa with a garden at Palaiseau; again in the midst of a rural paradise.

But poor Manceau has not long to live. Ever since he has had influenza, his pulmonary trouble has got worse. George Sand is at her old rôle: sitting by the bedside of her lover and attending to his wants. Sometimes Dumas comes, sometimes Borie, sometimes her son Maurice, and they bring relief to her lonely vigils. After a year at the new abode, comes the inevitable. Once more George Sand is alone. "I double the cape of bitterness," she says, "I enter the sea of isolation."

She had lived twelve years with him. It was on the whole a more satisfactory affair than she had experienced in her intimacies with the great. He was a simple soul, all devotion. Her last days would be alone.

5

Is an Epilogue necessary? Perhaps, the following story told by Monsieur Jules Claretie, will serve the purpose.

One evening, in the editorial office of the *Revue des Deux Mondes,* a bald little man, of military bearing and pensive manner, collided in the doorway with a fat lady with the dark complexion of a gipsy, and apologized to her politely.

"I beg your pardon, madame."

"I beg yours."

And then, when Jules Sandeau—for it was he, Sand's first lover—had taken his seat——

"Who is that lady?" he asked.

"What?" was the answer. "It is you who ask that question! Why, that is George Sand!"

GEORGE ELIOT—MID-VICTORIAN

THIS is not an exciting story, and if it had happened to-day it would have furnished a single item for the press. "Mr. So-and-so was yesterday granted a divorce from Mrs. So-and-so on grounds of adultery. The corespondent was Mr. So-and-so, who had deserted his own wife, Mrs. So-and-so." A few days later, perhaps, another item might have appeared to the effect that the recipient of the decree was yesterday married to Miss So-and-so, for whom he had long entertained an affection, and that immediately after the ceremony the happy couple started on a honeymoon for Italy or some equally pleasant place. But this did not happen in our own day, but in the days of Queen Victoria, that monument of virtue in whose shadow vice and immorality lay quiescent, not daring to raise their heads to the light in those regal eyes. Divorce was practically unknown, certainly rare, and available only to those whose purse allowed indulgence in what was then a luxury, and what is to-day a commodity.

The story concerns one George Henry Lewes and one Mary Ann Evans, better known as George Eliot, who, under conditions indicated above, finding the doors of legal marriage closed to them, had dared, in a day when such things aroused horror in the hearts of the virtuous, to live together "in a state of sin" without those felicities conferred by the formalities of the law. That they were happy together, and remained to the last a devoted couple, doubtless, in the eyes of some of their contemporaries, intensified their wickedness—since it is on record that not a few of their former friends had persisted in refusing to acknowledge them. It is equally certain that a more tolerant posterity, taking into consideration the facts of the case and the really conventional nature of the gifted lady, who has left some works behind so rich with the moral tone of her time, has not only accepted the attitude of the devoted lovers but is determined to justify it by results. Not only were Lewes and George Eliot happy and devoted, but to the union the English-speaking world is indebted for those literary creations which are to-day employed as "classics" of English in every schoolgirl's curriculum.

Can goodness proceed from "wickedness"? The world has decided that Lewes and George Eliot were good, in spite of the fact that some of their "friends" had judged them to be bad and refused to know them. The large public of her own day, to be sure, unaware of the identity of the author writing under a masculine pseudonym, had acclaimed her almost immediately, and it is doubtful whether personal knowledge of her would have changed the verdict. Arbitrary moralities are, after all, created by certain classes, with which the heart of the people, especially in England, by no means concurs. One has but to recall the case of Lord Nelson, and more recently that of King Edward, to realize that popularity is not always on the side of the conventional battalions. The discussion of the merits of this or that side need not enter here. But a statement of the true facts is pertinent.

Miss Mary Ann Evans was a conventional woman. She came from the middle class which, most of all, clings to convention as the very foundation of its existence. She was brought up in a typical Victorian household, traditional in its outlook, and secure in the integrity of established religion. Her father, whom she was later to immortalize in *Adam*

Bede, was a man strong of his kind, politically a Tory. "I was accustomed," says his daughter, "to hear him utter the word 'Government' in a tone that charged it with awe and made it part of my effective religion in contrast with the word 'rebel,' which seemed to carry the stamp of evil in its syllables, and, lit by the fact that Satan was the first rebel, made an argument dispensing with more detailed inquiry." Fortunately for him, he did not live to see his daughter a "rebel" against established morality and law. He would, doubtless, have thought that the discomfort she never ceased to suffer from her arrangement with the man of her choice was well deserved.

Education in those days for girls was not what it is now. There was no outlet for natural energies in games and exercise, and introspection was the result. Mary Ann, passionately longing for beauty and "yearning for something that would link together the wonderful impressions of this mysterious life, and give her soul a sense of home in it," was bound to suffer, and, indeed, turned as she was on herself, her young life was far from happy. Of books she read plenty, mostly of a serious kind, until, in 1839 at the age of twenty, her mind, in her own words, presents "an assemblage of disjointed specimens of history, ancient and modern; scraps of poetry picked up from Shakespeare, Cowper, Wordsworth, and Milton; newspaper topics; morsels of Addison and Bacon, Latin verbs, geometry, entomology, and chemistry; Reviews and metaphysics—all arrested and petrified and smothered by the fast-thickening everyday accession of actual events, relative anxieties, and household cares and vexations."

In short, she is a "highbrow," and one typical of her period.

But quite apart from this, she day-dreams, but as yet she does not know that this faculty in her is an indication of latent creative power which is to make her the great novelist of her day. Indeed, at this time she is chary of novels, and limits her reading of them to so-called "classics," and this only for the sake of understanding common allusions. Such standard works include Scott, and *Don Quixote,* and, of course, Shakespeare, though one must be as nice as a bee "to suck anything but honey from his pages." But on the whole, novel-reading is a bad habit; and in her case it leads to building fancies which are better discouraged. Only those works are good from which one derives something serviceable, be it knowledge or morals.

In a word, she had the Victorian mind, prescient of the epoch about to be ushered in, with its shibboleths of "evolution" and "progress." It was, perhaps, inevitable that young women with minds repressedly active should be aware of something portentous as far as their sex was concerned, though Florence Nightingale had not yet appeared and John Stuart Mill's *Subjection of Women* had not yet been published. But a common, often unspoken despair seized the more sensitive feminine minds at their exclusion from that larger world which had hitherto been man's undisputed province, and Mary Ann, ruminating over her housework, was perhaps more conscious than others of the limitations of the woman's world. She was asking questions in her own mind which, working slowly, was not to find a solution for some time to come.

In religion, too, dissensions appeared. Values were weighed in the balance; the spirit of change, than which nothing was more constant (as Huxley was to say), penetrated orthodoxy. Mary Ann, who had been strongly Evangelical, rationalizes her faith to a point which justifies the change in her to be called a "conversion." "What a pity," she writes to a correspondent, "that while mathematics are indubitable, immutable, and no one doubts the properties of a triangle or a circle, doctrines infinitely important to man are buried in a charnel heap of bones, over which nothing is heard but the barks and growls of contention." So strongly does she feel this that she decides to stop going to church, which stirs her father to wrath. She can not see that salvation can in any sense be connected with the acceptance of a dogma, and she is not blind to the fact that admired qualities by no means belong exclusively to any one creed. Thus she arrives at the sensible conclusion that "the great lesson of life is tolerance," which, in itself, is an excellent thing for one destined to become a novelist, since it allows for the necessary detachment, not to say pity, in dealing with a variety of characters.

Though she manages to think for herself, her emotional nature finds an outlet in devotion. Just as when a child, she had been attached to her brother Isaac, who was three years her senior, and later to Miss Lewis, her principal school governess, so now she gives years of arduous nursing to her stricken father, which is a terrible strain on her health and spirits. At this time she finds her only distraction in translating Spinoza's *Tractatus Theologico-Politicus,* which shows what an earnest young lady she is.

The French Revolution of 1848 attracts her sympathy, and she dreams of the time "when this miserable reign of Mammon shall end." She is aroused to fury "by the loathsome fawning, the transparent hypocrisy, the systematic giving as little as possible for as much as possible, that one meets with here at every turn." She feels that "society is training men and women for hell." Coincidently with this, she expresses herself with no little ardor concerning Rousseau and George Sand. Rousseau's genius has "sent that electric thrill through my intellectual and moral frame which has awakened me to new perceptions, which has made man and nature a fresh world of thought and feeling to me;

and this not by teaching me any new belief." She is thankful to George Sand for "that 'great power of God manifested in her,' " and she can not read six pages of hers without feeling "that one might live a century with nothing but one's own dull faculties and not know so much as those six pages will suggest." She acquires an "Imitation of Christ," and "it makes one long to be a saint for a few months."

Her devotion suffers a shock when her father dies. This is in the spring of 1849. "What shall I do without him?" she asks. "It will seem as if a part of my moral nature is gone."

This is followed by a visit to the Continent with friends. At Geneva she ponders on the superiority of that city over Coventry. But at Coventry, she consoles herself, there are some people "better than lake, trees and mountains." And the human factor alone reconciles her to a return to her native country. "It looks to me like a land of gloom, of ennui, of platitude, but in the midst of all this it is the land of duty and affection; and the only ardent hope I have for my future is to have given me some woman's duty, some possibility of devoting myself where I may see a daily result of pure calm blessedness in the life of another."

Such, in broad outlines, is the mental portrait of Mary Ann at the time she falls into the social circle in which she is to meet both the blessedness she craves and that duty which she so ardently seeks.

"In physique," wrote her friend, Herbert Spencer, "there was, perhaps, a trace of that masculinity characterizing her intellect; for though of but the ordinary feminine height, she was strongly built. The head, too, was larger than is usual in women. It had, moreover, a peculiarity distinguishing it from most heads, whether feminine or masculine; namely, that its contour was very regular. . . . Her face was remarkably transfigured by a smile. The smiles of many are signs of nothing more than amusement; but with her smile there was habitually mingled an expression of sympathy, either for the person smiled at or the person smiled with." At the same time he noted her intense domestic affections. "The activity of these last conduced to the leading incidents of her subsequent life." Moreover, he observed that "she had a remarkable capacity for abstract thinking, which so seldom goes along with capacity for concrete representation, even in men." He added: "Among women, such a union of the two as existed in her, has, I should think, never been paralleled."

At one time, undoubtedly, Mary Ann—or Marian, as she began to call herself—had a fondness for the great philosopher who had so accurately gaged her nature; she, for her part, declared him to be "a good delightful creature," and that she always felt better for being with him. It was rumored that they would marry, and this rumor was promptly denied by him. He introduced her to George Henry Lewes, a popularizer of current ideas and science, of whom, in the early days of their acquaintance, she writes: "People are very good to me. Mr. Lewes especially is kind and attentive, and has quite won my regard after having had a good deal of vituperation. Like a few other people in the world, he is much better than he seems. A man of heart and conscience wearing a mask of flippancy."

As for the rest, the story is simple.

During the ten years preceding his meeting with Miss Evans, Lewes had been living with his wife in an "advanced" Bohemian set, by no means conventional in their conduct. The set embraced several young couples who lived in a large house in the Bayswater district in London and saw much of one another. Apart from the Lewes couple, Thornton Hunt (Leigh Hunt's son) and his wife lived there. Agnes

Lewes, described as "that pretty rose-bud woman," left her husband and three children for Hunt, who forsook his wife, "one of the sweetest and best women that ever lived." Lewes forgave his wife, and took her back, but she once more deserted him and made it clear that this time it was for good.

This happened in 1854. Had Lewes and Miss Evans waited another three or four years, they might have married conventionally, for it was not until 1857-58 that marriage in England could be dissolved without a special Act of Parliament. But when the law went into effect, it was too late for Lewes to get the benefit of it.

For a woman steeped in convention as Miss Evans was, her decision to unite her fate with Lewes was a step not easily taken. It must be remembered, too, that she was not yet George Eliot, a great novelist, for whom a point might be stretched. She was, in fact, a woman who had her way to make, and whose very livelihood might conceivably be at stake. Considering the accepted morality of the time, the step might well have ended in disaster. Even as it was, her early training had left its mark, and she was never to feel quite comfortable in the position she had accepted of her own choice. But her mind was never in doubt as to the justice of her decision. More than a year after it had been made, she wrote to a woman friend, Mrs. Bray:

"If there is one action or relation of my life which is and always has been profoundly serious, it is my relation with Mr. Lewes. . . . We can not set each other right in this matter in this letter, but one thing I can tell in a few words. Light and easily broken ties are what I neither desire theoretically nor could live for practically. Women who are satisfied with such ties *do not* act as I have done. That any unworldly, unsuperstitious person who is sufficiently acquainted with the realities of life can pronounce my relation to Mr. Lewes immoral, I can only understand by remembering how subtle and complex are the influences that mold opinion. But I *do* remember this; and I indulge in no arrogant or uncharitable thoughts about those who condemn us, even though we might have expected a somewhat different verdict. From the majority of persons, of course, we never looked for anything but condemnation. We are leading no life of self-indulgence, except indeed that, being happy in each other, we find everything easy. We are working hard to provide for others better than we provide for ourselves, and to fulfill every responsibility that rests upon us."

The "others" are the three sons of Mr. Lewes, the oldest being eighteen, who call her "Mother," and she expresses the opinion that she has a right to be called by her "husband's" name. That, in spite of the absence of marriage papers, she fully regards herself as the wife of Mr. Lewes, she shows in the dedication of the manuscript of *Adam Bede*:

"To my dear husband, George Henry Lewes, I give the MS. of a work which would never have been written but for the happiness which his love has conferred on my life."

For his part, Lewes was tireless in his devotion to Marian. Not only, by his love and powers of divination, had he started her on a novelist's career, but throughout their common lives he encouraged her to greater and greater efforts. He gave himself wholly to her and staunchly stood between her and outside worries. He cheered her in moments when her temperament disposed her to fits of despair.

She was heart-broken when Lewes died in the autumn of 1878, and for a while her life was one of utter desolation. Her New Year's entry in 1879 simply reads: "Here I and sorrow sit." Her life seemed broken, she did not see how she could go on without the devotion that had been hers for so long. "Each day seems a new beginning—a new acquaintance with grief."

In the spring of 1880, however, she married Mr. John Walter Cross, a friend of the Lewes for many years, but she died toward the end of the same year. Though Cross married George Eliot by sanction of the law, it can not be said that he was more devoted to her than Lewes, but devoted to her he certainly was.

THE COMPARISON OF SAND WITH ELIOT

"A MAN's mind in a woman's body," has been said of George Sand, and that holds equally true of George Eliot. It is certain that deliberate rather than unconscious symbolism dictated to the two Georges their masculine names. Their emotions alone are feminine, a fact obviously conditioned by their women's bodies. Hence, it is clear that any comparison in their differences of racial temperaments must be sought in their minds. These, as it happens, are quite representative of the races and times which produced them.

The French mind works out each problem by some inexorable logic, ultimate in its goal; little wonder, then, that it so often arrives at an impasse, leaving to the traveler the only recourse: retreat; as often as not it means a complete rout whose objective is the other extreme. It has been seen how Arthur Rimbaud's mind had worked its way out of a bourgeois environment and reached a new altitude in the range of the arts hitherto unscaled and how it ultimately returned to bourgeois levels. It has also been seen how Anatole France, having found his Ivory Tower too confining for all its perfect beauty, descended to talk to men lest he cease to be human.

George Sand shares this faculty of logic peculiar to the French genius; if she rises to its heights, she also suffers from the inevitable reaction. That "our final impression of her always is that she is a woman and a French-woman," as Henry James puts it, only serves to give intellectual piquancy to the admission that at the same time "there is something very liberal and universal in her genius, as well as very masculine." The admission is significant, as it indicates that George Sand's eccentric conduct in her love-affairs is due to errors of the mind rather than of the heart. The mind plays an important part in French life; it makes existence more interesting, but it also has a way, in the course of experiment (which is its nature, alien to the heart), of playing tricks not in the province of simple impulse and sentiment. As Henry James says:

"George Sand's was a French mind, and as a French mind it had to theorize; but if the positive side of its criticism of most human institutions was precipitate and ill-balanced the error was in a great measure atoned for in later years. The last half of Madame Sand's career was a period of assent and acceptance; she had decided to make the best of those social arrangements which surrounded her—remembering as it were the homely native proverb which declares that when one has not got what one likes one must like what one has got."

This is very well put, and it sums up the George Sand who ran nearly the whole gamut of amorous experience, which began with Sandeau and Musset and ended with Manceau. The word "nearly" is used deliberately, since George Sand's own words, "I have known many kinds of love; the woman's love, mother-love, sister-love, nun's love, poet's love," include, after all, everything but profane love. Balzac, who knew women's hearts, and was to draw her portrait in *Beatrix,* perhaps more than any other of all her contemporaries, saw the chaste mind behind all her amours. One night when they had talked together, he said:

"I have sounded your soul to-night. Love for you is not an imperious need for the satisfaction of a passing pleasure, that is plain. With all your mental sophistication, your soul is pure; you are chaste, you know the theory but not the grossness of passion. Your idea of love is a sort of Heaven, full of noble sentiments and spiritual flowers and exalted morality, where two creatures, united into one angel, can fly on pure wings of rapture and poetry." He saw her great, generous, chaste: all manly qualities. But she hadn't a particle of coquetry. Hence, "her male was hard to find." He must have recalled another night when he had tried to read to her from his *Contes Drolatiques*. She had refused to listen because it was so full of Rabelaisean indecencies, and, on his persisting, she had snatched the manuscript and had thrown it at him, whereupon he left in anger, after calling her a prude and a fool.

In her novels, George Sand portrayed human beings not as they were but as they ought to be; this she did on principle. Thus, also, she had sought superior beings for her intimate relation, and, indeed, for a while she had imagined them to be such, until time found them out. Theory failing her, she had as a last experience an "affair" with Manceau, a simple, humble, devoted man; was it not, in the last analysis, a retreat from her former altitudinous position, in short, a compromise?

George Eliot began at the point where George Sand ended. She had neither cause to advance nor to retreat, but remained invulnerable in the security of her position, which was permanent and quite beyond action and reaction, curiously symbolic of the inviolable insularity of the British Isles. If she had any theories she made them fit her affections; it was at no cost to her spirit that she entered into a lasting union with a man who was neither better nor worse than Manceau and lived happily with him in a relationship which owed its felicity to the circumstance that it was thoroughly human and unspoiled by any preconceived notions of "superiority" common to romantic minds.

This is not to say that the one or the other attitude is, in itself, superior, but the comparison serves to distinguish between thought sprung from simple impulse and thought engendered by theory; between the English mind and the French. Both procedures are, in their way, direct enough, with this distinction: English action proceeds from the heart, the French from the mind. And this may account for the greater reticence of the English which, rightly or wrongly, has more than once brought charges of hypocrisy against them. The mind, *convinced* of the rightness of its deductions by processes purely logical, culminating in the creation of pure abstraction, is less diffident. What George Sand's mind created was love in the abstract, a love which existed neither on land nor sea. Such a love is apt to flaunt itself, in the sense that Don Quixote's chivalry, oblivious of ridicule, flaunted itself, and it must be remembered that his chivalry had been evoked by a mind surfeited on books concerned with the gallant deeds of the knights, just as George Sand's love had been evoked by a mind saturated with the spirit of the Romantics which then charged the air of France. To be a perfect Knight or a perfect Romantic one must be immune against ridicule, and our own age is too analytical to be either chivalrous or romantic.

The starting point of the Romantics of George Sand's day was Rousseau. How, then, is to be explained the abysmal difference between George Sand and George Eliot, since the Englishwoman also confessed her debt to Rousseau, who "sent that electric thrill through my intellectual and moral frame which has awakened me to new perceptions"? And the answer is that the great French nature lover affected more her moral than intellectual frame, and that he had precisely the opposite effect on George Sand. Each took from Rousseau exactly what her national temperament allowed her to take, neither more nor less.

English reserve, so often interpreted by Continentals as hypocrisy, a charge too sweeping to be wholly justifiable, would never have allowed George Eliot to be "sublime." The charge of hypocrisy might have been made more justly

George Sand

From a portrait by Delacroix

George Eliot

From a portrait by Sir Frederick Burton in the National Portrait Gallery, London

against critics of her morality, but here again we are called upon to touch on two attitudes which clash not because one is honest and the other dishonest, but because even were the honesty of the critics not in question it must be granted that both attitudes are dictated by two national temperaments whose approaches to morality have little in common. Charges and countercharges against each other by nations will lead nowhere. And, perhaps, the actions of a Frenchman or a Frenchwoman can best be understood by a French mind, or a mind akin to the French. Mr. Francis Gribble, in his flippant and amusing book on *George Sand and Her Lovers,* illustrates this point admirably. In commenting on George Sand's visits to Liszt, Heine, Madame Allart, Sainte-Beuve and others, to get some light on her failure with Alfred de Musset, he says:

"It is characteristically and supremely French. If we could imagine the greatest English authoress of the day (whoever that may be), with a similar past behind her, discussing the state of her heart in the office of, say, the *Fortnightly Review,* with any of the contributors who happened to be present, reporting progress daily to the editor, and imploring him to intercede for her, and then jumping into a cab and driving off to ask advice from, say, Mr. Paderewski, Mr. Swinburne, and the Countess of Warwick, we should have an approximately exact English parallel, inadequate only because insufficiently absurd. But George Sand, of course, could no more see that anything she did was absurd than she could admit that anything that she did was wrong."

What is interesting about this quotation is not that George appears absurd but that all who listen to her and give her of their counsel must be judged equally absurd, since, indeed, in countenancing it, they are parties to her absurdity. (Mr. Gribble, an Englishman, does not stress this point.)

And, pray, what is wrong in being absurd? It is certain that these Frenchmen and Continentals would have considered the Eliot-Lewes affair quite absurd, so much ado about nothing. It is equally certain that the so-called absurd, the so-called ridiculous, is not without its merits, apart from that of entertaining us. It may seem absurd to give the only shirt off your back to a stranger who hasn't one, but one must admit that the act is not without elements of the sublime, and has indeed the sanction of a great moral Teacher. A whole cult has sprung up in Spain from Unamuno whose chief aspiration is to inspire men with the religion of quixotism, the right and the need of being ridiculous. The idea is, perhaps, not so absurd as it seems. If "from the sublime to the ridiculous is but a step," then it is also true that the ridiculous is seldom without elements of the sublime. George Sand, in spite of her many lovers (who were, after all, so many mile-stones in the quest of the absolute love, which she never found), was, if we would believe her admirers, a chaste woman, sublime in her way even if exciting the ridicule of the sensible. But the sensible may at least find one merit in her suitable to their own mood, and that is, her insistence upon woman's right to lead her own life. She is the first great Feminist, and if it be a fault in her that she carried her idea too far, the result of an excess of French logic, the disgruntled ones may turn for comfort to her more moderate English sister whose courage in living her life in a more restricted atmosphere by no means met with the unanimous approval of minds steeped in English sentiment.

There are some who like French wines, some who prefer English ale, and again there are some who would have neither. It is a thankless task to compare the minds of nations as represented by individuals.

ROBERT E. LEE—STRONG IN DEFEAT

1

A SHADED lamp stood on the table in an upper chamber of an old Virginian house, full of old-fashioned comfort, and in the penumbral shadows there paced a man, up and down, up and down, plunged in contemplation. He was tall, broad-shouldered, graceful, and he walked with easy yet firm step. His bearded face, no longer young, was handsome; even in the shadows its leonine dignity made itself felt; one had no need to see its features clearly. He was fifty-four, but as he ceased from his peregrinations and sat down in the full light, it was to be seen that he looked much younger. He was a man of whom other men say that he is "in his prime." As he sat down he leaned his elbows on the table and buried his face in his hands, and, in this position, remained long and motionless, like an austere bronze from a sculptor's mold. Serene it seemed, outwardly, yet suggesting an inward agitation, an agony of thought, alien to the serenity of its outward form.

Suddenly, the man rose, shook himself, and once more resumed his pacing up and down, up and down.

Then, as suddenly, the big man dropped on his knees, and prayed and prayed. He implored God, his Father, for guidance; he entreated Him to help him come to a decision. Never had he prayed so hard, never had it been so needful to do the right thing. His honor was at stake. Come what may, be the cost ever so great, he must do his duty. It was not always easy to know what one's duty was. To this question there were two sides. On which side did his duty lie?

Several times he resumed his pacing, several times he sat down burying his face in his hands, several times he dropped on his knees to pray.

On the floor below, his wife heard the dull thuds of the big form falling on its knees, and, aware of her husband's dilemma, prayed that his prayer be answered. Only she knew the crisis he was called upon to face. Although she prayed, she had no doubt that what he should decide would be right.

It was that night a solemn household. Much depended on his decision, but whichever way he should decide to go, it would be hard.

It was the night of April 20, 1861; the place was Arlington, Virginia; the man who prayed was Robert E. Lee, then colonel in the United States Army; his prayer implored guidance as to whether, in the coming conflict, now inevitable, he should throw in his lot with the North or the South.

The dilemma he faced was as hard as any which ever faced a man.

For years past clouds had been gathering. There had been faint rumblings which presaged a storm. But two years before it had fallen to Colonel Lee's lot to apprehend that northern fanatic, John Brown, and as John Brown, a rope around his neck, was swung into eternity, Colonel Lee had watched, and near the gibbet had stood "Stonewall" Jackson, his companion-in-arms to be. Did Jackson then, as he "sent up a fervent petition to Heaven" to save John Brown's soul from perdition, comprehend how well his prayer had been answered? Had Lee an inkling of the force resident in that soul released from its earthly envelope? Had Lee known then, it would have made no difference in the decision he now had to make.

During the past three months things had happened quickly. In February, seven cotton states which had seceded from the Union met in convention in Montgomery, Alabama, and formed themselves into the Confederate States of America. On April twelfth Fort Sumter was fired on; on the following day President Lincoln called on the unseceded states for quotas of seventy-five thousand troops; on the seventeenth Virginia, hitherto staunch to the Union, had broken off her allegiance.

It was no longer a question whether one half of the country should maintain slaves and the other half be free. The question now was one of states' rights: whether a state, finding its welfare incompatible with the Union, had a right to secede. The larger issue swallowed up the lesser.

Colonel Lee was Virginia's proudest citizen. The son of "Lighthorse Harry" Lee, a gallant warrior who had, besides, the gift of eloquence, he had blood connections with the finest families in Virginia and in England. The Virginia Lees had for generations provided the state with councilors and governors. Richard Lee, the first to come to Virginia, which circumstance gave him the appellation of "the immigrant," belonged to an old family, "ancient enough to have fought at Hastings and to have followed Richard of the Lion Heart to the Holy Land." And in Robert there was at least one strain of blood which had come from Washington himself.

The military tradition was strong in the Lee family. Robert "seemed to have come a soldier from his mother's womb," his own son, General Charles Lee himself an accomplished soldier, was aptly to describe him later. He went to West Point "both to relieve his mother and to have a military education." He had patterned himself on George Washington, whom he so much resembled in character and demeanor and military gifts, that even at West Point the resemblance of the young cadet to Virginia's greatest son had already been remarked. At West Point, as later in the Mexican War, in which he performed distinguished service, he had unknowingly met his future foes and companions-in-arms, and he was enabled to gauge their faults and gifts to his later advantage. He had made so great a reputation that when a difficult task was in hand, Brevet Captain Lee was the man assigned to it. "He is young," wrote General Scott of him, when appealed to by the city of St. Louis for a man to save it from inundation, "but if the work can be done, he can do it." And he did it, as it happened, in opposition to those whom he came to succor and who thought they understood better than he how it should be done.

He had won the title of colonel in active service in the War with Mexico. General Scott was yet to say of him that he was the "very best soldier he ever saw in the field." General Scott went further than that, and asserted that Lee was "the greatest living soldier in America." As if that were not enough, the old general, years before the great conflict, made the startling declaration tantamount to a prophecy:

"If I were on my death-bed to-morrow, and the president of the United States should tell me that a great battle was to be fought for the liberty or slavery of the country, and asked my judgment as to the ability of a commander, I would say with my dying breath, 'Let it be Robert E. Lee.' "

And now, this very night, he faced the situation projected speculatively by General Scott.

The command of the United States Armies had already been offered him, and, tempting as the offer had seemed, he had rejected it. He was opposed to secession, and he deprecated war, but he could not, and he would not, take part in an invasion of the Southern States. He had said so frankly. He had watched the cleft widening, and as he saw the irrevocable acts taking place and the inevitable approaching, he grew more and more sad. He could do nothing except in-so-far as it concerned himself. He was no friend of slavery; he had already freed what slaves he had held in his own right. But even if all the slaves were freed, he saw no immediate solution to the problem; what, after all, was to be done with them? Like many Virginians, he thought that "the relation of master and slave, controlled by humane laws and influenced by Christianity and an enlightened public sentiment, is the best that can exist between the white and black races while intermingled, as at present, in this country."

Weeks of agony had gone by, and while other states had seceded Virginia maintained a neutrality. And now, President Lincoln's demand for quotas of seventy-five thousand men from unseceded states drove Virginia to its decision to resist the demand, and to defend, if need be, its sovereign rights. States' rights were a tradition in Virginia, and most of all in the Lee family. Robert's father, three times governor of Virginia, had said in public debate: "Virginia is my country: her will I obey, however lamentable the fate to which it may subject me." And he had, on other occasions, given similar expression to his feelings on the subject of states' rights. Robert E. Lee passionately esteemed the traditions of Virginia and of his family, and his political principles were as sacred to him as his religion.

Yet the question which now faced him, on this night of April twentieth, was not an easy one. He foresaw clearly that Virginia, in the event of a conflict, would be the inevitable battle-ground. It was the great border state; he shuddered at the prospect. He evoked a vision of conflagration, ruin, suffering . . . his beautiful state mutilated by incessant battle. The war, if war came, would be long . . . strife would stretch through the years. And who knew the outcome? The North had by far the most men, the greater resources; it had all the factories, munition-making would be relatively easy for them; he was an engineer, he knew what this meant. And the North had the whole navy, with which it might blockade the southern ports. The prospect was terrifying. . . . His eyes gazed down a vista of suffering, of horror, stretching through endless years. . . .

God, he prayed, open the eyes of these blind politicians that they might see whither their blindness leads; open the eyes of men in the North and in the South that they might become aware of their folly and avert disaster. . . .

Even as he prayed he knew it was too late. Feeling on both sides ran high, the blood of the protagonists was inflamed.

He searched his conscience. But one thing remained. To do his duty. Duty, as he once said, in a letter to one of his sons, was "the sublimest word in our language." And he recalled that magnificent story which he had used in the letter to illustrate the matter to his son. A hundred years ago there was a day of remarkable darkness and gloom, still remembered as the dark day—a day when the light of the sun was slowly extinguished, as if by an eclipse. The legislature of Connecticut was in session, and as its members saw the unexpected and unaccountable darkness coming on, they shared the general awe and terror. It was supposed by many that the last day—the day of judgment—had come. Some one in consternation moved an adjournment. Then there arose an old Pilgrim legislator, Davenport of Stamford, and said that if the last day had come he desired to be found at his place doing his duty, and therefore moved that candles be brought in so that the House could proceed with its duty. There was quietness in that man's mind, the quietness of heavenly wisdom and inflexible willingness to obey present duty. . . . "Do your duty in all things," he had advised his son, "like the old Puritan. You can not do more; you should never wish to do less. Never let me or your mother wear one grey hair for lack of duty on your part."

What, then, was his duty? That was all that mattered. He was a devoted Union man. He did not want to see the Union his forefathers helped to make broken up. He thought both sides had been precipitate. There was right on both sides (wrong too!); any sacrifice, short of honor, was worth making rather than plunge the nation into an ocean of blood. It was tragic and unnecessary. But such thought led to nothing. Human nature was weak, and blood was hot. Neither side would give away, not even a little. It was heart-breaking. His wife's family were strong adherents of the Union, and they had spoken and written to him, urging good reasons for his adherence to the Union side. They were honest and sincere, like himself.

All night he wrestled with the problem, weighing this and that in the balance, and in the intervals between his thoughts he gave himself up earnestly to supplication and prayer. This was better. Reason led nowhere, decided nothing. Something beyond, a mood growing out of an impulse in his deepest deeps, increasing rather than diminishing, swept over him, and destroyed the reason-erected dikes, until there was no longer any need to ask where his duty lay. Loyalties rose uppermost—loyalty to state, to family and to self—and where loyalties decide, there the path to duty is cleared.

Virginia had given him birth, he would die for Virginia.

Once he had come to this decision, a burden seemed lifted from his soul, an inward calm possessed him, a quiet determination to follow the path he had chosen, if need be, to the bitter end. Though blood flow, and hell's horrors are let loose, he must go through with it, and they all must go through with it, the foe as well as the friend. He was a tender-hearted man, and what was to come would need all his compassion. Was he sure of victory? By no means. But whether victory should crown their efforts, or defeat, it was God's will.

It was morning when the light had come.

No longer in doubt, he walked to the writing table, and sat down to write. He wrote quickly, and, without folding the paper, descended below, where his wife was waiting. He was collected, almost cheerful, and said:

"Well, Mary, the question is settled. Here is my letter of resignation, and a letter I have written to General Scott."

It was his resignation from the United States Army. "It would have been presented at once," he wrote, "but for the struggle it has cost me to separate myself from a service to which I have devoted the best years of my life and all the ability I possessed." After thanking the general for all the kindness he had received, and expressing regret for having to sever himself from his comrades, he added: "Save in the defense of my native state, I never desire again to draw my sword."

He wrote letters to relatives with Union sympathies and for all he had the same answer: he was doing his duty in following the dictates of his conscience. "I know you will blame me," he wrote to his sister, whose husband and son espoused the cause of the North, "but you must think as kindly of me as you can, and believe that I have endeavored to do what I thought right."

He had no desire to force any one's hand. Every one, even his own son, must follow his own true inclination. "Tell Curtis," he wrote to his wife, nearly a month later, "he must consult his own judgment, reason and conscience as to the course he may take. I do not wish him to be guided by my wishes or example. If I have done wrong, let him do better. The present is a momentous question which every man must settle for himself and upon principle."

Thus spoke the man who was the strangest combination of Puritan and Cavalier, the best of both. No description of the man could furnish a better portrait than that conveyed by his words: "Duty is the sublimest word in our language."

The time had come when he must suit the action to the word. He must make the word live a flaming life, full of sadness and wonder.

2

Three days following his resignation, Robert E. Lee is appointed major-general of the Virginian Army, and, in a modest acceptance, expresses the wish "that their choice had fallen upon an abler man." He concludes his short speech in words so characteristic of him:

"Trusting in Almighty God, an approving conscience, and the aid of my fellow citizens, I devote myself to the service of my native state, in whose behalf alone will I ever again draw my sword."

Here is no mock modesty, no sanctimonious avowal of the Godhead. That very day, he shows his modesty, his willingness to serve as to command.

It so happens that the Honorable Alexander H. Stephens, the Vice-President of the Confederate States, is present at the ceremony which has conferred the command of the Virginian forces on Lee. He has come to Richmond with the purpose of inducing Virginia to join the Confederacy, and it is to be seen at once that the proposed compact as it stands will eliminate Lee from the position newly conferred on him. It is clear, too, that a word or a look of disapproval from Lee will terminate the negotiations with which Mr.

Stephens has been entrusted. In the latter event, the Border States will act independently and either they will protect the Confederacy's lines or the battle-field will be moved at once to South Carolina and the borders of Georgia. Mr. Stephens, therefore, proposes to Lee "that he resign, without any compensation or promise therefor, the very honor and rank he had that same morning received."

So unselfish is the man who hardly a week before had rejected the command of all the Union forces that, seeing how matters stand, he, without a moment's hesitation, agrees, declaring that no personal ambition or emolument shall be considered to stand in the way!

And so Virginia joins the Confederacy, and General Lee takes a subordinate position "which for a time places him nearly out of sight."

It is a curious position for a man whom General Scott has called the greatest living soldier in America and whose campaigns are later to be judged with those of the world's greatest military captains. If he had been given his chance at once, the outcome of the war, even in the face of superior forces and equipment, might have proved different. As it is, his ultimate defeat does not tarnish his glory, and his achievements, not to detract from the victor, stand higher than those of Grant.

For a military genius, General Lee is a strange man. He is thinking of neither fame nor glory. With all his gifts for war, he is too well aware of the folly of strife and too richly equipped with compassion to desire the crown of a Cæsar or a Napoleon; in this sense, he is unique among great commanders. Here are his thoughts penned to his wife in those early days when he is in command of the forces in West Virginia:

"I enjoyed the mountains as I rode along. The views

were magnificent. The valleys so peaceful, the scenery so beautiful. What a glorious world Almighty God has given us! How thankless and ungrateful we are!"

What are we to think of a great general whose letters to his wife are full of such observations as this:

"Since I had been thrown in such immediate relations with him [Fitzhugh Washington], I had learned to appreciate him very highly. Morning and evening have I seen him on his knees praying to his Maker. 'The righteous perisheth, and no man layeth it to heart; the merciful men are taken away, none considering that the righteous are taken away from the evil to come.' May God have mercy on us all."

He is for ever thinking of those under him, and the petty amenities of life do not escape his notice. "We are without tents," he writes, "and for two nights I have lain buttoned up in my overcoat. To-day my tent came up, and I am in it, yet fear I shall not sleep for thinking of the poor men. I have no doubt the socks you mentioned will be very acceptable to the men here and elsewhere. If you can send them here I will distribute to the most needy." Duly he apprizes Mrs. Lee of the arrival of the socks and of his personal distribution of them. Self-imposed tasks like these do not hinder him from preparing well-calculated, precise plans for confounding the enemy.

He is at this time charged with incompetence, with being "too tender to shed blood." His "showy presence" and "historic name" are held as detrimental; demands are raised for a real soldier. Such outcries come from south of Virginia. The governor of Carolina protests against General Lee being sent there. But the president, Jefferson Davis, knows better. "If General Lee is not a soldier," he writes, "I have none to send you." General Lee himself remains silent, and proceeds with his duty of creating defenses, the results of which are to be seen later. To his wife he writes: "We must make up our minds to meet with reverses and overcome them. But the contest must be long, and the whole country has to go through much suffering. It is necessary we should be humble and taught to be less boastful, less selfish, and more devoted to right and justice to all the world."

Meanwhile, General McClellan is preparing to move on to Richmond, the Confederacy's capital, with an immense well-equipped army which he had been getting ready for months. As the situation becomes threatening, the tongues of fools are silenced and all eyes are turned to the one man who can avert impending disaster. The Confederate Congress creates for General Lee the office of commander-in-chief. President Davis vetoes the act as unconstitutional, he himself, by virtue of the constitution, being the head of the military and naval forces of the Confederacy. This is no time for playing at government and war, but official minds will have their way. As a substitute for the vetoed office, President Davis, on March 13, 1862, issues the following order:

"General Robert E. Lee is assigned to duty at the seat of government, and, under the direction of the President, is charged with the conduct of the military operations in the armies of the Confederacy."

"Under the direction of the President!" Mark you that! The ironic gods smile. The foolish man does not know that by vetoing the original act and tying General Lee's hands he has in all likelihood (who can tell?) signed away the tenancy of the Confederacy and of his own office.

Even so, the son of "Lighthorse Harry" Lee is to perform marvels. But at the moment he takes charge things look dark for the southern cause. The "little Napoleon" is almost at the gates of Richmond with an army of one hundred and ten thousand, with additional forces of sixty thousand under General McDowell and Frémont not many miles away.

Lee, with a force of barely eighty thousand, and with an equipment not to be compared with that of the foe, begins his work which is to confound not only the confident enemy but the world.

General Stonewall Jackson is his Ney; the other names to shine with his are J. E. B. Stewart, Joseph E. Johnston, Richard S. Ewell; should one include James C. Longstreet? His name is suggestive of his character: it takes him a long time to get anywhere. A good general in many ways, he fails at crucial moments. General Robert E. Lee contains them all, what is best in them; for a great commander he has one fault all his own: he is kind to his generals when they have blundered. He is generous to attribute victory to them; in the hour of setback or failure, because some one has not followed the precise plan, he accepts the whole blame. A queer sort of general is this who on the battlefield has time to be "a Christian gentleman." He would be a Hannibal or a Napoleon if he were not Robert E. Lee. In all the annals of war there is none like him.

3

Must one speak of his battles? That one must is a pity, for the man interests us more. But military students the world over are obliged to study Lee's campaigns as they study the campaigns of Cæsar and Napoleon. "According to my notions of military history," says Field-Marshal Viscount Wolseley, "there is as much instruction both in strategy and in tactics to be gleaned from General Lee's operations of 1862 as there is to be found in Napoleon's campaign of 1796."

Let us unroll, then, the scroll, and relate briefly the achievements of Lee in-so-far as they emphasize that contradiction in his character which enables him to be a good general without forfeiting the title of good Christian. Sadness and compassion do not forsake him in the hour of victory, but even in victory he is too well aware of the vast resources of the enemy in materials and men; he knows that time is against him, and he has inklings that in the "war of attrition" it is not on his banner that ultimate victory shall perch. But for the time being, with inferior forces and equipment, he performs marvels, to the profound chagrin of the North.

He begins by disposing of General McClellan's vast army around Richmond. By a series of carefully planned battles the northern commander is made to depart much more quickly than he came, and only the blunders of Lee's generals save his army from complete destruction. The usually reliable Stonewall Jackson makes his mistakes; as for Longstreet, he turns into the wrong road. The patient Lee takes the blame. Even so, the victory is his. The South is jubilant. Richmond is saved.

In the North President Lincoln calls for three hundred thousand more men. McClellan is deprived of the chief command; General Halleck takes his place. The cry grows louder: "On to Richmond!"

New armies are massed against Richmond under Major-General John Pope, an able man, but vain and something of a bully, who, as a beginning, issues orders outlawing southern non-combatants who refuse to take the oath of allegiance to the Union. Even the charitable Lee expresses contempt for the new leader in his message to Jackson, "I want Pope suppressed." And he immediately proceeds with measures of suppression which are to surprise that overconfident gentleman. The stroke he plans is audacious; he is to repeat it in the future with equally brilliant effects. If his strategy is audacious, it is also simple, as all great strategy always is. To be sure, it involves danger; the risks he must run are great, and Richmond itself is at stake in the event of failure. The safety of the city hangs on precarious threads, but these threads are held by genius whose perfect equilibrium is all that keeps them from snapping. Those in power are aware of this. "Confidence in you," writes President Davis to Lee, "overcomes the view which would otherwise be taken." Briefly, his plan is to hold Richmond with but two brigades while massing his forces elsewhere on one of the enemy's flanks with such effect as virtually to destroy Pope's forces before they could join hands with those of McClellan. Only the capture of one of Stuart's officers with the plans of battle saves Pope from complete destruction; as it is, his force of eighty thousand nearly melts away before the onslaught of Lee's fifty-five thousand and must flee in wild disorder.

Thus Pope passes out from the scene; McClellan once more takes command. As far as Lee is concerned, the battles for the defense of Richmond form but a prelude for greater achievements. He comes off with glory at Antietam, in spite of a second curious mishap. His plan of battle, wrapped around a handful of cigars, is found on the site of a deserted camp and is delivered to McClellan, who notwithstanding this advantage and the superiority of his forces against Lee's—eighty-seven thousand against thirty-five thousand men—is forced to retire, discomfited after sanguinary battles in which both sides lose heavily. But because the dispatch is lost by some careless officer, Lee is compelled to forego the main object of the campaign: the winning of Maryland. Even at this early date, his army already suffers from lack of necessities, and many of the men are without boots or shoes.

The feeling in the North is strong that McClellan should have won this battle, and it is not long before he is again relieved of his command and General Burnside takes his place, only a little later to give way to "Fighting Joe" Hooker.

General Lee's victories do not provide him with joy. "What a cruel thing is war," he writes to his wife in his letter of Christmas Day, 1862, "to separate and destroy families and friends, and mar the purest joys and happiness God has granted us in this world, to fill our hearts with hatred instead of love for our neighbors, and to devastate the fair face of this beautiful world! . . . My heart bleeds at the death of every one of our gallant men." This is only a fortnight after he had put Burnside to flight at Fredericksburg, at the zenith of his own fame.

Then Chancellorsville . . . Hooker has one hundred and thirty thousand men and four hundred and forty-eight guns; Lee sixty-two thousand men and one hundred and seventy guns. Hooker has a fine plan, and his "own ground," "the strongest position on the planet." Lee admits as much, but tries one of his audacious flanking movements while facing Hooker with a mere ten thousand men. Once more victory . . . Hooker's army escapes complete destruction by one of those tragic ironies with which the fates bestrew the life of Lee. Stonewall Jackson, his right hand, in the hour of victory, is shot by accident by one of his own men. Any victory is "dear at such a price," says Lee on hearing this.

Another general is found wanting. Hooker gives way to Meade.

Gettysburg . . . the first and only battle in northern territory, the war's turning-point. Lee might have won it, but Longstreet is at fault. . . . If only Stonewall Jackson were not dead! A great victory would be his. As it is, it is the beginning of the end. He takes the whole blame of it on himself. He writes to President Davis and asks to be relieved. President Davis refuses and says that there is no better man. Still, it is the beginning of the end.

Though other victories await him, Lee knows this. How can an army fight with lessening numbers, without food, or shoes, or guns, or other equipment? The North is rich, its armies increase, its resources are inexhaustible.

Lee sees the end, but before that comes he will show his foe the stuff the South is made of. The northerners, too, are brave, but he feels assured that the South is the greater cause and in its defense they will wage the better fight.

A great army is being gathered in the North; this army at last finds a worthy head, the victor of Vicksburg, Ulysses S. Grant, a good fighter and a dogged man. His plans are: "persistent hammering," and "attack all along the line." He can do it: he has plenty of guns and plenty of men, and plenty of food for both. He is forty-two years old, his opponent fifty-seven. In the "war of attrition" the odds are his.

In the fighting to come, three facts stand forth preeminently, says the historian: "Lee's genius, Grant's resolution, and the infinite courage of the officers and men on both sides."

Yet this is also clear: the greater man must lose. Though still distant, Appomattox is in sight.

4

Appomattox. . . . Call it Golgotha. But Gethsemane comes first. A gallant general, one of the world's greatest, prays to his Father for mercy, but fights calmly on. Judas? It is the inevitable, that betraying fate which so often awaits the greatest.

Let us invade the agony of those bitter hours. He, the chief protagonist, is calm, but the spectator must quail before the picture of those hours. Hours? These hours stretch into weeks and months. The agony is long, the inevitable end always in sight.

Skill alone, great as that skill is, is not enough to save the South from overwhelming force—force, moreover, not without skill. Marvels of strategy and tactics can not resurrect vanishing battalions, nor create commissariats out of mere air. The fields, once fertile, are devastated; women as well as men have given their all, and are at the point of exhaustion. The northern General Sherman has performed his march to the sea, ruthlessly burning and pillaging—"War is hell!" said he, and proceeded to demonstrate this incontrovertible fact. His colleague, General Sheridan, has led his cavalry on some historic rides. The southernmost South is doomed. General Grant descends on Richmond with armies and guns, a host the like of which has never been seen.

Too late General Lee is given *carte blanche* by his government. Too late to repair the damage of years "under the direction of the president." For a full year Grant has had his hands free. Undaunted, collected as on the first day of his command, Lee sets to his tasks. His army is now but a bare remnant of its old self; it is without food, without shoes, without blankets. Ammunition is scarce. But still Lee is full of resources, energy, defiance, challenging the inexorable fates to do their worst. He takes the whole burden of the war on his own shoulders. He is sustained by one thing: duty, the sublimest thing he knows, the main thread in the woof of his integrity.

For many months he holds at bay an army more than twice as large and with an equipment beyond all comparison. There is that terrible winter of 1864, when Lee's army, having stopped the Union advance, the Confederate soldiers, across the space separating the trenches, shout their exasperating taunts, which at last bring forth the unanswerable retort from a Union soldier:

"Swap generals with us and we'll come over and lick h—l out of you!"

Is there not truth in this? Is there not epic virtue in a situation which can bring forth such a retort? The war for Troy could not have had moments more Homeric than this.

Put aside now the wrongs and rights of the case. What is at stake here? Slavery, the Union? Yes. But these are side issues, when looked at through the telescope of the more remote future. The triumph to be is the triumph which is to project a new world: the world of industry, the world of the machine. Romance—chivalry—is in the death throes; Lee is the last symbol of a vanishing world, whose supreme expression he is.

The last moments come, inevitably. Can the most superhuman effort defeat the Machine, with hosts of brave men for servants? Lee decides to gather his dwindling, starving remnants, and beat a retreat from Richmond, which, throughout the war, has been "a millstone round his neck." For a third time the ironic fates betray him. His complete plan of retreat falls by accident into Grant's hands. This time it is contained in a letter found at Richmond on its occupation on April 3, 1865, by Federal troops. It enables Grant to counter every move which Lee makes and eventually to apprehend him with his overwhelming force.

At this time Lee's forces number twenty-five thousand arms at the most. Even now his chance for eluding Grant is good, but a fatuous blunder puts an end to that. A provision train should await him at Appomattox, but when he arrives there he finds that the train had been there and had been sent on to Richmond.

Why prolong the agony?

Thenceforth a series of letters passes between Grant and Lee relative to surrender. While these communications pass, the fighting goes on. The last desperate drive takes place on the ninth; one of Lee's generals reports that he can do nothing more without support from another corps.

"Then," says Lee, "there is nothing left for me but to go and see General Grant, and I would rather die a thousand deaths."

On the same day, the two men meet, and quickly settle the details of surrender. Grant rises to the occasion with a magnanimity for which he will be remembered more than for his victories.

The victory is won. The long-sought quarry is caught. But there is no elation in the younger general's heart, rather a sense of shame at his part in a humiliating affair. Why should he feel glad at having caged this magnificent old lion, who had fought until his strength had wasted away? (This is literal: the actual number of muskets surrendered on the ninth is nine thousand!)

Lee appears at the sad ceremony in full-dress uniform. Grant is more modest in a simple fatigue suit—a private's blouse, with only a general's shoulder-straps to mark his rank; his boots are spattered to their tops. And, suddenly, Grant feels curiously abashed before his defeated adversary, as an incident from earlier days flashes across his mind. They had both been serving in Mexico under General Scott. It had happened that Grant had gone to headquarters in an ordinary fatigue uniform, rather worse for wear, and had reported to Lee who was serving on Scott's staff. After the business had been transacted, Lee said: "I feel it my duty, Captain, to call your attention to General Scott's order that an officer reporting at Headquarters should be in full uniform." And suddenly remembering this, General Grant has no other feeling but that of mortification lest Lee should recall it also and take his present appearance as an intended affront.

Can tribute to the defeated be greater?

This is not the end of Grant's magnanimity. Salutes of joy are forbidden to be fired, no public tokens of exultation are allowed.

Then—says the historian:

"Men who saw the defeated general when he came forth from the chamber where he had signed the articles of capitulation say that he paused a moment as his eyes rested once more on the Virginia hills, smote his hands together as though in some excess of inward agony, then mounted his gray horse, Traveller, and rode calmly away. . . .

"As he rode quietly down the lane leading from the scene of the capitulation, he passed into the view of his men—of such as remained of them. The news of the surrender had got abroad and they were waiting, grief-stricken and dejected, upon the hillsides, when they caught sight of their old commander on the gray horse. . . . In an instant they were about him, bareheaded, with tear-wet faces; thronging him, kissing his hand, his boots, his saddle; weeping; cheering amid their tears; shouting his name to the very skies. He said: 'Men, we have fought through the war together. I have done my best for you. My heart is too full to say more.' "

5

What is the secret of this man, Robert E. Lee, who was loved by his friends, and admired by his enemies? Why is posterity so anxious to do him abundant tribute?

Let one who knew him, Senator B. H. Hill, of Georgia, speak:

"He was Cæsar without his ambition, Frederick without his tyranny, Napoleon without his selfishness, and Washington without his reward."

This tribute would serve well for his epitaph.

SIMON BOLIVAR—LIBERATOR

1

ON DECEMBER 1, 1830, a small man seated in a chair was borne to shore by two sailors from a ship newly arrived at the port of Santa Marta, in New Granada, now known as Colombia.

The man in the chair could have been barely five feet, six inches, in height; he had a spare body, a narrow chest and lean legs, while his hands and feet were hardly larger than a woman's. A rough yellowish skin stretched over high cheek-bones; the nose was long, well shaped and sensitive; the high forehead was deeply furrowed. The very long upper lip and pointed chin, both unshaved, added to the impression one already had of an exceptionally long face and head. The hair was very black, streaked with gray, the eyebrows heavy, the eyes black and piercing, burning with curious flickers like the suddenly awakened flickers of a dying flame, inevitable tokens of a wasting disease. It would have been hard to tell his age; he was, in fact, forty-seven.

The man was none other than Simon Bolivar, the Liberator. Patriot, warrior and statesman, father of five nations, he was coming here to die, though he did not know how near the end really was.

For twenty-two years, with rare ardor, he had fought to free South America from the cruel Spanish yoke, sparing neither himself nor his fortunes,—he had given all,—and now he was incredibly weary in soul, tired in body and disillusioned, and the prospect of death had no terrors for him. He had done the impossible: in the face of the greatest odds, and with a constancy unsurpassed in heroic chronicles, he had created five nations, in the end only to encounter treachery and to witness strife and chaos where he had sought to impart peace and unity. He had had his dream of a free united America, and just when he saw his dream coming true, even then the awakening had come. . . . Ungrateful wretches, for whom he had given his life—were they worth working for?

God, how he had worked! How he had suffered to make men free! How many defeats he had sustained and overcome to achieve his goal! Another man would have long since given up the fight or died in his tracks. It was a long fifteen years ago that the Duke of Manchester, the governor of Jamaica, had said of him that "the flame had consumed the oil,"—that had been nonsense, of course!—he had, after all, kept going another fifteen years at a strenuous frightening pace, confounding his enemies as he had the well-meaning duke. It was natural, perhaps, that they should think he would crack; he had seemed so frail. But he wasn't frail, and his great cause had given him superhuman strength; it had been to him his food and drink.

But now——

It was not the prospect of death that hurt him. Death could only mean relief. It was the base treachery of men that stung him. He had brought them gifts—freedom and law and order—where before had been slavery and anarchy and chaos. He had removed all restrictions the mother country had imposed. Spain had governed her colonies wholly for her own profit; commerce was prohibited, taxes were imposed at will, industry was restricted, learning was forbidden, a native could not hold office. Why, a man couldn't even plant a vineyard or an olive tree if he so desired. He, Bolivar, had changed all that. . . .

Was there a vice worse than ingratitude? Human nature was strange, perverse, inscrutable.

His own country, Venezuela, reviled him most. The agony of Prometheus was nothing to this, Bolivar's ordeal in his declining days.

Sad were the thoughts of the now weazened man borne in a chair; he had come to Santa Marta to seek a little rest.

2

Here in Santa Marta he was with friends. Among them was a bishop.

Two doctors had looked him over. The case was hopeless. His lungs were in a bad way; tubercular phthisis was his malady. The hero of a thousand battles, forced to sit quietly, was indulging in backward glances over traveled roads. They were by no means pleasant reflections. To the Villa Pedro Alejandrino, where day by day he sat, his friends came, and now and then the bishop. He talked to them, but most of all to the bishop he unburdened his heart. He talked to the bishop of his childhood, of the one woman he had loved and lost, of his many battles, his defeats, his victories, his disappointments, his ecstasies, of his constancy of purpose which had permitted him to endure all for his ultimate goal.

He was born in 1783 in the ungrateful city of Caracas, which he had lived to liberate. His father had died when he was still very young; his mother had educated him, with the aid of a tutor, Simon Rodriguez, whom he grew to love. The Bolivars were Spanish nobles, among Venezuela's wealthiest. When he was fifteen his mother died, and he was sent by his uncle and guardian to Madrid to finish his education. There he mingled with the highest, even with royalty. There, also, he met Maria Teresa de Toro, whom he loved. They were too young to marry. In 1801 Bolivar went to Paris. Napoleon Bonaparte had already won some of his most notable victories, and, as First Consul, was working to reorganize France from the long chaos through which she had passed after the Revolution. Bonaparte had inspired him with a great ardor for that new world which he saw coming into being. He began to dream great dreams for his country's future.

In the same year he married Maria Teresa de Toro and, for the time being forgetting his dreams, returned with his wife to Caracas, where he drifted into a peaceful life and attended to his affairs. But the fates had been unkind, and took Maria from him but ten months after his arrival in Caracas.

"I vowed then and there never to marry again," he said to the bishop. "I vowed that I would give myself, heart and soul, to my country. I have kept my vow."

The bishop nodding assent, Bolivar went on:

"I went the same year back to Madrid. This was in 1803. From Madrid I went to Paris. Napoleon, you see, had been my hero. But alas! You know what happened. Napoleon accepted the crown, the Empire had come into being. I got an invitation to the coronation ceremony, but in my rage tore it up into bits. Why should I go? Since Napoleon had become a king it seemed to me that his glory was like the brilliancy of hell. But the liberty of America was to me a wonderful thing and I began to dream of liberty for my country. It is true that two years later I saw Napoleon crowned in Milan as King of Italy, and saw the great parade pass before the Emperor. Let me assure you: these pompous ceremonies only fearfully aroused my hatred of monarchy. I went to Florence, Venice, Rome and Naples, studying life and people, and all the while one dream pursued me: how to help my own people.

"Then a curious thing happened: one of those strange meetings which influence one's whole life. For in Rome I ran across my old tutor and compatriot, Simon Rodriguez. I hold the memory of that man with affection. For, in that talk we had together—I shall never forget it—he fired me with a love of our country such as I had never had before. I remember when we parted I took Rodriguez' hand and I made a solemn vow that I would not rest until I should free my country. I kept this vow too, Father. . . ."

"You have, my son. . . . Your country will remember you."

"They have already forgotten!" said Bolivar, with a contemptuous shrug, some of his old fire flashing from his eyes. "No sooner I turn my back than they are at their old tricks. I am old now. I have no more that youthful fervour with which I greeted Rodriguez. . . . I have worn myself out in their service. They hate me after all I have done for them. Colombia has been my dream. I joined Venezuela and New Granada and made one country of them, after freeing both from bondage. And now! Now they threaten to jump at each other's throats!"

The bishop nodded understandingly, while Bolivar went on:

"I have welded New Granada and Venezuela with my blood. They realized my dream of Colombia; only the beginning, mind you, of a still larger Colombia, which, one day, might stretch from the Isthmus to the Horn, and in which peace and amity would reign. What were these countries when I first came? Nothing! Worse than nothing! What were the people? Mere savages! Yes, even worse than savages! Because, beside their ferocity, they were slaves to boot! I have given them liberty and law, the two things by which civilization can exist; I have given them pride and dignity in being Americans; I have given them an opportunity to hold up their heads with the nations of the earth. . . . I have given my life and my fortune for them. What have I? My life is ebbing from me, I am forced to subsist on a pension granted me by the Government. . . ."

"You have been generous, son," said the prelate kindly. "You have given away all you've had, which will be accounted in your favour in the world to come. The commonest soldier under you can not say that you've ever sent him away without giving him of your last."

"Slaves! Slaves!" cried Bolivar, a hoarse cough choking him. "They weren't satisfied with freedom. They wanted to make me Emperor! Me, who has always fought against kings; whose one idea has always been to banish monarchy from the earth, who has scorned Napoleon because he had accepted a crown! How many crowns haven't I been offered, and refused! It has been against my principles to be dictator. . . ."

"Perhaps, it would have been better if you had. These people can not rule. . . ."

"Don't say that, Father! Don't say that!" interrupted Bolivar, with passion. "What is right is right, and what is wrong is wrong. The age for Emperors and Dictators is past. Despots belong to history, but not to the future! I have always held to that, as to a sacred vow. But I could have been an Emperor, a Dictator, a Despot. Yes, and by the desire of the people. I have rejected every chance. . . . Yet I have been called ambitious! Am still called ambitious. I have but done my duty, and what is it that I have asked? Nothing but an opportunity to be a citizen, a simple citizen. And still I am called ambitious. . . ."

"All great men have enemies, my son," said the bishop.

"What have I done to deserve them? There's Paez . . .

Paez is, in his way, a brave man. He was of incalculable help to me in war. But truly peace is more dangerous than war for some men. Paez had other ideas than mine. When I was in Peru he, with some friends, conspired to make me Emperor of the Andes. I refused. I wrote him then that I was not Napoleon and had no wish to be one; and that I hadn't the least desire to imitate Cæsar. Paez, you see, wanted to shine in a way that one can't shine in a Republic. To satisfy his ambition I appointed him head of one of the three military districts in Venezuela. I thought he would rest content. But in my absence in Peru he started no end of trouble. The people of Peru offered me all sorts of inducements to remain. But how could I? I started back to Colombia to straighten out the tangle. I was still strong, and Paez saw his mistake. He went so far as to ask to be tried for his misconduct. And what did I do? I forgave him, I tried to overlook all he did, and even called him the 'saviour of the country.' I did this because I did not want internal strife, and because I saw that peace, above all, was needed in the country. I called upon all Colombians to forget all that happened in that terrible year of 1826. They thought I did this because I was weak; at a banquet given me by Paez and his friends they tried to hint as much; but if they thought so, they were soon undeceived. To this day, I remember the words I said: 'Here is no other authority and no other power than mine. Among all my lieutenants I am like the sun; if they shine it is because of the light I lend them.' Ha! ha! ha! . . . Does that sound vainglorious, Father? There are times in life when for a great cause one must stop at no means to exercise authority."

"And what happened then?" asked the bishop, with a laugh.

"What happened? Nothing! They were silent as the

night. I was magnanimous. I gave my sword to Paez, who then made a speech. He'd rather die a thousand times, he said, and lose every drop of his blood than permit this sword to leave his hand, or ever attempt to shed the blood which up to now it has set free. 'Bolivar's sword is in my hands,' the fellow said. 'For you and for him I shall go with it to eternity. This oath is inviolable.' "

"I fear," said the bishop, with a smile, "the fellow's not to be trusted, for all his fine words and inviolable oaths. You've been too magnanimous."

"I fear you are right. Hardly two years have passed since he lifted my own sword against me. For once the people of New Granada were right in being incensed at my magnanimity. . . . I was kind to Santander too. And what was my reward? A plot against my life. They nearly got me too! It was the same as if they had got me. Perhaps, it would have been better if they really had. . . . Then I should have been spared every added treachery. . . . The murder of poor Sucre was the last. It did for me. Poor Antonio! I loved that man. He was my best general. An honester and more generous man never lived. What America and freedom owe to him they can never repay. His battle at Ayacucho but six years ago is our greatest glory. It ended that war for American freedom which began with the battle of Lexington in 1775. What the great Washington began Antonio José de Sucre completed. Poor, kind, generous Antonio! Think of it, Father, he was shot from ambush by his own countrymen! That is how South America rewards her best men and her greatest heroes. The shot that killed him killed me too. . . . Do you know, Father, I began to ail on the day when I first got the news of Antonio's death. I've never recovered from the blow. . . . They did things differently in North America. Such treachery has not been dreamt of there. . . . They appreciate liberty in the North, not like we of Spanish blood. . . ."

"Fear not, my son. Your work will live. . . ."

"Do you know," went on Bolivar, unheeding of the prelate's effort to assuage his final grief, "do you know what I consider the greatest honour of all honours I received? It is this!" The dying man undid his jacket and showed a tiny miniature which hung on his breast. "It is the head of noble Washington," he said. "General Lafayette sent it to me, together with a lock of Washington's hair. It is the crown of my rewards. . . . God have mercy on my country as God had mercy on the North. . . . Mercy . . . mercy . . . mercy . . ." Bolivar's voice broke, as his eyes appeared to penetrate something which was remote. "Do you know, Father, I myself have not always been merciful. Perhaps, I am being punished for my sins. But in those early days of my fighting for liberty I was once or twice quite pitiless. Once, as you know, I ordered some hundreds of Spanish prisoners shot. I was entreated to spare them, but to all entreaties I turned a deaf ear. Though my heart bled for what, through force of circumstances, I had to do, I had to be hard. That villain Boves at the head of the wild Llaneros was then our most formidable enemy. He made war a horror. There was no counting the atrocities of which he was the author. He did not stop at torture and mutilation, and he spared neither defenceless women nor children. That man was a monster, Father. Nothing short of reprisals would have availed here. In self-defence I had to be hard. One has to fight the devil with his own weapons. There are some who hold that against me today and on the score of it call me tyrant, and what not. Again, there are some who have criticised me with exercising too much mercy against my enemies. There is no pleasing men under the sun."

The dying man paused and sighed. His eyes, scanning the landscape through the window, seemed to lose themselves in the dim distance, while the friendly bishop studied him with a paternal eye. Presently, he tapped the frail man lightly on the shoulder, and said:

"My son, do not take your sorrow too much to heart. Your work is not lost. God, who sees all, will reward you. Your name will go down the ages as of one who has worked for humanity and has done nobly! The present phase will pass, and strife shall cease. You will be remembered for ever and ever as the Liberator."

Under the light touch of the prelate's hand, the Liberator's body quivered; an electric tremor seemed to pass down his wasted body. He straightened, held up his proud head, which suddenly appeared to resume its former virility, while to his eyes there sprang hidden fires. He began to talk rapidly, and his words came like sparks struck fresh from an anvil; it was as if he were possessed by a vision, as if everything in him had gathered itself for a final effort to speak his dream.

"Father——" he began, like one addressing the world. "Father—I can not believe that my dream will not come true. My faith in it alone has sustained me through all the setbacks, all the treacheries, all the perversities of human nature. I want to see this great continent from end to end united in one great society of sister nations, bound together by principles of freedom and justice and by a common need to defend that freedom against strong European aggressors who find it profitable to exploit weaker peoples. I want to see these vast green plains fertile and prosperous, and the men and women working them strong, free and happy. I want to see the very name of tyranny obliterated from the language of the world, and even forgotten. . . . I had once thought that I had fulfilled my mission. . . . I thought

I was sure of it when I and my brave army had crossed the impassable Andes; men who could achieve this feat are not to be despised. But blindness possesses them now, and they do not know what they are doing. But the day will surely come when their eyes will be opened to the truth, and my sacrifices will then not have been in vain. And, as surely, the day will come when the nations of the earth will look to the conventions of the Isthmus of Panama with admiration and respect; and, what I have said years ago I hold to now: What will the Isthmus of Corinth then be, compared with the Isthmus of Panama? . . ."

"A worthy dream, one bound to come true," said the bishop, thinking to stop the man, lest he get too tired.

"Peru offered me a million pesos for my dream!" said Bolivar with a mordant laugh. "Others wanted to give me . . ." He paused, as if to catch breath, then gasped out: "I rejected them all, all, Father! I am Don Quixote, the great Knight himself in the flesh. Did the good Lady Dulcinea, for whom he had fought, exist? No, there was only Aldonza. He saw Aldonza, and thought her Dulcinea! Do you understand? And I too saw Dulcinea in this Continent. Is she only Aldonza? I shall not live to see. I have an idea, Father, that if Aldonza can only go on long enough thinking herself Dulcinea she will become Dulcinea! What do you think?"

"Even so," was all the prelate said. "If Aldonza goes on thinking long enough that she is Dulcinea she will surely become Dulcinea. . . . But you had better rest, my son. I must go now. I shall return." And he helped the sick man to his couch.

3

A few days later, Simon Bolivar, feeling the approach

of death, proclaimed his last message. It read as follows:

"Colombians, you have witnessed my efforts to establish freedom where tyranny formerly reigned. I have worked unselfishly, giving up my fortune and tranquility. I resigned the command when I was convinced that you did not trust my disinterestedness. My foes availed themselves of your credulity and trampled upon what is most sacred to me—my reputation as a lover of freedom. I have been a victim of persecutors, who have led me to the border of the tomb. I forgive them.

"Upon disappearing from your midst, my love prompts me to express my last wishes. I aspire to no other glory than the consolidation of Columbia; all must work for the invaluable blessing of union; the peoples, obeying the present government, in order to free themselves from anarchy; the ministers of the Sanctuary, by sending prayers to Heaven; and the soldiers, by using their swords to protect the sanctions of social order.

"Colombians, my last wishes are for the happiness of our country. If my death can help to destroy the spirit of partisanship, and strengthen the union, I shall tranquilly descend to my grave."

Soon after this utterance Simon Bolivar entered into the last throes of death. The poor man's mind, dwelling on his enemies, was tormented with terrible thoughts of men's ingratitude. He called his servant, and in his delirium, he cried:

"Joseph, let us go away. They are throwing us out of here. Where shall we go?"

The question did not wait long for an answer, as far as it concerned Bolivar, for a week later the great man died.

THE COMPARISON OF LEE WITH BOLIVAR

IN CHAPTER after chapter of that wonderful novel, *War and Peace,* Count Tolstoi takes the great Napoleon to task for his presumption in pitting his little efforts against those ultimate inexorable forces which some men call the Fates, others God. He portrays him as a kind of chess-player sitting before his board and contriving all sorts of clever moves against what he imagines to be some stupid human adversary, not realizing that his real opponent is that Inevitable, which, not without irony, dictates the moves of both, to the confusion of the most arrogant player.

As a theory of history, this is interesting, but one wonders how, using it as a measure, Tolstoi could have explained Robert E. Lee.

Here was a man who, though a soldier, a war technician and a "chess-player" in the Tolstoian sense, was tender-hearted and compassionate, a Christian who abhorred war and all useless strife, and was wholly devoid of ambition. For a great soldier, he was curiously modest. Tyranny, the almost inevitable accompaniment of military genius, was absent from his composition. He performed his duty with ability (like the good military chess-player he was), but, unlike Napoleon, also with sorrow, with a Christian humility and with a constant submission "to God's will." His kindness to his subordinates, his readiness to take on his own shoulders the blame belonging to others, has been deemed his sole weakness as a soldier. In this "weakness" is to be sought the source of his nobility and strength as a human being and as a man. Tolstoi, indeed, in any portrayal of Lee, might have encountered some difficulty in reconciling the southerner's military genius (chess-like in its calculation) with his integrity of character and religious nature,—virtues having as their foundation, on the one hand, principles of law and order so dear to the Anglo-Saxon race; on the other, the Bible.

There is on record a conversation between General Lee and Senator B. H. Hill, of Georgia, quoted in that excellent *Life of Lee* by Mr. Thomas Nelson Page. Hill mentioned the possibility of Lee succeeding Davis as President of the Confederate States, in the event of victory over the North. Lee protested and expressed himself as unwilling to undertake civil duties for which he was unfitted. He was a soldier, not a statesman.

" 'Well—but, General,' persisted Hill. 'History does not sustain your view. Cæsar, Frederick of Prussia, and Bonaparte were great statesmen as well as great generals.'

" 'And great tyrants,' replied Lee promptly. 'I speak of the proper rule in republics, where I think we should have neither military statesmen nor political generals.'

" 'But Washington was both,' urged Hill, 'and yet not a tyrant.'

" 'Washington was an exception to all rules and there was none like him,' said Lee smiling."

The views expressed here were, curiously enough, the views of Simon Bolivar. The latter, to be sure, accepted the presidency of Venezuela, but he did it protestingly, and only because it was quite clear that the people were not yet fit to govern themselves. In a letter he wrote at the time he plainly stated that his ambition was that the verdict of history may be: "Bolivar took command to liberate his fellow-citizens, and, when they were free, left them to govern themselves by the law and not by his will." Again, in his message to the Congress of Rosario de Cúcuta, he reiterated his views even more strongly:

"A man like me is a dangerous citizen in a popular government. He is an immediate threat to the national sovereignty. I want to be a citizen in order to secure my own freedom and the freedom of everybody else. I prefer the title of citizen to that of Liberator, because the latter comes from war and the former from the law. Change, I beg you, all my titles for that of *good citizen*."

This was written in 1821 on the occasion of his election to the presidency of Colombia (the name given to the newly organized union of Venezuela and New Granada), when he desired to resign his military command. That he was not allowed to do so was natural, as his services were still sorely needed by the new Republics which he had helped to found.

At one time it was suggested that Bolivar be made Emperor of the Andes, a title to cover five countries with which his name is associated,—Venezuela, New Granada (now Colombia), Ecuador, Peru and Bolivia (named after him),—but he refused to listen to the temptation. "I am not Napoleon," he said. "Nor do I wish to be. Neither do I want to imitate Cæsar." Again: "I have fulfilled my obligations, for I have done my duty as a soldier, the only profession which I have followed since the first day of the Republic. . . . I was not born to be a magistrate. . . . Even if a soldier saves his country, he rarely proves a good executive. . . ."

Did not Robert E. Lee, nearly two generations later, echo these sentiments when the idea of his succeeding Jefferson Davis was broached to him? "Never, sir," he said. "That I will never permit. Whatever talents I possess (and they are but limited) are military talents. My education and training are military. I think the military and civil talents are distinct if not different, and full duty in either sphere is about as much as one man can qualify himself to perform. I shall not do the people the injustice to accept high civil office with whose questions it has not been my business to become familiar."

Thus, we see that Bolivar and Lee, in different ways, arrive at the same conclusion with regard to the military and political functions, though, to be sure, Bolivar, in the absence of real statesmen, has been constrained to employ both talents.

The relative merits of Bolivar and Lee in the military sphere are more difficult to judge, since the conditions of warfare which faced the two commanders were of a nature which do not allow of a comparison. The South American has fought engagements which dragged on through twenty-two years; they were mostly pitched battles and guerrilla skirmishes, but the crossing of the Andes speaks for the resolution and valor of the leader. What Bolivar might have done with real armies in Europe is a matter for speculation. Lee is quite another matter. For four years he fought war on a grand scale, and his generalship is comparable with that of the greatest commanders. In many respects, indeed, the Civil War was fought in a manner which presaged the greater conflict in 1914; for not only was the battle-line flung wide but trench fighting saw its first real development, and sea power was used by one side to starve out the other; more than that: modern industry entered for the first time as the main weapon in "a war of attrition," to be repeated on a larger scale in the war of 1914-18. Lee was not defeated by the superior generalship of the enemy but by superior forces and equipment.

In constancy of purpose the two men can stand comparison. For twenty-two years Bolivar had fought for the freedom of South America, and his intermittent defeats, complete at the time, did not dampen his ardor; each time he returned to fight more fiercely. Defeat only served to

SIMON BOLIVAR

From an engraving by M. N. Bate
in *Simon Bolivar, El Libertador* by F. Loraine Petre
John Lane, The Bodley Head, London

General Robert E. Lee
Photo from Ewing Galloway, New York

give new zest to his sword. As for Lee, the end of the war found him fighting as stubbornly as when he first took command, and only the absence of provisions and equipment and the wasting of his forces put an end to any further resistance. No man could have done more.

Lee has been charged with weakness toward his subordinates; where Napoleon would have promptly shot a general for serious negligence, Lee not only overlooked the fault but took the whole blame on himself. Bolivar brought about some of his own ultimate difficulties by his generosity to his enemies at home; nevertheless, there are blots in his career, for which his volcanic Latin temperament and the unreliable, the unprincipled savage natures of the contending forces, must be held responsible. The conditions, when he took matters in hand, were so anarchic, so chaotic from the Anglo-Saxon point of view, that, perhaps, he should not be judged too harshly. One can only wonder that he exhibited as much forbearance as he did. It is certain that as the conflict progressed and Spain put more humane and gallant leaders in the field, Bolivar met them on their own terms and his generous nature responded to theirs.

To his own generals he was loyal, and, in victory, was prompt to render them tribute. Lee's tribute to Jackson on the latter's death, "Any victory would be dear at such a price," has its parallel in Bolivar's tribute to Anzoátegui, "I would have preferred the loss of two battles to the loss of Anzoátegui." And the news of General Sucre's death affected him so deeply that it hastened his end. Instances of his loyalty could be multiplied.

Treachery against the Liberator darkened his last days. The unsuccessful attempt on the part of his own countrymen, whose benefactor he was, to assassinate him called forth from him the bitter remark: "I have really been murdered." And bitter must have been those days when the dying man, after twenty-two years of persistent endeavor, requiring great patience and courage, saw the beginning of internal strife in the states he had helped to make. The dissolution of Colombia into Venezuela and New Granada broke his heart. He died, feeling there was no place for him in the world he had created by his own valiant efforts. His life is a subject around which Shakespeare might have created one of his tragic histories.

Lee's life after the war was humble, but tranquil and collected as before. He was not the man to make complaints. He retained his marvelous integrity. Having lost all, he became the president of Washington College at a salary of fifteen hundred dollars a year. The story goes that he was once approached with an offer of the presidency of an insurance company at a salary of fifty thousand dollars a year. He declined it on the ground that it was work with which he was not familiar.

"But, General," said the man who represented the insurance company, "you will not be expected to do any work; what we wish is the use of your name."

"Do you not think," said General Lee, "that if my name is worthy fifty thousand dollars a year, I ought to be very careful about taking care of it?"

He kept his integrity to the last.

How shall one compare briefly Lee and Bolivar, so as to convey their racial differences? A single sentence will do it: they are different to the extent that an English gentleman is different from the Knight of the Mancha.

And if that conveys nothing, nothing will.

CECIL RHODES — EMPIRE BUILDER

1

GREAT men, to whom victory has become a habit, are an interesting spectacle in the hour of their defeat. Irony, bitter irony, crowns their efforts. Napoleon at Waterloo, Cecil Rhodes at his magnificent home at Groote Schuur,—where is the difference? For each his ultimate cup of bitterness, the reward of the quest for power.

But this portrait is not concerned with Napoleon, but with Cecil Rhodes, the "Colossus," Emperor in nearly all but in name of Bechuanaland, Cape Colony and Rhodesia, named after him, and with eyes on other South African vastnesses which he had dreamed of uniting into one autonomous country under the ultimate protection of the British flag, the one flag of which he took any cognizance. It was a great dream, but he did not think it impossible to make it come true; indeed, in the short years in which he had essayed the task he had already done wonders. And it was only a beginning, he thought. To him it seemed logical and necessary. In England, his mother country, he saw modern Rome, the great civilizer of our times, whose conquests were beneficent for the conquered. His library at Groote Schuur was filled with typewritten translations of Greek and Latin authors; it had been a whim of his; he had them especially prepared, at the sacrifice of a small fortune, that he might be able to read all the original authorities quoted by Gibbon (whom he admired) in *The Decline and Fall of the Roman Empire*. The grandeur of Rome he saw repeated in imperial Britain, and he regarded it the duty of every Englishman to play his predestined rôle in England's historic mission. When he happened to glance in a mirror, he liked to fancy that his massive, well-cut head had a likeness to that of the Roman Emperor Titus. There was no gainsaying: it had. And his dreams were not unlike the dreams of his ancient prototype. The extension of the British Empire: that was what he aimed at, and everything he did had this as its ultimate purpose.

Two well-thumbed books always lay on his table. They were Marcus Aurelius and the Bible. After all, the modern Roman must be a Christian of sorts.

The modern Roman does not make all his conquests by force of arms. A new force, hardly less potent, has arisen in the world, and it is called *money*. Money is power. Early in life Rhodes had learned the great secret, and all his preliminary efforts for the realization of his dream were directed to making money. And in this respect the fates had been propitious. When, in 1870, he first set foot on African soil, "a tall, lanky, anæmic, fair-haired boy, shy and reserved in bearing," the Kimberley diamond mines had just been discovered, and, together with his brother Herbert, he made a journey thither and began working out a claim.

A little later, another youngster, Barnett Isaacs, the grandson of a rabbi and the son of a little shopkeeper in Whitechapel, arrived in Kimberley with a capital of sixty boxes of cigars, the result of many years' savings. He sold his cigars at a good price and began dealing in diamonds. Some years later he was to become the famous magnate, Barney Barnato, and Rhodes' great rival for the possession of the rich diamond fields.

The ship which was bringing young Isaacs to Africa had passed the ship which was bringing the now twenty-year-old Rhodes back to England, for he had one other dream, that of going to Oxford. But even while at Oxford he had maintained a connection with his interests in South Africa, and his letters to his partner Rudd were rich with injunctions to "accumulate the ready." He saw in money a fulcrum wherewith he could move his particular world. He had been witness to its power in small ways, and on more than one occasion at Oxford had pulled out a pocketful of diamonds to induce a desirable man to join him at Kimberley. But for big objects one needed big money, and he would abide his time until he had it.

Not that he had wanted money for its own ends. He wanted it to make his dream come true. While at Oxford he had decided that there was something in the idea of evolution; he had more than a suspicion that God having devised the evolutionary principle, it was naturally His logical intention and desire to see the best race on top, and, certainly, the Anglo-Saxon race was, without doubt, the fittest to survive; therefore, the fittest to rule. He had always thought so; Oxford merely had confirmed his suspicion. He had listened, with delight, to the great Ruskin:

"There is a destiny now possible to us, the highest ever set before a nation to be accepted or refused. We are still undegenerate of race; a race mingled of the best northern blood. We are not yet dissolute of temper, but still have the firmness to govern and the grace to obey. . . . Will you youths of England make your country again a royal throne of kings; a sceptered isle, for all the world a source of light, a centre of peace; mistress of learning and of the Arts . . . and amidst the cruel and clamorous jealousies of nations, worshipped in her strange valour, of goodwill towards men? . . . This is what England must do, or perish; she must found colonies as fast and as far as she is able, formed of her most energetic and worthiest men; seizing every piece of fruitful waste ground she can set her foot on, and there teaching these her colonists that their chief virtue is to be fidelity to their country, and that their first aim is to be to advance the power of England by land and sea. . . ."

Rhodes had been fertile ground for such discourses. As a man of action, as "practical visionary," he would better the instruction.

Already, during his long vacation at Kimberley, at the age of twenty-four, he had drawn up his first will for the disposition of the millions which he did not yet possess but which he knew that destiny, with inevitable certainty, was storing up for him. It had stipulated the foundation of a Secret Society whose aim should be "the extension of British rule throughout the world . . . the colonization by British subjects of all lands where the means of livelihood are attainable by energy, labour and enterprise, and especially the occupation by British settlers of the entire continent of Africa, the Holy Land, the Valley of the Euphrates, the islands of Cyprus and Candia, the whole of South America, the islands of the Pacific not heretofore possessed by Great Britain, the whole of the Malay Archipelago, the sea-board of China and Japan, the ultimate recovery of the United States of America as an integral part of the British Empire . . . colonial representation in the Imperial Parliament, which may tend to weld together the disjointed members of the Empire, and finally, the foundation of so great a Power as to hereafter render wars impossible and promote the best interests of humanity."

For these modest objects he needed money, lots of it, and, equally, he needed powerful friends. With a single-heartedness, hardly equaled, he had set out to acquire these. He had made up his mind to do without a wife, since a woman might divert him from his purpose.

And, thus, the quest for money, and still more money, had

become the guiding principle, if not the motive power, of all his actions; so that any one who did not know his dream, his desire to paint the African map a British red, could be aware only of that all-pervading obsession of his for the acquisition of wealth. He had at last succeeded in absorbing all his rivals in the diamond fields but one: Barney Barnato. Barnato was a clever man and fought a hard fight, but in the end was forced to capitulate. The victor and the vanquished met afterward at the Kimberley Club, when Rhodes asked his guest to satisfy a whim: "I have always wanted to see a bucketful of diamonds; will you produce one?" And Barnato, with great pride, did as he was asked, to the great delight of Rhodes, who plunged his hands in and, lifting handfuls of the sparkling stones, let them stream between his fingers like water.

His victory had enabled him to establish a great corporation, which ultimately became a great chartered company, resembling the great East India and other trading companies, with special privileges and almost unlimited rights of a territorial and administrative nature. His plan was to obtain trading, mining, railway and other concessions, to populate the "conquered" districts with Englishmen; or, at all events, to put his countrymen in positions of power, and thus win Africa to British civilization—to his way of thinking, the greatest boon which could be conferred on humanity. He could accomplish this best by making the effort for any venturing Englishman profitable.

Charmed by his personality, men of money and worth had flocked to his standard. Barney Barnato he had won over to his side by sheer persistence; Alfred Beit, the great financier, had answered to the lure of his magnetic presence; Leander Starr Jameson, a brilliant, young Scottish doctor, also joined him and became his most intimate friend.

A great affection developed between Rhodes and Jameson; and as this affection, Rhodes' one surrender to sentiment, was to be fatal to him, it is meet that a sketch portrait be given of the favored friend who was to bring about his downfall.

If Rhodes' slow methodical mind was of the nature of iron, that of Jameson was of the nature of quicksilver; he was quick, sharp, alert. If he had neither the depth nor the fundamental integrity of his leader, he had the faculty of catching the drift of the other's thoughts and of illuminating them with a sympathy and understanding which quite endeared him to Rhodes. There was nothing deliberate about Jameson as there was about Rhodes; he was rash, impulsive and impetuous; he would delight Rhodes with his ingenuity in devising ways and means for carrying into execution particularly difficult plans. He did not care a fig for how much money Rhodes made, but he was heart and soul with him in any scheme which would further British power. There was no doubt about his devotion, and Rhodes came to love him as a brother.

Their common enemy was Paul Kruger.

Paul Kruger, President of Transvaal, a man nearly twice Rhodes' age, whose boast was that though he had little schooling he had learned "to distinguish between friends and foes," was a hard-headed, stiff-necked Dutchman, who had gleaned all the statecraft and philosophy of life he knew from the Bible. He had won popularity with the Boers by his simple manners, his feats of strength, his knowledge of his fellow-burghers, and by his narrow, uncompromising integrity. He did not hold the high opinion of the English that Rhodes held. On the contrary, he considered them ungodly interlopers, and he did not propose that the independence which he had helped his country to win should be surrendered to the devil in the guise of an Englishman. He granted the desired concessions to the Uitlanders grudgingly or not at all, and frowned on any suggestion of political privileges. He was adamant even where the encroachment promised benefit and profit to his countrymen, who, in consequence, did not always regard his attitude as wise. But no one could help but respect the stubborn old man who could show such a strong front to those whom he considered as dangerous enemies of his country.

And there was every reason why Rhodes should respect him. Did not Kruger have the same aims as himself? Kruger's object, like his own, was "to extend his country over the whole of the northern interior." They had sized each other up at their first meeting in 1885, and knew each other's worth. Rhodes saw in "that extraordinary man" a rival worthy of his steel. Kruger, with his singular faculty "of distinguishing friends from foes," admitted the younger man's capacity for creating situations. "That young man," he said, "will cause me trouble if he does not leave politics alone and turn to something else. Well, the race-horse is swifter than the ox, but the ox can draw the greater loads. We shall see."

It was a challenge. It was, indeed, to be seen.

Rhodes had had other meetings with the wily Boer. There was the time when he headed a delegation to the President and made representations on behalf of the miners. Undaunted by the vigor of the Englishman, Kruger pointed the stem of his pipe toward the speaker, and said in his native tongue: "Tell him I have heard all these stories before. I am here to protect my burghers as well as the Rand people. I know what I have to do and I will do what I consider right."

There was a later occasion when Rhodes came to see Kruger with a proposal which promised to benefit both parties. "We must work together," began Rhodes, over coffee. "I know the republic wants a seaport: you must have Delagoa Bay." "But the harbor belongs to the Portuguese," protested Kruger, "and they won't hand it over." "Then we must simply take it," was Rhodes' reply. "No," said the President, "I can't take other people's property. If the Portuguese won't sell the harbor, I wouldn't take it, even if you gave it to me: ill-gotten goods are accursed."

What was one to do with the man? Such was Kruger, but do we not also learn somthing from this about Rhodes? Rhodes was helpless before such an inexorable gesture. There were other like gestures; they were to drive the Englishman to madness. And Doctor Jameson, beloved Jameson, was there at his elbow, prompting his chief.

With protagonists such as these, the drama is bound to develop; what is to come is inevitable.

2

Time: evening, several years later. Place: study at Groote Schuur, the magnificent South African home of Cecil Rhodes.

The great man, now prime minister of his conquered country, paces up and down his spacious study in obvious distress. It is the first time he is called upon to play the rôle of the distressed. He is usually so calm, so phlegmatic, so resolute. His strong features, unaccustomed to the expression of the softer emotions, look unnatural and grotesque in this new attitude. If any one should look in now, he would be astonished to see the change so quickly wrought in the massive, well-chiseled head which might have passed for Cæsar's. His fair hair is tousled from the rufflings of nervous fingers, and his clear blue eyes, which have always given the impression of searching vast distances, are now turned in on themselves, or are fixed in an incomprehensible stare, such as an erstwhile victor might have in contemplating approaching defeat. His ill-fitting clothes, which hang loosely on the large ungainly form, add a touch of pathos to one for whom pathos had been an alien thing. Pride, natural here, in the crushing has become despair. He stops to peer through the window into the darkness, toward his beloved mountain, but nothing is visible. He turns, and runs his fingers through his hair for the hundredth time. He is in very great distress.

What has happened, then?

In confidence of his powers, a confidence intensified by constant successes, he had overreached himself. He had accumulated a fabulous fortune and, with the main object still in view, entered politics. As in the world of money, so in politics, he was not content until he had reached the top. He was prime minister. Englishman and Boer alike had faith in him. Shrewd men of Dutch extraction were among the members of his Cabinet. He had won over men like the sturdy Jan Hofmeyr who, good Dutchman though he was, threw in his lot with the man who had been described to him as "a regular beefsteak, John Bull Englishman." Hofmeyr believed in the Dutch as Rhodes believed in the English and, long before the Englishman appeared on the scene, had advocated a Dutch union of South African States. They had, indeed, started out as enemies. But, on meeting, they had become staunch friends. Then there was the incorruptible Schreiner, the famous Olive Schreiner's brother, who had likewise succumbed to the African Cæsar's personality. They had respected him and loved him and admired him as a civilizing force for Africa; had he not made Africa a great country, built railways, developed trade, encouraged workers and abolished "loafers"?

Then, at the very height of his powers, at the very moment that confidence in him was greatest, he made the fatal blunder. Cautious man that he was, he never would have made it but for his good friend and evil genius, Jameson, who was there at his side waiting to pounce upon any overt hint which might serve his own rash nature.

It all happened because Kruger had stood ever in the way of the grandiose plans for expansion which Rhodes had for so long nursed in his heart. And there was no getting around this stubborn rock of a man. There was the question of tariffs; Kruger would refuse to give way. There was the matter of railways; a concession would enable Rhodes to link up one line with another northward; Kruger would not listen to it. There was the problem of Uitlanders, treated by Kruger as pariahs; Kruger would turn a deaf ear to all protests. Kruger was becoming a serious problem. Rhodes had tried every peaceful means in his power; he had tried bluntness, diplomacy, conference, friendliness, patience; he had argued and expostulated; he had tried to point out the advantages for Transvaal of this or that, but the old man had remained obdurate. Once or twice Rhodes had lost patience. At last his mind had turned to more violent devices. And Jameson was at his elbow to encourage him, friendly Jameson who was ever ready to do something brilliant; to achieve a coup would suit him to perfection.

And, indeed, a coup was on the cards. Jameson would be the man to carry it out. He would ask no questions, but go ahead, once he knew what he was about. That was one reason why Rhodes liked him. He preferred men about him who wasted no time in futile preliminaries.

To bring the wily Boer to his senses, Rhodes and his associates began to plot a raid, and to foster a revolt against Kruger's rule in Transvaal. This was to be done by smuggling arms into Transvaal and concentrating a force on the frontier ready to enter the country and support the rebels in the event of a rising. As prime minister, Rhodes could not do this; he therefore proposed to furnish the arms as a private individual. Again, as managing director of the chartered company he was enabled secretly to place a force on the frontier, an act of treason to the Crown. Only one thing could save him, and that was the success of the venture. He knew human nature and his history well enough to grasp the salient fact: any reprehensible action of this nature could only be justified by success. It was a gambler's throw. Cæsar or Napoleon would have hazarded it, and Rhodes' fortune had thus far been fabulous enough to give him a measure of faith in his lucky star. If the coup succeeded, he would be in a fair way toward realizing his dream.

The question whether the revolt should be conducted under the Transvaal or the British flag had been debated by the leaders of the conspiracy. Rhodes had assured them that the object was to put an end to Kruger's obstructive policy, and that it did not matter which course of action was pursued to attain this. But the suspicion remained that Rhodes and Jameson would be better pleased with annexation. There was no doubt that Jameson, carried away by his late success in the conquest of Matabeleland, was ready for any eventuality and eager "to go the whole hog," as the saying goes. Throwing all caution to the winds, he entered the spirit of the enterprise with every determination to exceed his master's fondest expectations. He quite forgot that he was under orders and that his force had been assigned duties quite secondary to the scheme. British Army officers were in the plot, and they shared his faith in the outcome; they took their coming success for granted.

It was, however, quite clear to some sympathizers that the preparations were inadequate and that the venture might prove worse than a fizzle. Moreover, the question of the British flag appeared by no means settled. The more moderate adherents of the plan began to feel dubious of the whole affair. They infected Rhodes himself with their doubts. He had decided to wait for a more propitious moment, when the preparations were better perfected than they were. He feared a fiasco, which might set back his plans, perhaps put an end to them. And, to prevent a fiasco, he issued orders to Jameson more in harmony with his moderated attitude.

But he had not realized that he had already let loose a force which he could by no means control. Jameson's mind, long nurtured on Rhodes' dream, was impatient of delays. There was no moment like the present. He had been held in leash too long to withdraw now. It was better now, before Kruger got wind of the plot and prepared accordingly. "You may say what you like, but Clive would have done it!" he exclaimed; for he had happened just then to read Macaulay's essay. To be sure, Rhodes had issued new orders to him, and had enjoined upon him again and again to go slowly, but to this he had the flexible answer that he would "do the best he could as circumstances arise."

It was a case of giving the devil a bit of rope.

Not that Jameson had meant to do harm to his great friend. On the contrary he had intended adding to the glory of Cæsar. Never again would such a chance arise. He would make the most of it. England would thank him.

It happened on a Sunday, for Rhodes an unforgettable day. In the morning Jameson had wired him that he would start that night. Rhodes immediately telegraphed him not to move. The wires having been cut, Jameson never received the order. With six hundred troopers he had crossed the border into Transvaal. Rhodes hoped against hope that Jameson did not act rashly, that he had remained where he had been told to. But he really did not believe it. He felt utterly crushed, and knew that to-morrow he must resign his premiership. But one faint hope remained to him, and that was Jameson's success. Only success could justify him, only the accomplished fact. But the chances of that were slim, very slim.

And now—it was Monday—as he paced his large study at Groote Schuur, he was, for the first time in his life, wholly distraught. His life-work, all he had given himself to, seemed to tumble about his ears. He knew that his sympathizers were not prepared, that Jameson's force was inadequate. He loved Jameson as a brother. That the man he loved in this world above all men should bring this upon him! What irony! Yet he knew that Jameson was doing this for his sake; whatever happened, he, Rhodes, would forgive him. He only hoped Jameson himself should come to no grief. This would be adding sorrow to sorrow. Burdened under the weight of his thoughts, the Colossus crumpled up. He continued to pace the chamber like a lion newly caged. It was all an impossible nightmare. "England, my England!" What hadn't he tried to do for England? He had thought himself a Cæsar for England, and here he was nothing, worse than nothing! His country would chastise him for bringing disgrace upon her. And he would deserve it. Only a slight spark would suddenly light in his breast full of darkness; it was the faint hope that a miracle had happened, that Jameson had achieved the impossible, that his raid was a complete success. But the spark, lighting up, would go out as quickly at it came, leaving his heart in utter darkness.

There was a knock on the door. It was a knock against his own heart, filled with forebodings of the worst.

Schreiner entered with telegrams in his hand. On beholding Rhodes, he drew back, startled. He had never seen Rhodes looking like that, so wholly different, so dejected. Words were on Schreiner's lips, but, before he could utter them, Rhodes said:

"Yes, yes, it is true. Old Jameson has upset my apple-cart. It is all true."

Schreiner said that he had some telegrams. Rhodes said:

"Never mind, it is all true. Old Jameson has upset my apple-cart. . . ."

Schreiner was staggered. "What do you mean?" he said. "What can you mean? Why did you not say anything to me yesterday when I was here?"

"I thought I had stopped him," replied Rhodes. "I sent messages to stop him, and did not want to say anything about it if I stopped him."

"Why do you not stop him now? Although he has ridden in you can still stop him."

"Poor old Jameson," replied the dejected man. "Twenty years we have been friends, and now he goes in and ruins me. I can not hinder him. I can not go in and destroy him."

For three hours the two friends talked. Schreiner, who had been his partner in the ministry and a faithful follower, saw that the man was broken; he saw clearly that the ministry was doomed. He left in very great distress.

Left to himself, Rhodes lived through hours of agony, and only now and then a tiny spark lighted up his heart's darkness, and this spark was the hope that his friend Jameson had, after all, won his way through to Johannesburg. But this hope of a miracle only intensified the torment, like a false dawn in the night.

3

Days went by without definite news. Everybody, of course, knew of the raid. Rhodes sent in his resignation, but it was not immediately accepted.

His friend Hofmeyr was wroth. "If Rhodes is behind this, he is no more friend of mine," he said. When they met, Hofmeyr said: "Mere resignation is not enough. You must issue a manifesto repudiating Jameson, suspending him as administrator of Rhodesia, and declaring that the law be set in force against him."

No, Rhodes couldn't quite do that. Jameson, after all, was such an old friend.

"I quite understand," returned Hofmeyr, "that is quite enough, and you need not say more."

Thus ended a fifteen-year-old friendship. Rhodes felt its loss bitterly. They met once more at Groote Schuur. The meeting did not improve matters. Rhodes was left under the impression that his charter was in danger from his erstwhile friend. As for Hofmeyr, he was not at all pleased with Rhodes' attitude. Rhodes, to his mind, should have admitted his guilt. Instead: "He imagines himself a young king, the equal of the Almighty . . . a Clive and a Warren Hastings rolled into one."

Whatever hope Rhodes had in Jameson's success was soon snuffed out by the news that Jameson and his whole force had surrendered to the Boers at Doorn Kop but twenty miles from Johannesburg. It had been a lost cause from the start, and not a Johannesburger lifted a finger to help him.

At this time Rhodes had one piece of luck. This was the German Kaiser's telegram of congratulation to President Kruger. It was interpreted, as Rhodes knew and every one else knew, as a challenge to England. It was to serve Rhodes' cause well later. But for the moment Kruger had won the battle. His words, "the race-horse is swifter than the ox, but the ox can draw the greater loads," sounded like a prophecy come true.

For the moment, too, the cause Rhodes had so much at heart, the union of South Africa, suffered a blow from which it did not look as if it would recover soon. It was a terrible setback, and even his friends, who believed in the integrity of his cause, turned from their leader.

For the while, Rhodes set his whole energies to help the raiders who had been turned over to a British tribunal for trial. Jameson and others were sentenced to terms of imprisonment. Frank Rhodes, his brother, and a few others, were sentenced to death. Their sentences were ultimately commuted for fines of twenty-five thousand pounds apiece, which Rhodes paid cheerfully; he also, with Beit, paid other expenses connected with the raid, which amounted in all to over a quarter of a million sterling. Then he offered his own person up for trial for his part in the affair.

He was censured by a Committee of the Cape House of Assembly in 1896, and accepted the verdict, though he was not present in person, as he was busy at the time putting down the rebellion in Matabeleland. But the following year he sailed to "face the music" before the British South Africa Committee of the House of Commons.

Now it was Kruger who was making mistakes. His grudging mercy to Reform prisoners, his persistence in treating Uitlanders as pariahs unworthy of generosity, robbed him of that sympathy which would have been his; as it was, he incurred only hostility, and his obstinate conduct did more than anything else to reestablish Rhodes in Africa as in England. And, in consequence, his biographer is able to state that "his journey was more like a triumphal progress than the penitential pilgrimage of a culprit going to meet his judge." He had gained much from his defeat, Kruger had lost something by his victory. When all is said and done, the strengths of the two protagonists contained seeds of their weakness. In the face of his reception, Rhodes was able to say at Port Elizabeth, a stopping point on his way to England:

"If I may put to you a thought, it is that the man who is continuously prosperous does not know himself, his own mind or character. It is a good thing to have a period of adversity. You then find out who are your real friends. . . . I am confident enough to say that I do not feel that my public career has closed. . . . I am determined still to strive for the closer union of South Africa. . . ."

Elsewhere, he admitted his error, and promised to do his best to make atonement "by untiring devotion to the best interests of South Africa." He had wanted to make admission of his guilt at the public reception at Cape Town, but just as he was on the point of beginning his apology such tumultuous applause greeted him that he was not able to make it. And this attitude of worship put him in a mood to "face the music" in England with music of his own. He was no longer the repentant Rhodes, but Colossus ready to do a little castigation of his own.

This was not so apparent on the first morning of the sitting, when, facing the greatest officials and lawyers in the land for whose glory he had worked, he seemed nervous and shy and half-dazed, and his whole appearance and manner did not impress his judges and auditors as consistent with his fame as Cæsar.

"The first unfavorable impression," says his biographer, "was confirmed when he began to speak. His voice was squeaky and staccato, he sat humped up in his chair and was obviously ill at ease before his inquisitors. The answers he gave seemed involved and sometimes off the point. One began to wonder if this were really the great Colossus who bestrode half a continent. He seemed heavy, even stupid."

Then his moment came. It was during luncheon. They all ate off little trays, and while they ate the proceedings went on. Rhodes bit into his sandwich, took one long draught from his tankard of stout; then, suddenly, like one awakened from a long sleep, shook himself and faced his tormentors with a flash of fire in his eye that had not been there before. In a mere twinkling he became master of the situation. It was his turn to ask questions. Of course, he didn't shirk his responsibility in the raid! But what did they know about South Africa? There were a few things he thought they ought to know about it, and he was willing to tell them. And he went on to tell them, and he had a good time in doing it. He had made his mistakes, he admitted it, but what were his mistakes in Africa compared with theirs? He had had to fight his fight single-handed. Had he been helped by them? By no means. Only hindered. Their ignorance and their policy of obstruction had helped to bring about the situation he had found himself in.

There was Germany. The committee seemed to think that Germany's feelings had to be considered. Damn diplomacy! He was a realist, and he had some facts to put before them.

Undaunted by the distinguished advocates who sat in judgment upon him, he proceeded with a narration of these facts, and gave his critics more than they asked. He blandly admitted to making money, yes, lots of it, but then he had always paid for his patriotism out of his own pocket. After that no one ventured to ask him if he expected to profit materially by the Jameson adventure. Besides, the fellow had a way of asking uncomfortable questions of his own. After five days, the committee was only too delighted to put an end to the inquiry. Would they like to have him up again? Rhodes asked cheerfully. Of course, his work in Rhodesia kept him very busy. Still, he should be happy to come. The committee thought they might call on him later. But they never did.

The committee did the only thing it could do. It condemned the raid, and censured Rhodes for the misuse of his office as prime minister of the Cape and managing director of the chartered company. The House of Commons, however, refused to remove his name from the list of Privy Councilors; and the raid was not generally condemned in England. "I found all the busmen smiling at me when I came to London," said Rhodes, and added: "so I knew it was all right."

And he went back to fight for his dream of a united Africa.

4

It was barely two years later that the South African War broke out. Rhodes, who was tired and ill from his long exertions, had little part in the immediate events which brought it about. The obstinate, relentless Kruger, undoubtedly, had a hand in them. The integrity of the old Boer need not be called into question here. But if "character is fate," then, surely, he can not be altogether held guiltless for the conflict of arms which followed.

The result, favorable to his policy, brought no cry of triumph from Rhodes. Krugerism was beaten, but he had always a respect for the Dutch, and he called upon his followers to honor the "vigorous and unconquered" Boer peasants and to work with them for the country which belonged to them as much as to the English. His years of hard experience, of intimate contacts with both races had made him a more balanced man than he had been. No longer was he the youth, fresh from Oxford, with jingoistic ideas for "the extension of British rule throughout the world . . . the ultimate recovery of the United States of America as an integral part of the British Empire . . ." and so forth, stipulations of his first will. His new will honored the British Empire and Oxford in quite a different fashion. The object of the Rhodes scholarships is too well known to go into detail, but their general aim, that of encouraging and fostering an appreciation of the advantages which he implicitly believed would result from the union of the English-speaking people throughout the world, is a dream which many people besides Rhodes still ardently believe in.

His active life was not without its intimate, tender moments, and there are many stories of his numerous acts of kindness. These undoubtedly were remembered when, on his death-bed, his old ally, Hofmeyr, sent him a message of reconciliation, and friends rallied round him in his last days of physical agony.

He himself seemed to realize how far he was from having accomplished his dream. He died in March, 1902; he was but forty-nine, worn out by his endeavors, and almost his last words were:

"So little done, so much to do."

He was buried on his favorite mountain, the View of the World, in the Matoppos. This mountain he used to call "his church," and it has been called the Westminster Abbey of Rhodesia.

FERDINAND DE LESSEPS—DREAMER IN STEEL

1

SOMETIME during the year 1831 a vessel called the *Diogenes,* commanded by a Captain Pilate, arrived at Alexandria, in Egypt, and was put in quarantine. It had come from Tunis, and had had a miserable voyage of thirty-seven days. Among its passengers was the young French diplomatist, Ferdinand de Lesseps. After so long and wretched a journey, it was irksome to be forced to remain in confinement. The French Consul, Monsieur Minault, visited him and, to relieve the tedium of the visitor's stay, had brought him Denon's great work on *The Expedition to Egypt.* The book proved absorbing. It contained, among other things, the engineer Lepère's report on the project of a canal at Suez. He studied it carefully. He then read of all the attempts that he had made to solve the problem.

The project of a canal across the Suez had attracted the ancients as well as the moderns. The Pharaoh, Rameses II, was the first to dig a canal between the Nile Delta and the Red Sea. Afterward, owing to neglect, it was filled up and fell into disuse. The Persian King, Darius I, re-opened it, and it was used by the Arab conquerors of Egypt. Napoleon, also, appears to have had the idea of connecting the Mediterranean and the Red Seas by a canal which would admit the passage of ocean-going ships. Engineer Lepère, whom he had engaged to examine its practicability, reported in the negative. His opinion that the surface of the Red Sea was nearly thirty feet higher than that of the Mediterranean caused the project to be abandoned. But his opinion was founded on error.

During the period between 1831 and 1838, Lesseps had passed much of his time at Alexandria, where, as it chanced, a curious and persevering English adventurer, Lieutenant Waghorn, more than once had paused on journeys from England to India. This Waghorn greatly attracted Lesseps, who saw in the traveler a brave man carrying on a vain contest with the cautious stupidity of the age. He was at the time trying to demonstrate to the British Government that the overland route to India was in every sense more practicable than the route round the Cape which was then followed. It usually took the mails four to six months to arrive by the Cape route, and the lieutenant was bent on proving, by practical example, the superiority of a direct road. He was doing his journeys at his own expense and in the face of the most cruel discouragements. After fabulous efforts, the best he could obtain from his ungrateful government was the privilege of carrying duplicates of dispatches at his own cost. He devoted seven years of his life to this labor, and succeeded in wasting all his substance.

Tireless and daring, Waghorn tried every possible route; sometimes he arrived at Alexandria by way of Marseilles, sometimes by the way of Trieste. Once at Alexandria, he would lose no time in setting out for Suez either on a dromedary's back or in a canal boat; at Suez, if luck was with him, he would find a steamer.

Lesseps saw him arrive like this many a time, and his sympathy went out to the man, for he recognized in the intrepid spirit something of his own nature.

In England, Lieutenant Waghorn passed for a man with a bee in his bonnet. But to Lesseps it seemed that he had undertaken a worthy project which he had worked out with courage and devotion; for its success he had ruined his health and his fortune and had left his family to beggary but for the generosity of the Peninsular and Oriental Company which awarded them a pension.

Waghorn's experiments had been a complete success. He had amply demonstrated to the satisfaction of the Bombay Government, which engaged him, that it was possible to deliver dispatches by the overland route. It was doubted at the time whether steamers could navigate the Red Sea. Men of professional experience, such as admirals and politicians, particularly politicians, testified before the English Parliament that steamers were useless there, though sailing vessels might make their way. While the discussion was going on, Waghorn opened up the route to India over land.

The man's endeavors against all manner of discouragements had impressed Lesseps, who was later to confess that he had served him as an example.

Waghorn had begun his career in the navy, in which as a mere lad he had received a lieutenancy. He had bravely fought for his country and received honorable wounds. The idea of an overland route to India had taken possession of him early, and at twenty-seven he dedicated all his energy to it. He addressed meetings all over the kingdom, and became a nuisance to the Post-Office and the Admiralty, who considered him something of a bore. From the official world he met with nothing but obstruction; at every step it checked and thwarted him. After two years of unwearied effort, to rid themselves of his importunities, the authorities commissioned him to carry dispatches as an experiment. He made great haste, and by traveling night and day he reached Suez, where he expected to find a steamer. As luck would have it, the steamer had broken down. Undaunted, the young man hired an open boat, and for six and a half days faced many perils as he proceeded down the Red Sea to Aden.

There was something of the imperturbable Phineas Fogg

about his efforts, and he might have well served as a model for Jules Verne's hero.

He carried out his performance, however, for no mere wager and for no ends of his own, but was moved by the spirit of public benefaction. Largely with his own money, though assisted by a committee at Bombay, he at once proceeded to make the route available to other travelers. He formed the eight halting-places in the desert between Cairo and Suez, which subsequently marked every map of Egypt, built three large hotels, and established regular caravans. He also introduced English carriages, which took the place of camels hitherto used by passengers, and brought the use of small steamers on the Nile. In a day before Cook's Tours were known, one may imagine what a boon this pioneer had conferred.

Officialdom itself had to yield, if reluctantly, before such a practical demonstration. By 1831 Waghorn had his arrangements in working order; yet governments are proverbially slow, and the Overland Route was not established until six years later. Not satisfied with this, he worked to improve the route, with the object of shortening the journey. He reached the apex of his success in 1845, when, traveling by way of Trieste, he arrived at Suez on October nineteenth, whereupon proceeding to Alexandria he arrived there the following day and reached London at four o'clock in the morning of October thirty-first, a startling achievement for those days. Shortly afterward, his health and means failed, and in 1850, at the age of fifty, he died.

He bequeathed his example to Lesseps, who always thought tenderly of the man, the memory of whom served him well in his great effort to build the Suez Canal and in overcoming the opposition he was to encounter to the great engineering project whose object was to unite two seas and the peoples of the East and the West.

2

Ferdinand de Lesseps, who was born in 1805 at Versailles, came of a family famous for having produced diplomatists and adventurers. The spirit of action and love of country were in the blood of the race. Some of his ancestors collaborated intimately with such men as Mazarin and Choiseul. French diplomacy, which had attained a high rank in the seventeenth and eighteenth centuries, owed a great deal to them. Ferdinand's father, Mathieu de Lesseps, had held many important positions. He had been Governor of the Ionian Islands; and at one time Consul-General to the United States. Napoleon himself had esteemed him.

Ferdinand was one of a large family. It is told that the Czar Alexander I, meeting the elder Lesseps one day asked him about his wife. "Sire, she was happily confined yesterday. "What? Again? But how many children have you now?" "An infinite number, sire—like to the sands of the desert!"

The Lesseps clan had produced many famous men, of whom Ferdinand was to attain the greatest glory. He was but twenty years old when he was appointed attaché to the French Consulate at Lisbon; shortly afterward he was transferred to Tunis, and somewhat later to Algiers. He was instrumental in perpetuating French power in these regions. The years 1832 to 1838 saw him in Egypt, where, as diplomatic agent, he not only made a thorough study of the country and its people but acquired great influence and popularity with its ruler, Mehemet Ali and his court. And this was not surprising, for he was sympathetic to the struggle of the Viceroy and his son Ibrahim against Turkish domination. The friendship was to stand him in good stead later.

Courage and distinction marked Lesseps' diplomatic career. At the age of thirty he was made a Chevalier of the Legion of Honor for conduct during the Syrian war of 1834 and the terrible pestilence of the following year. His subsequent diplomatic duties took him to Rotterdam, Malaga and finally in 1842 to Barcelona. He carried them all out with such éclat as to cause honors to be showered on him not only by the French Government but also by the governments to which he had been assigned as the French representative.

After serving as minister plenipotentiary at Madrid, a position to which he had been appointed after the French Revolution of 1848, he was in the following year chosen to carry out a particularly difficult and delicate mission to Italy. The situation was very muddled there. A new Republican Government had been established under Mazzini and two other triumvirs. The French President, Prince Louis Napoleon, wanted his emissary to propitiate the clericals and win the Vatican to his side. Such an outcome was bound to assist him in augmenting the power of the French Empire. There was an element of double-dealing in the matter, of which Lesseps was ignorant. But as he was a straightforward man, he tried to solve the difficulties by fair means and treated both sides impartially. This was not to the liking of the prince. He ultimately disavowed his envoy, who, in the course of negotiations, barely escaped assassination from his own countrymen. The story of this mission would make its own fascinating narrative, but here it is enough to say that Lesseps, unwilling to betray his mission, resigned from the diplomatic service after twenty-nine years of devoted labors.

Released from politics, he gave himself up to his first studies of the East and Egypt, and to his farm at Berry. This lasted for some years, during which his mind worked on the project of the Suez Canal. He remembered, too, the example of Waghorn, and thought often of that dauntless spirit.

3

For five years Lesseps worked in obscurity on his farm and thought of his favorite project. During those years he studied everything about the trade between the West and the East. He had calculated that the traffic doubled every ten years, and he saw clearly that a canal across the Isthmus of Suez would increase that traffic manyfold. The time was opportune for a revelation of his plans. Already in 1852 he had a definite plan. Loath to submit it to the pleasure-loving viceroy of Egypt, he laid it before the ruling powers at Constantinople, who replied that the project was not within the scope of the Porte.

There was nothing to do but abandon the scheme for the time being. Lesseps went on working on his farm, and the thought of Waghorn often returned to him.

Two years later, the ruling Viceroy of Egypt, Abbas Pasha, died. And good fortune placed a more amiable governor over that country in the person of Said Pasha, who was none other than the son of Lesseps' old friend, Mehemet Ali, creator of modern Egypt. Lesseps happened to have been instrumental in contributing to the rise of Mehemet Ali, and the grateful prince had felt tenderly toward the Frenchman. Mehemet Ali's son, Said, had been a pupil of Lesseps, and a meeting between them was easily arranged at Alexandria. The Pasha welcomed him and gave him one of his palaces for a residence. Then the two went on to Cairo, where the Viceroy was going to assume power.

The Frenchman's proposal met with the enthusiastic approval of the imaginative Pasha, who asked to see the plan in a form which he might lay before his government. And Lesseps had the necessary document ready in his pocket. The document, which still exists to-day, is a brief but clear statement giving the history of the project from the Pharaohs to Napoleon and showing the advantages which would accrue to humanity from its execution. He does not for an instant doubt its feasibility. Modern science can cope with problems hitherto thought impossible. "It is merely a question of money, which the spirit of enterprise and cooperation will soon solve, if the profits which are to result from it are in proportion to the cost." And he is certain "that the cost of the Suez, taking the highest estimate, is not out of proportion with the usefulness and the profits of this great work, which would abridge, by more than half, the distance between the principal countries of Europe, America and the Indies."

At this point, the author of the project breaks into dithyrambs, suited to the mood of the Oriental potentate to whom the message is addressed. Not that it isn't a true statement of facts!

"Mohammed Said has not been slow to see that there was no work which, as regards the grandeur and utility of results, could compare with this.

"What a glorious record for his reign! What an inexhaustible source of wealth for Egypt it will be! The names of the Egyptian sovereigns who erected the Pyramids, those monuments of human pride, remain unknown. The name of the prince who opens the great maritime canal will be blessed from century to century, down to the most distant posterity.

"The pilgrimage of Mecca secured for all time, and made easy the future of the Mohammedans. An immense impulse given to steam navigation and long voyages; the countries along the Red Sea and the Persian Gulf, the eastern coast of Africa, India, the kingdom of Siam, Cochin China, Japan, the vast Chinese Empire, the Philippine Islands, Australia, and that vast archipelago towards which the emigration of ancient Europe and America;—such are the sudden and immediate results of piercing the Isthmus of Suez."

He ends:

"May we not conclude that this great work, far more important for the future of the world, is henceforth secure from all serious opposition, and that the efforts made to realize the project will be sustained by the universal sympathy and active assistance of the enlightened men of all countries?"

The report convinced the viceroy and his generals, but Lesseps was yet to learn that Waghorn had been no accident and that it takes more than a convincing document to convince official minds.

For the moment he had his concession. What was he to do with it? Bricks are not to be made without straw, and canals are not to be built without money. Millions of pounds sterling were necessary. "I am not a financier, or a man of business," said Lesseps to the viceroy. "What do you think I had best do?" We do not know the viceroy's answer. But Lesseps had many rich colleagues and friends, and as a beginning a hundred of them contributed a share each of two hundred pounds. (A little more than twenty years later each of these shares was worth no less than forty thousand pounds!) This initial sum was used in studying the ground. The investigation conclusively proved the projector's contention that the Red and the Mediterranean Seas were on the same level and that a simple cut across the Isthmus would do, without calling in the aid of the Nile.

That much settled, Lesseps turned to the viceroy. Should he now put himself in the hands of French financiers, who would probably get the better of him? Said replied that there was ample money in the Egyptian treasury, which would bear all the cost.

The matter seemed simple. But just as it was being arranged and the engineers set to work making surveys, the opposition of England was so strong as to put the viceroy in a dilemma. Lesseps began to feel the pressure of that senseless obstruction which must have ultimately driven poor Waghorn to his untimely grave. He took a leaf out of Waghorn's book, and started a campaign for informing the British public—publicity, we should call it nowadays. It was to engage him for years; the hindrances he was to meet would have driven a less persistent man to despair.

He began by writing to Richard Cobden, M. P., famous free-trade advocate and promoter of Anglo-French commerce. He expressed astonishment at the hostility the canal project was said to have aroused in England, which country, he pointed out, had the most to gain from the execution of the project. Surely, England, who had one-half of the general trade with the Indies and China and possessed an immense empire in Asia, saw the advantage of reducing by a third the cost of her trade and by one-half the distance. Surely, she would not refuse to do so, simply because the nations bordering on the Mediterranean might benefit by their geographical situation to do a little more trade in Eastern waters than they were doing at the time. England, it was said, feared that the canal, by shortening the journey to India, would reduce the number of her merchantmen. This was a fallacious theory, replied Lesseps. "The experience of railways has surely proved, to an extent exceeding the boldest estimates, that a shortening in the distance and an abbreviation in the length of a journey increase, to an extent exceeding all calculation, the business relations and traffic."

In 1855, just in the thick of the Crimean War, Lesseps went to Constantinople. Here he found that Reshid Pasha and his ministers approved the project but were afraid to express themselves publicly owing to the influence and power exerted by the English Ambassador, Lord Stratford de Redcliffe; or Sultan Stratford, as he was known by the Turkish public.

Everywhere he found England the one obstacle to his plans. If poor Waghorn, an Englishman, had found difficulty with a relatively lesser project, what hope had he, a Frenchman, against the stubborn might of the British Empire? He went doggedly on.

He ultimately decided that the canal project should retain its private character and that the company should be organized as an universal concern, since if it assumed a national character it might invite the wrath of some one belligerent power. This, however, did not appease England, which continued its hostility chiefly in the person of her Prime Minister, Lord Palmerston, who, in a private interview with Lesseps, stated his apprehensions. They were that the canal being open to the navigation of all nations it would deprive England of the advantages which she possessed, and that though England was on friendly terms with France now one never knew what would happen after the Emperor was gone.

To Lesseps such reasons seemed puerile and unworthy, and he took energetic steps to educate English opinion; he thought the leading men and the public would be with him if they knew the nature of the benefits which would accrue to England in the event of the construction of the canal. He was not far wrong here. The great men of commerce, a few far-sighted politicians, Lord Rothschild himself, and the Geographical Society, listened to the great engineer and were favorably impressed. The matter ultimately came up in Parliament and elicited an attack from Lord Palmerston; as it contained a personal implication Lesseps rushed to England to defend himself against the charge. He had no designs on English money, he said, and his allotment of a fifth of the needed capital of eight million pounds sterling, he declared, was merely a courtesy to such a power as England. He was sure of getting the money elsewhere, and did not want an unwilling penny from England. His English allies continued to increase, and in 1857, Mr. Gladstone, then a member of the House of Commons, expressed himself in favor of the canal and condemned the government for opposing a scheme which had the support of the nation.

The fight continued. Lesseps energetically interviewed persons in power in Egypt, Turkey and on the Continent; he addressed meetings in the United Kingdom. In 1858 the House of Commons declared definitely against the project, though sixty-eight members voted in favor of it. Then efforts were made to induce Turkey and Egypt to act independently of England. The end of the year 1858 saw the Universal Company of the Maritime Suez Canal in action.

Lesseps approached Rothschild, to whom he had been of some service while minister at Madrid, and asked him if he would open a subscription.

Of course! He would be glad to accommodate Lesseps, and placed his offices at the engineer's disposal.

"And what will you ask for it?" asked Lesseps.

"Good heavens!" replied Rothschild. "It is plain you are not a man of business. It is always five per cent."

Lesseps made a rapid mental calculation. "Five per cent. on eight million pounds; why, that makes four hundred thousand pounds!" He laughed. "I shall hire a place for twelve hundred francs, and do my own work equally well!"

And he did. France alone took four million, four hundred thousand pounds of the shares. Several countries participated in the enterprise, England and America being among the smallest subscribers. The Khedive of Egypt contributed the remainder of the necessary fund.

The year 1859 saw the work on the canal in actual progress. It was not long before twenty-five thousand to thirty thousand men were at work excavating, to the great annoyance of Lord Palmerston, who still hoped that something could be done to prevent it. With the aid of new gigantic inventions, 2,763,000 cubic yards of earth were removed each month, bringing the two seas nearer and nearer. But even while progress was being made in construction, attempts were made to discredit the enterprise, in Paris as elsewhere.

By 1869, however, the work had gone so far forward that the day of inauguration was fixed for November seventeenth of that year. Actually, the festivities began on the sixteenth.

It was a day of triumph. Important visitors from all parts of the earth flocked to Port Said for the ceremony. Among the guests of the Khedive were the Empress of the French, the Emperor of Austria, the Crown Prince of Prussia, the Crown Prince of Holland, Prince William of Hesse, the British Ambassador to Egypt, the British Ambassador to Turkey, and there were dozens of others belonging to the diplomatic and military corps. There were also great merchants and manufacturers, and not a few politicians from nearly every country. The Crescent and the Star of the Moslem and the Cross of the Christian, emblazoned on banners, were flung side by side to the winds, as were also the flags of many nations. An old sheik of the Moslem faith began the ceremony, a Mussulman prayer was chanted, a discourse in Arabic was read by the Grand Ulema. Then followed a procession of the clergy of the Christian churches, headed by the Archbishop of Alexandria. Monseigneur Bauer, Almoner to the Empress Eugénie, followed by priests, slowly marched through an immense crowd, chanting a *Te Deum*. The impossible had been accomplished, "there was no longer an Old World and a New," he then declared in an address. Trumpets sounded, cannon boomed, the din of the multitudes filled the air.

On the next day, the canal was opened. The French steamer *Aigle,* with Empress Eugénie on board, led the maritime pageant; the emotional lady broke into sobs at the thought of the wonder that had been wrought by Frenchmen. It was followed by the Austrian, Prussian and Dutch royal steam yachts. Duke Michael was on board a Russian war-ship, a Swedish yacht bore Prince Oscar of Sweden. Forty vessels in all, carrying important personages, left Port Said that day and arrived at Ismailia, without delay or accident.

Lesseps, now sixty-four, was a proud man that day; he was proud because the inauguration ceremonies brought a young lady visitor, a Creole lady of English extraction, Mlle. Héléne Autard de Bragard. A few days later she became Madame Ferdinand de Lesseps, the second wife of the engineer.

On the day he saw the ships go through the canal he did not forget to give a thought to Lieutenant Waghorn. Certainly he, Ferdinand de Lesseps, was a more fortunate man.

4

Nations began to shower honors on him. The Emperor

Napoleon conferred on him the rank of the Cross of the Legion of Honor; the Italian Government presented him with the cordon of the Order of St. Maurice; Queen Victoria nominated him an Honorary Knight Grand Commander of the Order of the Star of India. Other honors came, thick and fast. He was the lion of the day.

A particularly gratifying acknowledgment of his achievement came from the Earl of Clarendon, English Minister of Foreign Affairs. Lesseps then paid a visit to England, where he met with a reception such as is only accorded to princes in fairy tales. Gladstone's prophecy that it would be England who would cover Lesseps with glory when he had successfully carried through his great work had come true. Those who had most fiercely opposed him now made haste to do him tribute.

There was the crowning honor in 1884, when he was elected to the French Academy in the place left by the death of the historian, Henri Martin. Among those who sponsored the new member was Victor Hugo, and it was the great Renan who replied to the simple if impressive address made by Lesseps with a speech the equal of any he had ever before delivered.

"When you excite the enthusiasm of a meeting," said Renan, addressing himself to Lesseps, "and succeed in reducing that which is the most obdurate thing in the world to metaphors, and the most refractory to the artifices of the so-called art of fine talking,—I mean capital,—it is not your words but your individuality which attracts; or, I should rather say, your whole person speaks. You exercise a charm. You have that supreme gift which works miracles like faith, and which is in truth of the same order. Charm has its secret motives, but not its definite reasons. Its action is wholly spiritual. You obtain the same success at Chicago, a city which is not a third your age, as you do in the ancient cities of Europe. You convince the Turk, the Arab, the Abyssinian, the Paris speculator, and the Liverpool merchant, by reasons which differ only in appearance. The true reason for your ascendancy is that people detect in you a heart full of sympathy for all that is human, a genuine passion for ameliorating the lot of your fellow-creatures. . . .

"The persons who were at first surprised to hear of your election were but imperfectly acquainted with the spirit which governs our company. You have cultivated the most difficult of styles—one which has for a long time been abandoned amongst us—that of action. You are of the small band of those who have maintained the ancient French tradition of a brilliant and glorious existence, one useful to all your fellow-men. . . ."

The speaker went on to say that Lesseps was one of those fortunate workers who had been taken into the confidence of what the genius of civilization required at a given moment. If man was really master of the planet he inhabited it was his first duty "to rectify, in view of his requirements, the combinations, in many cases opposed to those requirements, which the revolutions of the globe, ignoring altogether the interests of humanity, have inevitably produced. . . . For a planet is only ripe for progress when all its inhabited parts have reached that stage of close relationship which constitute a living organism, so that no one part can enjoy, suffer, or act without the other parts feeling in harmony." Such was the critical stage reached in the history of our planet. This was evident in the way the stock exchanges of Paris and London were affected by what occurred at Peking, in the Congo, in Kordofan, or in California; there were but few dead parts in the body of humanity. The telegraph and the telephone had annihilated distance as regards the things of the mind, while railways and steam navigation had multiplied tenfold the facilities of bodily movement. Was it not inevitable, then, that the century should regard as an essential part of its work the removal of the obstacles to rapid communication? "It was impossible, surely, that the generation which had tunnelled the Mont Cenis and the St. Gotthard should be arrested by a few sandbanks of rock at Suez, Corinth and Panama!"

Then, again, Renan directly addressed Lesseps:

"You were born to pierce isthmuses, and antiquity would have made a myth of you. You are the man of our age upon whose forehead is most clearly the sign of an unmistakable vocation. The principle of great deeds is to take possession of force where it is to be found, to purchase it at its proper price, and to know how to make use of it."

The work of Lesseps, the speaker said, was in the nature of religion by reason of the enthusiasm he aroused, and he gave numerous intimate instances of this nature. And he assured the new member of the Academy that, having improved the Creator's work, the Creator had cause to be pleased with him.

This tribute of Renan has been declared to be the most just estimate ever made of the genius of Lesseps.

Even while these honors were being showered in abundance on the great engineer's head, now gray with eighty winters, the ironic fates were preparing an overwhelming calamity. And such is the destiny of great men that the fates furnish their victims with weapons of their own choosing wherewith to wreak misfortune on their heads. It is for the Chorus of Pities to pronounce a fitting lament.

5

The story can be told briefly and simply.

Lesseps, being an energetic man, "a man of action," as

Renan pronounced him, was moved to make an effort to conquer new worlds. The Suez Canal had been a complete success. Why not Panama?

He had not sufficiently realized the difficulty of the project. He had made an estimate that it would take eight years to accomplish the task, and that it would cost twenty million, five hundred thousand pounds sterling. So great was the confidence in him that he had little difficulty in getting the money. Even men of moderate means subscribed for the shares. There were 102,230 stockholders, of whom 16,000 were women. The work began in February, 1881.

The project was beset from the start with misfortunes. The climate was vile, snakes and scorpions lurked in the swamps, the place bred disease. Thousands found untimely graves. A severe earthquake inflicted great damage to the works in 1882. A tidal wave added to the confusion. Insurrections in 1885 were calamitous. The resident heads wasted money on palatial homes and comforts. Above all, the physical difficulties of construction seemed at times insurmountable. Progress was slow. Notwithstanding immense expenditures, far exceeding the original estimates, by the end of 1886 only thirty millions of cubic feet of excavation had been accomplished, hardly a fifth of the total amount of excavation required. An investigator in 1887 wrote that "half buried in mud lie about wrecks of costly machinery, consumed by rust, sent out under lavish orders, and found unfit for the work for which they were intended." One expert declared that another thirty million pounds sterling would be required to finish the work!

Rumors were spreading in Paris, the shareholders were beginning to be alarmed, an early liquidation of the company was spoken of.

Lesseps energetically set to work to get more money,

and he declared that the canal would surely be opened by July, 1890. But there were limits even to his powers of persuasion. After 1888 no more money was to be had. The canal had already cost something like fifty million pounds sterling. Another thirty million pounds might finish it, but then there would be no money to the investors on the immense outlay.

Soon the crash came.

In 1892 there was the startling news that the French Government had decided to institute a prosecution against Lesseps and his co-directors. Charles de Lesseps, son of the engineer, was among them. As the possession of the Grand Cross of the Legion of Honor provided exemption from trial before magistrates, the law was changed to allow a summons to be issued to Lesseps. But his presence in court could hardly be insisted on. The old man, now eighty-seven, at his country home at Chesnaye, was ill. He had lost his memory, and was hardly aware of what was going on. Only once, before the proceedings had been instituted, did he give a sign of his former energy. That was while he was still in Paris and a summons arrived for him to appear before Monsieur Prinet, the examining magistrate. Then something happened which astonished all who were in the house. He, who had been so ill for days that he could not move without assistance, suddenly rose from his bed and, calling for his clothes, hastily dressed and put on his Grand Cordon of the Legion of Honor. Then he issued forth, descending the stairs with a firm tread. He returned home, and took to bed with fever. "What a terrible nightmare I have had!" he said the next day to his wife. "I imagined I was summoned before the examining magistrate." But conscious moments came when he knew it had not been a dream, and again, he lapsed into a torpor. Never again did he speak of Panama. But sometimes, as in a half-sleep, he murmured incoherently; some one thought he had heard him repeat the name of one Waghorn.

The Panama scandals convulsed the political world. One ministerial cabinet fell, the squabbles in the Chamber went on, there were deaths, duels, condemnations; a thousand things happened. Lesseps' own son, Charles, was given a prison sentence, with others. There was a final interview between father and son, but the father did not know that the police inspectors were behind the door. There was one affectionate instant of greeting, that was all. The old man relapsed into his customary state of semiconsciousness. He was not for long in this world.

On December 7, 1894, death released the old man, at the age of eighty-nine, from his earthly travail.

Neither Ferdinand de Lesseps, nor his son Charles, was guilty of dishonesty in any but the legal sense of the word. As one of the liquidators of the Panama Company put it: "They certainly put no money into their own pockets. They were guilty of weakness and of not taking care of other people's money. M. Charles de Lesseps was made a scapegoat for others."

Ferdinand never cared for money for its own sake, but he thought a great deal of the glory of France. He had parted with his one founder's share of his Suez property in order to pay the liquidator six hundred and seventy-five thousand francs as amends for his mistake. He would have left his family quite without resources, and only the generosity of the Suez Canal Company in setting aside a sum for them saved them from destitution.

Ferdinand de Lesseps had built one canal; another destroyed him. Here is a theme for Shakespeare.

THE COMPARISON OF RHODES WITH DE LESSEPS

Money, as a medium of exchange, reached its highest development in the nineteenth century. The first men could not boast of so complicated a system, but exchanged one kind of goods for another kind of goods: potatoes for lentils, fowl for mutton, or cloth for wine. In our own day, money has become a commodity of its own, and one kind of money is often exchanged for another kind of money. We hear a great deal about money being "the root of all evil." Certainly, money is responsible for a great many tragedies. Balzac drew a typical picture of one of these tragedies as long ago as in *César Birotteau*.

We have two such tragedies in the lives of Cecil Rhodes and Ferdinand de Lesseps.

Money to-day is such an international affair, and the money of this or that country is so intrinsic a part of the world organism that it would be difficult nowadays to draw purely national distinctions without stretching the point. Increasingly rapid methods of intercommunication have made certain types universal, and there would seem to be little distinction between a French, German, English and American financier.

Without money, in the sense that the nineteenth century began to understand this dangerous commodity, Rhodes and Lesseps could not have been what they were; they might have been great generals, great diplomatists, great engineers, even great artists, but not the great Cæsars they were.

Rhodes gave expression to a new conception: the economic empire; that is to say, universal domination by the acquisition of material concessions, such as mines, railways, oil-wells, and so forth. He discovered that it was not absolutely necessary to make conquests by force of arms, but if you had the financial concessions in a country you practically ruled it and could gradually, by force of material power, insinuate your own national culture into the country from which you exacted tribute under another name. His one deviation from this plan proved disastrous, but not ultimately so, since a war intervened and consolidated all his campaigns of peace. He was, surely, a Roman in modern dress.

Lesseps had also the Roman mind. The Romans had a genius for building. They built roads, aqueducts and viaducts wherever they went, and left everywhere footprints of their creation. By these efforts they knit the world closer; the canals of Lesseps had the same object. He was a great civilizer.

What are, then, the distinctions of national temperament which separate Rhodes from Lesseps? They exist, though they are very subtle.

Rhodes, not for nothing called the "Colossus," was the realistic Englishman, with his feet firmly entrenched in the ground. He saw early the power of money, and set out, first of all, "to accumulate the ready," so that his patriotic plans for making the world English might not go amiss. He allowed his dreams to wait on his fortune.

Lesseps, once he had his dream and faith in it, depended entirely on firing people's imaginations with its possibilities. His plan, like all things French, was logical and practical, and money came to him as by a miracle, by sheer charm and suasion. As Renan had said in his famous address:

"You have renewed in our time the miracles of ancient days. You possess in the highest degree the secret of all

CECIL RHODES

From an etching by Mortimer Menpes

Ferdinand de Lesseps

Photo by Goupil et Cie

greatness, the art of making yourself beloved. You have succeeded in forming out of incoherent masses a small but compact army, in which the best qualities of the French race have appeared in all their éclat. Thousands of men have found in you their conscience, their reason of being, their principle of nobility or of moral renovation."

Might not Renan have addressed the same words to Napoleon?

Another thing: the French temperament is reflected in the election of Lesseps to the Academy, which is, on the whole, an institution created for thought and literature. His selection is a tribute to imagination, which the French hold in high regard in whatever walk of life it may appear. And thus money finds its place as a side issue, where it belongs.

"The evil that men do lives after them, the good is oft interred with their bones." The opposite is sometimes the case. The Panama scandals are nearly forgotten, the Jameson Raid is wholly forgiven, and only the good that Lesseps and Rhodes have done is more and more remembered.

AFTERWORD

THE French sculptor, Auguste Rodin, said somewhere that the genius which was moved to create the marvelous Gothic temples of France with their multifold spires, each rising above the other in the effort to reach heaven, was the same genius which later made the French such fine aviators.

Two interesting ideas are implied in this statement. One, that a nation possesses its own specific genius. Two, that it can not escape this genius and that in different epochs it merely changes in appearance, consistent with the age, but not in that essence which belongs to itself, which is eternal and defiant of all change. This integral changeless quality we may call the national or racial temperament, or, if you like, character. At all events, Rodin meant to convey by his statement that though the centuries have changed, Frenchmen as a race and as individuals have retained their specific character. And what is true of Frenchmen is true of members of other nations.

All that is surely true. Yet the fact remains that, since the Renaissance, the individual has gained a predominant rôle in society, and what great achievements have been carried out may be credited to the individual rather than to the race. Whole races have poured themselves into the Bible and Homer and into the Gothic cathedrals, but though it may be argued that a whole epoch is represented in Shakespeare, it nevertheless remains true that Shakespeare is one man.

It is to express this point of departure from ancient

standards that the author of a new Plutarch may begin his work. Great men must assume importance not because they are great individuals but because, by means of unconscionable creative processes, they do, like Shakespeare, represent and give voice to what is best in the mind of the race at a given epoch, and sum up that epoch in terms of action or art. If they merely expressed themselves, the interest they would have for men would be temporary and limited; they would be a one-day wonder like the sword-swallower or the bearded lady of the traveling circus, abnormal phenomena without other meaning than any sport of nature may have for us. They would excite our curiosity, provide a little diversion for our minds, and pass on, leaving our hearts and the best part of our minds untouched.

The virtue of great men is that, far from being monstrosities, they are the most normal of men, "abnormally normal" indeed, as Mr. Arthur Symons has said of Tolstoi. The maddest of them have an abundance of common sense; it is this very abundance of sense, assuming an exaggerated form, that passes for madness. Clear sight and far sight are given to few, and he who has both is likely to appear mad to one of limited vision. Men of limited vision are unfortunately many. When Blake looks at a sunrise and exclaims, "What! You will tell me that when the sun rises you see a little round golden spot like a guinea—and I tell you I see all the hosts of heaven, singing *Holy, Holy, Holy, Lord God Almighty*!" he expresses something of that humanity which once really worshiped the sun as a deity but, through oversophistication, has lost the art of worship. When Thoreau builds himself a hut in the woods and sings the joys of gliding in a canoe across the smooth waters of the lake, he says in effect: "Ah, men, you who work in factories, you who work in all manner of sterile labors, you who clutter your houses with useless, ugly possessions, you who have nothing but petty thoughts for the morrow and forget to live to-day—you have lost the art of happiness, you have lost Paradise!" Does he not, by his example and his words, awaken a dim echo in the hearts of many of a nostalgia for some deep-hidden treasure over-crusted with time and well-nigh forgotten? When Herman Melville longs for the great things potential in life, for a woman he may pedestal, for the superior friendship of a superior man, for the absolute he may not reach, for that warm contact of humanity which may cause his rich gifts to come forth like a flower under the sun, does he not ultimately awaken the conscience of humanity he desired to enrich to a vision of Prometheus who having given fire to men is crucified on a rock and exposed to the talons of the cruel eagle? Of such stuff are legends made, and great men are one of the few noble myths left to us. If this sounds highfalutin, the least that can be said is that "great men, taken up in any way, are profitable company," which are the words of Carlyle, who could be on occasion a Scotsman of hard sense.

A great man, then, is something more than an individual. He is the essence of life, and however individual, however selfish he may appear in his life, willy-nilly he lives for the many. If, in the ultimate sense, he did not, he would have little interest in achievement. Even the pessimist Schopenhauer, writing of the folly of reading books, proceeds to write them. And Anatole France, if with better humor, does the same. For all his abstract love of beauty, for all his skepticism, he is forced to confess, that like Rabelais, Montaigne, Molière, Voltaire, Renan, like all skeptics of the French tradition, he writes with a purpose. "They attacked everything which put the intelligence and the will in bondage. They struggled against ignorance which stupefies, against error which oppresses, against intolerance which tyrannizes, against cruelty which tortures, against hatred which kills. . . . All our skeptics were full of fervor, all strove to deliver their fellow-creatures from the chains which bound them. In their way, they were saints." A people are a subsoil which grows and nourishes its finest flower, called genius, and in these words of Anatole France we have a glimpse of the French mind and temperament, which in their ultimate expression, have lodged themselves in an individual, a great man. And, in this sense, Anatole France not merely represents France; he *is* France.

English genius, on the other hand, is less the result of such rational ramifications. It is, on the whole, insular, and what it lacks in precision, polish and breadth, it makes up in directness and in depth. In comparison with the French mind, the British mind is inarticulate, but then, when its genius expresses itself it gushes forth with a freshness and spontaneity denied to the French, and Shakespeare is the result. It is true that Voltaire called Shakespeare a barbarian, and that Tolstoi took umbrage at his so-called feudal attitude toward life. Without going into the merits of these strictures, it is certain that Shakespeare was the most perfect expression of his age and race. In short, Shakespeare can not be assailed without assailing in his person the country and the age which gave him birth. What, indeed, both Voltaire and Tolstoi find fault with is that Shakespeare is not a thinker, but a poet. Young energetic races find their expression not in thought but in action and in poetry, terms which translate into one another, as at least one Frenchman, Ernest Renan, recognized in his speech on the admission of Ferdinand de Lesseps, builder of the Suez Canal, into the French Academy. How came this man, Lesseps, to sit by the side of Victor Hugo, as a fellow-member in an institution primarily designed for artists and scholars? And Renan, addressing himself to the great engineer, gives answer: "You have cultivated the most difficult of styles—one which has for a long time been abandoned among us—that of action." It must be remembered that Shakespeare was a contemporary of the great adventurer, Francis Drake; Shakespeare was a Francis Drake who expressed himself in letters. Abstract thought is alien to the Anglo-Saxon mind, but action is quite natural to it, and poetry, rather than prose, is its expression in literature. The English have produced a body of poetry unequaled in Europe.

A modern biographer who wishes to do more that state facts about his subjects is here confronted with a difficulty. The man of action who is that and nothing more lives his life so intensely that the only opportunity he offers the biographer is a bare recital of facts. The man of thought likewise provides a meager chance, since he has already adequately expressed the processes of his mind. To the first category belong men like Garibaldi who, though he was the greatest romantic character of the nineteenth century and had won by his achievements the title of "demigod," lived a life which leaves nothing to the imagination. To the second belong men like Amiel and Henry Adams who have thought so deeply and recorded their thought so well (and hardly acted at all) that any biographer who should seek to depend on them would find his occupation soon gone. The subject interesting for biography is he who has both lived and acted, whose thought has influenced his action and whose action has influenced his thought, in whom the two things have merged as day into night. If Hamlet had acted at the start, if his will had not been "sicklied o'er with the pale cast of thought," there would have been no play. Hamlet, to be sure, is an extreme example; he is, besides, a legendary personage; nevertheless, the nineteenth century is peculiarly rich in these dual types who offer fine quarry to the biographer. In their duality, with the consequent effort to reconcile two often contradictory natures, lies the ominous seed of their ultimate disruption and that tragic irony which makes them the sport of gods and a fascinating spectacle to men. The theater of life offers dramas which, considering the heroic stature of the protagonists, are in no wise behind the tragic portrayals (with the Fates pulling the strings) of Æschylus and Euripides.

Consider the list, in any case a partial one, of these nineteenth-century Titans, going willingly or blindly, as the case may be, to their doom, through some whimsical or perverse note in their character: Paul Gauguin, sick of civilization, and in quest of some dream Eden; John Brown, practical Yankee, driven by an idea of a heaven of equality until he nobly puts his head into a noose; Ferdinand Lassalle, prince and democrat, man of iron will, who like Samson of old is shorn of his locks by a woman to his undoing; Simon Bolivar, liberator, South American Don Quixote, who spends a lifetime liberating five countries from Spanish tyranny, only to witness from his death-bed the dissipation of his victories; Robert E. Lee, master general, a man of men, whose fortitude and integrity deserved better of the fates which guide the destiny of men. All these men, and a great many others, represented something of the minds of nations, and the story of their lives is not only biography; it is also history. A chronicle of the efforts of these individuals is a true history of humanity's success and failure.

There is no better example of the power of the great individual to incarnate in himself a whole race than that of Cervantes, whose novel, *Don Quixote*, the supreme work of fiction, expresses the genius and the mind of the Spanish people as no formal history may hope to do. It happens to be a spiritual autobiography of Cervantes himself, but a great man may take a country to his bosom, and so it also happens to be Spain herself made articulate. He has absorbed the unformed background of his age and race and he has poured it into a form at once beautiful and comprehensible.

In a noble tribute to Cervantes, in his *The Soul of Spain,* Mr. Havelock Ellis, a sage of our time, dwells on the interesting fact that Cervantes was a man of letters only by accident.

"He was a soldier, a man of action, who would never have taken up the pen, except in moments of recreation, if a long chain of misfortunes had not closed the other avenues of life. It is a singular fact that nearly every great Spanish author has been a soldier or an adventurer, at least as familiar with the pike as with the pen. 'The lance has never blunted the pen, nor the pen the lance,' said Don Quixote, therein expressing the conviction of all Spanish writers. Italian men of letters have often been keen politicians, French men of letters brilliant men of the world, English and American good business men, or capable men of affairs, but nowhere save in Spain do we find the soldier supreme in literature." Cervantes, we are told, lived his whole life in the spirit of the knight errant, "and *Don Quixote* swept away the romances of chivalry, not because it was a satire of them, but because it was itself a romance of chivalry and the greatest of them all, since its action was placed in the real world."

The meaning of this should not escape the reader; it simply means that not only had Cervantes sublimated his own adventure, hitherto active, by producing a great work of art, but that he had also poured into his book the chivalrous nature of a whole people.

It is curious that nowhere outside of Spain was the book sooner appreciated than in England, and the reasons for this have already been indicated: it was as with *King Lear,* published in the same year, surplus energy transformed into poetry. England and Spain were both the great active nations of the time, and their art was but one outlet for their superabundant energy. Both Shakespeare and Cervantes are the supreme types of genius, because in their work one may read not only the minds of their nations but also see revealed those mainsprings of action which give rise to the peculiarities of these minds.

But even in respect of this, there are subtle racial distinctions. The Spaniard (witness again *Don Quixote*) begins with ideas of honor and action, and the consciousness of these is never lost. The Englishman (Shakespeare, the supreme example) doesn't, in a sense, begin at all: he is all action, and the transition from one form of it into another, from active adventuring into a work of art, is an invisible process of which one is never consciously aware; plays like *Macbeth* and *King Lear* are pieces of pure action. In our own day, Charles M. Doughty, author of *Arabia Deserta*, is an equally characteristic example of this; the English mind is supreme here; what thought there is merges in action with such a measure of integrity that there is no telling where the one ends and the other begins. The Frenchman (Molière or Anatole France is an equally good example) begins with an idea, which he conveys by a series of actions, reasoned with lucid precision, to its ultimate logic; that is to say, the initial idea leads to action, and this action is almost mathematically progressive and inevitable. *The Misanthrope* and *Thais*, in different genres, equally reveal this quality of the French mind. In actual life, there was Arthur Rimbaud, who pendulated between one extreme and the other, between ultimate art and the ultimate bourgeois attitude; he was a great artist in Europe (begetting the later Verlaine and Mallarmé), and to escape corrupt Europe he went to Africa where he became a pure bourgeois. Molière and Anatole France and Arthur Rimbaud are France.*

This brings us to the mooted question of tradition. Frenchmen, whether men of action or poets, are proud of being in the Latin tradition, which, in its turn, is presumed to hark back to the Greek tradition. The beauty of the French genius Anatole France attributes to the classics, Homer, Virgil, Horace and the rest. "We are Latins. The milk of the she-wolf is in our blood." This would be quite true, were it not that Frenchmen, in their pride, too often bulk the Greeks with the Latins. The French, it would seem, have taken from the Greco-Latin tradition that part which was common both to the Greeks and to the Latins: balance, harmony, the pagan attitude toward living (even when it is tempered with Christianity), the lighter virtues, the Aristophanic delight in the comic and the profane, but by no means that somber character, that deep sense of tragic horror, which so vividly stamps the work of Æschylus, Sophocles and Euripides. This is in greater evidence in the productions of Shakespeare and Marlowe, and even more in those of Mr. Thomas Hardy, whose attitude toward the relentless fates which dog the footsteps of man has been compared to that of Æschylus himself. This simple, tragic note is even more clear in the work of some of the Russians, especially in that of Dostoievsky; and it is not difficult to trace the kinship that exists between the pathological types as drawn in *Œdipus Rex* and those in *The Brothers Karamazov.*

We are not concerned here however with the Russians,

*Since this essay was written there has appeared Mr. Salvador de Madariaga's altogether admirable *Englishmen, Frenchmen, Spaniards* (Oxford University Press), significant for the ramifications it presents concerning national temperaments and its effect on life and letters.

but with the differences which exist between the Latin and the Anglo-Saxon types of mind. And these differences, it must be said, arise chiefly from the different attitudes assumed by the two races toward the Bible. The Latins temper their relation toward the Bible with Homer, and at one period, the period of the Italian Renaissance, the conflict between the two was so far reconciled as to cause the Church and Art to flower at the same time. Since then the conflict has entered into life, and one can not say that the Latins are not a happier people than the Anglo-Saxons for the balance created by its successful issue. In Anglo-Saxon communities, notably in America, there has been a greater adherence to the Bible. Puritanism has been the issue, and whether one likes it or not, it must be admitted that, in a larger sense, puritanism is an effort on the part of man to shake off earthly fetters and "be nearer to God," as the saying goes. That the effort is doomed to failure is, after all, due to the circumstance that man is man. The Latins understand this, and accept it, and it is by no means certain that they would have it otherwise. "Let us drink and be merry, for to-morrow we die!" "Let us spend our time in prayer and repentance, for we have not long to live!" Thus, roughly, may be summed up the two attitudes. It is not for us to discuss their relative merits. But it must be noted that one attitude and the other are best expressed in the great men of both races, and to understand the best that any race has to give one must study its great men.

The present tendency to minimize the great, on the one hand, by lingering on their human failings, on the other, by explaining their conduct by purely mechanical processes, which reduce them to merely superior pieces of mechanism without personal responsibility for their actions, is a sad commentary on an age which would dispense with greatness.

The adherents of the new "psychology" have not yet ventured to attribute the "Sermon on the Mount" to glands. This must be said for the sensible Latins: they do not allow themselves to be taken in by new fads, even when they pass under the name of "science."

It was a great Greek, Sophocles, who said: "Either noble life or noble death befits one of generous strain." And that should hold good to this day.

BIBLIOGRAPHY AND ACKNOWLEDGMENTS

BIBLIOGRAPHY AND ACKNOWLEDGMENTS

Special acknowledgments for sources of *A Modern Plutarch* are indicated by an asterisk.

Mark Twain (1835-1910).

*MARK TWAIN. A BIOGRAPHY. By Albert Bigelow Paine. 3 vols., New York and London: Harper & Bros. 1912. (A thorough, authoritative, well-documented biography, indispensable for students.)

*MARK TWAIN'S AUTOBIOGRAPHY. 2 vols. Harper & Bros. 1924. (Fragments of varying merit, some disappointing, others intensely interesting. No biographer can overlook the essay, "The Character of Man.")

*THE ORDEAL OF MARK TWAIN. By Van Wyck Brooks. New York: E. P. Dutton & Co. 1920. English edition entitled: *The Tragedy of Mark Twain*. London: Heinemann. 1922. (A brilliant essay in the psycho-analyst method.)

Anatole France (1844-1924).

*ANATOLE FRANCE: THE MAN AND HIS WORK. By J. Lewis May. London: John Lane. New York: Dodd, Mead & Co. 1924. (A straightforward "essay in critical biography.")

*ANATOLE FRANCE AND HIS CIRCLE. Being His Table Talk Collected by Paul Gsell. London: John Lane. New York: Dodd, Mead & Co. 1922.

*THE GARDEN OF EPICURUS. By Anatole France. London: John Lane. New York: Dodd, Mead & Co. 1908. (A beautiful book of fragmentary thoughts, embodying an exposition of the master's philosophy.)

PENGUIN ISLAND. By Anatole France. London: John Lane. New York: Dodd, Mead & Co. 1909. (A satirical history of France.)

JOAN OF ARC. By Anatole France. 3 vols. London: John Lane. New York. Dodd, Mead & Co. 1909.

THE LATIN GENIUS. By Anatole France. London: John Lane. New York: Dodd, Mead & Co. 1924.

ANATOLE FRANCE. By Georg Brandes. London: Heinemann. 1908.

Paul Gauguin (1848-1903).

*PAUL GAUGUIN: HIS LIFE AND HIS ART. By John Gould Fletcher. New York: N. L. Brown. 1921. (A terse, well-written biography).

NOA NOA. By Paul Gauguin. New York: N. L. Brown. 1919.

*LETTERS OF PAUL GAUGUIN TO GEORGES DANIEL DE MONFRIED. New York: Dodd, Mead & Co. 1922. London: Heinemann. 1923.

Henry Thoreau (1817-62).

*WALDEN. By Henry Thoreau. Boston: Houghton, Mifflin & Co.

HENRY THOREAU: BACHELOR OF NATURE. By Léon Bazalgette. New York: Harcourt, Brace & Co. 1924. London: Jonathan Cape. 1924. (A charming biography, with the lyrical note predominating.)

*LIFE OF HENRY D. THOREAU. By F. B. Sanborn. Houghton, Mifflin & Co.
FAMILIAR STUDIES OF MEN AND BOOKS. (Essay on Thoreau.) By R. L. Stevenson.

Ferdinand Lassalle (1825-64).

*FERDINAND LASSALLE. By Georg Brandes. London: Heinemann. 1911. New York: Bernard G. Richards Co. 1925. (The best available exposition of the man and his ideas.)
*PRINCESS HELÉNE VON RACOWITZA: AN AUTOBIOGRAPHY. London: Constable. 1910.
*IMMORTAL MEMORIES. (Essay: The Private Life of Ferdinand Lassalle.) By Clement Shorter. New York: Harper & Bros. 1907.

Charles Stewart Parnell (1846-91).

*CHARLES STEWART PARNELL. By Katharine O'Shea. 2 vols. London: Cassell & Co. New York: George H. Doran Co. 1914.
*PARNELL. By St. John Ervine. London: Ernest Benn. Boston: Little, Brown & Co. 1927. (An excellent book, with emphasis on the dramatic aspects of Parnell's life.)

Honoré de Balzac (1799-1850).

*BALZAC. By Frederick Lawton. London: Grant Richards. 1910. (In some respects the best existing biography in English.)
*WOMEN IN THE LIFE OF BALZAC. By Juanita Helm Floyd. New York: Henry Holt. 1921.

HONORÉ DE BALZAC. By Margaret F. Sandars. London: John Murray. 1904.

BALZAC. By René Benjamin. New York: Alfred A. Knopf. London: Heinemann. 1927. (A creative biography.)

Herman Melville (1819-91).

*HERMAN MELVILLE: MARINER AND MYSTIC. By Raymond M. Weaver. New York: George H. Doran Co. 1921. (A pioneer biography which still waits to be bettered.)

*HERMAN MELVILLE. (English Men of Letters — New Series.) By John Freeman. London and New York: The Macmillan Co. 1925. (An excellent, short critical biography.)

*THE REBELLIOUS PURITAN: PORTRAIT OF MR. HAWTHORNE. By Lloyd Morris. New York: Harcourt, Brace & Co. 1927. London: Constable & Co. 1928. (The pages about Melville are exceptionally interesting.)

Arthur Rimbaud (1854-91).

*RIMBAUD: THE BOY AND THE POET. By Edgell Rickword. London: Heinemann. 1924. (The only existing biography in English, and very good of its kind. But it is a pity that the French phrases are not always translated.)

*THE SYMBOLIST MOVEMENT IN LITERATURE. (Essay on Rimbaud.) By Arthur Symons. London: Constable. 1908. (An excellent piece of interpretation.)

*THE BOOK OF GALLANT VAGABONDS. (Essay on Rimbaud.) By Henry Beston. New York: George H. Doran Co. 1925.

Charles M. Doughty (1843-1926).

*Arabia Deserta. By Charles M. Doughty. With an Introduction by Colonel T. E. Lawrence. London: the Medici Society and Jonathan Cape. New York: Boni & Liveright. 1924.

John Brown (1800-59).

*John Brown. By Oswald Garrison Villard. Boston: Houghton Mifflin Co. 1910. (A monument of painstaking scholarship, not likely to be surpassed, and bound to remain for all time the source-book for all future biographers and historians.)

Giuseppe Garibaldi (1807-82).

Garibaldi's Defence of the Roman Republic. By George Macaulay Trevelyan. London: Longmans. 1907.

*Garibaldi and the Thousand. Ibid. 1909.

Garibaldi and the Making of Italy. Ibid. 1911.

*Liberation of Italy. 1815-1870. By Countess E. Martinengo Cesaresco. London: Seeley, Service & Co. 1915.

*Autobiography of Giuseppe Garibaldi. 2 vols. With a supplementary volume by Jesse White Mario. London: Walter Smith and Innes. 1889.

*Creative Spirits of the Nineteenth Century. (Essay on Giuseppe Garibaldi.) By Georg Brandes. Thomas Y. Crowell & Co. 1923.

*The Life and Times of Cavour. By William Roscoe Thayer. 2 vols. Boston: Houghton Mifflin Co. 1911.

Builders of United Italy. (Essay on Garbaldi.) By Rupert Sargent Holland. Boston: Houghton Mifflin Co. 1908.

THRONE MAKERS. (Essay on Garibaldi.) By William Roscoe Thayer. Boston: Houghton Mifflin Co. 1899.

Henri-Frédéric Amiel (1821-81).

*AMIEL'S JOURNAL. With an Introduction and Notes by Mrs. Humphry Ward. 2 vols. New York and London: Macmillan Co. 1893.

Henry Adams (1838-1918).

*THE EDUCATION OF HENRY ADAMS: AN AUTOBIOGRAPHY. Boston: Houghton Mifflin Co. 1918. London: Constable & Co. (One of the most important books for thinking men that America has produced.)

*THE DEGRADATION OF THE DEMOCRATIC DOGMA. By Henry Adams. With an Introduction by Brooks Adams. New York: The Macmillan Co. 1919. (Extremely valuable for ideas as well as for biographical data by Adams' brother. Not a book for infants.)

AMERICAN PORTRAITS, 1875-1900. (Essay on Henry Adams.) By Gamaliel Bradford. Boston: Houghton Mifflin Co. (Interesting and readable, but judgments not always reliable.)

George Sand (1804-76).

*GEORGE SAND AND HER LOVERS. By Francis Gribble. London: Eveleigh Nash. 1910. (An amusing account of Sand's life, with stress on the intimate.)

*THE SEVEN STRINGS OF THE LYRE. THE LIFE OF GEORGE SAND. By Elizabeth W. Schermerhorn. London: Heinemann. Boston: Houghton Mifflin Co.

1927. (A dignified, sympathetic biography, valuable for the background of the time which the author succeeds in conveying.)

GEORGE SAND: THE SEARCH FOR LOVE. By Marie Jenney Howe. New York: John Day Co. 1927. (The story of George Sand told simply, apparently for popular consumption.)

GEORGE SAND. By Mary F. Sandars. London: Robert Hoden. 1927.

George Eliot (1819-80).

*GEORGE ELIOT AND HER TIMES. By Elizabeth S. Haldane. New York: D. Appleton & Co. 1927. (An illuminating study, in which the relation of Eliot to her epoch is considered.)

*GEORGE ELIOT. (In the English Men of Letters series.) By Leslie Stephen. London and New York: Macmillan Co. 1902.

Robert E. Lee (1807-70).

*ROBERT E. LEE: MAN AND SOLDIER. By Thomas Nelson Page. Charles Scribner's Sons. 1911. (An excellent, sympathetic biography.)

Simon Bolivar (1783-1831).

*SIMON BOLIVAR, "EL LIBERTADOR." By F. Loraine Petre. London: John Lane. 1910. (A thorough but somewhat prejudiced record of Bolivar's life and activities.)

*SIMON BOLIVAR. By Guillermo A. Sherwell. Washington, D. C.: Press of Byron S. Adams. 1921. (A less involved effort than Mr. Petre's, easy to follow. Mr. Sherwell is as sympathetic to Bolivar as Mr. Petre appears to be hostile. The lay reader will, in all likelihood, share Mr. Sherwell's sympathies.)

Cecil Rhodes (1853-1902).

*CECIL RHODES. By Basil Williams. London: Constable. New York: Henry Holt. 1821. (All that any lay reader may want to know about the man.)

Ferdinand de Lesseps (1805-94).

*RECOLLECTIONS OF FORTY YEARS. By Ferdinand de Lesseps. 2 vols. London: Chapman & Hall. 1887.

*LIFE AND ENTERPRISES OF FERDINAND DE LESSEPS. By G. Barnett Smith. London: W. H. Allen & Co. 1894.

*THE GREAT CANAL AT SUEZ. By Percy Fitzgerald. 2 vols. London: Tinsley Bros. 1876.

General.

MAIN CURRENTS IN NINETEENTH CENTURY LITERATURE. By Georg Brandes. 6 vols. London: William Heinemann Ltd. New York: Boni & Liveright. 1924.

FRENCH POETS AND NOVELISTS. By Henry James. London: Macmillan Co. 1878.

THE SOUL OF SPAIN. By Havelock Ellis. London: Constable & Co. 1924.